Bible Time Line

Key

▨	Major event
c.	Circa (about)
‖	10 years between lines
○	Year marker
▨	Time span marker

Many dates listed are approximate and may vary according to different scholars.

Bible History

World History

Middle East History

Books of the Bible are listed by date of events on the time line. →

2200 BC   2100 BC   2000 BC   Egypt

Bible History

ABRAHAM c. 2166-1991
Some scholars place Abraham's birth at 1952 BC. In this case, biblical events through Joseph would slide to the right 214 years.

JOSEPH c. 1914-1805
○ **JOSEPH BECOMES AN OFFICIAL IN EGYPT** c. 1884
○ **JACOB AND HIS FAMILY GO TO EGYPT** c. 1876
Sons of Jacob (Israel)—Reuben, Simeon, Levi, Judah, Dan, N
Grandsons (sons of Joseph)—Manasseh, Ephraim

▨ **ABRAHAMIC COVENANT**
○ **JOB** (dates unknown)

ISHMAEL c. 2080-1943
ISAAC c. 2066-1886
JACOB (ISRAEL) c. 2005-1859
○ **JACOB FLEES TO HARAN** c. 1929

World History

○ The city of Ur falls c. 2004

Earliest forms of writing (cuneiform) c. 3200
First Ziggurats built by Ur-Nammu c. 2112-2095

Hammurapi (Hammurabi) reigns in Bab
○ Law code of Hammurapi

▨ Creation to Abraham

NOAH 950 (The Flood)
○ (The Fall) **ADAM** 930*
SHEM 600
SETH 912
ARPHAXAD 438
ENOS 905
SALAH 433
KENAN (CAINAN) 910
EBER 464
MAHALALEEL 895
PELEG 239
JARED 962
REU 239
ENOCH 365 (God took him.)
SERUG 230
METHUSELAH 969
NAHOR 148
LAMECH 777
TERAH 205
ABRAHAM 175

* The numbers indicate the age of the person at death.
The red lines indicate the life span of the person in relationship to the others.

Code of Hammurapi   Beni Hasan-Mu

EGYPT

Old Kingdom Pyramids built c. 2700-2200

Middle Kingdom (11th-12th Dynasty) in Egypt c. 2050-1800

Second Intermediate Period (13th-17th Dy

Middle East History

2200 BC   2100 BC   2000 BC   1900 BC   1800 BC

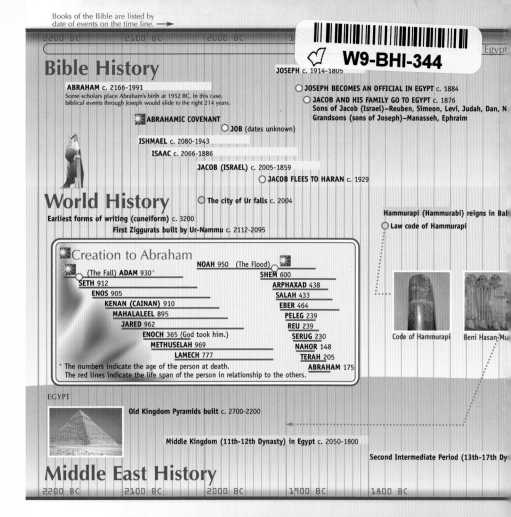

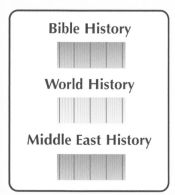

---

1 KINGS, ECCLESIASTES, SONG OF SOLOMON, PROVERBS, 2 CHRONICLES, 2 KINGS | **JONAH, AMOS, ISAIAH, HOSEA, MICAH** | **NAHUM, JEREMIAH, LAMENTATIONS, Z EZEKIEL, HABAKKUK, OBADIAH, ZECHA/**

1000 BC   900 BC   800 BC   700 BC   600 BC

United Kingdom | Divided Kingdom

Bible History

NATHAN

JEROBOAM I 931-910
NADAB 910-909
BAASHA 909-886
ELAH 886-885
○ **ZIMRI** 885
TIBNI 885-880
OMRI 885-874
AHAB 874-853
KINGS OF ISRAEL (NORTHERN)
▨○ **DIVISION OF THE KINGDOM** 931

AHAZIAH 853-852
JORAM (JEHORAM) 852-841
JEHU 841-814

JEHOASH 798-782
JEROBOAM II 793-753
○ **ZECHARIAH** 753
○ **SHALLUM** 752
MENAHEM 752-742
PEKAHIAH 742-740
PEKAH 752-732
HOSHEA 732-722
JEHOAHAZ 814-798

▨○ **ISRAEL (NORTHERN KINGDOM) FALLS TO THE ASSYRIANS** 722
NAHUM c. 658-615
JEREMIAH c. 650-582
ZEPHANIAH c. 640-626
HABAKKUK c. 608-
EZEKIEL c. 620-570
DANIEL c. 620-540
○ **OBADI**

KINGS OF JUDAH (SOUTHERN)
KING SOLOMON c. 971-931
REHOBOAM I 931-913
ABIJAH 913-911
ASA 911-870
JEHOSHAPHAT 873-848
JEHORAM (JORAM) 853-841
AHAZIAH 841
QUEEN ATHALIAH 841-835
JOASH 835-796

AMAZIAH 796-767
UZZIAH (AZARIAH) 792-740
JOTHAM 750-732
AHAZ (JEHOAHAZ) 735-716
HEZEKIAH 716-687
MANASSEH 697-643
AMON 643-641
JOSIAH 641-609

○ **JEHOAHAZ (SHA**
JEHOIAKIM (ELIA
▨○ **FIRST EXILE OF**
JEHOIACHIN
ZEDEKIAH (
▨○ **JUDA**
TEMP

World History

▨○ **SOLOMON'S TEMPLE COMPLETED** 960

ELIJAH c. 870-845
ELISHA c. 845-800

○ City of Samaria founded c. 879

Hiram, king of Tyre c. 978-944
Battle of Qarqar–Israel and Syria clash with Assyria 853 ○
Syria oppresses Israel
Assyria forces Israel to pay tribute 841 ○
○ King Mesha of Moab 830

○ **JONAH** c. 781
AMOS c. 765-754
ISAIAH c. 760-673
HOSEA c. 758-725
MICAH c. 738-698

○ First recorded Olympic games 776
○ Traditional date for the founding of Rome 753
Homer c. 800-701
Assyria rules Egypt 671-652

○ GEDA

○ Nineveh, capital o
Babylon fa

Middle East History

ASSYRIAN EMPIRE

Asshurnasirpal II 883-859
Shalmaneser III 858-824
Shamsi-Adad V 823-811
Ada-Nirari III 810-783

Shalmaneser IV 783-773
Ashurdan III 772-755
Ashur-Nirari V 754-745
Tiglath-Pileser III 744-727

Shalmaneser V 726-722
Sargon II (722-705) takes Samaria, exiles people to Babylon 722
Sennacherib 704-681
Esarhaddon 680-669
Asshurbanipal 668-627

NEO-BABYLON EMPIRE
Nabopolassar I 625-605
Nebuchadnezzar

Captives shown on Shishak Relief
Mesha Stele
Shishak I 945-924

1000 BC   900 BC   800 BC   700 BC   600 BC

THE IRON AGE

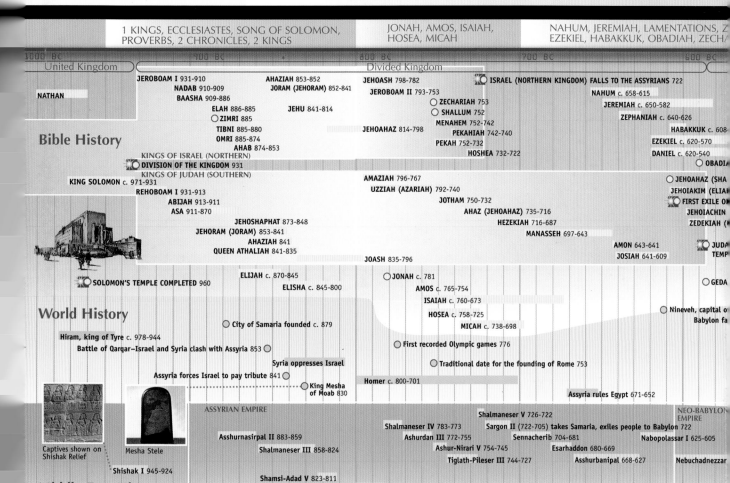

1700 BC   1600 BC   1500 BC   1400 BC

Moses and the Exodus

SLAVERY IN EGYPT (dates uncertain)

AARON c. 1529-1407

MOSES c. 1526-1406

ERA OF THE JUDGES BEGINS
Judges: Othniel, Ehud, S...

FIRST PASSOVER c. 1446

"HIGH DATE" FOR THE EXODUS & WILDERNESS WANDERINGS c. 1446

TEN COMMANDMENTS AND OTHER LAWS GIVEN

TABERNACLE

JOSHUA LEADS ISRAELITES INTO CANAAN

RAHAB HELPS SAVE SPIES

...htali, Gad, Asher, Issachar, Zebulun, Joseph, Benjamin

...lon 1792-1750

Hittites sack Babylon 1595

Tabernacle

Shang Dynasty in China c. 1450-1027

Ruins at Jericho

King Tutankhamen

18th Dynasty begins in Egypt 1570

Ahmose 1570-1545

Amenhotep 1545-1529

Thutmose 1529-1517

Thutmose II 1517-1504

Thutmose III 1504-1453

Queen Hatshepshut 1504-1483

Amenhotep II 1453-1426

Thutmose IV 1426-1416

Amenhotep III 1416-1377

Amenhotep IV (Ikhnaton) 1377-1360

Tutankhamen ("King Tut") 136...

Ay 1350-1347

Horemhab 1347-1318

19th Dy...

Hyksos rule Egypt c. 1670-1570

Rameses...

...asties) begins c. 1800-1570

Seti I 13...

Ra...

1700 BC   1600 BC   1500 BC   1400 BC

THE BRONZE AGE

---

500 BC   400 BC   300 BC   200 BC

Exile   Restoration of Jerusalem   Palestine ruled by Egyptian Ptolemies, the Syrian Seleucids, the Macc...

ZECHARIAH c. 522-509

HAGGAI c. 520

CYRUS'S EDICT ALLOWS JEWS TO RETURN TO THEIR LAND 538
EXILES BEGIN TO RETURN TO JERUSALEM

REBUILDING OF TEMPLE BEGINS 536

TEMPLE COMPLETED 516

ZERUBBABEL AND JESHUA LEAD THE JEWS
TO FINISH REBUILDING THE TEMPLE 520-516

ESTHER c. 478

MALACHI c. 465

EZRA SENT TO JUDAH 457

JOEL c. 450

NEHEMIAH GOVERNS JUDAH 444-432

NEHEMIAH IN BABYLON c. 432-430

PTOLEMAIC EGYPT CONTROLS PALESTINE 331-198

The Syrian Seleucids begin to rule Palestine 198

Jewish priests on good terms with the Seleucids

The Seleucid ruler Antiochus IV tries to force Jews to abandon their law, desecrates the temple 175-163

Judas Maccabeus leads a Jewish revolt against the Seleucids 166-160

Temple in Jerusalem rededicated, Hanukkah 164

Jonathan, brother of Judas Maccabeus continues revolt 1...

Hasmoneans take control of the priesthood 15...

Simon, brother of Judas Maccabeus, governs Ju...

John Hyrcan...

John Hyrcanus I becomes ruler...

Aristobulus I declares him...

Alexander Jann...

...c. 590

...UM) 609

...M) 609-598

...EWS TO BABYLON 605

...ECONIAH) 598-597

...ATTANIAH) 597-586

..., THE SOUTHERN KINGDOM, FALLS TO BABYLON
...E AND JERUSALEM DESTROYED 586

...AH, GOVERNOR OF JUDAH 586

Edict on Cyrus
Cylinder 536 BC

Ephesus ruins

Vesuvius Erupts
AD 79

Masada AD 73

Roman Colosseum
built AD 71-80

Rosetta Stone Tri...
written in Greek,
and Egyptian dem...

...Assyria, falls to the Babylonians and the Medes 612

...s to Persia 539

Persia regains control of Egypt 342-332

Pericles 500-429

Darius (Gubaru) the Mede, governor of Babylon 539

Egypt ruled by the Persians 525-405

Roman Republic established 509

Buddha, India 550-480

Herodotus 485-424

Confucius, Chinese philosopher 551-479

Peloponnesian War between Athens & Sparta 431-404

Alexander the Great conquers Egypt and Palestine, Hellenization begins 332

First Punic War; Romans control Italy 264-241

Septuagint (scriptures translated into Gree...

Second Punic War; Hannibal in...

...le
13
...le?
...hat
...ong
...em.
...em.
...set
...ord
...uilt
400
the
...s of
...nt.

...AN   PERSIAN EMPIRE   ALEXANDRIAN EMPIRE   PTOLEMIES OF EGYPT   SELEUCIDS OF SYRIA   An...

Cyrus the Great 559-530

Cambyses 529-522

Darius I 522-486

Artaxerxes II 404-359

Gauls sack Rome 390

Xerxes I (Ahasuerus) 485-465

Artaxerxes III 358-337

Xerxes I (Ahasuerus) makes Esther queen c. 478

Artaxerxes 464-424

Darius II 423-405

Egypt independent from Persia 405-342

Alexandrian Empire

Alexander the Great 336-323

Ptolemy I 323-285

Seleucus I 312-280

Ptolemy II 285-246

Alexandrian Empire divided; Ptolemy rules Egypt, Seleucus rules
Persia and Syria, Antigonus rules Macedonia and Greece 323

Antiochus I 280-261

Antiochus II 261-247

Ptolemy III 246-221

Ptolemy IV 221-203

Ptolemy V 203-181

Antiochus VI

Antiochus III the Great 223-187

Seleucus IV Phi...

Antiochu...

...604-562

n, Inc.

.com

500 BC   400 BC   300 BC   200 BC

THE IRON AGE

ROSE BOOK OF
BIBLE CHARTS,
MAPS AND
TIME LINES

- Full-Color Bible Charts
- Illustrations of the Tabernacle, Temple, and High Priest
- Then and Now Bible Maps
- Biblical and Historical Time Lines

Rose Publishing, Inc.
Torrance, California

Rose Book of Charts, Maps, and Time Lines
© Copyright 2005 RW Research, Inc.
All rights reserved.
Rose Publishing, Inc.
4733 Torrance Blvd., #259
Torrance, California 90503 USA
www.rose-publishing.com

Conditions of Use

Photographs, Illustrations and Other Credits

"100 Well-Known Events from Acts to Revelation," "100 Well-Known Old Testament Events," "100 Well-Known People in the Bible," and "100 Well-Known Prayers in the Bible," used by permission, © 2005 Dr. Harold Willmington.

Exodus Map, © 2003, Hugh O. Claycombe; Herod's Temple aerial view, © 1983 Hugh O. Claycombe; Herod's Temple cutaway, © 1998, Hugh O. Claycombe; Jesus' Hours on the Cross, © 2000, Hugh O. Claycombe; Palm Sunday to Easter, © 2002, Hugh O. Claycombe; Solomon's Temple, © 2003, Hugh O. Claycombe; Tabernacle aerial view, © 1997, Hugh O. Claycombe; used by permission

Middle East and Central Asia Map. Used by permission, © 2002, Global Mapping International.

Photographs and Illustrations of: Asherah idol, Ashkelon, Astarte Plaque, Beth Shemesh, Beersheba, Beni Hasan tomb painting, edict on Cyrus cylinder, flood story fragment from Megiddo, Galilee boat, horned altar, "House of David" Inscription, Ishtar Gate, Isaiah Scroll, ivory pomegranate, Law Code of Hammurapi, nail in heel bone, ossuary of Caiaphas, Masada, Megiddo, Merneptah Stele, Mesha Stele, mud-brick Gate of Dan, "Place of Trumpeting" inscription, Seal of SHLOMO, Siloam Tunnel Inscription, Silver Amulets, and warning to the Gentiles fragment, Zev Radovan, Jerusalem; used by permission

Photographs and Illustrations of: Arch of Titus, Bethsaida, Cana, Church of the Nativity, Damascus, Tiberias, and "Politarch" Inscriptions, Dr. John McRay; used by permission

Photographs of: Arabic translations of *Injil* and *Taurat* and Trinity ring, Peter Commandeur; used by permission

Some Scripture taken from THE HOLY BIBLE: NEW INTERNATIONAL VERSION®.NIV® © 1973, 1978, 1984 by International Bible Society. Used by permission of Zondervan Publishing House. All rights reserved.

Library of Congress Cataloging-in-Publication Data

Rose book of Bible charts, maps, and time lines : full-color Bible charts, illustrations of the
     tabernacle, temple, and High Priest, then and now Bible maps, biblical and historical time lines.
          p. cm.
     Includes indexes.
     ISBN 1-59636-022-4 (alk. paper)
     1. Bible--Handbooks, manuals, etc. 2. Bible--Geography--Maps. 3.
Bible--Chronology--Charts, diagrams, etc. I. Title: Book of bible charts, maps, and time
lines. II. Rose Publishing (Torrance, Calif.)

BS417.R67 2005
220'.022--dc22

                                                                    2005049047

Printed by Regent Publishing Services Ltd.
Shenzhen, China
May 2010, 14th printing

TABLE OF CONTENTS

TABLE OF CONTENTS

Many Bible charts, maps, drawings, and time lines featured in this book are available individually as wall charts and/or pamphlets. Visit www.rose-publishing.com for details.

GENERAL BIBLE CHARTS

Bible Bookcase

LAW
Genesis
Exodus
Leviticus
Numbers
Deuteronomy

HISTORY
Joshua
Judges
Ruth
1 Samuel
2 Samuel
1 Kings
2 Kings
1 Chronicles
2 Chronicles
Ezra
Nehemiah
Esther

POETRY
Job
Psalms
Proverbs
Ecclesiastes
Song of Solomon

MAJOR PROPHETS
Isaiah
Jeremiah
Lamentations
Ezekiel
Daniel

MINOR PROPHETS
Hosea
Joel
Amos
Obadiah
Jonah
Micah
Nahum
Habakkuk
Zephaniah
Haggai
Zechariah
Malachi

GOSPELS
Matthew
Mark
Luke
John

HISTORY
Acts

EPISTLES TO CHURCHES
Romans
1 Corinthians
2 Corinthians
Galatians
Ephesians
Philippians
Colossians
1 Thessalonians
2 Thessalonians

EPISTLES TO FRIENDS
1 Timothy
2 Timothy
Titus
Philemon

GENERAL EPISTLES
Hebrews
James
1 Peter
2 Peter
1 John
2 John
3 John
Jude
Revelation

OLD TESTAMENT

THE LAW

The first five books of the Bible are called "The Law" or the Pentateuch or the Torah. The Law contains stories about the creation of the world, the flood, Abraham, Isaac, Jacob, the children of Israel in Egypt, the Exodus, and the time the children of Israel spent in the wilderness before entering the Promised Land. The books of the Law also recorded the law God gave to the people on Mt. Sinai which laid down the regulations for sacrifice, worship, and daily living.

GENESIS
Who: Moses
What: The Beginnings
Where: Egypt and Canaan
When: c. 1450 BC–1400 BC
Why: To demonstrate that God is sovereign and loves his creation.

Outline (Chapter)
- Creation, Fall, and Flood (1-11)
- Abraham (11-25)
- Isaac and Jacob (25-36)
- Joseph (37-50)

Key Verse: I will establish my covenant as an everlasting covenant between me and you and your descendants after you for the generations to come, to be your God and the God of your descendants after you. (Genesis 17:7)

EXODUS
Who: Moses
What: Deliverance from Slavery
Where: Egypt and Canaan
When: c. 1445 BC–1440 BC
Why: To show God's faithfulness to the covenant and provide Israel with guidelines for healthy living.

Outline (Chapter)
- Moses (1-7)
- The Plagues (7-13)
- The Exodus (14-18)
- The Law (19-24)
- Tabernacle and Worship (25-40)

Key Verse: God said to Moses, "I am who I am. This is what you are to say to the Israelites: 'I AM has sent me to you'."(Exodus 3:14)

LEVITICUS
Who: Moses
What: Law and Sacrifice
Where: Sinai and Canaan
When: c. 1445 BC–1400 BC
Why: To instruct Israel on how to be holy and to be a blessing to others.

Outline (Chapter)
- Sacrifice (1-7)
- Priesthood (8-10)
- Clean and Unclean (11-15)
- Day of Atonement (16)
- Laws for Daily Life (17-27)

Key Verse: Consecrate yourselves and be holy, because I am the LORD your God. Keep my decrees and follow them. I am the LORD, who makes you holy. (Leviticus 20:7, 8)

NUMBERS
Who: Moses
What: Census and History
Where: Borders of Canaan
When:c. 1445 BC–1400 BC
Why: A reminder of what happens when people rebel against God

Outline (Chapter)
- Census (1-9)
- Sinai to Canaan (10-12)
- Spies and Rebellion (13-19)
- Moab (20-36)

Key Verse: The LORD bless you and keep you; the LORD make his face shine upon you and be gracious to you; the LORD turn his face toward you and give you peace. (Numbers 6:24-26)

DEUTERONOMY
Who: Moses
What: Sermons by Moses
Where: Plains of Moab
When: c. 1401 BC–1400 BC
Why: To remind the people what God expects from them.

Outline (Chapter)
- Sermon 1: Journey Review (1-4)
- Sermon 2: Laws (5-28)
- Sermon 3: Covenant (29-30)
- Final Farewells (31-34)

Key Verse: Hear, O Israel: The LORD our God, the LORD is one. Love the LORD your God with all your heart and with all your soul and with all your strength. (Deuteronomy 6:4, 5)

HISTORY

The 12 History books continue with the story of the people of Israel and the conquest of the Promised Land in the book of Joshua, the continuous cycle of disobedience in the book of Judges, the first kings and the United Kingdom, Divided Kingdom, the Assyrian invasion, Babylonian invasion, the years in exile, and the return from exile during the Persian rule.

JOSHUA

Who: Unknown (Joshua)
What: History of Conquest
Where: Canaan
When: c. 1405 BC–1383 BC
Why: To assure the people that obedience to God is rewarded.

Outline (Chapter)
• The Conquest (1-12)
• Dividing the Land (13-22)
• Joshua's Farewell (23-24)

Key Verse: Be strong and very courageous. Be careful to obey all the law my servant Moses gave you; do not turn from it to the right or to the left, that you may be successful wherever you go. (Joshua 1:7)

JUDGES

Who: Unknown (Samuel)
What: History before Kings
Where: Canaan
When: c. 1086 BC–1004 BC
Why: To stress the importance of remaining loyal to God.

Outline (Chapter)
• Reasons for Failure (1)
• The Judges: Othniel, Ehud, Shamgar, Deborah, Gideon, Tola, Jair, Jephthah, Ibzan, Elon, Abdon, and Samson (2-16)
• Days of Lawlessness (17-21)

Key Verse: In those days Israel had no king; everyone did as he saw fit. (Judges 21:25)

RUTH

Who: Unknown (Samuel)
What: Story of Faithful Foreigner
Where: Canaan
When: c. 1046 BC–1035 BC
Why: To demonstrate the kind of faithfulness, godliness, loyalty, and love that God desires for us.

Outline (Chapter)
• Naomi and Ruth (1)
• Ruth meets Boaz (2)
• The Threshing Floor (3)
• The Marriage (4)

Key Verse: But Ruth replied, "Don't urge me to leave you or to turn back from you. Where you go I will go, and where you stay I will stay. Your people will be my people and your God my God." (Ruth 1:16)

1 SAMUEL

Who: Unknown
What: History of Events
Where: Israel and Judah
When: c. 1050 BC–750 BC
Why: To record how Israel got a king.

Outline (Chapter)
• Samuel (1-7)
• Saul (8-15)
• Saul and David (16-31)

Key Verse: But Samuel replied: "Does the LORD delight in burnt offerings and sacrifices as much as in obeying the voice of the LORD? To obey is better than sacrifice, and to heed is better than the fat of rams." (1 Samuel 15:22)

2 SAMUEL

Who: Unknown
What: History of Events
Where: Israel and Judah
When: c. 1050 BC–750 BC
Why: To demonstrate the prominence of David's line.

Outline (Chapter)
• David's Reign in Judah (1-4)
• David Unites Israel (5-10)
• David and Bathsheba (11-12)
• Family Problems (13-20)
• Conclusions (21-24)

Key Verse: I have been with you wherever you have gone, and I have cut off all your enemies from before you. Now I will make your name great, like the names of the greatest men of the earth. (2 Samuel 7:9)

HISTORY

1 KINGS
Who: Unknown
What: Evaluation of the Kings
Where: In Exile in Babylon
When: 590 BC–570 BC
Why: To demonstrate the value of obeying and the danger of disobeying God.

Outline (Chapter)
- King Solomon's Reign (1-4)
- Temple Construction (5-8)
- Queen of Sheba (9-10)
- Kingdom Splits (11-16)
- Prophet Elijah (17-22)

Key Verse: So give your servant a discerning heart to govern your people and to distinguish between right and wrong. (1 Kings 3:9a)

2 KINGS
Who: Unknown
What: Evaluation of the Kings
Where: In Exile in Babylon
When: 590 BC–550 BC
Why: To demonstrate the value of obeying God.

Outline (Chapter)
- The Prophet Elisha (1-8)
- Kings of Judah and Israel (9-16)
- Fall of Israel (17-21)
- King Josiah (22-23)
- Fall of Judah; Exile (24-25)

Key Verse: And Hezekiah prayed to the LORD: "O LORD, God of Israel, enthroned between the cherubim, you alone are God over all the kingdoms of the earth. You have made heaven and earth." (2 Kings 19:15)

1 CHRONICLES
Who: Ezra
What: Review of David's Reign
Where: Judah
When: c. 450 BC–425 BC
Why: To encourage the remnant.

Key Verse: "Oh, that you would bless me and enlarge my territory! Let your hand be with me, and keep me from harm so that I will be free from pain." (1 Chronicles 4:10)

2 CHRONICLES
Who: Ezra
What: Highlights Kings of Judah
Where: Judah
When: c. 450 BC–425 BC
Why: To show the benefits that come from obedience.

Key Verse: As for us, the LORD is our God, and we have not forsaken him. (2 Chronicles 13:10a)

EZRA
Who: Ezra
What: History of Reconstruction
Where: Judah
When: c. 457 BC–444 BC
Why: Provide a detailed account of the exiles' return and the rebuilding of the Temple.

Outline (Chapter)
- The Exiles Return (1-2)
- Rebuilding the Temple (3-6)
- The Work of Ezra (7-10)

Key Verse: With praise and thanksgiving they sang to the LORD: "He is good; his love to Israel endures forever. And all the people gave a great shout of praise to the LORD, because the foundation of the house of the LORD was laid." (Ezra 3:11)

NEHEMIAH
Who: Nehemiah
What: History of Reconstruction
Where: Judah
When: c. 445 BC–430 BC
Why: Rebuilding of the walls of Jerusalem.

Outline (Chapter)
- Nehemiah Returns (1-2)
- The Rebuilding of the Walls (3)
- Threats and Persecution (4-7)
- Renewal of Covenant (8-10)
- Dedication and Laws (11-13)

Key Verse: Nehemiah said, "Go and enjoy choice food and sweet drinks, and send some to those who have nothing prepared. This day is sacred to our Lord. Do not grieve, for the joy of the LORD is your strength." (Nehemiah 8:10)

ESTHER
Who: Unknown
What: Story of Redemption
Where: Persia
When: c. 464 BC–435 BC
Why: To demonstrate that, in all circumstances, God is in control.

Outline (Chapter)
- Search for a new Queen (1-2)
- Haman's Plot (3)
- Esther's Plan (4-6)
- Haman's Downfall (7)
- Esther saves the Jews (8-10)

Key Verse: For if you remain silent at this time, relief and deliverance for the Jews will arise from another place, but you and your father's family will perish. And who knows but that you have come to royal position for such a time as this? (Esther 4:14)

POETRY & WISDOM

The five Poetry and Wisdom books include hymns, proverbs, poems, and dramas. They illustrate the creative ways the people of Israel expressed themselves to God and to each other.

JOB

Who: Unknown
What: Story of Perseverance
Where: Mesopotamia (Uz)
When: Unknown
Why: To show the sovereignty of God and to illustrate faithfulness in the midst of suffering.

Outline (Chapter)
- Job Tested (1-3)
- Job's Friends (4-31)
- Elihu's Speech (32-37)
- God's Answer (38-42)

Key Verse: I know that my Redeemer lives, and that in the end he will stand upon the earth. And after my skin has been destroyed, yet in my flesh I will see God. (Job 19:25, 26)

PSALMS

Who: David, Moses, Asaph, Solomon, Ethan, Sons of Korah
What: Poetry and Song
Where: Ancient Israel
When: c. 1410 BC–430 BC
Why: To communicate with God and worship him.

Outline (Chapter)
- Book I: Psalms 1-41
- Book II: Psalms 42-72
- Book III: Psalms 73-89
- Book IV: Psalms 90-106
- Book V: Psalms 107-150

Key Verse: My mouth will speak in praise of the Lord. Let every creature praise his holy name for ever and ever. (Psalm 145:21)

PROVERBS

Who: Solomon and others
What: Wisdom
Where: Israel
When: c. 950 BC–700 BC
Why: To provide wisdom and guidance for God's children.

Outline (Chapter)
- Lessons in Wisdom (1-9)
- Proverbs of Solomon (10-22)
- Other Wise Sayings (23-24)
- Solomon's Sayings (25-29)
- Other Proverbs (30-31)

Key Verse: Trust in the LORD with all your heart and lean not on your own understanding; in all your ways acknowledge him, and he will make your paths straight. (Proverbs 3:5, 6)

ECCLESIASTES

Who: Solomon
What: Wisdom
Where: Jerusalem
When: c. 935 BC
Why: A search to discover truth.

Outline (Chapter)
- The Meaning of Life (1-2)
- Life is Not Always Fair (3-6)
- Wisdom (7-8)
- No One Knows the Future (9-10)
- Obedience to God (11-12)

Key Verse: Fear God and keep his commandments, for this is the whole duty of man. For God will bring every deed into judgment, including every hidden thing, whether it is good or evil. (Ecclesiastes 12:13, 14)

SONG OF SOLOMON

Who: Solomon
What: Love Poem
Where: Jerusalem
When: c. 965 BC
Why: To illustrate the joy of authentic love found in marriage.

Outline (Chapter)
- The Courtship (1-3)
- The Wedding (3-4)
- The Lasting Relationship (5-8)

Key Verse: Many waters cannot quench love; rivers cannot wash it away. If one were to give all the wealth of his house for love, it would be utterly scorned. (Song of Solomon 8:7)

MAJOR PROPHETS

The five Major Prophets are not called "major" because of their message or quality, but rather because of the length of the books. The prophets brought God's word which included warning of judgment, warnings and hope for the immediate future (as well as warnings and hope for the distant future), and hope in the coming Messiah.

ISAIAH

Who: Isaiah
What: Prophecy and Judgement
Where: Judah
When: c. 740 BC–680 BC
Why: To convince the people that salvation was possible through repentance and hope in the coming Messiah.

Outline (Chapter)
- Condemnation (1-39)
- Comfort in Exile (40-55)
- Future Hope (56-66)

Key Verse: For to us a child is born, to us a son is given, and the government will be on his shoulders. And he will be called Wonderful Counselor, Mighty God, Everlasting Father, Prince of Peace. (Isaiah 9:6)

JEREMIAH

Who: Jeremiah
What: Prophecy and Judgement
Where: Judah
When: c. 626 BC–580 BC
Why: To warn Judah of their destruction, to remind them of their sin, and convince them to submit to the Babylonian invaders.

Outline (Chapter)
- Jeremiah (1-10)
- Prophetic Warnings (11-28)
- New Covenant (29-39)
- The Fall of Jerusalem (40-52)

Key Verse: "For I know the plans I have for you," declares the LORD, "plans to prosper you and not to harm you, plans to give you hope and a future." (Jeremiah 29:11)

LAMENTATIONS

Who: Jeremiah
What: Dirge Poem (Lament)
Where: Babylon
When: c. 586 BC–584 BC
Why: To express the despair of the people of Judah over the loss of their land, city, and Temple.

Outline (Chapter)
- Sorrows of Captives (1)
- Anger with Jerusalem (2)
- Hope and Mercy (3)
- Punishment (4)
- Restoration (5)

Key Verse: Because of the LORD's great love we are not consumed, for his compassions never fail. They are new every morning; great is your faithfulness. (Lamentations 3:22, 23)

EZEKIEL

Who: Ezekiel
What: Prophecy and Warning
Where: Babylon
When: c. 587 BC–565 BC
Why: To confront people about their sin, give them one last chance to repent, and offer hope.

Outline (Chapter)
- Ezekiel (1-3)
- Judgment of Judah (4-24)
- Judgment on the Nations (25-32)
- The End of the Age (33-39)
- Restoration of Temple (40-48)

Key Verse: I will give you a new heart and put a new spirit in you; I will remove from you your heart of stone and give you a heart of flesh. (Ezekiel 36:26)

DANIEL

Who: Daniel
What: Prophecy and Apocalyptic
Where: Babylon
When: c. 605 BC–530 BC
Why: To convince the Jewish exiles that God is sovereign and to provide them with a vision of their future redemption.

Outline (Chapter)
- Daniel and His Friends (1-6)
- Apocalyptic Visions (7-12)

Key Verse: In the time of those kings, the God of heaven will set up a kingdom that will never be destroyed, nor will it be left to another people. It will crush all those kingdoms and bring them to an end, but it will itself endure forever. (Daniel 2:44)

MINOR PROPHETS

The 12 Minor Prophets, called "The Book of the Twelve" in the Hebrew Bible, are just as important as the Major Prophets. They are called "minor" because of the shorter length of the books. The Minor Prophets also brought God's word to the people regarding judgment and hope.

HOSEA
Who: Hosea
What: Prophecy and Warning
Where: Israel
When: c. 755 BC–710 BC
Why: To illustrate Israel's spiritual adultery and warn of destruction.
Outline (Chapter)
• The Unfaithful Wife (1-3)
• The Unfaithful Nation (4-14)
Key Verse: Because you have rejected knowledge, I also reject you as my priests; because you have ignored the law of your God, I also will ignore your children. (Hosea 4:6)

JOEL
Who: Joel
What: Prophecy and Judgment
Where: Judah
When: Unknown
Why: To call Judah to repentance in order to avoid judgment.
Outline (Chapter)
• Locusts (1)
• Blessings and Curses (2-3)
Key Verse: And afterward, I will pour out my Spirit on all people. Your sons and daughters will prophesy, your old men will dream dreams, your young men will see visions. (Joel 2:28b)

AMOS
Who: Amos
What: Prophecy and Judgment
Where: Israel
When: c. 760 BC–750 BC
Why: To accuse and judge Israel for injustice and lack of mercy.
Outline (Chapter)
• Neighbors Punished (1-3)
• Israel's Destruction (3-8)
• Future Hope (9)
Key Verse: Seek good, not evil, that you may live. Then the LORD God Almighty will be with you, just as you say he is. (Amos 5:14)

OBADIAH
Who: Obadiah
What: Prophecy
Where: Judah
When: c. 586 BC
Why: To prophesy against Edom.
Outline: (Verses)
• Judgment on Edom (1-9)
• Edom's Violations (10-14)
• Israel's Victory (15-21)
Key Verse: Because of the violence against your brother Jacob, you will be covered with shame; you will be destroyed forever. (Obadiah 10)

JONAH
Who: Jonah
What: Story of God's Mercy
Where: Nineveh
When: c. 783 BC–753BC
Why: To show that God loves all.
Outline (Chapter)
• Jonah Flees (1)
• Jonah Prays (2)
• Jonah's Anger with God's Mercy
Key Verse: I knew that you are a gracious and compassionate God, slow to anger and abounding in love, a God who relents from sending calamity. (Jonah 4:2b)

MICAH
Who: Micah
What: Prophecy and Judgment
Where: Israel and Judah
When: c. 739 BC–686 BC
Why: To warn people of judgment and to offer hope.
Outline (Chapter)
• Judgment and Deliverance (1-5)
• Confession and Restoration (6-7)
Key Verse: He has showed you, O man, what is good. And what does the LORD require of you? To act justly and to love mercy and to walk humbly with your God. (Micah 6:8)

NAHUM
Who: Nahum
What: Prophecy and Judgment
Where: Judah and Nineveh
When: c. 664 BC–612 BC
Why: To pronounce judgment on Nineveh and the Assyrian Empire.
Outline (Chapter)
• Judgment (1)
• Hope for Judah (1)
• Nineveh's Destruction (2-3)
Key Verse: The LORD is good, a refuge in times of trouble. He cares for those who trust in him. (Nahum 1:7)

HABAKKUK
Who: Habakkuk
What: Prophecy and Judgment
Where: Judah
When: c. 609 BC–597BC
Why: To affirm that the wicked will not prevail and to remind Judah that God is in control.
Outline (Chapter)
• Tough Questions (1-2)
• Praise to the Lord (3)
Key Verse: ...yet I will rejoice in the LORD, I will be joyful in God my Savior. (Habakkuk 3:18)

ZEPHANIAH
Who: Zephaniah
What: Prophecy and Judgment
Where: Judah
When: c. 640 BC–628 BC
Why: To motivate repentance.
Outline (Chapter)
• Judgment on Judah (1)
• Judgment on the Nations (2)
• Promise of Restoration (3)
Key Verse: The great day of the LORD is near— near and coming quickly. Listen! The cry on the day of the LORD will be bitter, the shouting of the warrior there. (Zephaniah 1:14)

HAGGAI
Who: Haggai
What: Prophecy and Hope
Where: Judah
When: c. 520 BC
Why: To urge the people to complete rebuilding the Temple.
Outline (Chapter)
• Rebuild Temple (1)
• Blessings (2)
• David's Throne (2)
Key Verse: This is what I covenanted with you when you came out of Egypt. And My Spirit remains among you. Do not fear. (Haggai 2:5)

ZECHARIAH
Who: Zechariah
What: Prophecy and Hope
Where: Judah
When: c. 520 BC–519 BC
Why: To give hope to the remnant.
Outline (Chapter)
• Zechariah's Visions (1-8)
• Messianic Prophecy (9-12)
Key Verse: Rejoice greatly, O Daughter of Zion! Shout, Daughter of Jerusalem! See, your king comes to you, righteous and having salvation, gentle and riding on a donkey, on a colt, the foal of a donkey. (Zechariah 9:9)

MALACHI
Who: Malachi
What: Prophecy and Judgment
Where: Judah
When: c. 430 BC–400 BC
Why: To examine Judah's actions and make sure God has priority.
Outline (Chapter)
• Sins Identified (1-3)
• Rewards for the Righteous (4)
Key Verse: But for you who revere my name, the sun of righteousness will rise with healing in its wings. (Malachi 4:2)

NEW TESTAMENT

GOSPELS & ACTS

The Gospels, which are the first four books of the New Testament, record the good news of God's plan for a Savior through the life, ministry, death, and resurrection of Jesus Christ. Each writer has a particular method or style to communicate the life and message of Jesus Christ.

Acts is the record of the radically changed "acts" or "actions" of the followers of Jesus Christ after the resurrection. Acts opens with the out-flowing of the Holy Spirit and describes the missionary efforts of the early followers of Jesus as they spread the message of the gospel to Judea and Samaria. Acts also records the actions of the apostle Paul as he and other courageous believers continued to spread the good news of Jesus to the Jews and Gentiles of the Roman Empire.

MATTHEW

Who: Matthew (also called Levi)
What: Gospel
Where: Judea
When: C. AD 60
Why: To show Jesus as the Son of David, the Kingly Messiah who fulfills prophecy.

Outline (Chapter)
- Birth and Early Life (1-4)
- Ministry of Christ (5-20)
- Death and Resurrection (21-28)

Key Verse: Then Jesus came to them and said, "All authority in heaven and on earth has been given to me. Therefore go and make disciples of all nations, baptizing them in the name of the Father and of the Son and of the Holy Spirit." (Matthew 28:18-19)

MARK

Who: John Mark
What: Gospel
Where: Rome
When: C. AD 58
Why: To show Jesus as the Suffering Son of Man sent to serve and not be served.

Outline (Chapter)
- Introduction (1)
- Ministry of Christ (2-10)
- Death and Resurrection (11-16)

Key Verse: ...Instead, whoever wants to become great among you must be your servant, and whoever wants to be first must be slave of all. For even the Son of Man did not come to be served, but to serve, and to give his life as a ransom for many. (Mark 10:43-45)

LUKE

Who: Luke (The Physician)
What: Gospel
Where: Caesarea
When: C. AD 60–AD 62
Why: To show Jesus as the Savior of the World who has compassion for all human beings.

Outline (Chapter)
- Birth and Early Life (1-4)
- Ministry of Christ (5-19)
- Death and Resurrection (20-24)

Key Verse: Then he said to them all: "If anyone would come after me, he must deny himself and take up his cross daily and follow me. For whoever wants to save his life will lose it, but whoever loses his life for me will save it." (Luke 9:23,24)

JOHN

Who: John (The Beloved Disciple)
What: Gospel
Where: Asia Minor
When: C. AD 85–AD 95
Why: To show Jesus as the Son of God, the Word made flesh, who provides eternal life for all who believe in him.

Outline (Chapter)
- Introduction (1)
- Ministry of Christ (2-12)
- Private Ministry (13-17)
- Death and Resurrection (18-21)

Key Verse: For God so loved the world that he gave his one and only Son, that whoever believes in him shall not perish but have eternal life. (John 3:16)

ACTS

Who: Luke (The Physician)
What: History of Early Church
Where: Caesarea and Rome
When: C. AD 60–AD 62
Why: To record how the Holy Spirit acted through believers to spread the Word of God.

Outline (Chapter)
- Jerusalem (1-8)
- Judea and Samaria (8-12)
- Paul's Journeys (13-20)
- Paul Taken to Rome (21-28)

Key Verse: But you will receive power when the Holy Spirit comes on you; and you will be my witnesses in Jerusalem, and in all Judea and Samaria, and to the ends of the earth. (Acts 1:8)

PAUL'S LETTERS (EPISTLES)

The apostle Paul wrote 13 letters to young churches, pastors, and friends in order to guide, encourage, and correct them. Most of these letters served a specific purpose or addressed a specific question or problem.

ROMANS

Who: Paul
What: Letter to Roman Christians
Where: Corinth
When: C. AD 57
Why: To illustrate law, faith, and salvation, and righteous living.

Outline (Chapter)
• Christian Gospel (1-8)
• Israel (9-11)
• Christian Life (12-16)

Key Verse: Therefore, I urge you, brothers, in view of God's mercy, to offer your bodies as living sacrifices, holy and pleasing to God—this is your spiritual act of worship. Do not conform any longer to the pattern of this world, but be transformed by the renewing of your mind. (Romans 12:1, 2a)

1 CORINTHIANS

Who: Paul
What: Letter to Church in Corinth
Where: Ephesus
When: C. AD 56
Why: To address division and immorality and to encourage them to love each other.

Outline (Chapter)
• Divisions (1-4)
• Morality (5-11)
• Spiritual Gifts (12-14)
• The Resurrection (15-16)

Key Verse: Love is patient, love is kind. It does not envy, it does not boast, it is not proud. It is not rude, it is not self-seeking, it is not easily angered, it keeps no record of wrongs. (1 Corinthians 13:4, 5)

2 CORINTHIANS

Who: Paul
What: Letter to Church in Corinth
Where: Philippi
When: C. AD 56
Why: To defend Paul's call as an apostle, to address deceivers.

Outline (Chapter)
• Apostolic Characteristics (1-7)
• Giving (8-9)
• Paul's Defense (10-13)

Key Verse: But he said to me, "My grace is sufficient for you, for my power is made perfect in weakness." Therefore I will boast all the more gladly about my weaknesses, so that Christ's power may rest on me. (2 Corinthians 12:9)

GALATIANS

Who: Paul
What: Letter to Churches in Galatia
Where: Asia Minor
When: C. AD 50–AD 55
Why: To warn against legalism and defend justification by faith as well as Paul's apostolic authority.

Outline (Chapter)
• Paul's Defense (1-2)
• Justification by Faith (3-4)
• The Christian Life (5-6)

Key Verse: But the fruit of the Spirit is love, joy, peace, patience, kindness, goodness, faithfulness, gentleness and self-control. Against such things there is no law. (Galatians 5:22, 23)

EPHESIANS

Who: Paul
What: Letter to Church in Ephesus
Where: Prison in Rome
When: C. AD 60–AD 64
Why: To show believers what it means to be a follower of Christ and encourage them in their spiritual walk.

Outline (Chapter)
• Spiritual Blessings (1-3)
• The Christian Life (4-6)

Key Verse: For it is by grace you have been saved, through faith—and this not from yourselves, it is the gift of God—not by works, so that no one can boast. (Ephesians 2:8, 9)

PHILIPPIANS

Who: Paul
What: Letter to Church in Philippi
Where: Prison in Rome
When: C. AD 60–AD 64
Why: To express Paul's love and affection for the Philippians.

Outline (Chapter)
• Joy of Life (1)
• Humility of Christ (2)
• Finish the Race (3)
• Thanks and Greetings (4)

Key Verse: Do everything without complaining or arguing, so that you may become blameless and pure, children of God without fault in a crooked and depraved generation, in which you shine like stars in the universe. (Philippians 2:14, 15)

COLOSSIANS

Who: Paul
What: Letter to Church in Colossae
Where: Prison in Rome
When: C. AD 60–AD 64
Why: To counteract heretical teachings and exhort believers

Outline (Chapter)
• Thanksgiving (1)
• Work of Christ (1-2)
• Finish the Race (3-4)
• Final Greetings (4)

Key Verse: For in Christ all the fullness of the Deity lives in bodily form, and you have been given fullness in Christ, who is the head over every power and authority. (Colossians 2:9, 10)

PAUL'S LETTERS (EPISTLES)

1 THESSALONIANS

Who: Paul
What: Letter to the Church in Thessalonica
Where: Corinth
When: c. AD 49–AD 54
Why: To emphasize Christ's return and to stress commitment.

Outline (Chapter)
• Faith and Example (1-3)
• Living for God (4)
• Christ's Return (4-5)

Key Verse: Be joyful always; pray continually; give thanks in all circumstances, for this is God's will for you in Christ Jesus. Do not put out the Spirit's fire; do not treat prophecies with contempt. Test everything. Hold on to the good. Avoid every kind of evil. May God himself, the God of peace, sanctify you through and through. May your whole spirit, soul and body be kept blameless at the coming of our Lord Jesus Christ. (1 Thessalonians 5:16-23)

2 THESSALONIANS

Who: Paul
What: Letter to the Church in Thessalonica
Where: Corinth
When: c. AD 50–AD 54
Why: To emphasize Christ's return and to encourage believers.

Outline (Chapter)
• Praise and Encouragement (1)
• Christ's Return (2)
• Pray and Work (3)

Key Verse: We have confidence in the Lord that you are doing and will continue to do the things we command. May the Lord direct your hearts into God's love and Christ's perseverance. In the name of the Lord Jesus Christ, we command you, brothers, to keep away from every brother who is idle and does not live according to the teaching you received from us. (2 Thessalonians 3:4-6)

1 TIMOTHY

Who: Paul
What: Letter to Timothy
Where: Rome
When: c. AD 64
Why: To remove false doctrine and suggest proper leadership for the church in Ephesus.

Outline (Chapter)
• Trouble in Ephesus (1)
• Church Leadership (2-3)
• False Teachers (4)
• Discipline (5)
• Paul's Advice to Timothy (6)

Key Verse: Don't let anyone look down on you because you are young, but set an example for the believers in speech, in life, in love, in faith and in purity. Until I come, devote yourself to the public reading of Scripture, to preaching and to teaching. (1 Timothy 4:12, 13)

2 TIMOTHY

Who: Paul
What: Letter to Timothy
Where: Prison in Rome
When: c. AD 65–AD 67
Why: To encourage Timothy to remain faithful in ministry even in the midst of suffering.

Outline (Chapter)
• Thanksgiving (1)
• Call to Remain Faithful (2)
• Authority of God's Word (3)
• Lead a Godly Life (3-4)

Key Verse: …from infancy you have known the holy Scriptures, which are able to make you wise for salvation through faith in Christ Jesus. All Scripture is God-breathed and is useful for teaching, rebuking, correcting and training in righteousness, so that the man of God may be thoroughly equipped for every good work. (2 Timothy 3:15-17)

TITUS

Who: Paul
What: Letter to Titus
Where: Rome
When: c. AD 64
Why: To encourage the church in Crete to do good works.

Outline (Chapter)
• Instruction for Titus (1)
• Living the Faith (2-3)
• Final Instructions (3)

Key Verse: But when the kindness and love of God our Savior appeared, he saved us, not because of righteous things we had done, but because of his mercy. He saved us through the washing of rebirth and renewal by the Holy Spirit, whom he poured out on us generously through Jesus Christ our Savior, so that, having been justified by his grace, we might become heirs having the hope of eternal life. (Titus 3:4-7)

PHILEMON

Who: Paul
What: Letter to Philemon
Where: Prison in Rome
When: c. AD 60
Why: To appeal to Philemon to forgive and receive Onesimus, a runaway slave.

Outline (Verses)
• Salutations (1-3)
• Philemon's Love and Faith (4-7)
• Paul's Appeal (8-22)
• Final Greetings (22-25)

Key Verse: So if you consider me a partner, welcome him as you would welcome me. If he has done you any wrong or owes you anything, charge it to me. I, Paul, am writing this with my own hand. I will pay it back–not to mention that you owe me your very self. (Philemon 17-19)

GENERAL EPISTLES & REVELATION

The eight General Epistles were written by other apostles and leaders including Simon Peter, James, John, and Jude. The General Epistles were addressed to the early Christians to provide guidance, encouragement through persecution, and warnings of false teachings.

HEBREWS
Who: Unknown (Paul)
What: Letter to Hebrew Believers
Where: Unknown
When: C. AD 60–AD 69
Why: To emphasize the superiority of Christ over the Old Covenant.

Outline (Chapter)
• Supremacy of Christ (1-4)
• The New Covenant (4-10)
• The Life of Faith (11-13)

Key Verse: Let us fix our eyes on Jesus, the author and perfecter of our faith, who for the joy set before him endured the cross, scorning its shame, and sat down at the right hand of the throne of God. (Hebrews 12:2)

JAMES
Who: James
What: Letter to Jewish Believers
Where: Jerusalem
When: C. AD 48
Why: Encouragement to live out one's faith within the Christian community.

Outline (Chapter)
• Living a Life of Faith (1-2)
• Faith without Works (2-3)
• Speech and Wisdom (3-4)

Key Verse: My dear brothers, take note of this: Everyone should be quick to listen, slow to speak and slow to become angry, for man's anger does not bring about the righteous life that God desires. (James 1:19, 20)

1 PETER
Who: Peter
What: Letter to All Christians
Where: Rome
When: C. AD 64–AD 65
Why: To call Christians to holiness.

Outline (Chapter)
• Holiness and Submission (1-2)
• Suffering (3-4)

Key Verse: The end of all things is near. Therefore be clear minded and self-controlled so that you can pray. (1 Peter 4:7)

2 PETER
Who: Peter
What: Letter to All Christians
Where: Rome
When: C. AD 64–AD 70
Why: To warn against false teachers.

Outline (Chapter)
• Living Like Christ; False Teachers (1-2)
• The Return of Christ (3)

Key Verse: For prophecy never had its origin in the will of man, but men spoke from God as they were carried along by the Holy Spirit. (2 Peter 1:21)

1 JOHN
Who: John
What: Letter to All Christians
Where: Ephesus
When: C. AD 85–AD 95
Why: To emphasize love in Christ.

Outline (Chapter)
• Living in the Light (1-2)
• Living in Love (3-4)
• Living by Faith (5)

Key Verse: Whoever does not love does not know God, because God is love. (1 John 4:8)

2 JOHN
Who: John
What: Letter to the Elect Lady
Where: Ephesus
When: C. AD 85–AD 95
Why: To warn against heresy and false teachers

Key Verse: Watch out that you do not lose what you have worked for, but that you may be rewarded fully. (2 John 8)

3 JOHN
Who: John
What: Letter to Gaius
Where: Ephesus
When: C. AD 85–AD 95
Why: To praise Gaius for his loyalty to the truth and criticize Diotrephes for his pride.

Key Verse: I have no greater joy than to hear that my children are walking in the truth. (3 John 4)

JUDE
Who: Jude
What: Letter to all Christians
Where: Unknown
When: C. AD 60–AD 95
Why: To warn against heresy

Key Verse: To him who is able to keep you from falling and to present you before his glorious presence without fault and with great joy. (Jude 24)

The book of Revelation addressed seven churches in Asia Minor (Turkey today). It encourages believers who are experiencing persecution. Revelation illustrates that God is in control and that all people were created to love and worship God.

REVELATION
Who: John
What: Letter to Seven Churches
Where: Island of Patmos
When: C. AD 96 or c. AD 69
Why: To give hope to persecuted Christians and provide a vision of Christ's return.

Outline (Chapter)
• The Seven Churches (1-4)
• Visions (5-16)
• God's Triumph (17-20)
• The New Creation (21-22)

Key Verse: Then I saw a new heaven and a new earth, for the first heaven and the first earth had passed away, and there was no longer any sea. (Revelation 21:1)

How We Got the Bible
Ten Key Points

1. The Bible is inspired by God (2 Timothy 3:16-17; 2 Peter 1:20-21).

2. The Bible is made up of 66 different books that were written over 1600 years (from approximately 1500 BC to AD 100) by more than 40 kings, prophets, leaders, and followers of Jesus. The Old Testament has 39 books (written approximately 1500-400 BC). The New Testament has 27 books (written approximately AD 45-100). The Hebrew Bible has the same text as the English Bible's Old Testament, but divides and arranges it differently.

3. The Old Testament was written mainly in Hebrew, with some Aramaic. The New Testament was written in Greek.

4. The books of the Bible were collected and arranged and recognized as inspired sacred authority by councils of rabbis and councils of church leaders based on careful guidelines.

5. Before the printing press was invented, the Bible was copied by hand. The Bible was copied very accurately, in many cases by special scribes who developed intricate methods of counting words and letters to insure that no errors had been made.

6. The Bible was the first book ever printed on the printing press with moveable type (Gutenberg Press, 1455, Latin Bible).

7. There is much evidence that the Bible we have today is remarkably true to the original writings. Of the thousands of copies made by hand before AD 1500, more than 5,300 Greek manuscripts from the New Testament alone still exist today. The text of the Bible is better preserved than the writings of Caesar, Plato, or Aristotle.

8. The discovery of the Dead Sea Scrolls confirmed the astonishing reliability of some of the copies of the Old Testament made over the years. Although some spelling variations exist, no variation affects basic Bible doctrines.

9. As the Bible was carried to other countries, it was translated into the common language of the people by scholars who wanted others to know God's Word. Today there are still 2,000 groups with no Bible in their own language.

10. By AD 200, the Bible was translated into seven languages; by AD 500, 13 languages; by AD 900, 17 languages; by AD 1400, 28 languages; by 1800, 57 languages; by 1900, 537 languages; by 1980, 1,100 languages. Source: *The World Christian Encyclopedia*.

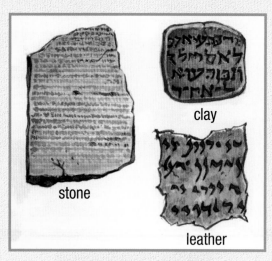

clay

stone

leather

Old Testament Written
(approx. 1500-400 BC)

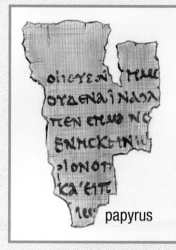

The oldest New Testament fragment (from John 18) that we have today was copied in Greek on a papyrus codex around AD 110-130.

papyrus

New Testament Written
(approx. AD 45-100)

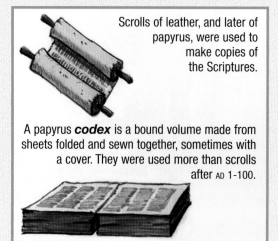

Scrolls of leather, and later of papyrus, were used to make copies of the Scriptures.

A papyrus **codex** is a bound volume made from sheets folded and sewn together, sometimes with a cover. They were used more than scrolls after AD 1-100.

Bible Copied on Papyrus

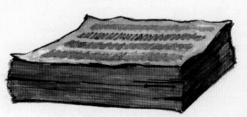

Fine quality animal skins from calves or antelope (vellum) and sheep or goats (parchment) were used for over 1000 years to make copies of the Bible approximately AD 300-1400.

Two of the oldest vellum copies (AD 325-350) that exist today are the Vatican Codex and the Sinaitic Codex.

Bible Copied on Fine Animal Skins

Wycliffe Bibles were inscribed by hand on vellum in the 1300s-1400s. Some copies took ten months to two years to produce and cost a year's wage.

The Bible was the first book to be printed with Gutenberg's printing press in 1455.

Bible Printed by Printing Press after 1455

The Bible is now printed on paper in many versions and languages. It is also on tape recordings, compact discs and computers.

The Bible, God's Word to The World

2000 BC

Old Testament events

are written down in Hebrew (portions in Aramaic) over centuries. In Exodus, the Lord tells Moses to write in a book. Other Old Testament writers, inspired by God, include leaders, kings and prophets. Together, these writings on leather scrolls and other materials are called the Hebrew Scriptures or Old Testament.

500 BC

Ezra,

a priest and scribe, collects and arranges some of the books of the Hebrew Bible—the Old Testament about 450 BC, according to Jewish tradition.

200 BC

The books are arranged by subject: historical, poetic, and prophetic. The Septuagint includes the Apocrypha (meaning "hidden") referring to seven books that were included in the Hebrew Bible until AD 90 when they were removed by Jewish elders.

The Septuagint is the

Greek translation of the Hebrew Bible (the Old Testament). It is translated in 250-100 BC by Jewish scholars in Alexandria, Egypt. (The word *Septuagint* means seventy, referring to the tradition that 70 or 72 men translated it. It is often abbreviated LXX, the Roman numeral for seventy.)

A Scribe

AD 1

Time of Jesus 4 BC-

AD 33? Jesus quotes the Old Testament (Scriptures) often. He says that He did not come to destroy the Scriptures, but to fulfill them. He says to his disciples, "These are the words which I spake unto you,...that all things must be fulfilled, which were written in the law of Moses, and in the prophets, and in the psalms, concerning me." Then opened he their understanding, that they might understand the scriptures. *Luke 24:44-45*

Papyrus,

a plant, is cut into strips and pressed into sheets of writing material and can be made into a scroll or a codex. The New Testament books were probably first written on papyrus scrolls. Later Christians begin to copy them on sheets of papyrus which are bound and placed between two pieces of wood for covers. This form of early book is known as a codex.

Papyrus

AD 100

Followers of Jesus

Matthew, Mark, Luke, John, Paul, James, Peter, and Jude write the Gospels, history, letters to other Christians, and the Revelation between AD 45 and 100. The writers quote from all but eight of the Old Testament books. These writings in Greek are copied and circulated so that by about AD 150 there is wide enough use of them to speak of the "New Testament" ("New Covenant"). The new covenant God made with people was promised in Jer. 31:31-34 and referred to by Jesus (Lk. 22:20) and Paul (1 Cor. 11:25) and in the letter to the Hebrews.

AD 200

Old Testament Apocrypha

Evidence derived from first century AD writers Philo and Josephus indicates that the Hebrew canon did not include the Apocrypha.

Earliest Translations

AD 200-300 Latin, Coptic (Egypt), and Syriac (Syria).

Church fathers accept

the writings of the Gospels and Paul's letters as *canonical* (from a Greek word referring to the *rule* of faith and truth). Origen lists 21 approved New Testament books. Eusebius lists 22 accepted books.

Early Coptic Translation

AD 300

The New Testament books

are collected and circulated throughout the Mediterranean about the time of Constantine, the Roman emperor who legalizes Christianity in AD 313. By AD 400 the standard of 27 New Testament books is accepted in the East and West as confirmed by Athanasius, Jerome, Augustine and three church councils. The 27 books of the New Testament were formally confirmed as canonical by the Synod of Carthage in AD 397, thus recognizing three centuries of use by followers of Christ.

Saint Matthew
Lindisfarne Gospels
Approximately AD 900

Jerome starts translating the

Scriptures into Latin in AD 382 and finishes 23 years later. This translation, called the Latin Vulgate, remains the basic Bible for many centuries.

Jerome

AD 500   AD 600   AD 1300

Roman Empire declines. Germanic migrations (AD 378-600) cause new languages to emerge.

The Masoretes are special Jewish scribes entrusted with the sacred task of making copies of the Hebrew Scriptures (Old Testament) approximately AD 500-900. They develop a meticulous system of counting the number of words in each book of the Bible to make sure they have copied it accurately. Any scroll found to have an error is buried according to Jewish law.

Christianity reaches Britain before AD 300, but Anglo-Saxon pagans drive Christian Britons into Wales (AD 450-600). In AD 596, Augustine of Canterbury begins evangelization again.

Caedmon, an illiterate monk, retells portions of Scripture in Anglo-Saxon (Old English) poetry and song (AD 676).

Aldhelm of Sherborne, AD 709, is said to have translated the Psalms.

Bede

Bede, a monk and scholar, makes an Old English (Anglo-Saxon) translation of portions of Scripture. On his deathbed in AD 735, he finishes translating the Book of John.

Alfred The Great, King of Wessex, 871-901, translates portions of Exodus, Psalms, and Acts.

Aldred, Bishop of Durham, inserts a translation in the Northumbrian dialect between the lines of the Lindisfarne Gospels (950).

Aelfric, 955-1020, translates portions of the Old Testament.

John Wycliffe

First English Bible is translated from Latin in 1382 and is called the Wycliffe Bible in honor of priest and Oxford scholar John Wycliffe. During his lifetime, Wycliffe had wanted common people to have the Bible. He also criticized a number of church practices and policies. His followers, derisively called Lollards (meaning "mumblers") included his criticisms in the preface to the Wycliffe Bible. This Bible is banned and burned. Forty years after Wycliffe's death, his bones are exhumed and burned for heresy.

Normans conquer England (1066) and make French the official language. No English translation work produced until the 1300s.

Middle English emerges, popularized by works such as the *Canterbury Tales* and Richard Rolle's *Psalter* (1340).

AD 1500

In 1408, in England, it becomes illegal to translate or read the Bible in common English without permission of a bishop.

World's first printing press with moveable metal type is invented in 1455 in Germany by Johann Gutenberg. This invention is perhaps the single most important event to influence the spread of the Bible.

The Gutenberg Bible is the first book ever printed. This Latin Vulgate version is often illuminated by artists who hand paint letters and ornaments on each page.

Gutenberg Bible Page

Erasmus, a priest and Greek scholar, publishes a new Greek edition and a more accurate Latin translation of the New Testament in 1516. His goal is that everyone be able to read the Bible, from the farmer in the field to the weaver at the loom. Erasmus' Greek text forms the basis of the *"textus receptus"* and is used later by Martin Luther, William Tyndale, and the King James translators.

Erasmus

Martin Luther translates the New Testament into German in 1522.

William Tyndale, priest and Oxford scholar, translates the New Testament from Greek (1525), but cannot get approval to publish it in England. He moves to Germany and prints Bibles, smuggling them into England in sacks of corn and flour. In 1535 he publishes part of the Old Testament translated from Hebrew. In 1536, Tyndale is strangled and burned at the stake. His final words are "Lord, open the King of England's eyes."

Tyndale is called the "Father of the English Bible" because his translation forms the basis of the King James Version. Much of the style and vocabulary we know as "biblical English" is traceable to his work.

William Tyndale

AD 1500

The Coverdale Bible
is translated by Miles Coverdale (1535) and dedicated to Anne Boleyn, one of King Henry VIII's wives. This is the first complete Bible to be printed in English.

Tyndale's Initials printed in the Matthew's Bible

The Matthew's Bible,
translated by John Rogers under the pen name "Thomas Matthew," is the first Bible published with the king's permission (1537). Printed just one year after Tyndale's death, its New Testament relies heavily on Tyndale's version, and even has a tribute to him on the last page of the Old Testament. Tyndale's initials are printed in 2 ½ inch block letters. Later Thomas Cromwell, advisor to King Henry VIII, entrusts Coverdale to revise Matthew's Bible to make the Great Bible.

1539 Great Bible is
placed in every church by order of Thomas Cranmer, archbishop under King Henry VIII. It is read aloud except during services and sermons. This Bible is chained to the church pillars to discourage theft.

The "Chained Bible"

AD 1555

England's Queen Mary
bans Protestant translations of the English Bible. John Rogers and Thomas Cranmer are burned at the stake. Later some 300 men, women and children are also burned.

The Geneva Bible
Exiles from England flee to Geneva, Switzerland, and in 1560 print the Geneva Bible, a complete revision of the Great Bible with the Old Testament translated from Hebrew. The Geneva Bible contains theological notes from Protestant scholars

Bishops Bible
A new translation begins under Queen Elizabeth in 1568. It is translated by several bishops of the Church of England in answer to the Geneva Bible.

Rheims-Douay Bible
was translated into English from the Latin Vulgate by Catholic scholar Gregory Martin, while in exile in France (1582/1609). It becomes the standard translation for the Catholic church.

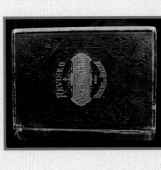

Queen Mary

John Calvin, Beza, Knox, and Whittingham. It is the first Bible to use Roman type instead of blackletter. This is the Bible of Shakespeare and the one carried to America by the Pilgrims in 1620. The 1640 edition is the first English Bible to omit the Apocrypha.

AD 1600

King James Version or Authorized Version
King James I of England commissions 54 scholars to undertake a new Bible translation. Over the next six years, six teams of scholars using the Bishops Bible and Tyndale's Bible, as well as available Greek and Hebrew manuscripts, complete the new version in 1611. The King James Version (also called the "Authorized Version," even though King James never gave the finished version his royal approval) is revised several

King James Bible Page from 1611 version

AD 1800

Older Manuscripts Discovered!
Between 1629 and 1947, several of the earliest known copies of the Bible are found.

Codex Alexandrinus,
a copy of the New Testament from AD 400 approx., perhaps the best copy of the book of Revelation, is made available to western scholars in 1629.

Codex Sinaiticus
(earliest complete copy of the New Testament, copied in AD 350 approx.) is found in St. Catherine's Monastery near Mt. Sinai.

times. The edition used today was revised in 1769. It is the most popular Bible for more than 300 years.

King James

reflect the findings from the manuscripts discovered the two previous centuries. Their goal is to use better Hebrew and Greek texts and to retranslate words based on new linguistic information about ancient Hebrew.

Codex Vaticanus
(earliest and probably best copy known of the New Testament from AD 350 approx.) is released to scholars in 1889 by the Vatican Library.

The Revised Version

The Revised Version
(AD 1885) In 1870, scholars in England decide to revise the King James Version to

AD 1900

AD 1900

The Dead Sea Scrolls, found in a cave in 1947 by a shepherd, contain the oldest known copies of portions of the Old Testament. These copies were made between 100 BC and AD 100.

A Qumran Cave near the Dead Sea

A Scroll of Isaiah that is part of the Dead Sea Scrolls is the oldest complete manuscript of any book of the Bible (copied around 100 BC). The copies of Isaiah discovered in the Qumran caves prove to be remarkably close to the standard Hebrew Bible, varying slightly in the spelling of some names. They give overwhelming confirmation of the reliability of the Masoretic copies.

During the 1900s more than a hundred New Testament manuscripts are found in Egypt.

Scroll of Isaiah

A Ugaritic Grammar is published in the 1960s. Ugaritic is an ancient language similar to Hebrew and helps scholars understand Hebrew vocabulary and poetry.

Modern Translations The knowledge from newly discovered manuscripts has led to hundreds of new translations.

1885 The English Revised Version A British revision of the King James Version.

1901 American Standard Version (ASV) Revision of the King James Version in American English.

1926 Moffatt Bible A very popular modern-language version.

1931 Smith-Goodspeed, An American Translation Modern American English.

1952 The Revised Standard Version (RSV) A revision of the A.S.V. New Testament revised 1971.

1958 J.B. Phillips' New Testament in Modern English A paraphrase, originally made for youth.

1965 The Amplified Bible Uses word-for-word ASV with added words to communicate insights on original texts.

1966 Jerusalem Bible Translation by Catholic scholars in Jerusalem. The New Jerusalem Bible, 1985.

AD 2000

AD 2000

1970 New English Bible "Timeless" modern English. Revised in 1989.

1970 New American Bible (NAB) Official version of the Catholic Church. Revised New Testament in 1986.

1971 New American Standard Bible Literal word-for-word translation. Updated in 1995.

1971 The Living Bible Popular paraphrase.

1976 The Good News Bible (Today's English Version) Vernacular English translation.

1978 New International Version (NIV) Dignified, readable.

1982 New King James Version Modernization of the KJV using the same manuscripts.

1989 Jewish New Testament English translation using traditional Jewish expressions.

1989 New Revised Standard Version "Gender neutral" revision of the RSV.

1991 Contemporary English Version "Natural, uncomplicated" English.

1995 God's Word Contemporary English.

1996 New Living Translation A revision of *The Living Bible* to make it a translation.

1996 New International Reader's Version (NIrV) A simplified version of the NIV with a 3rd or 4th grade reading level.

2001 English Standard Version (ESV) Literal update of the RSV.

2001 Today's New International Version (TNIV) (New Testament) Modernization of the NIV

2002 The Message (MSG) A paraphrase from the original languages.

2004 Holman Christian Standard Bible (HCSB) Balance between word-for-word and thought-for-thought.

The Origin and Growth of the English Bible

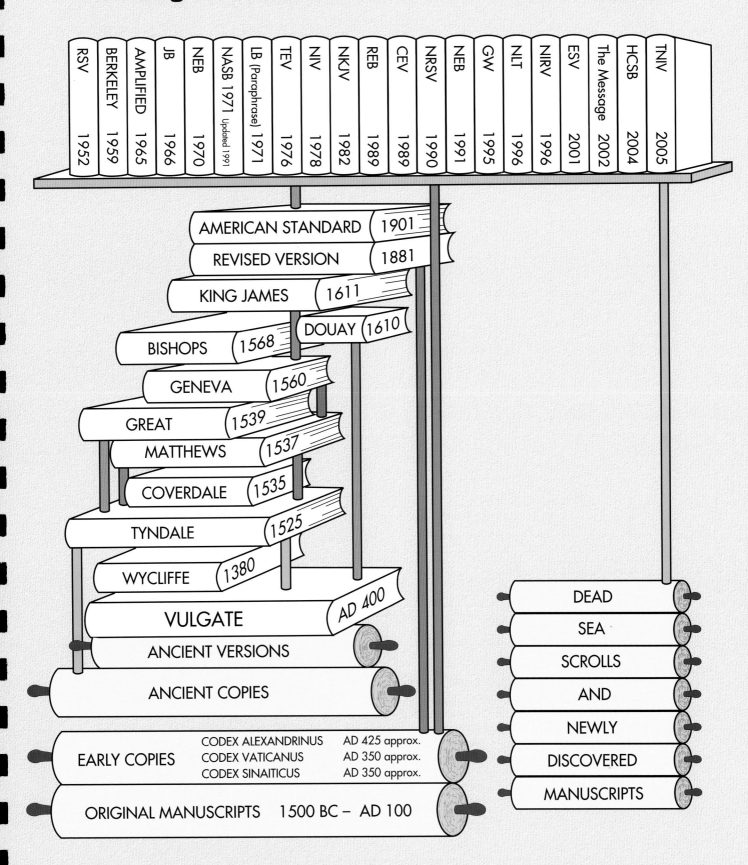

RSV	1952
BERKELEY	1959
AMPLIFIED	1965
JB	1966
NEB	1970
NASB 1971 Updated 1991	
LB (Paraphrase) 1971	
TEV	1976
NIV	1978
NKJV	1982
REB	1989
CEV	1989
NRSV	1990
NEB	1991
GW	1995
NLT	1996
NIRV	1996
ESV	2001
The Message	2002
HCSB	2004
TNIV	2005

AMERICAN STANDARD 1901
REVISED VERSION 1881
KING JAMES 1611
DOUAY 1610
BISHOPS 1568
GENEVA 1560
GREAT 1539
MATTHEWS 1537
COVERDALE 1535
TYNDALE 1525
WYCLIFFE 1380
VULGATE AD 400
ANCIENT VERSIONS
ANCIENT COPIES

EARLY COPIES
CODEX ALEXANDRINUS   AD 425 approx.
CODEX VATICANUS   AD 350 approx.
CODEX SINAITICUS   AD 350 approx.

ORIGINAL MANUSCRIPTS   1500 BC – AD 100

DEAD
SEA
SCROLLS
AND
NEWLY
DISCOVERED
MANUSCRIPTS

Adapted from the chart by BACK TO THE BIBLE BROADCAST, Lincoln, Nebraska

English Translations of the Bible

Translation/Version	Type of Translation	Description	Year Released
American Standard Version (ASV)	A formal or word-for-word translation.	Revision of the King James Version in American English.	1901
The Revised Standard Version (RSV)	A formal or word-for-word translation.	A revision of the A.S.V in 1952. The New Testament was revised again in 1971.	1952
The Living Bible (TLB)	A paraphrase	Very popular paraphrase with both adults and children.	1971
New American Standard Bible (NASB)	A formal, very literal, word-for-word translation.	Translation from original languages.	1971
The Good News Bible (Today's English Version) (GNT)	A dynamic or thought-for-thought translation.	A vernacular English translation.	1976
New International Version (NIV)	A balance between formal and dynamic translation.	A dignified and readable translation.	1978
New King James Version (NKJV)	A formal or word-for-word translation.	Modernization of the King James Version using the same manuscripts.	1982
New Living Translation (NLT)	A dynamic or thought-for-thought translation.	A revision of The Living Bible to make it a translation.	1996
The Message (MSG)	A paraphrase	Popular with new believers and those who desire more modern terminology.	2002

Important Terms to Know

Formal Translation (word-for-word): Translates the words and structures of the original languages.

Dynamic Translation (thought-for-thought): Translates the meaning and concepts of the original languages.

Paraphrase: Rewording of an existing translation in the same language or a free translation.

Comparisons of the Old Testament Canon

(Catholic, Orthodox, and Protestant Bibles all contain the same 27 New Testament books)

Hebrew Bible	Roman Catholic	Greek Orthodox	Protestant
Genesis	Genesis	Genesis	Genesis
Exodus	Exodus	Exodus	Exodus
Leviticus	Leviticus	Leviticus	Leviticus
Numbers	Numbers	Numbers	Numbers
Deuteronomy	Deuteronomy	Deuteronomy	Deuteronomy
Joshua	Joshua	Joshua	Joshua
Judges	Judges	Judges	Judges
1 Samuel	Ruth	Ruth	Ruth
2 Samuel	1 Samuel	1 Samuel	1 Samuel
1 Kings	2 Samuel	2 Samuel	2 Samuel
2 Kings	1 Kings	1 Kings	1 Kings
Isaiah	2 Kings	2 Kings	2 Kings
Jeremiah	1 Chronicles	1 Chronicles	1 Chronicles
Ezekiel	2 Chronicles	2 Chronicles	2 Chronicles
Hosea	Ezra	1 Esdras	Ezra
Joel	Nehemiah	Ezra	Nehemiah
Amos	Tobit	Nehemiah	Esther
Obadiah	Judith	Esther (includes additions to Esther)	Job
Jonah	Esther (includes additions to Esther)	Judith	Psalms
Micah	1 Maccabees	Tobit	Proverbs
Nahum	2 Maccabees	1 Maccabees	Ecclesiastes
Habakkuk	Job	2 Maccabees	Song of Solomon
Zephaniah	Psalms	3 Maccabees	Isaiah
Haggai	Proverbs	Psalms (plus Psalm 151)	Jeremiah
Zechariah	Ecclesiastes	Prayer of Manasseh	Lamentations
Malachi	Song of Songs (Song of Solomon)	Job	Ezekiel
Psalms	Wisdom of Solomon	Proverbs	Daniel
Proverbs	Sirach (Ecclesiasticus)	Ecclesiastes	Hosea
Job	Isaiah	Song of Songs (Song of Solomon)	Joel
Song of Songs	Jeremiah	Wisdom of Solomon	Amos
Ruth	Lamentations	Sirach (Ecclesiasticus)	Obadiah
Lamentations	Baruch (includes Letter of Jeremiah)	Hosea	Jonah
Ecclesiastes	Ezekiel	Amos	Micah
Esther	Daniel (includes Susanna and Bel and the Dragon)	Micah	Nahum
Daniel	Hosea	Joel	Habakkuk
Ezra	Joel	Obadiah	Zephaniah
Nehemiah	Amos	Jonah	Haggai
1 Chronicles	Obadiah	Nahum	Zechariah
2 Chronicles	Jonah	Habakkuk	Malachi
	Micah	Zephaniah	
	Nahum	Haggai	
	Habakkuk	Zechariah	
	Zephaniah	Malachi	
	Haggai	Isaiah	
	Zechariah	Jeremiah	
	Malachi	Baruch	
		Lamentations	
		Letter of Jeremiah	
		Ezekiel	
		Daniel (includes Susanna and Bel and the Dragon)	
		4 Maccabees (in Appendix)	

100 WELL-KNOWN PEOPLE IN THE BIBLE
Sixty Old Testament People

1. Aaron The older brother of Moses and Israel's first high priest (Numbers 26:59; Exodus 28:1)

2. Abel Adam and Eve's second son, killed by his brother Cain (Genesis 4:2, 8)

3. Abraham Father of the Hebrew nation and the ultimate role model for faith (Genesis 12:1-3; 1 Chronicles 1:34; 2:1; Hebrews 11:8-10)

4. Adam The first human being God created (Genesis 1:27; 2:7)

5. Balaam A false prophet who attempted to curse Israel and prevent them from entering the Promised Land (Numbers 22–24)

6. Bathsheba The wife of King David and mother of Solomon (2 Samuel 12:24)

7. Belshazzar A Babylonian king condemned by God for his blasphemy through written message on a wall during a drunken banquet. The message was interpreted by Daniel the prophet (Daniel 5)

8. Boaz The husband of Ruth, great-grandfather of King David and ancestor in the line leading to Jesus Christ (Ruth 4:13, 21, 22; Matthew 1:5-16)

9. Cain He was the first baby to be born on the earth and later murdered his younger brother Abel (Genesis 4:1, 8)

10. Caleb Joshua's faithful partner who urged Israel to enter the Promised Land at Kadesh-barnea as opposed to the 10 cowardly spies (Numbers 14:6-9)

11. Cyrus The Persian king issued the return decree allowing the Jews to go back and rebuild Jerusalem (2 Chronicles 36:22, 23)

12. Daniel Prime minister in Babylon under King Nebuchadnezzar and King Darius. Interpreted the handwriting on the wall to King Belshazzar (Daniel 2:48; 6:1-3; 5:25-28)

13. David Israel's greatest king, the father of Solomon. Author of more than one half of the Psalms (Psalms 78:70-72; 2 Samuel 12:24; 23:1, 2)

14. Deborah Israelite prophetess and judge who helped Barak to defeat the Canaanites (Judges 4:4, 8, 9)

15. Eli Israel's high priest who helped raise Samuel in the Tabernacle and died in great sorrow upon hearing that the Ark of the Covenant had been captured by the Philistines (1 Samuel 1:17-20; 4:12-18)

16. Elijah A fearless and rugged Israelite prophet who defeated his enemies on Mt. Carmel and was later caught up into heaven without dying (1 Kings 18:16-40; 2 Kings 2:1-18)

17. Elisha Elijah's successor who parted the Jordan River, raised the Shunammite's son from the dead, and healed Namaan of his leprosy (2 Kings 2:9-14; 5:10-14)

18. Enoch The first of two people taken from the earth without dying (Genesis 5:23, 24; Hebrews 11:5)

19. Esau Jacob's brother and the father of the Edomites (Genesis 25:26; 36:43)

20. Esther The Jewish Persian Queen who saved her people from destruction (Esther 7:3-6; 8:3-8)

21. Eve Adam's wife and the world's first woman. She was successfully tempted by Satan (Genesis 2:22; 3:1-6; 4:1, 2; 1 Timothy 2:14)

22. Ezekiel Prophet and priest became the key religious leader to the Jewish people in Babylon during the Babylonian captivity (Ezekiel 1:3; 2:3, 4)

23. Ezra A learned Jewish scribe and priest who led the second of three Jewish returns from the Babylonian captivity back to Jerusalem (Ezra 7:1, 6-10)

24. Gideon He was Israel's sixth military leader during the days of the Judges who defeated a vastly superior enemy army with just 300 chosen men (Judges 6:12-14; 7:22; 8:10-12)

25. Hagar She was Abraham's second wife and mother of Ishmael (Genesis 16:1-3, 15)

26. Hannah The godly woman who cried out to God to give her a child. She gave birth to Samuel (1 Samuel 1:20)

27. Hezekiah The thirteenth king of Judah and was on the throne when God saved the city of Jerusalem from the Assyrian army by the death angel (2 Kings 19)

28. Hosea Israelite prophet whom God commanded to marry a harlot named Gomer to illustrate Israel's spiritual adultery (Hosea 1:2)

29. Isaac Abraham's promised son and father of Jacob (Genesis 17:19; 25:21-26)

30. Isaiah Prophet who predicted the virgin birth of Jesus, His spirit-filled mission, His dual nature (Isaiah 9:6), His death, and His millennial reign (Isaiah 7:14; 11:13; 53:1-12; 2:2-4; 65:25)

31. Ishmael Abraham's first son (Genesis 16:15)

32. Jacob Isaac's son and the father of 12 sons from whom Israel's 12 tribes would come (1 Chronicles 2:1, 2)

33. Jeremiah Known as Judah's weeping prophet and author the book of Jeremiah. He later wrote a funeral song mourning the destruction of Jerusalem (Book of Lamentations)

34. Job God permitted this wealthy, righteous believer to be tormented by Satan to demonstrate God's presence and authority even in the midst of suffering. (Job 1, 2, 40-42)

35. Jonah A prophet who was punished by God for refusing to go preach in Nineveh. He was swallowed by a fish and later preached in Nineveh which resulted in a city-wide revival (Jonah 1-3)

36. Jonathan King Saul's son and David's closest friend (1 Samuel 14:1; 18:1)

37. Joseph Jacob's favorite son, sold into slavery by his own brothers, who would later use his position in Egypt to save his brothers and father from famine (Genesis 37:3, 28; 45:7-11)

38. Joshua Moses' successor who led Israel into the Promised Land (Joshua 1:1-3; 3:1-17)

39. Josiah This sixteenth king of Judah who used the discovery of the only remaining copy of the Law of Moses to lead his people in a great revival (2 Chronicles 34:1, 14-33)

40. Leah Jacob's first wife who bore him six sons (including Judah and Levi) and one daughter Dinah (Genesis 30:21; 35:23)

41. Melchizedek The king/high priest of Salem to whom Abraham paid tithes. His priestly work later being associated with the high priestly ministry of Jesus Christ (Genesis 14:18-20; Psalms 110:4)

42. Methuselah Died at the age of 969, the longest life span recorded (Genesis 5:27)

43. Miriam The elder sister of Moses who helped lead the Israelites through the wilderness (Exodus 15:20)

44. Mordecai Queen Esther's cousin who helped her save the Jewish people from slaughter. He later became prime minister of Persia (Esther 2:7; 4:14; 10:3)

45. Moses Israel's deliverer and law giver who led his people from Egypt to the border of the Promised Land. The author of scripture's first five books (Exodus 14; 20; Deuteronomy 31:9; 34:4)

46. Naaman Syrian military leader who was healed of leprosy by the prophet Elisha (2 Kings 5:14; Luke 4:27)

47. Naomi Ruth's mother-in-law and the great-great-grandmother of King David (Ruth 1:3-6; 4:18-21)

48. Nebuchadnezzar Founder/king of the Neo-Babylonian Empire who who had the three godly Hebrew men thrown into a fiery furnace. Later, he promoted both them and Daniel (Daniel 3–4)

49. Nehemiah Led the final of three return trips from Persia to Jerusalem after the Babylonian captivity. He rebuilt the walls around the city (Nehemiah 7:1)

50. Noah Constructed a ship at God's command and survived the great Flood along with his wife, three sons, and their three wives (Genesis 6:9; 8:19)

51. Rachel The beloved wife of Jacob and mother of Joseph and Benjamin (Genesis 29;18; 30:23, 24; 35:16-20)

52. Rahab The former harlot who saved the lives of two Israelite spies in Jericho and later was included in the genealogy of Jesus Christ (Joshua 2:6; Matthew 1:5)

53. Rebekah She was the wife of Isaac and mother of Esau and Jacob (Genesis 24:67; 25:24-26)

54. Ruth Naomi's daughter-in-law, Boaz's wife, and King David's great grandmother. (Ruth 1:14-17; 4:21, 22; Matthew 1:5, 16)

55. Samson Israel's thirteenth military leader during the time of the Judges. The strongest man who ever lived (Judges 14:6, 19; 15:14)

56. Samuel A prophet who was raised as a Nazarite in the Tabernacle and later anointed Saul and David as kings over Israel (1 Samuel 1:11, 20, 24; 9:27-10:1; 16:13)

57. Sarah Abraham's wife and Isaac's mother (Genesis 11:29; 21:1-7)

58. Saul Israel's first king who turned away from God (1 Samuel 10:17-27; 13:13, 14; 1 Chronicles 10:13)

59. Solomon King David's son and the wisest man who ever lived. He was the author of Proverbs, Ecclesiastes, and Song of Solomon (2 Samuel 12:24; 1 Kings 3:11, 12)

60. Zerubbabel A political leader who organized and led the first of three return trips from Babylon and Persia following the Babylonian captivity (Ezra 2:2)

Forty New Testament Individuals

1. Ananias A devout and well respected believer living in Damascus who ministered to the blinded Saul of Tarsus following his conversion (Acts 9:10-18; 22:12-16)

2. Andrew A former fisherman and one of the twelve apostles who brought his brother Peter to Christ (Mark 1:16; Matthew 10:2; John 1:40-42)

3. Apollos A gifted teacher and preacher from Alexandria who ministered in Ephesus, Greece, and Corinth (Acts 18:24-28; 1 Corinthians 1:12; 3:6)

4. Barnabas A godly teacher, the cousin of John Mark, who initially ministered in Antioch and later joined up with Paul during his first missionary journey (Acts 4:36; 11:22-26; 13:1-3)

5. Caiaphas The wicked high priest who plotted the death of Jesus and who later persecuted the leaders of the early church (Matthew 26:3-5, 62-65; Acts 4:6, 7)

6. Cornelius A God-seeking military commander living in Caesarea who was eventually led to Christ by Simon Peter (Acts 10)

7. Elizabeth The wife of Zacharias the Jewish high priest who supernaturally gave birth to John the Baptist in her old age (Luke 1:5-7, 57-60)

8. Herod Antipas The ruling son of Herod the Great who beheaded John the Baptist and later ridiculed Jesus during one of the Savior's unfair trials (Matthew 14:10, 11; Luke 23:10, 11)

9. Herod the Great King of Judea. A great builder who remodeled the second Jewish Temple and later attempted to kill the infant Jesus in Bethlehem (Matthew 2)

10. James the Apostle A former fisherman, the brother of John, and the first of the twelve apostles to be martyred for Christ (Matthew 4:21;10:2; Acts 12:1, 2)

11. James the Brother of Jesus An unbeliever prior to Jesus' resurrection, pastored the Jerusalem church, and authored the book of James (John 7:3-5; 1 Corinthians 15:7; Acts 15:13; 21:17, 18; James 1:1)

12. John the Apostle A former fisherman, the brother of James, the beloved disciple of Jesus, and author of the Gospel of John, First, Second, and Third John, and the book of Revelation (Matthew 4:18-22; Revelation 1:1)

13. John the Baptist The miracle child of elderly Elizabeth. The Nazarite evangelist who introduced Jesus, baptized him, and was martyred for his preaching (Luke 1:5-17; John 1:29; Matthew 3:13-17; 14:1-11)

14. Joseph The husband of Mary, and the godly, legal (but not physical) father of Jesus (Matthew 1:18-35)

15. Judas Iscariot The dishonest and demon-possessed apostle of Jesus who betrayed his master for 30 pieces of silver and then committed suicide (John 12:4, 5; 6:70, 71; Matthew 26:14, 15; 27:5)

16. Lazarus The brother of Mary and Martha whom Christ raised from the dead at Bethany (John 11)

17. Luke A Gentile physician who travelled with Paul. The author of the gospel of Luke and the Book of Acts (Acts 16:8, 10; Luke 1:1-4; Acts 1:1)

18. Lydia A business woman and Paul's first female convert in Greece (Acts 16:14, 15)

19. Mark The cousin of Barnabas who initially failed in the ministry. He was later restored and wrote the gospel of Mark (Acts 13:13; 2 Tim. 4:11)

20. Martha The sister of Mary who reaffirmed her faith in Jesus during the funeral of her brother Lazarus and then witnessed him being raised from the dead by the Savior (John 11)

21. Mary, the Mother of Jesus The virgin wife of Joseph who was chosen to give birth to the Savior of the world (Luke 1:26-38; 2:7)

22. Mary Magdalene A demon-possessed woman who was delivered by Jesus and later became the first person to see the resurrected Christ (Luke 8:2; John 20:16)

23. Mary, sister of Martha She worshiped at the feet of Jesus, witnessed Him raising her dead brother Lazarus, and would later anoint the body of the Savior (Luke 10:39; John 11:43; 12:1-3)

24. Matthew A former tax collector, called by Jesus to become an apostle. He would later author the book of Matthew (Matthew 9:9; 10:3)

25. Nathanael Also known as Bartholomew. He was introduced to Christ and later was called to become one of the twelve apostles (Jn. 1:45-51; Mt. 10:3)

26. Nicodemus A well known Pharisee and teacher. He was introduced to Christ during a midnight visit and would later help prepare His crucified body for burial (John 3:1-15; 19:39)

27. Paul A missionary, church planter, soul-winner, and theologian. He authored at least 13 of the 27 New Testament books before being martyred in Rome (Acts 13:2, 3; 20:17-21; 2 Timothy 4:6-8)

28. Peter A fisherman who became a disciple of Jesus, denied Jesus three times, and became the spokesman at Pentecost. He authored 1 and 2 Peter (Matthew 4:18; Luke 22:54-62; Acts 2:14-40)

29. Philemon He received a letter from the apostle Paul, urging him to forgive and restore his escaped slave Onesimus, a new convert who was returning home. (Book of Philemon)

30. Philip the Apostle He led his friend Nathanael to Christ shortly after his own conversion and later was called to serve as one of the twelve apostles (John 1:43; Matthew 10:3)

31. Philip the Evangelist He was one of the original seven deacons in the Jerusalem church who later became a powerful evangelist (Acts 6:3-5; 8:6-8, 27-39)

32. Pilate The Roman governor who was pressured by the Jewish leaders to release the guilty Barabbas and to scourge and crucify the innocent Jesus (Matthew 27:2, 15-26)

33. Priscilla She and her husband, tent-makers by trade, instructed Apollos in the scriptures and assisted the apostle Paul in his ministry (Acts 18:1-3, 24-26; Romans 16:3, 4)

34. Silas Paul's faithful companion during the second missionary journey (Acts 15:40)

35. Stephen He served as one of the original seven deacons. He ministered as an evangelist, was arrested, condemned, and stoned to death. He was the church's first martyr (Acts 6-7)

36. Thomas Known as the doubting apostle. He initially did not believe in Christ's resurrection until Jesus personally appeared to him. He had an unnamed twin brother (John 20:19-29)

37. Timothy One of Paul's most faithful associates. Paul addressed 1 and 2 Timothy to this godly undershepherd (1 Tim. 1:2; 6:11; 2 Tim. 1:5)

38. Titus A Greek Gentile, pastoring on the Isle of Crete. One of Paul's most trusted associates who later received a letter from Paul (Book of Titus)

39. Zacchaeus This dishonest tax collector met Jesus while in a sycamore tree and immediately accepted Him as Savior (Luke 19:1-10)

40. Zacharias A priest who was visited by the angel Gabriel. The angel Gabriel predicted his wife would present him with a son, John the Baptist (Luke 1:5-25, 57-80)

100 WELL-KNOWN PRAYERS IN THE BIBLE

Genesis	**1.** Abraham's prayer for Sodom (18:16-19)
	2. Abraham's servant's prayer regarding the solution of a bride for Isaac (24:12-14)
	3. Jacob's prayer as he wrestled with God at the brook of Jabbok (32:9-12)
	4. Jacob's prayer in Egypt for his two favorite grandsons (48:15-16)
Exodus	**5.** Moses' prayer beside the burning bush as God instructs him to return to Egypt (3-4)
	6. Moses' prayer at Rephidim regarding water for his people to drink (17:4, 5)
	7. Moses' prayer at Rephidim that God would give Joshua victory over the Amalekites (17:16)
	8. Moses' prayer that God would forgive Israel for worshiping the Golden Calf (32:11-14, 31)
	9. Moses' prayer to view God's glory (33:18)
Numbers	**10.** Moses' prayer that God's glory would continue to guide and protect Israel (10:35, 36)
	11. Moses' prayer for strength and help in governing Israel (11:10-15)
	12. Moses' prayer that God would heal Miriam of leprosy (12:13)
	13. Moses' three-fold prayer for Israel, pleading with God that he not destroy the people: a. Following their refusal to enter the Promised Land (14) b. Following Korah's rebellion (16) c. Following their complaint regarding lack of bread and water (21:6, 7)
	14. Moses' prayer that God would bless his successor, Joshua (27:15-17)
Deuteronomy	**15.** Moses' unsuccessful prayer to enter the Promised Land (3:23)
	16. Moses' prayer for Israel and Aaron following the Golden Calf episode (9:18-21)
Joshua	**17.** Joshua's prayers as he meets the captain of the Lord's hosts (5:13-15)
	18. Joshua's prayer following Israel's defeat at Ai (7:6-9)
	19. Joshua's prayer for additional sunlight at Aijalon (10:12-15)
Judges	**20.** Gideon's prayer for a sign (6:17, 18)
	21. Manoah's prayer for his unborn son Samson (13:8)
	22. Samson's prayer for supernatural strength that he might destroy his enemies (16:28)
First Samuel	**23.** Hannah's prayer of petition; asking God to give her a son (1:10, 11)
	24. Hannah's prayer of praise; thanking God for giving her a son (2:1-10)
Second Samuel	**25.** David's prayer thanking God for the permanent establishment of his kingdom (7:25)
	26. David's prayer asking God to permit his infant son to live (12:16)
First Kings	**27.** Solomon's prayer asking God for wisdom (3:9)
	28. Solomon's prayer of dedication at the completion of the Temple (8:23, 24)
	29. Elijah's three-fold prayer a. That God would raise up a dead child (17:20, 21) b. That God would send fire to consume a sacrifice (18:36-38) c. That God would take away his life (19:3, 4)
Second Kings	**30.** Elisha's prayer that God would raise up a dead child (4:33)
	31. Elisha's prayer that his servant see the angelic army that was protecting them (6:17)
	32. Hezekiah's prayer that God would save Jerusalem from the Assyrian army (19:14-19)
First Chronicles	**33.** Jabez's prayer that God would change his border (4:10)
	34. David's prayer that Jerusalem not be destroyed by a plague (21:17)

First Chronicles	**35.** David's prayer at the dedication of the building materials for the new temple (21:26)
Second Chronicles	**36.** Asa's prayer that God would deliver Jerusalem from the Ethiopian army (14:11)
	37. Manasseh's prayer for forgiveness regarding his many wicked acts (33)
Ezra	**38.** Ezra's prayer, confessing the sins of the Jewish remnant following the exile (8:21-23)
Nehemiah	**39.** Nehemiah's two-fold prayer: a. In Persia: that God would forgive the returning Jews already in Jerusalem b. To give him favor in the sight of King Artaxerxes (1)
	40. The prayer of praise and confession by the Levites after rebuilding Jerusalem's wall (9)
Job	**41.** Job's two-fold prayer after hearing and seeing God (42:1-6) a. Job's worthlessness b. God's sovereignty
Psalms	**42.** The psalmist thanks God who cared for him as an earthly father and mother would (27)
	43. The psalmist thanks God for encouragement in the time of great discouragement (28)
	44. The psalmist thanks God for the permanence of the divine king and kingdom (45)
	45. David confesses his sins of adultery and murder and prays for cleansing (51)
	46. The psalmist asks God to judge all enemies of righteousness and truth (69)
	47. The psalmist contrasts the morality of man with the eternality of God (90)
	48. The psalmist offers up a prayer of praise (103)
	49. The psalmist thanks God for His word (119:11)
	50. The psalmist thanks God for His omniscience, omnipotence, and omnipresence (139)
Isaiah	**51.** Isaiah's prayer that God would use him (6:8)
	52. Israel's prayer of praise during the millennium (12)
Jeremiah	**53.** Jeremiah's prayer of protest regarding his call to preach (1:6)
	54. Jeremiah's questions regarding God's dealing with Israel (12:1-6)
	55. Jeremiah's prayer regarding Israel's sin (14:1-10)
	56. Jeremiah's questions regarding his own ministry (15:5-21)
	57. Jeremiah's bitter complaint to God (20:7-8)
Lamentations	**58.** Jeremiah's prayer of total despair (3)
Daniel	**59.** Daniel's confessional prayer for both himself and his people (9)
Jonah	**60.** The prayer by some frightened pagan sailors (1:14)
	61. Jonah's prayer of rededication from the belly of a fish (2:2-9)
Micah	**62.** Micah's prayer of praise for God's forgiveness of His people (7)
Habakkuk	**63.** Habakkuk's prayer thanking God for His mercy, power, and salvation (3)
Matthew, Mark, Luke, John	Prayers prayed by Jesus:
	64. Before choosing His twelve disciples for wisdom in their selection (Luke 6:12, 13)
	65. Thanking the Father for revealing great truths to the 70 disciples (Matthew 11:25-30)
	66. Asking that Lazarus be raised to prove the Father had sent the Son (John 11:41, 42)
	67. Asking the father to comfort His troubled soul and glorify the Father's name (John 12:27, 28)
	68. He prays for Himself, His disciples, and all believers (John 17)

Matthew, Mark, Luke, John	**69.** Asking that His Father's will be done three times in the Garden of Gethsemane (Mark 14:35-41)
	70. His three-fold prayer on the cross: a. First prayer: "Father, forgive them" (Luke 23:24) b. Second prayer: "My God, my God, why hast thou forsaken me?" (Mark 15:34) c. Third prayer: "Father, into thy hands I commend my spirit" (Luke 23:46)
Luke	Prayers not prayed by Jesus:
	71. Zacharias' prayer for a son (1:11-20)
	72. Simeon's prayers at the dedication of the infant Jesus (2:29, 30)
	73. The publican's prayer for forgiveness (18:13)
Acts	**74.** The prayer session of the 120 in the Upper Room just prior to Pentecost (1:14)
	75. The apostles' prayer of thanking God for the privilege of suffering for Him (4:23-30)
	76. The apostles' prayer for the newly selected deacons (6:6)
	77. The prayer of the dying Stephen asking God to forgive those who were stoning him (7:59, 60)
	78. The prayer of Peter and John that the Samaritans would receive the Holy Spirit (8:15)
	79. Paul's prayer of submission upon seeing the resurrected Christ en route to Damascus (9:5)
	80. Peter's prayer that God would raise up Dorcas from the dead (9:40)
	81. Cornelius' prayer that he might be saved (10:2)
	82. The prayer of the Jerusalem church that Peter might be released from prison (12:5)
	83. The prayer of the Antioch church for the missionary efforts of Paul and Barnabas (13:1-3)
	84. The midnight prayer of the imprisoned Paul and Silas at Philippi (16:25)
	85. Paul's prayer for the Ephesian elders who had met him in Miletus (20:32)
	86. Paul's prayer for some disciples at Tyre (21:5)
	87. Paul's prayer for the healing of Publius' sick father on the Isle of Malta (28:8)
Romans	**88.** Paul's prayer for Israel's salvation (10:1)
Second Corinthians	**89.** Paul's prayer that God would remove his thorn in the flesh (12:8)
Ephesians	**90.** Paul's first prayer for the Ephesian church (1:17-23)
	91. Paul's second prayer for the Ephesian church (3:14-19)
Colossians	**92.** Paul's prayer for the church at Colosse (1:9-14)
Philemon	**93.** Paul's prayer for Philemon (4-7)
Hebrews	**94.** The author of Hebrews' prayer for believers (13:20, 21)
Revelation	**95.** Heaven's two-fold prayer of praise to God: a. Thanking Him for His great work in creation (4:11) b. Thanking Him for His great work in redemption (5:9-14)
	96. The prayer of the martyred souls in heaven (6:10)
	97. The prayer of the saved multitude during the Great Tribulation (7:10-12)
	98. The prayer of the heavenly saints thanking God for Christ's millennial reign (11:15)
	99. The heavenly saints thanking God for the marriage of Christ and His bride the church (19:6-8)
	100. The prayer of John that Christ would soon appear (22:20)

Table of Weights and Measures

Bible	American/British	Metric
Old Testament Weight & Modern Equivalent		
talent (60 minas)	75 pounds	34 kilograms
mina (50 shekels)	1.25 pounds	0.6 kilogram
shekel (2 bekas)	0.4 ounce	11.3 grams
pim (0.66 shekel)	0.33 ounce	9.4 grams
beka (10 gerahs)	0.2 ounce	5.7 grams
gerah	0.02 ounce	0.6 gram
New Testament Weight & Modern Equivalent		
pound (Roman litra)	12 ounces	340.2 grams
Old Testament Length & Modern Equivalent		
cubit (2 spans)	18 inches	46 centimeters
span (3 handbreadths)	9 inches	23 centimeters
handbreadth (4 fingers)	3 inches	7.6 centimeters
finger	0.75 inch	1.9 centimeters
New Testament Length & Modern Equivalent		
mile (8 stadions)	4858 feet	1.5 kilometers
stadion (100 fathoms)	200 yards	183 meters
reed (3 paces)	9 feet	2.7 meters
fathom (2 paces)	6 feet	1.8 meters
pace	3 feet	0.91 meters
Old Testament Liquid Measures & Modern Equivalent		
cor or homer (10 baths)	58 gallons	220 liters
bath (6 hins)	5.8 gallon	22 liters
hin (12 logs)	1 gallon	3.8 liters
kab or cab	1.3 quarts	1.23 liters
log	0.7 pint	0.3 liter
New Testament Liquid Measure & Modern Equivalent		
firkin	10 gallons	39.9 liters

Table of Weights and Measures

Bible	American/British	Metric
Old Testament Dry Measure & Modern Equivalent		
cor or homer (10 ephahs)	6 bushels	218 liters
lethek (5 ephahs)	3 bushels	109 liters
ephah (10 omers)	23 quarts	18.9 liters
seah	7.7 quarts	7.3 liters
omer	2.3 quarts	2.2 liters
kab or cab	1.3 quarts	1.2 liters
New Testament Dry Measure & Modern Equivalent		
bushel	7.7 quarts	7.3 liters
measure	1.2 quarts	1.1 liters
pots	1.2 pints	0.6 liter

Money in the Bible

Name (Equivalent)	Value
Old Testament Monetary Values & Modern Equivalent	
shekel	$0.32 – $9.60*
mina (50 shekels)	$16.00 – $480.00
talent (60 minas)	$960.00 – $28,000.00
*value depends on weight of currency (light or heavy) and type of currency (silver or gold)	
New Testament Monetary Values & Modern Equivalent	
mite or lepton	$0.0012
farthing or quadran (2 mites)	$0.0024
penny (1 Roman danarius)	$0.16 (daily wage of a laborer)
mina or pound (100 Roman danarii)	$16.00
Talent (240 Roman aurei)	$960.00

Life of Jesus. Early Church. Age of the Apostles and Church Fathers.

AD1

4? BC Birth of Jesus Christ in Bethlehem of Judea.

AD 29? Beginning of Jesus' public ministry, about age 30. He preaches, does miracles and claims to be God.

AD 33? Jesus crucified, resurrected, appears to more than 500 disciples at one time (I Cor. 15:6). Jesus gives his followers the Great Commission: "Go ye therefore and teach all nations . . ." (Matt. 28:19). After 40 days, he ascends into heaven (Acts 1:3, 9).

33 Pentecost: the Holy Spirit descends on the disciples in Jerusalem. Some 3,000 people become Christians. They spread the Gospel (the good news about redemption through Jesus) throughout the Roman Empire (Acts 2:8).

35 Stephen, the first Christian martyr, is stoned to death in Jerusalem. Believers scatter through Judea, Samaria.

35 Conversion of Paul, formerly Saul, the persecutor of Christians. Paul goes on three missionary journeys starting in AD 48 to preach to Jews and Gentiles. He writes 13 letters (epistles) to the new churches.

41 Conversion of Roman centurion, Cornelius. Peter and other Christians evangelize Gentiles. Converts among Roman soldiers return to Italy and preach.

Followers of Christ first called Christians at Antioch.

44 Christians are persecuted under King Herod Agrippa. James is executed, Peter is imprisoned. Famine strikes Judea; Christians in Antioch send relief.

45-100 The Gospels (Matthew, Mark, Luke and John) and the other New Testament books are written.

49-50 Council of Jerusalem agrees with Paul that Gentile converts are not required to follow Jewish law. Paul's work with Gentiles recognized.

53 Jews expelled from Rome. Jewish believers Priscilla and Aquila flee. They meet Paul in Corinth during his second missionary journey.

64 Great fire in Rome blamed on Christians. Emperor Nero tortures and kills thousands of Christians.

67-68? Peter and Paul taken to Rome. Paul evangelizes while under house arrest. Both executed under Nero.

66-70 Jewish revolt against Romans. Emperor Titus destroys the Temple in Jerusalem. Jews and Christians flee to all parts of the empire, including Alexandria, Carthage, and Rome. Antioch becomes the center for Christianity.

71-81 Colosseum in Rome built. Christians thrown to beasts.

81 Roman persecution of Christians under Domitian. Jews oust followers of Jesus from synagogues.

85-150 Writings of apostolic fathers (early church leaders) Barnabas, Clement of Rome, Ignatius, Polycarp.

90 Rise of Gnostic heresies within the church. Some gnostics deny Jesus' humanity (Docetism), saying that he merely appeared to have a body. Gnostics claim to have secret knowledge beyond divine revelation and faith.

Christianity spreads to Egypt (Mark), Sudan (Ethiopian eunuch), Armenia (Thaddaeus, Bartholomew), France, Italy, Germany, Britain, Iraq, Iran, India (Thomas), Greece, Yugoslavia, Bosnia, Croatia (Titus), Asia Minor (Turkey today), Albania, Algeria, Libya, and Tunisia (Africa).

AD100

c. 100 Death of John, the only one of Jesus' 12 disciples to die a natural death. All others are martyred.

c. 107 Martyrdom of Ignatius, bishop of Antioch, who wrote letters of encouragement to the early churches.

c. 125 Gnosticism spreads.

132-135 Second Jewish rebellion. Jerusalem destroyed. Most of the population dies or flees.

c. 144 Marcion is excommunicated for heresy. He taught that there was no connection between the Old and New Testament, between the God of the Jews and the God of the Christians. He rejected the Old Testament. The heresy persists in some areas for several centuries.

Early Christians create this mosaic floor in a church in Galilee to depict Jesus' miracle of the loaves and fishes.

c. 155 Justin Martyr, theologian, writes his first *Apology*, a rebuttal to Greek philosophers.

Polycarp, bishop of Smyrna and disciple of the apostle John, is burned at the stake at age 86+. Polycarp refers to Old and New Testament books as "scriptures."

c. 156 Montanus of Phrygia preaches a form of religious extremism called Montanism.

c. 180 Irenaeus of Lyons, student of Polycarp and great theologian, writes *Against Heresies*. He lists 20 New Testament books as *canonical* (officially accepted and recognized as authoritative).

193 Roman persecution under Septimius Severus.

196 Easter controversy concerning the day to celebrate Christ's resurrection. Western Christians prefer Sunday; eastern Christians prefer linking Easter with the Jewish Passover regardless of the day of the week.

197 Christianity sweeps the empire. Tertullian writes "There is no nation indeed which is not Christian."

The Apostles Creed and the *Didache* (an important document describing Christian beliefs, practices, and church government) are written during this century.

By AD 200 the church recognizes 23 New Testament books as canonical, but it is unlikely these are collected yet into one volume.

Christianity expands to Morocco, Bulgaria, Portugal, and Austria. Widespread conversion to Christianity in North Africa.

Christianity Legalized. Byzantine Era.

AD200

200 The Scriptures now are translated into seven languages, including Syriac and Coptic (Egyptian).

Christians in Egypt viciously persecuted, thousands martyred.

215 Clement of Alexandria, theologian, dies.

c. 220 Origen, theologian and student of Clement, founds a school in Caesarea. He writes many works, including commentaries on most of the New Testament books. Origen writes, "The gospel of Jesus Christ has been preached in all creation under heaven."

235-270 Roman persecution under several emperors. Christianity grows rapidly.

Carthage becomes a major center for Christianity in Africa.

c. 242 Manichaeism originates in Persia (Iran today). This dualistic heresy denies the humanity of Christ, and reappears in different forms over the centuries.

261 First church buildings erected as rectangular shaped basilicas. Previously Christians met in homes.

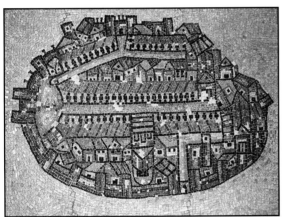

The Madaba map, a mosaic from the 500s, shows basilicas built by early Christians in Jerusalem.

During this century, monasticism begins in Egypt: eremitical (individual hermits) and cenobitic (religious groups or orders).

287 Mass conversion of Armenia under Gregory the Illuminator; King Tiridates makes Christianity the state religion.

c. 292 Diocletian divides Roman Empire into East and West. Regions are different culturally and politically. Rome's influence wanes in the East.

295 Some Christians refuse military service and are executed. Galerius begins to doubt that Christians in the army will obey orders. He persuades Diocletian to expel Christians from the Roman legions.

The phrase "catholic" is used to mean all churches that agree with the whole apostolic teaching, as opposed to the heretical groups that follow a "secret revelation" or knowledge based on one teaching.

Christianity expands to Switzerland, Sahara, Belgium, Edessa, Qatar, Bahrain (Assyrian Church), Hungary, and Luxembourg.

AD300

303-4 Violent persecution of Christians under Diocletian. Scriptures burned; thousands killed.

311-411 Donatist schism in North Africa. Christians who stayed faithful during Diocletian's persecution oppose leniency toward those who lapsed.

312 Constantine (emperor of the western provinces) sees a vision of the cross of Jesus that he credits for giving him victory in battle.

Constantine I, legalizes Christianity. His mother, Helena, a devout Christian, goes to the Holy Land to locate key places in Jesus' life, and builds many churches.

313 Edict of Milan (Toleration). Constantine and Licinius (emperor of the eastern provinces) agree to end the persecution of Christians, but it continues in the East.

320 Arius claims that Jesus Christ is a created being and not God by nature. His beliefs are called Arianism.

324 Eusebius writes *Church History*.

325 Council of Nicaea is convened in response to numerous heresies. It condemns Arianism and produces an early version of the Nicene Creed—a clear definition of the Trinity.

330 Constantine establishes the capital of the empire at Byzantium and renames it Constantinople.

337 Constantine baptized a few days before death.

339 Severe persecution of Christians in Persia (Iran).

346 Death of Pachomius, father of monasticism in the East and founder of the monastery at Tabennisi, Egypt.

350 Eastern church is mostly Arian. Arianism spreads to the Goths.

361 Emperor Julian the Apostate attempts unsuccessfully to restore paganism to the Roman Empire.

364 Basil, bishop of Caesarea, opposes Arian teachings.

367+ Canon of the New Testament slowly collected and confirmed. Books recognized as authoritative by Athanasius, bishop of Alexandria, in the East, and the Council of Carthage in the West.

c. 376 Goth and barbarian invasions of the Roman empire begin.

381 Council of Constantinople I finalizes the Nicene Creed and condemns heresies about Jesus.

391 Theodosius makes Christianity the official religion.

398 John Chrysostom, great orator, becomes bishop of Constantinople.

Christianity expands to Afghanistan and Ethiopia.

Fall of the Roman Empire. Rise of the Eastern Orthodox Church. Middle Ages. Rise of Monasticism.

AD400

395-430 Augustine, bishop of Hippo (N. Africa), authors numerous theological works including *City of God* and arguments against Donatists, Pelagians, and Manichaeans. His writings dominate Christian theology in the West for centuries.

405 In Bethlehem, Jerome finishes translating the Old and New Testament into Latin after 23 years of work. The Vulgate, as it is known, is the Bible used for the next 1000 years.

410 Arian Visigoths sack Rome.

428 Nestorius, patriarch of Constantinople, teaches that there are two distinct Persons in Jesus Christ (Mary is mother of the human part only), therefore some of Jesus' actions were human and some were divine.

431 Council of Ephesus condemns Nestorianism and Pelagianism (which claims man can attain salvation by works). The council defines Mary, Jesus' mother, as *Theotokos*, "bearer of God" to show that Jesus has *one* nature that is fully human and fully divine.

432 Patrick evangelizes Ireland. Over the next 30 years most of the country has been converted.

440 Leo the Great becomes pope. He persuades Attila the Hun to spare a weakened Rome.

451 Council of Chalcedon focuses on the divine and human natures of Christ. It confirms Pope Leo's *Tome* and condemns Appolinarianism, Nestorianism, and Monophysitism (also known as Eutychianism, which denies the humanity of Christ). Copts of Egypt and Ethiopia divide, the majority form monophysite or "One Nature" churches.

Early Christians commemorate this location on the Mt. of Olives, as the place where Jesus wept over Jerusalem.

476 Fall of the western Roman Empire. Emperor ousted. This marks the beginning of the Middle Ages.

496 Clovis, king of the Franks, converts to Christianity.

499 By the end of this century, the Scriptures have been translated into 13 languages.

Christian spreads to Western No. Africa, the Isle of Man, San Marino, Liechtenstein, the Caucasus, Ireland, and tribes in Central Asia.

AD500

500 Syrian Orthodox church establishes a monophysite monastery in Ethiopia.

520 Irish monasteries flourish as centers of learning, spiritual life, and training for missionaries to other parts of the known world.

Nestorians gain converts throughout Asia and continue to influence religious life for many centuries.

The monastery of St. George of Koziba in the Judean Wilderness is built in 480.

525 Christianity spreads throughout the Middle East, including the Arabian Peninsula (Saudi Arabia, Yemen, and Oman today).

529 Monk Benedict of Nursia, founder of Monte Cassino Abbey in Italy, writes the *Rule*, a guide for monastic life. Benedict is considered the father of monasticism in the West.

545? Death of Dionysius Exiguus, a monk, who was the first to date history by the life of Christ, leading to the B.C. and A.D. designations. His calculations were off by at least four years.

553 Council of Constantinople, convened by Emperor Justinian, condemns the "Three Chapters," (the writings of several theologians including Theodore of Mopsuestia) for alleged heresies.

589 Third Council of Toledo. Visigoth king renounces Arianism, accepts church teachings.

590 High ranking Roman official, Gregory, resigns his post and donates his wealth to church relief efforts for the poor in 574. He is elected pope in 590. Known as Gregory the Great (or Gregory I), he institutes reforms and sends missionaries (including Augustine of Canterbury) to re-evangelize England, after Angle and Saxon pagans force Christian Britons to Wales. He also promotes liturgical music and the growth of monasticism. He is the first of the medieval popes.

597 Death of Columba, evangelist of Scotland and founder of an important monastery at Iona, Scotland.

Christianity spreads to North Yemen, Ceylon, Malabar, Nubia (Sudan), Channel Islands, and Andorra.

Rise of Islam. Islamic Conquest in Europe.

AD600

600 Plainsong "Gregorian" chants begin to develop.

610? Muhammad declares himself to be Prophet of God, after claiming to receive divine revelations. He founds the religion of Islam. In 622 he is persecuted and flees (*hegira*) from his home in Mecca to the oasis of Medina. There he founds a Muslim community. In 630 he launches a military campaign and defeats his opponents in Mecca. His teachings and deeds are called the Qur'an (Koran). By Muhammad's death in 632, Islam has spread to much of Arabia.

632 Islam sweeps through Palestine and Syria. Muslims (those who follow Islam) conquer Jerusalem. By 640 Islam invades Egypt and North Africa, almost eradicating Christianity (which had numbered more than one million believers). Three hundred years later very few Christians remain in the region.

663 The Synod of Whitby aligns the English church with Rome for the next nine centuries.

676-709 Earliest Old English (Anglo-Saxon) translations and paraphrases of portions of the Bible are made by Caedmon and Aldhelm.

680-692 Eastern and Western churches drift further apart due to differences in church practices and expression of theology. On clergy celibacy: the Eastern church allows priests to be married, provided that they are married before ordination. The Western church discourages it.

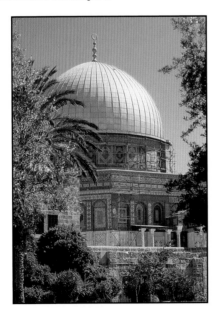

688-691 The Dome of the Rock, gold domed shrine of Islam, is built on the Temple Mount in Jerusalem by caliph Abd al-Malik. Its ornate interior and location were designed to impress travelers. Some of the beautiful columns in the shrine are adorned with crosses, indicating that they were removed from Christian churches.

Christianity spreads to China, Andorra, Netherlands, Indonesia, Niger, Mongolia. Christianity declines in Northern Africa.

AD700

711 Muslim Moors invade Spain and Portugal, their first foothold in Europe. They are driven out in the 1200s.

716 Boniface, an English missionary, known as the "Apostle to the Germans," evangelizes southern and central German cities and establishes Benedictine monasticism.

720 Bede translates the Gospel of John into English; writes *Ecclesiastical History*.

The use of icons is debated throughout the East for 100 years. In 787 the Second Council of Nicaea decides in favor of those who venerated icons.

726 Controversy over the use of icons in the East. Emperor Leo condemns the veneration of sacred images and relics (supports *iconoclasm*, "image-breaking"). In 731, Pope Gregory III condemns iconoclasm and supports the veneration of icons.

732 Charles Martel defeats the Muslims in France, stopping the Muslim advance in Europe for 100 years.

754 A council of 300 Byzantine bishops endorse iconoclasm. The council is condemned by the Lateran synod of 769.

754 Pepin, son of Charles Martel, unites and rules the Franks. At the request of Pope Stephen II (III), Pepin invades Italy to defend it against Lombard invaders. Pepin gives conquered land to the church (called the Donation of Pepin) which establishes the papal states.

768-814 Charlemagne, son of Pepin, expands his empire through military conquest to almost all of what is now France, Germany, and Italy. He forces the German Saxons to convert.

787 Council of Nicaea II condemns iconoclasm (the belief that venerating sacred images is idolatry) and Adoptionism (belief that Jesus was not Son of God by nature). This is the last council that is recognized as binding by both the eastern and western churches.

Christianity spreads to Iceland, Pakistan, and East Germany.

Charlemagne. Islam Spreads to Italy. Church Schism.

AD800

800 Charlemagne crowned Roman emperor by Pope Leo III. His administration reforms the law and church organization. He also encourages all monasteries to teach reading and writing. Through the influence of the scholar Alcuin, schools are founded and scriptoria set up to copy the Bible and Latin classics. This commitment to culture is known as the Carolingian Renaissance. The Western church's prominence begins to increase; the Eastern church's declines.

800 Egbert, king of the West Saxons, unifies England and becomes the first king.

814 Charlemagne dies.

829 Sweden is evangelized by Anskar, "Apostle of the North."

837 Christians in Egypt are persecuted and forced to wear 5-pound crosses around their necks.

843 Charlemagne's empire is split between his three grandsons.

845 Nestorians are persecuted in China.

846 Muslims attack Rome.

857 Photian Schism: communion between Eastern and Western church broken when Patriarch Photius of Constantinople (Orthodox Church) rejects the Roman pope's claim of primacy among the bishops of the East as well as the West.

861 Slavs are converted by Greek missionary brothers Cyril and Methodius, who translate the Scriptures and other works into the Slavonic language.

868 Count Vimara Peres drives Moors out of Portugal.

871 Alfred the Great, king of Wessex, translates portions of the Psalms, Exodus, and Acts into Old English (Anglo-Saxon).

876 Byzantine Empire retakes Italy.

Built near the Pools of Bethesda in Jerusalem, the Church of St. Anne, is one of the finest examples of Crusader architecture.

AD900

Christianity spreads to Tibet, Burma, Denmark, Czechoslovakia, Sweden, and Norway.

902 Muslims gain complete control of Sicily.

909 William, Duke of Aquitane, founds the Benedictine Abbey of Cluny, France, which becomes the center for reform under Abbot Odo (926).

950-999 Conversion of royalty across the empire, including Olga of Kiev, Miesko of Poland, and Stephen of Hungary.

962 Otto I, the Great, founder of the Holy Roman Empire, is crowned by Pope John XII. This empire continues until 1806.

988 Conversion of Vladimir of Kiev, grandson of Olga, to Eastern (Orthodox) Christianity. According to tradition, Vladimir considered other religions, but chose Orthodoxy because the splendor of the worship at the Church of St. Sophia in Constantinople convinced him that "God dwells there among men." Vladimir orders the population of Kiev to choose Christianity. He wipes out paganism, builds churches, and establishes schools. At his death, he donates all of his possessions to the poor.

The iconostasis of an Orthodox church separates the nave (the central area of the church) and the altar.

996 In Egypt, Caliph El Hakim persecutes Copts, destroying thousands of churches and forcing people to convert to Islam.

999 Leif Ericson converts to Christianity while in Norway. The next year he brings the Gospel to his father's colony in Greenland.

Christianity in western North Africa virtually wiped out by Islam.

Christianity spreads to Hungary, Kiev (Russia today), Greenland, Bohemia , and Poland.

AD**1000**

1000 Greek Catholicism (Melkite) introduced in Nubia.

1009 Nestorians convert northern Mongolians. Their beliefs spread to Persia (Iran today), India, and China.

1054 Great Schism between the church in the West and the East. Roman Cardinal Humbart, envoy of Pope Leo IX, excommunicates Patriarch Michael Cerularius in the Church of St. Sophia (Hagia Sophia) in Constantinople. Despite this, there is some cooperation between the Eastern (Orthodox) and Western (Roman Catholic) church against the Seljuk Turks.

1066 Normans (French Christians) conquer Britain, Sicily, and evangelize the Celts.

1071 Seljuk Turks (converts to Islam) from Central Asia conquer Persia (Iran today) and move west toward the Byzantine capital, Constantinople (Turkey today).

1073 Gregory VII (Hildebrand) becomes pope. He works to revive and reform the church. He prohibits simony (the buying or selling of church offices), sexual immorality in the clergy, and lay investiture (the custom of emperors and local rulers choosing local church leaders).

1096 Pope Urban II calls for volunteers for a crusade to repel the Turks: specifically to help Eastern Christians in Constantinople, to liberate the Church of the Holy Sepulchre in Jerusalem, and to reopen the Holy Land to Christian pilgrims.

Church of the Holy Sepulchre in Jerusalem. Considered by many scholars to be the location of Jesus' tomb.

1097-99 The First Crusade. More than 70,000 people inspired by both noble and lesser motives, join the ranks and head for the Holy Land. In their zeal they slaughter Jews in Germany and pillage villages en route. They capture Jerusalem in 1099 and brutally massacre their opponents. They set up the Latin Kingdom of Jerusalem under Godfrey of Bouillon, and build castles and churches.

AD**1100**

1115 Bernard founds a monastery at Clairvaux, which becomes the influential center of Europe.

1116 Peter Abelard, philosopher and theologian.

1122 Concordat of Worms focuses on the controversy over lay investiture. (Worms, pronounced "vormps," is a city in Germany)

1123 Lateran Council ratifies the Concordat of Worms.

1129 The Knights Templar, an order of monastic soldiers sworn to protect Holy Land pilgrims, is recognized.

1130 Disputed election of Popes Innocent II and Anacletus II. Innocent becomes pope.

1139 Second Lateran Council focuses on pseudo-popes (popes elected by unauthorized councils).

1146 Second Crusade is preached by Bernard of Clairvaux in response to the Muslim conquest of Edessa, the crusader capital (Turkey today). The crusade, led by Louis VII of France and Emperor Conrad III of Germany, fails.

1150 Syrian Orthodox church reaches zenith.

College of Cardinals is established by pope.

1162 Thomas Becket becomes archbishop of Canterbury. A close friend of Henry II and chancellor of England, Becket resigns his chancellorship after conflicts with Henry over the power of the church and the throne.

1170 Becket is murdered by knights of Henry II.

1174 French merchant and reformer Peter Valdes gives his wealth to the poor and becomes an itinerant preacher, the beginning of the Waldensians. His beliefs are accepted by the church, but his practice of appointing ministers and preaching without permission draws criticism and eventually excommunication.

1177 Third Lateran Council denounces the Waldensians and Albigensians. (Albigensians were heretics that believed that Jesus was an angel with a phantom body, and therefore did not die or rise again.)

1187 Muslim general Saladin defeats Crusaders at the Horns of Hattin (Galilee) and captures Jerusalem.

The Horns of Hattin (flat mountain, center)

1189-92 The Third Crusade, led by Richard I (the Lion-Heart) of England, Philip II of France, and Barbarossa the Holy Roman Emperor, captures Cyprus, Acre, and Jaffa. Richard negotiates access to Jerusalem for Christian pilgrims.

Christianity spreads to Finland.

Middle Ages. Bubonic Plague. Crusades. Papal Schism.

AD1200

1201 Pope Innocent III claims the right of the pope to oversee the moral conduct of heads of state and to choose rulers, including the emperor. The height of papal authority.

1202 Innocent III launches Fourth Crusade to defeat Egypt. After some setbacks, Crusaders defy the pope and sack Constantinople, center of the Orthodox church. A three-day massacre by the Crusaders alienates the eastern and western church for centuries.

1208 Church declares a crusade against Albigensians.

1209 Francis of Assisi gives away his wealth and starts group of traveling preachers (Franciscans).

1211 Mongol Genghis Khan, whose mother is a Nestorian, rises to power. Conquers China, Iran and Iraq.

1212 Children's Crusade disaster. Thousands of children die at sea or are sold into slavery.

1212 Alfonso VII of Castile leads a coalition against the Moors and drives them out of Spain (the battle of Las Navas de Tolosa).

1215 Fourth Lateran Council condemns Waldensians and Albigensians; affirms doctrine of transubstantiation. In 1231, the Papal Inquisition is established.

1216 Dominican order forms, dedicated to spiritual reform.

1217 Fifth Crusade to defeat Egypt fails. Francis of Assisi crosses enemy lines to preach to the sultan.

The seaport Acre, the last Crusader stronghold, falls to Egyptian Mamluks in 1291.

1229 Crusaders recover Jerusalem by negotiation. In 1244 the Muslims recapture Jerusalem by force.

1255 Thomas Aquinas, the most influential medieval theologian, writes *Summa Theologiae*.

1266 Mongol leader, Kublai Khan, asks the pope to send 100 Christian teachers to baptize him and teach his people. The pope sends seven. In 1295 the Mongols begin to convert to Islam.

AD1300

1274 Byzantine Empire rebuilt. Second Council of Lyon decrees unification of the eastern and western church, but unification is rejected in the East.

1302 Pope claims supremacy over secular rulers.

1302 Franciscans active in Mongol empire.

1309 The "Babylonian Captivity": for the next 70 years, the papacy resides in Avignon, France. The new pope favors French policies; convenes the Council of Vienne that abolishes the Order of Knights Templar and gives their wealth to King Philip IV of France.

1312-1324 Marsilius of Padua writes *Defensor pacis*, stating that the church should be ruled by general councils. He is condemned as heretical.

1348-51 The Bubonic plague, also known as the Black Death, kills 33% of the people in Europe (about 40 million). People blame the disease (which is transmitted by fleas living on rats) on the Avignon papacy, the Jews, or personal immorality.

John Wycliffe

1371 John Wycliffe, English priest and diplomat, proposes that papal taxation and civil power should be limited. He challenges some church doctrines, including transubstantiation. He believes Scripture should be available to the people in their own language. People inspired by Wycliffe (derisively called "Lollards," meaning mumblers), translate the entire Bible into English (1382) from Latin, and call it the Wycliffe Bible.

1373 Julian of Norwich, English mystic.

1376 Catherine of Sienna, mystic, sees a vision calling the new pope, Gregory XI, to return the papacy to Rome, which he does in 1377.

1378 Great Papal Schism: Two or three popes at one time. The College of Cardinals elects an Italian pope, Urban VI, but later denies the validity of the decision and elects Clement VII instead. Urban remains in Rome. Clement goes to Avignon, France. The schism continues until 1417.

AD 1400

1408 In England, it becomes illegal to translate or read the Bible in English without permission of a bishop.

1413 Jan Hus of Bohemia (Czechoslovakia) writes *De Ecclesia*, which supports ideas popularized by Wycliffe.

1414-1418 Council of Constance rejects Wycliffe's teachings and burns Jan Hus at the stake as a heretic. It affirms that general councils are superior to popes (conciliarism), a decision later overturned. Pope Martin V is elected; the Great Papal Schism ends.

1418 Thomas À Kempis, a German monk, writes the *Imitation of Christ*, a devotional.

1431 Joan of Arc, a French peasant girl during the Hundred Years' War, sees visions and hears voices telling her to save France. She leads a successful military expedition at Orleans. Later she is taken prisoner, tried for witchcraft, and is burned. In 1456, the verdict is reversed.

Joan of Arc

1438 Council of Florence affirms the primacy of the pope over general councils. It declares reunion between the Roman and Orthodox churches, but is not accepted by the Orthodox.

c. 1450 Beginning of the Renaissance. The popes of the Renaissance (1447-1521) are notable more for their intrigues and quest for power than for their pastoral care or desire for reform.

1453 Ottoman Turks capture Constantinople and make the Church of St. Sophia (Hagia Sophia) a mosque. Scholars flee to the West with Greek literary and scientific manuscripts, including manuscripts of the Bible. These manuscripts help to revive classical learning during the Renaissance.

Plans to build a new St. Peter's Basilica in Rome begin, including efforts to raise funds for construction.

1456 Johann Gutenberg prints the Latin Vulgate, the first book printed using moveable metal type. The invention of printing makes the Bible accessible to more people who previously could not afford handmade copies, which cost a year's wage.

Page from the Gutenberg Bible

1479 The Spanish Inquisition begins at the initiation of King Ferdinand V and Queen Isabella of Spain, and is approved by the pope. It is established to investigate and punish heretics. Its cruel methods (torture, death by burning), secret trials, and favoritism toward the Spanish monarchy continue despite protests from Rome. The Franciscan and Dominican friars who serve as judges often misuse their power. Thousands of Jews are deported. Later the Inquisition is used against Protestants. It is finally suppressed in 1820. Catholics today condemn the methods used.

1492 The last of the Muslim Moors are removed from Spain by Ferdinand and Isabella.

Columbus discovers the Americas.

Peak of papal corruption: Rodrigo Borgia buys cardinals' votes and becomes Pope Alexander VI.

1493 Pope Alexander VI avoids war by dividing newly discovered lands in the Americas and Africa between Spain and Portugal. Vast colonizing of the New World by explorers for the next 150 years. Settlers wishing to exploit the land and the people conflict with missionaries (Dominicans, Franciscans and Jesuits) who spread the Gospel and advocate for the Indians.

1497-8 Dominican friar Savonarola preaches reform. He encourages the people of Florence, Italy, to burn luxury items and return to a humbler Christian life. He sells church property and gives the proceeds to the poor. Despite his initial popularity with the common people, he is caught in a political conflict with Alexander VI and is excommunicated. His popularity wanes and later he is executed for heresy.

Christianity reaches Senegal, Guinea Bissau, Mauritania, Haiti, Dominican Republic, Kenya, and Equatorial Guinea.

Protestant Reformation. Age of Exploration.

AD 1500

1500 Decline of Christianity in China, Persia, Nubia (So. Egypt and Ethiopia), and areas influenced by Islam.

Moscow claims to be the center of Christianity after the fall of Constantinople.

1503-12 Pope Julius II commissions Michelangelo to finish painting the Sistine Chapel. In 1506, the foundation stone of St. Peter's Basilica is laid.

1512-17 Council of Lateran V is held to address a variety of concerns, including church reform.

1516 Erasmus, priest and Greek scholar, publishes a Greek translation of the New Testament. Later editions of his Greek text form the basis of the *textus receptus* and are used by Martin Luther, William Tyndale, and the King James Bible (Authorized Version).

Martin Luther, becomes convinced that faith alone justifies the Christian, without works (Eph. 2:8-9) —a doctrine supported by Augustine's writings.

1517 Martin Luther posts his *95 theses* on the door of the church in Wittenberg. They call for an end to abuses involved in methods of selling indulgences. The Protestant Reformation begins.

1519 Swiss Ulrich Zwingli spreads reform.

1522 Luther translates the New Testament into German.

1525 William Tyndale makes an English translation of the New Testament from Greek without permission and smuggles copies into England. He is burned at the stake.

1525 The Anabaptist movement, predecessor to Brethren and Mennonite churches, teaches believers' baptism only, democratic decision making, and separation of church and state.

1529 The term Protestantism becomes associated with Lutheranism, Zwinglianism, and Calvinism. Protestant characteristics: acceptance of the Bible as the only source of revealed truth, the doctrine of justification by faith alone, and the priesthood of all believers.

1530 Augsburg Confession adopted by Lutherans.

1534 Act of Supremacy makes British monarch Henry VIII head of the English church, breaking away from Roman Catholic control. The new "Church of England" (Anglican Church) sets forth a doctrinal statement: *The 39 Articles.*

1535 The Munster Rebellion. Anabaptists take over Munster and are slaughtered. Later, under the leadership of Menno Simons, the group adopts pacifism.

1537 The Matthew's Bible is the first English Bible published with the king's permission. On the last page of the Old Testament, the translator prints Tyndale's initials in 2½ inch letters to honor him. Many Bibles in common languages begin to appear.

1536 John Calvin's *Institutes of the Christian Religion* explains Protestant beliefs, including predestination.

1540 Ignatius Loyola's Society of Jesus (Jesuits) approved. They vow to evangelize the heathen.

1545-63 Council of Trent (Catholic Counter-Reformation) condemns indulgence sellers, immorality of clergy, nepotism (appointing family members to church offices), and Protestantism.

1549 The Church of England's *Book of Common Prayer* unites most English churches in a middle route between Catholicism and Protestantism.

Jesuit Francis Xavier begins missionary efforts in the Indies and Japan: 100,000 converts attributed to him.

1555 Queen Mary Tudor restores Roman Catholicism to England, bans Protestant translations of the Bible, and persecutes Protestants. Many Protestants flee to Geneva, Switzerland, where they print the Geneva Bible (1560).

1560 John Knox's Reformed church begins in Scotland.

1558 Queen Elizabeth I becomes queen of England and Supreme Governor of the Church of England. She aims for a compromise between Catholics and Protestants. In 1570, she is excommunicated by the pope, and in turn persecutes Catholics.

1562 Heidelberg Catechism is formed. It is the most widely held Protestant doctrinal statement for centuries.

1568 Bishops Bible, Church of England translation.

1577 Formula of Concord defines Lutheran beliefs.

1582/1609 Catholic scholar Gregory Martin translates the Rheims-Douay Bible from the Vulgate (Latin) while in exile in France.

1596 Council of Brest-Litovsk. Most Orthodox in Kiev, Czechoslovakia, Hungary, and Polish Galatia (Uniat Churches) join communion with Roman Catholic church.

1598 Edict of Nantes grants freedom of worship to French Protestants (Huguenots) after 30 years of persecution. In 1685, the Edict is revoked by Louis XIV.

Christianity spreads throughout Thailand, Cambodia, Macao, South Korea, South America and Africa through Catholic missionary efforts (through monastic orders), conquest, and colonization. Few Protestant efforts during the next 200 years.

King James Bible. Galileo.

AD1600

1601 Jesuit missionary and scholar, Matteo Ricci, starts evangelizing China by befriending intellectuals in the emperor's court in Peking (Beijing). Ricci is one of the first missionaries to adopt the dress and customs of the land he seeks to evangelize. His methods are criticized by other Catholics as too tolerant toward the idolatrous Confucian custom of ancestor worship.

1603 Dutch Reformed theologian Jacobus Arminius's studies of the Epistle to the Romans lead him to doubt Calvin's doctrine of predestination. He sets forth doctrines that emphasize man's ability to choose Christ and Christ's death for all people (Arminianism).

1605 Gunpowder Plot fails. Catholic fanatics attempt to kill England's King James I and blow up the houses of Parliament in order to seize the government.

1609 The first Baptist church is founded in Amsterdam by John Smyth, who baptizes himself (by pouring).

1611 King James Version Bible (KJV), also known as the Authorized Version (AV), is published. King James I of England commissions 54 scholars to undertake a new Bible translation, which takes six years to complete. The scholars use the Bishops Bible and Tyndale's Bible as well as available Greek and Hebrew manuscripts. After slow initial acceptance, this becomes the most popular Bible for the next 300 years.

A page from the King James Bible, also known as the Authorized Version (even though it never received official royal authorization).

1618 Dutch Reformed Synod of Dort denounces Arminianism and responds to Arminius's five criticisms of Calvinism with five points of Calvinism. They are (using the mnemonic *tulip*): the **t**otal depravity of mankind (mankind's inability to choose Christ), **u**nconditional election, **l**imited atonement, the **i**rresistibility of grace, and the final **p**erseverance of the saints (an elect person cannot "lose" his salvation).

1622 Creation of the Congregation de *Propaganda Fide* for Roman Catholic missionary efforts.

1620-30s Separatists reject the Church of England and sail to America on the *Mayflower*. Later Puritans, who wish to cleanse the church, arrive and start colonies.

1629 Orthodox Patriarch of Constantinople, Cyril Loukaris (Lucar), befriends Protestants and presents the earliest known copy of the Bible in Greek (*Codex Alexandrinus*, fifth century AD) to Charles I of England.

1630 Catholicism wiped out in Japan, thousands of martyrs.

Coptic and Syrian Orthodox churches decline.

1633 The Sisters of Charity founded by Vincent de Paul.

Galileo

1642 Death of Galileo, scientist, who agreed with Copernicus's theory that the earth moved around the sun. He was censured by the church and kept from teaching his views because his proofs were inadequate. The case was closed in his favor in 1992.

Power struggles between Charles I and the Parliament lead to civil war in England. Puritan member of Parliament, Oliver Cromwell, defeats the king's troops. Later as Lord Protector, he seeks tolerance for many Protestant groups.

1646 Westminster Confession accepted as the statement of Presbyterianism in Scotland and England.

1647 Beginnings of the Quaker movement (the Society of Friends) under preacher George Fox.

1648 End of the Thirty Years' War. Catholics and Protestants given equal rights in most of the Holy Roman Empire.

1649 In America, Iroquois Indians destroy Huron Indians and their Jesuit mission.

1654 Conversion of Blaise Pascal, French mathematician and theologian.

1655 Waldensians break from Roman Catholicism and embrace Protestantism. Catholics launch persecutions.

1667 John Milton writes *Paradise Lost*.

1673 The British Test Act bans Catholics from holding public office unless they deny certain doctrines.

1678 John Bunyan's *Pilgrim's Progress* published.

1685 Edict of Nantes revoked. Huguenots flee France.

1689 English Parliament issues Toleration Act (tolerating all Protestant groups, but not Roman Catholics).

1692 Chinese emperor officially allows Christianity. Ricci's initial 2,000 converts multiply to 300,000.

1698 First missionary societies formed by Protestants.

Christianity spreads to Bermuda, Uruguay, Taiwan, Barbados, St. Kitts-Nevis, Laos, Montserrat, Antigua, Virgin Islands, Grenada, Anguilla, Belize, Gambia, Polynesia, Chad, Micronesia, Gabon, Bahamas, Benin.

Great Awakening. French Revolution. American Independence.

AD1700

1700 Slave trafficking from Africa increases.

1704 Pope Clement XI condemns "Chinese Rites," the mixture of Confucianism and ancestor worship with Christianity in China. Persecution against Christians begins; thousands are killed.

1705 Death of Philipp Jakob Spener, the "father of Pietism." Pietism emphasizes feelings, a personal religious experience, and living a life of intense devotion.

1706 First Presbyterian church in America. It is governed by a board of elders (presbyters).

1707 Isaac Watts writes more than 600 hymns in his life.

1721 Peter the Great appoints the Holy Synod to head the Russian Orthodox church, putting the church under the state's control until 1917.

1722 Count Nikolaus Ludwig von Zinzendorf welcomes fleeing Hussites from Moravia (Moravian Brethren) to live on his lands. The pietistic colony that forms, "Herrnhut," sends out missionaries to Africa, India, and the Americas.

1724 Greek Catholic (Melkite) church established in what is now Lebanon. Primarily located in Ethiopia and parts of Egypt, the Melkite church had accepted the Council of Chalcedon in 451, rejecting monophysitism.

1729 Jonathan Edwards, one of America's greatest preachers and theologians, preaches in Northampton.

Anglican minister John Wesley and his brother Charles are converted through contact with Moravians.

1738 Conversions of John and Charles Wesley. Their emphasis on living a holy life by doing specific spiritual disciplines each week is derided as "methodist." Eventually the descriptive is accepted with pride, and Methodism spreads rapidly in the Church of England.

Charles Wesley pens more than 6,000 hymns, including "And Can It Be" and "O For a Thousand Tongues to Sing," and "Hark, the Herald Angels Sing."

Freemasonry condemned by Pope Clement XII (and later popes). The pope forbids Catholics to join.

1739 George Whitefield, Anglican preacher, gives open-air evangelistic messages.

John Wesley travels throughout Britain on horseback, reportedly giving 40,000 sermons during his lifetime.

1740 The Great Awakening in New England, led by Whitefield. Revival spreads throughout colonial America.

1741-2 George Frideric Handel writes the *Messiah*.

1759 Powerful Jesuit order suppressed. In 1773, it is dissolved by the pope. In 1814, Jesuits are reestablished.

1764 John Newton, former slave trader converts, writes "Amazing Grace."

1769 Serra founds the first of nine missions in California.

1771 John Wesley sends Francis Asbury to preach in America. The American Methodist Church becomes a separate organization in 1784.

1773 First independent Black Baptist church is established in America.

1780 "Sunday school" is developed in England by Robert Raikes out of concern for urban poor.

1781 Immanuel Kant's *Critique of Pure Reason*. Reason cannot deny the existence of God, the soul, or eternity.

1784 "Conference of Methodists" forms a group within the Church of England.

The Russian Orthodox send missionaries to Alaska.

1785 Korean Christianity expands, then is exterminated.

1789 The French Revolution results in a new government and a new religion hostile to Christianity, "The Cult of Reason." Thousands of Catholic and some Protestant clergy are executed. Ten years later the French invade Rome, and take Pope Pius VI prisoner to France.

1792 Second Great Awakening: revival sweeps New England for 30 years.

William Carey, often called the father of modern Protestant missions

1793 William and Dorothy Carey of England sail for India. Carey writes a significant work on the Great Commission and offers strategies for fulfilling it at a time when many Protestants believe that "when God pleases to convert the heathen, he'll do it without consulting you or me."

The Baptist Missionary Society and other missionary societies formed during this century.

1795 Many American churches, including the Baptists, begin to divide over the issue of slave holding.

1797 Methodists separate from the Church of England to form a distinct church.

Christianity spreads to Nepal, Seychelles, Falkland Islands, Turks and Caicos Islands, Pitcairn Island, Sierra Leone, Norfolk Island, and Tonga.

Abolition. Industrial Revolution. Darwin.

AD 1800

1801 French leader Napoleon Bonaparte reconciles with new pope temporarily (Concordat of 1801) and makes himself emperor in 1804. France reinvades Rome and takes Pius VII to France as a prisoner.

1807 William Wilberforce, member of Parliament and devout Christian, leads Parliament to abolish the slave trade in the British Empire. He and other Christians also address social problems including exploitative child labor, illiteracy, prison reform, education, and reinstating civil rights for Jews and Catholics.

1811 Thomas and Alexander Campbell's Restoration Movement gives rise to the Disciples of Christ and some Church of Christ groups.

1813 Adoniram and Ann Judson arrive in Burma.

Richard Allen, founder of the AME Church

1816 The African Methodist Episcopal Church (AME) is founded by Richard Allen, a free Black, in Philadelphia. In 1821, the African Methodist Episcopal Zion Church forms.

1822 Congregation for the Propagation of the Faith (reestablished by Pope Pius VII) spurs Roman Catholic missionary efforts in Ethiopia, Mongolia, North Africa (Charles Lavigerie, founder of the White Fathers) and Hawaii (Fr. Damien, works with lepers 16 years and dies of leprosy).

1827 John Nelson Darby of the Plymouth Brethren creates the first dispensational system (dividing history into spiritual eras or *dispensations*), which influences Cyrus Scofield's teachings of the 1900s.

1830 Friedrich Schleiermacher, the "Father of Liberal Protestant Theology," teaches that God is *within* human reality, not above it.

Joseph Smith, Jr., founds the Church of the Latter-day Saints (Mormonism), which denies the Trinity.

1833 Oxford Movement calls the Church of England to return to "high church" practices and doctrines.

1835 Charles Finney leads revival in New York.

1836 George Müller opens faith orphanage in England.

1840 David Livingstone, missionary, goes to Africa.

1844 Søren Kierkegaard's *Philosophical Fragments*.

The YMCA and YWCA (Young Men's/Women's Christian Association) form in London during the Industrial Revolution to introduce Christianity to new large populations in urban areas.

Adventist Movement begins with William Miller.

1854 Baptist preacher Charles H. Spurgeon draws such great crowds that a church is built for him in England.

Immaculate Conception dogma is pronounced by Pope Pius IX. It states that Mary, Jesus' mother, was free from original sin, a belief debated since the Middle Ages.

Dwight L. Moody

1855 Dwight L. Moody, shoe salesman in Chicago, converts and works with the YMCA. He develops a simple message of repentance and salvation and the work of the Holy Spirit ("higher life"). Moody, Finney, and singer Ira Sankey mark the beginning of "revivalism": revival meetings held in urban areas.

1859 Charles Darwin writes *Origin of the Species*.

1863 Seventh-Day Adventist Church founded.

1864 Catholics in Korea persecuted by revolutionaries.

1865 Hudson Taylor begins China Inland Mission.

1865 After the U.S. Civil War, many former slaves join with other African-Americans to start denominations in America, including the Black Baptists and the Colored Methodist Episcopal Church (CME, later the C is changed to mean Christian).

1870 First Vatican Council (Roman Catholic) on faith and the church declares papal infallibility dogma.

1875-9 Christian Science and Jehovah's Witnesses (Watchtower Bible and Tract Society) founded. Both deny Christ's deity.

1878 The Salvation Army is founded by William Booth and his wife, Catherine Munford, both Methodist preachers, to minister to the poor.

1880 Moody leads the nondenominational Northfield Conferences, which emphasize holiness, dispensationalism, missions, evangelism, and the Spirit-filled life.

1887 B.B. Warfield, Reformed theologian at Princeton.

1895 The five "fundamentals" of the faith are set forth by the Evangelical Alliance to define the line between fundamentalism and modernism (radical liberalism). They are the inerrancy of Scripture, the deity of Jesus, the Virgin birth, Jesus' death providing substitutionary atonement, Jesus' physical resurrection, and his imminent return.

1895 Turks massacre 300,000 Armenian Christians.

Christianity spreads to Botswana, Madagascar, Djibouti, Somalia, Zambia, Rwanda, Liberia, Samoa, Transkei, New Hebrides, Lesotho, Uganda, Hong Kong, and Pacific Islands.

World Wars. Rise of Communism. Space Travel. Computer Age.

AD1900

1901 Amy Carmichael, Irish missionary to India for 53 years, starts work at Donavur for children in danger.

Boxer Rebellion: Chinese kill missionaries and converts.

Many revivalists now preach premillennialism.

1906 Azusa Street revivals, led by William Seymour, emphasize living a holy life demonstrated by Spirit baptism and evidenced by speaking in tongues. Beginnings of Pentecostalism.

Albert Schweitzer writes *Quest for the Historical Jesus*.

1909 Scofield Bible published. Cyrus Scofield links verses from various books of the Bible in an attempt to explain God's actions in human history—fitting history into seven distinct spiritual eras (dispensations).

1914 Assemblies of God, and later Church of God and Four-Square Gospel denominations, form in the wake of the Azusa Street revivals.

1917 Communism spreads anti-religious ideology through Europe, Asia, and Latin America. Christianity is eradicated from education and worship. Millions are imprisoned and killed.

1919 Karl Barth's *Commentary on Romans*. Birth of neo-orthodoxy, which challenges liberalism with an emphasis on the Bible and on God's transcendence.

1925 Billy Sunday, the "baseball preacher," preaches salvation and temperance revivals.

Scopes "Monkey" Trial (State of Tennessee v. John Scopes) on the teaching of evolution.

1930-1950 Many Protestant denominations split over issues involving modernism, higher life, or dispensationalism, including the Presbyterian Church in the USA and the Northern Baptist Convention.

1934 Wycliffe Bible Translators is founded by Cam Townsend. Wycliffe and other organizations translate the Bible into other languages. In 1914 there are portions of the Bible in 600 languages. By 1980, the Bible is translated into more than 1600 languages.

1941 Rudolf Bultmann leads movement to "demythologize" the Bible.

1933-45 Rise of Nazism, leading to World War II and the death of 6 million Jews and millions of Christians.

Dietrich Bonhoeffer leads the seminary of the Confessing Church in Germany during the Nazi regime.

1945 Dietrich Bonhoeffer, Lutheran pastor and a leader of the underground church in Germany, is hanged for plotting to kill Adolph Hitler.

1945 Franciscan priest Maxmilian Kolbe, prisoner in Auschwitz, volunteers to die and is executed in place of a fellow prisoner.

1948 Discovery of the Dead Sea Scrolls, the oldest known copies of portions of the Bible (c. 100 BC).

Modern political State of Israel established.

1949 Organized Christian churches exist in every country in the world except for Afghanistan, Saudi Arabia and Tibet, according to *World Christian Encyclopedia*.

Billy Graham, a Southern Baptist minister, preaches the largest crusade in history—1.1 million people in Seoul, Korea, in 1973.

Billy Graham's Los Angeles Crusade launches his ministry. Over the next five decades, he preaches to more people than any evangelist in history.

World Council of Churches formed by representatives from all major Christian denominations except the Roman Catholics.

1954 Scientology and Unification Church founded. Neither accepts the Trinity or the deity of Jesus Christ.

1950-1960's Explosion of Christianity in newly independent African countries. Approximately 200 million Christians by 1980.

1962 Second Vatican Council (Roman Catholic) accepts Protestants as "separated brethren," encourages translating and reading the Bible, revokes the excommunication of the Great Schism (1054), upholds papal infallibility and encourages services (the Mass) to be held in each common language rather than in Latin.

1963 C.S. Lewis, author of *Mere Christianity*, dies.

1964 Baptist minister Martin Luther King, Jr., receives Nobel Peace Prize for civil rights efforts.

1970s Many major national and international crusades held: Latin America (Luis Palau), worldwide Here's Life crusade (Campus Crusade), Korea (Billy Graham). Jesus Movement in the USA; charismatic movement.

Largest church in the world is now in Seoul, Korea.

1997 Death of Mother Teresa of Calcutta, Catholic nun, who spent 50 years caring for the poor and dying.

Pope John Paul II apologizes for the Roman Catholic Church's lack of moral leadership during the Holocaust.

1998 *The Jesus Film*, an evangelistic film, is seen by more than 5 billion people since 1979.

2004 *The Passion of the Christ* movie released. Depicts Jesus' suffering, death, and resurrection.

Persecution of Christians continues around the world.

Christianity spreads to the Antarctic. There are still 2000 groups of people who have no portion of the Bible in their own language.

OLD TESTAMENT CHARTS

The Creation

In the beginning, God created the heavens and the earth.

Genesis 1:1

Day 1

God made light.
He called the light Day
and the darkness
He called Night.
Genesis 1:3-5

Day 2

God made the sky.
He called the sky
Heaven.
Genesis 1:6-8

Day 3

God made the seas
and the dry land.
He called the land
Earth. He also made
plants of every kind.
Genesis 1:9-13

Day 4

God made the sun
for the day and the
moon for the night.
He also set stars
in the sky.
Genesis 1:14-19

Day 5

God made fish
and other creatures
of the sea. He made
birds of the air.

Genesis 1:20-23

Day 6

God made animals
of the land.
He made one man
and one woman.

Genesis 1:24-31

Day 7

God rested from all
His work. He blessed
the seventh day and
made it holy.

Genesis 2:1-3

100 WELL-KNOWN OLD TESTAMENT EVENTS

Event 1	Creation of All Things (Genesis 1)
Event 2	Institution of Marriage (Genesis 2:18-25)
Event 3	Fall of Man and Promise of a Redeemer (Genesis 2:15-17; 3:1-24)
Event 4	Murder of Abel and Birth of Seth (Genesis 4:1-25)
Event 5	Removal of Enoch to Heaven without Dying (Genesis 5:18-24)
Event 6	Protection of Noah, His Family, and Selected Animals During the Great Flood (Genesis 6–8)
Event 7	Giving of the Rainbow Covenant (Genesis 9:1, 11-13)
Event 8	Tower of Babel Judgment (Genesis 11:1-9)
Event 9	Conversion, Call, and Commission of Abraham (Genesis 12:1-3)
Event 10	Meeting Between Abraham and Melchizedek (Genesis 14:18-20)
Event 11	Confirmation of the Abrahamic Covenant (Genesis 15:1-9)
Event 12	Birth of Ishmael (Genesis 16)
Event 13	Institution of Circumcision and Changing of Abram's and Sarai's names (Genesis 17)
Event 14	Destruction of Sodom and Gomorrah (Genesis 19)
Event 15	Birth of Isaac (Genesis 21:1-7)
Event 16	Offering Up of Isaac (Genesis 22:1-14)
Event 17	Marriage of Isaac and Rebekah (Genesis 24)
Event 18	Birth of Esau and Jacob (Genesis. 25:21-26)
Event 19	Transfer of Birthright and Blessing from Esau to Jacob (Genesis 27:6-16)
Event 20	Flight of Jacob and His Marriages to Leah and Rachel (Genesis 28:10– 29:28)
Event 21	Wrestling match between Jacob and a "Man" (Genesis 32:6-32)
Event 22	Selling of Joseph in Slavery and His Rule in Egypt (Genesis 37:3-28; 41:1-44)
Event 23	Joseph Reveals Himself to His Brothers and Jacob's Family Moves to Egypt (Genesis 45:1-11; 46:1-7)
Event 24	The Dying Jacob Blesses His 12 Sons in Egypt (Genesis 49:1-28)
Event 25	The Sufferings of Job and the Sovereignty of God (Job 1:1–2:7; 42:10-12)
Event 26	Slavery of the Israelites in Egypt (Exodus 1:8-14)
Event 27	Rescue of the Baby Moses from the Nile (Exodus 2:1-10)
Event 28	Call of Moses at the Burning Bush (Exodus 3:1-10)
Event 29	The Ten Plagues and the First Passover (Exodus 7:14–13:16)
Event 30	The Red Sea Crossing (Exodus 14:16-30)
Event 31	Giving of Manna (Exodus 16:14-18, 31, 35)
Event 32	Institution of the Sabbath (Exodus 16:25-30; 31:14-17)
Event 33	Moses Strikes the Rock at Rephidim and Prays for Israel (Exodus 17:1-14)

Event 34	The Ten Commandments Given at Mt. Sinai (Exodus 20:3-17; 34:29-32)
Event 35	Worship of the Golden Calf at Sinai (Exodus 32:1-4, 6)
Event 36	Moses Intercedes for Israel and View's God's Glory (Exodus 32:30-32; 33:18-23)
Event 37	Building of the Tabernacle and Anointing Aaron as the First High Priest (Exodus 25:1-9; 29:4-9)
Event 38	Giving of the Levitical Feasts and Ordinance of the Red Heifer (Leviticus. 23:4-27; Numbers 19:2-9)
Event 39	Miriam's Leprosy (Numbers 12:1-13)
Event 40	The Unfavorable Report from the Spies (Numbers 13:1–14:10)
Event 41	Korah's Rebellion and Aaron's Rod that Budded (Numbers 16:1-33; 17:6-8)
Event 42	Moses' Sin and Aaron's Death (Numbers 20:7-29)
Event 43	People are Healed by Looking at the Serpent of Brass (Numbers 21:5-9)
Event 44	Balaam's Futile Attempts to Curse Israel (Numbers 22:26; 23:8-23; 24:2-17)
Event 45	Repeating of God's Law to Israel's Next Generation (Deuteronomy 1:3; 6:1-5)
Event 46	Completion of the Pentateuch (Deuteronomy 31:9, 24-26)
Event 47	Transfer of Leadership from Moses to Joshua (Deuteronomy 31:7-14; 34:9)
Event 48	Moses Blesses the 12 Tribes, Views the Promised Land, and Dies (Deuteronomy 33:1–34:1-12)
Event 49	Jordan River Crossing and Fall of Jericho (Joshua 1–3; 6:2-20)
Event 50	Setting Up of the Tabernacle at Shiloh and the Division of the Land (Joshua 18:1-10)
Event 51	Final Words of Joshua to Israel (Joshua 23:1-11; 24:14, 15)
Event 52	Four Key Judges (Deborah/Barak, Gideon, Jephthah, Samson) (Judges 4; 6–8; 11; 13–16)
Event 53	The Marriage of Boaz and Ruth (Ruth 4:13-17)
Event 54	Prayer of Hannah. Birth, Call, and Ministry of Samuel (1 Samuel 1:11-28; 3:1-20)
Event 55	Anointing of Saul as Israel's First King (1 Samuel 8:4–9:1-17; 10:1)
Event 56	Rejection of Saul and the Anointing of David as King (1 Samuel 13:13, 14; 15:22, 23; 16:1-14)
Event 57	David's Victory Over Goliath (1 Samuel 17:4-49)
Event 58	Saul's Persecution of David and David's Kindness to Saul (1 Samuel 18:10-12; 24:1-12; 26:5-18)
Event 59	Saul's Visit to the Witch of Endor and Subsequent Death on the Battlefield (1 Samuel 28:7-16; 31:1-6)
Event 60	David's Kingship Over All Israel (2 Samuel 2:4; 5:1-5)
Event 61	David Captures Jerusalem from the Jebusites and Recovers the Ark of the Covenant (2 Samuel 5–6)
Event 62	Giving of the Davidic Covenant (2 Samuel 7:1-16)
Event 63	David's Sins of Adultery and Murder (2 Samuel 11:2-5, 14, 15)
Event 64	Punishment of David. Birth of Solomon (2 Samuel 12:7-25)
Event 65	Rebellion of David's Son Absalom (2 Samuel 15:1-6)
Event 66	David's Sin in Numbering the People (1 Chronicles 21:1-27)
Event 67	Solomon's Request for Wisdom (1 Kings 3:5-10)

Event 68	Completion of Israel's First Temple (1 Kings 6:1, 38; 8:1, 6)
Event 69	Queen of Sheba's Visit with King Solomon (1 Kings 10:1-7)
Event 70	Solomon's Many Wives, His Idolatry, and God's Anger Against Him (1 Kings 11:1-13)
Event 71	The United Kingdom Divides (1 Kings 12:1-20)
Event 72	Elijah Raises the Widow of Zarephath's Dead Son (1 Kings 17:1-24)
Event 73	Elijah's Confrontation on Mt. Carmel (1 Kings 18:20-40)
Event 74	Elijah's is Carried to Heaven in a Chariot of Fire (2 Kings 2:1-11)
Event 75	The Healing of Namaan (2 Kings 5:1-3, 9-14)
Event 76	Deliverance of Starving Samaria (2 Kings 6:24-29; 7:1-16)
Event 77	Jehoshaphat's Prayer for Deliverance (2 Chronicles 20:1-17)
Event 78	Isaiah's Vision of God's Glory (Isaiah 6:1-8)
Event 79	The Divine Sign Refused by Ahaz (Isaiah 7:1-14)
Event 80	The Protection of Joash from Athaliah's Bloody slaughter of the Royal Family (2 Kings 11:1-16)
Event 81	The Stoning of Zechariah, Judah's Godly High Priest (2 Chronicles 24:15-22)
Event 82	Jonah and the Great Revival and Repentance in the City of Nineveh (Jonah 3:1-10)
Event 83	The Extension of Hezekiah's Life (2 Kings 20:1-11)
Event 84	Conversion of Wicked King Manasseh (2 Chronicles 33:1-16)
Event 85	Assyrian Captivity of the Ten Northern Tribes (2 Kings 18:9-12)
Event 86	The Deliverance of Jerusalem from the Assyrians (Isaiah 37:33-36)
Event 87	Discovering the Law of Moses in Josiah's Reign (2 Kings 22:1-11; 23:1-3)
Event 88	Call of Jeremiah and the Burning of His Scroll (Jeremiah 1:4-10; 36:1-32)
Event 89	Prophecy of the New Covenant When God Will Forgive His People (Jeremiah 31:31-34)
Event 90	Call of Ezekiel and the Departure of the Glory Cloud (Ezekiel 1:3-28; 3:16, 17; 10:3, 4, 18; 11:22, 23)
Event 91	Destruction of Jerusalem, the First Temple and the Babylonian Captivity (2 Chronicles 36:14-21)
Event 92	Interpretation of Nebuchadnezzar's Dream by Daniel (Daniel 2:27-45)
Event 93	Divine Protection of Three Hebrew Men in a Furnace of Fire (Daniel 3:23-28)
Event 94	Interpreting by Daniel of the Handwriting on the Wall (Daniel 5:1-28)
Event 95	Divine Protection of Daniel in a Den of Lions (Daniel 6:16-23)
Event 96	The Return Decree of King Cyrus (2 Chronicles 36:22, 23; Ezra 1:5; 2:64)
Event 97	Completion of the Second Temple (Ezra 3:10-13; 6:14, 15)
Event 98	Revivals Under Ezra and Nehemiah (Ezra 9:1-6; 10:1-5; Nehemiah 8:1-12)
Event 99	Deliverance of the Jews From Their Enemies in Esther's Time (Esther 8:7-11; 9:1-5)
Event 100	Rebuilding of the Jerusalem Walls (Nehemiah 2:5-18; 6:15)

The Families of Abraham, Isaac, and Jacob (Israel)

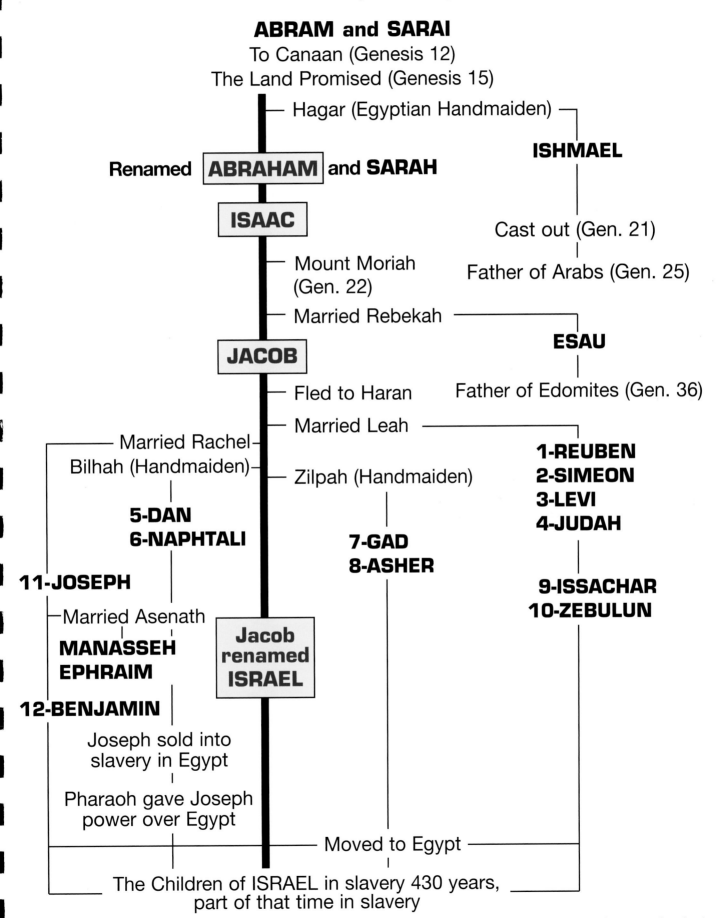

ABRAM and SARAI
To Canaan (Genesis 12)
The Land Promised (Genesis 15)

— Hagar (Egyptian Handmaiden) —

ISHMAEL

Renamed **ABRAHAM** and **SARAH**

ISAAC

— Mount Moriah (Gen. 22)

Cast out (Gen. 21)

Father of Arabs (Gen. 25)

— Married Rebekah —

ESAU

JACOB

— Fled to Haran

Father of Edomites (Gen. 36)

— Married Leah —

— Married Rachel
Bilhah (Handmaiden) —

— Zilpah (Handmaiden)

1-REUBEN
2-SIMEON
3-LEVI
4-JUDAH

5-DAN
6-NAPHTALI

7-GAD
8-ASHER

11-JOSEPH

9-ISSACHAR
10-ZEBULUN

— Married Asenath

MANASSEH
EPHRAIM

**Jacob
renamed
ISRAEL**

12-BENJAMIN

Joseph sold into
slavery in Egypt

Pharaoh gave Joseph
power over Egypt

— Moved to Egypt —

The Children of ISRAEL in slavery 430 years,
part of that time in slavery

Name of God	Meaning	Application
ADONAI	The Lord My Great Lord	God is the Master and majestic Lord. God is our total authority.
EL	The Strong One	He is more powerful than any false god. God will overcome all obstacles. We can depend on God.
EL ELOHE YISRAEL	God, the God of Israel	The God of Israel is distinct and separate from all false gods of the world.
EL ELYON	The God Most High	He is the Sovereign God in whom we can put our trust. El Elyon has supremacy over all false gods.
ELOHIM	The All-Powerful One Creator	God is the all-powerful creator of the universe. God knows all, creates all, and is everywhere at all times. The plural of "El".
EL OLAM	The Eternal God The Everlasting God	He is the Beginning and the End, the One who works His purposes throughout the ages. He gives strength to the weary.
EL ROI	The God Who Sees me	There are no circumstances in our lives that escape His fatherly awareness and care. God knows us and our troubles.
EL SHADDAI	The All Sufficient One, The God of the Mountains, God Almighty	God is the all-sufficient source of all of our blessings. God is all-powerful. Our problems are not too big for God to handle.
IMMANUEL	God With Us "I AM"	Jesus is God in our midst. In Him all the fullness of Deity dwells in bodily form.
JEHOVAH (YHWH, see comments)	"I AM," The One Who Is The Self-Existent One	God never changes. His promises never fail. When we are faithless, He is faithful. We need to obey Him.
JEHOVAH-JIREH	The Lord Will Provide	Just as God provided a ram as a substitute for Isaac, He provided His son Jesus as the ultimate sacrifice. God will meet all our needs.
JEHOVAH-MEKADDISHKEM	The Lord Who Sanctifies	God sets us apart as a chosen people, a royal priesthood, holy unto God, a people of His own. He cleanses our sin and helps us mature.
JEHOVAH-NISSI	The Lord is My Banner	God gives us victory against the flesh, the world and the devil. Our battles are His battles of light against darkness and good against evil.
JEHOVAH-RAPHA	The Lord Who Heals	God has provided the final cure for spiritual, physical, and emotional sickness in Jesus Christ. God can heal us.
JEHOVAH-ROHI	The Lord is My Shepherd	The Lord protects, provides, directs, leads, and cares for His people. God tenderly takes care of us as a strong and patient shepherd.
JEHOVAH-SABAOTH	The Lord of Hosts The Lord of Armies	The Lord of the hosts of heaven will always fulfill His purposes, even when the hosts of His earthly people fail.
JEHOVAH-SHALOM	The Lord is Peace	God defeats our enemies to bring us peace. Jesus is our Prince of Peace. God brings inner peace and harmony.
JEHOVAH-SHAMMAH	The Lord is There The Lord My Companion	God's presence is not limited or contained in the Tabernacle or Temple, but is accessible to all who love and obey Him.
JEHOVAH-TSIDKENU	The Lord Our Righteousness	Jesus is the King who would come from David's line, and is the one who imparts His righteousness to us.
YAH, OR JAH	"I AM," The One Who Is The Self-Existent One	God never changes. His promises never fail. When we are faithless, He is faithful. God promises His continuing presence.
YHWH	"I AM," The One Who Is The Self-Existent One	God never changes. His promises never fail. When we are faithless, He is faithful.

Bible Reference	Comments
Psalm 8; Isaiah 40:3-5 Ezekiel 16:8; Habakkuk 3:19	**Pronounced: ah-doe-NI** *Adonai* (plural) is derived from the singular *Adon* (Lord). This term was pronounced in substitution of *YHWH* (considered too sacred to be uttered).
Exodus 15:2; Numbers 23:22 Deuteronomy 7:9 (Mark 15:34)	**Pronounced: el** Occurs more than 200 times in the Old Testament (including compounds). Generic Semitic name for God, used by other cultures to refer to their gods. *El* is used in compound proper names such as Isra-*el* (wrestles with God), Beth-*el* (House of God), and *El*-isha (God is salvation).
Genesis 33:20; Exodus 5:1 Psalm 68:8; Psalm 106:48	**Pronounced: el el-o-HAY yis-raw-ALE** The name of the altar that Jacob (Israel) erected after his encounter with God and God's blessing upon him. (Genesis 32:24-30; Genesis 33:19, 20)
Genesis 14:17-22; Psalm 78:35 Daniel 4:34 (Acts 16:17)	**Pronounced: el EL-yuhn** Melchizedek, the king of Salem (Jeru "Salem") and the priest of God Most High, referred to God as "El Elyon" three times when he blessed Abram.
Genesis 1:1-3; Deuteronomy 10:17 Psalm 68 (Mark 13:19)	**Pronounced: el-o-HEEM** Plural form of *El*. This name is usually associated with God in relation to His creation. Some people use the plural word "Elohim" as proof for the Trinity. (Genesis 1:26) *Elohim* is also used to refer to false gods and even human judges. (Psalm 82:6, 7; John 10:34)
Genesis 21:33; Psalm 90:1, 2 Isaiah 40:28 (Romans 1:20)	**Pronounced: el o-LAHM** Jesus Christ possesses eternal attributes. He is the same yesterday and today and forever. (Hebrews 13:8) He obtained eternal redemption for us. (Hebrews 9:12)
Genesis 16:11-14; Psalm 139:7-12	**Pronounced: el ROY** Hagar called the Lord by this name beside a fountain of water in the wilderness. God knows all of our thoughts and feelings. Jesus knew the thoughts of those around him, demonstrating that he is *El Roi*. (Matthew 22:18; 26:21, 34; Luke 5:21-24)
Genesis 17:1-3; 48:3; 49:25 Genesis 35:11; Psalm 90:2	**Pronounced: el-shaw-DIE** Some scholars suggest that *Shaddai* refers to God's power evident in His judgment. Others suggest that *El Shaddai* means "God of the Mountains." God refers to Himself as "El Shaddai" when he confirms his covenant with Abraham.
Isaiah 7:14; 8:8-10 (Matthew 1:23)	**Pronounced: ih-MAN-u-el** This name indicates that Jesus is more than man. He is also God. Isaiah said that the child born to the virgin would be called "Immanuel." (Isaiah 7:14; 9:6) He is the radiance of God's glory and the exact representation of His nature. (Hebrews 1:3)
Exodus 3:14; Exodus 6:2-4 Exodus 34:5-7; Psalm 102	**Pronounced: juh-HO-vah** A 16th century German translator wrote the name *YHVH (YHWH)* using the vowels of *Adonai*, because the ancient Jewish texts from which he was translating had the vowels of *Adonai* under the consonants of *YHVH*. By doing this, he incorrectly came up with the name Jehovah (*YaHoVaH*).
Genesis 22:13, 14; Psalm 23 (Mark 10:45; Romans 8:2)	**Pronounced: juh-HO-vah JI-rah** Also known as YHWH-Jireh. Abraham called the place "The Lord will provide" where God provided a ram to be sacrificed instead of his son Isaac. Jesus said that He was the bread of life and anyone who comes to Him will be provided for. (John 6:35)
Exodus 31:12, 13 (1 Peter 1:15, 16 Hebrews 13:12; 1 Thessalonians 5:23, 24)	**Pronounced: juh-HO-vah mek-KAH-dish-KIM** Also known as YHWH-Mekaddishkem. We have been set apart, made holy, and redeemed by the blood of Jesus Christ, our *Jehovah-Mekaddishkem*. Therefore, we are to continue to live our lives holy and pleasing to God. (1 Peter 1:13-25)
Exodus 17:15, 16; Deuteronomy 20:3, 4 Isaiah 11:10-12 (Ephesians 6:10-18)	**Pronounced: juh-HO-vah NEE-see** Also known as YHWH-Nissi. Name of the altar built by Moses after defeating the Amalekites at Rephidim. Isaiah prophesies that the "Root of Jesse" (Jesus) will stand as a banner for the peoples. (Isaiah 11:10)
Exodus 15:25-27; Psalm 103:3 Psalm 147:3 (1 Peter 2:24)	**Pronounced: juh-HO-vah RAH-fah** Also known as YHWH-Rapha. Jesus demonstrated that He was *Jehovah-Rapha* in his healing of the sick, blind, lame, and casting out demons. Jesus also heals His people from sin and unrighteousness. (Luke 5:31, 32)
Psalm 23:1-3; Isaiah 53:6 (John 10:14-18 Hebrews 13:20; Revelation 7:17)	**Pronounced: juh-HO-vah RO-hee** Also known as YHWH-Ra'ah (RAH-ah). Jesus is the good shepherd who lay down His life for all people.
1 Samuel 1:3; 1 Samuel 17:45; Psalm 46:7 Malachi 1:10-14 (Romans 9:29)	**Pronounced: juh-HO-vah sah-bah-OATH** Also known as YHWH-Sabaoth. Many English versions of the Bible translate *Sabaoth* as Almighty. "Jehovah-Sabaoth" is often translated as *The Lord Almighty*. *Sabaoth* is also translated as *Heavenly Hosts* or *Armies*.
Numbers 6:22-27; Judges 6:22-24 Isaiah 9:6 (Hebrews 13:20)	**Pronounced: juh-HO-vah shah-LOME** Also known as YHWH-Shalom. Name of the altar built by Gideon at Ophrah to memorialize God's message "Peace be unto thee." Isaiah tells us that the Messiah will also be known as the "Prince of Peace," our *Jehovah-Shalom*. (Isaiah 9:6)
Ezekiel 48:35; Psalm 46 (Matthew 28:20; Revelation 21)	**Pronounced: juh-HO-vah SHAHM-mah** Also known as YHWH-Shammah. God revealed to Ezekiel that the name of the New Jerusalem shall be "The Lord is there." Through Jesus Christ, the Spirit of God dwells in us. (1 Corinthians 3:16)
Jeremiah 23:5, 6; 33:16; Ezekiel 36:26, 27 (2 Corinthians 5:21)	**Pronounced: juh-HO-vah tsid-KAY-noo** Also known as YHWH-Tsidkenu. All people sin and fall short of God's glory, but God freely makes us righteous through faith in Jesus Christ. (Romans 3:22, 23) God promised to send a King who will reign wisely and do what is just and right. The people will live in safety. (Jeremiah 23:5, 6)
Exodus 3:14; 15:2; Psalm 46:1 Psalm 68:4; Isaiah 26:4	**Pronounced: Yah** Shorter form of *Yahweh*. It is often used when combined with other names or phrases. *Hallelujah* means "Praise Yah (the Lord)," *Elijah* means "God is Yah (the Lord)," and *Joshua* means "Yah (the Lord) is my salvation."
Exodus 3:14; Malachi 3:6	**Pronounced: YAH-way** God's personal name given to Moses. Also called the tetragrammaton ("four letters"). Occurs about 6,800 times. Translated "LORD" in English versions of the Bible, because it became common practice for Jews to say "Lord" (Adonai) instead of saying the name *YHWH*.

Jesus and the Names of God

The New Testament alludes to Jesus' divine nature by comparing Jesus to several names and attributes used for God. Here are a few examples of Jesus being compared to God:

Jesus is God	In the beginning was the Word, and the Word was with God, and the Word was God. ...(John 1:1-5)
Jesus is one with God	"I and my Father are one." (John 10:30)
Jesus is eternal	[Jesus] said, "Fear not; I am the First and the Last." (Revelation 1:17b)
Jesus is omnipresent Omnipresent means "present everywhere"	And [God] hath put all things under his feet, and gave him to be the head over all things to the church, which is his body, the fullness of him that filleth all in all. (Ephesians 1:22, 23)
Jesus is omniscient Omniscient means "all-knowing"	"Lord, thou knowest all things...." (John 21:17)
Jesus is life giving	In him was life; and the life was the light of men. (John 1:4)
Jesus is El Olam	The Beginning and the End: "I am Alpha and Omega, the beginning and the end, the first and the last." (Revelation 22:13)
Jesus is YHWH-Jireh	The Lord will Provide: ..."I am the bread of life. He that cometh to me shall never hunger, and he that believeth on me shall never thirst." (John 6:35)
Jesus is YHWH-Rohi	The Lord is my Shepherd: "I am the good shepherd: the good shepherd giveth his life for the sheep." (John 10:11)
Jesus is YHWH-Tsidkenu	The Lord is Righteousness: For he hath made him to be sin for us, who knew no sin; that we might be made the righteousness of God in him. (2 Corinthians 5:21)
Jesus is YHWH-Rapha	The Lord Who Heals: Who his own self bare our sins in his own body on the tree, that we, being dead to sins, should live unto righteousness: by whose stripes ye were healed. (1 Peter 2:24)
Jesus is El Shaddai	The All Sufficient One: ..."My grace is sufficient for thee: for my strength is made perfect in weakness..." (2 Corinthians 12:9)
Jesus is Immanuel	God With Us: ...they shall call his name Emmanuel, which being interpreted is, God with us. (Matthew 1:23)
Jesus is YHWH-Shalom	The Lord is Peace: "Peace I leave with you; my peace I give unto you...." (John 14:27)

The Ten Commandments and You

	Commandment	Bible Example	Modern Example
RESPECT FOR GOD — You shall love the Lord your God with all your heart.	**1.** You shall have no other Gods before me.	The Exodus Exodus 34:11-14	Put God first! Today a "god" may be anything a person allows to rule his daily life: deities of other religions, superstitions, horoscopes, bad habits or addictions, friends, heroes, desire for money, fame or power.
	2. You shall not make for yourself an idol.	Golden Calf Exodus 32:1-8	Put your faith in God only. Worshipping or serving any man-made thing that is thought to have supernatural power: statues of gods of other religions, crystals, pictures, jewelry, amulets, charms, rabbit's foot, or objects thought to have power or "good luck."
	3. You shall not misuse the name of the LORD your God.	Don't use God's name in a false oath. Lev. 19:12	Treat God's name with respect. Don't use God's name lightly in making promises or in any other way. This is the name that raised people from the dead, caused blind to see, and made the paralyzed to walk. It is a powerful name and needs to be used with the right attitude.
	4. Remember the Sabbath day by keeping it holy.	God provides enough on the sixth day for the seventh. Exodus 16:23-30	In Jesus' time, very religious people obeyed this commandment by refusing to do any kind of work—even to the point of not helping people in need. Jesus said that Sabbath was made for man's benefit. People should rest from their normal work, but also be available to do good to others. Today Christians set aside the day to worship God and meet with other Christians.
RESPECT FOR PEOPLE	**5.** Honor your father and your mother so that you may live long in the land the LORD your God is giving you.	Jesus was obedient to Mary and Joseph. Luke 2:51	Treat your parents with respect no matter what. Your parents have made many sacrifices to raise you. They have changed diapers, lost sleep, bought food, toys and clothes, paid doctor bills and changed their schedules to help you. Even if you don't get along with your parents, they deserve your gratitude. If your parents ask you to do something wrong, respectfully tell them no and suggest a good alternative that they might consider.
	6. You shall not murder.	Each person is made in God's image. Genesis 9:6	Personal revenge belongs to God. God will make things right in the end. God has set up governments and rules to deal with murders. Life and death are in God's hands. Examples: no revenge killing, murder, suicide, abortion or euthanasia (mercy killing). Jesus said we should love our enemies and pray for them.
	7. You shall not commit adultery.	Joseph runs from temptation. Genesis 39:1-13	Stay true to your husband or wife. Marriage vows made before God should be kept in spite of difficulties. Sex only within marriage relationship. No rape or incest. Avoid sexual temptation: provocative videos, movies, television, magazines, computer games or programs, pictures and books. Jesus said that even thinking about another person lustfully is wrong.
	8. You shall not steal.	Achan steals. Joshua 6:17-19 Joshua 7:1-5	Respect other's possessions. Don't take things that don't belong to you. Examples: shoplifting (taking candy, toys, or anything from a store), taking money or valuables from others, cheating on tests and taxes, photocopying music or any printed material without permission.
	9. You shall not bear false witness against your neighbor.	Honesty toward neighbors. Leviticus 19:13	Be trustworthy. Don't falsely accuse or blame someone else. Don't lie about them or to them. Don't gossip. Don't lie to God and to yourself by believing you are perfect. Keep your promises.
	10. You shall not covet...anything that belongs to your neighbor.	Life is more than possessions. Eccl. 5:9-18; 6:12	Be content with what you have. Don't long for things that belong to others. Example: their house, car, job, bike, toys, jewelry, clothing, or friends. Ask God to give you what you need. He promises that He will take care of your needs! Seek wisdom and good character, not riches.

HOLIDAY	DATE OBSERVED	SCRIPTURE BASIS	GENERAL INFORMATION
PASSOVER (Pesach) and	**14 NISAN** *(MARCH OR APRIL)*	**Leviticus 23:4, 5 Exodus 12:1-4**	**Passover and Unleavened Bread: Commemorates God's Deliverance of Israel Out of Egypt** *Pesach* (PAY-sahk) means to "pass over." The Passover meal, seder (SAY der), commemorates the Israelites' deliverance from slavery in Egypt. The LORD sent Moses to lead the children of Israel from Egypt to the Promised Land. When first confronted by Moses, Pharaoh refused to let the people go. After sending nine plagues, the LORD said the firstborn males of every house would die unless the doorframe of that house was covered with the blood of a perfect lamb. That night, the LORD "passed over" the homes with blood on the doorframes. The tenth plague brought death to the firstborn sons of Egypt, even taking the life of Pharaoh's own son. Finally, Pharaoh let the children of Israel go. Passover was to be a lasting ordinance for generations to come. In Leviticus, the LORD said that on the fourteenth day of the first month (of the religious new year) the LORD's Passover was to begin at twilight.
UNLEAVENED BREAD (Hag Hamatzot)	**15-21 NISAN** *(MARCH OR APRIL)*	**Leviticus 23:6-8 Exodus 12:15-20**	In Leviticus 23, *Hag HaMatzot* (Hawg Hah MAHT zot) or *Hag HaMatzah*, also known as the "Feast of Unleavened Bread," is mentioned as a separate feast on the fifteenth day of the same month as Passover. Today, however, the feasts of Pesach, Unleavened Bread, and Firstfruits have all been incorporated into the celebration of Passover, and reference to *Passover* means all three feasts. Passover is celebrated for eight days, Nisan 14-21. The LORD said that for seven days the children of Israel must eat unleavened bread. This bread, made in a hurry without yeast, represents how the LORD brought the Israelites out of Egypt in haste. In Scripture, leaven also represents sin. Orthodox Jews believe that not only is eating bread with leaven unlawful during the Feast of Unleavened Bread, but even having leaven present in one's house or apartment is forbidden. Today, cleansing the house before Passover is often a symbolic search to remove any hypocrisy or wickedness. Unleavened Bread is one of the three pilgrimage feasts when all Jewish males were required to go to Jerusalem to "appear before the LORD." (Deut. 16:16)
FIRSTFRUITS (Yom HaBikkurim)	**16 NISAN** *(MARCH OR APRIL)*	**Leviticus 23:9-14**	**Firstfruits: Offerings are Given for the Spring Barley Harvest** On *Yom HaBikkurim* (Yome Hah-Bee-koo-REEM) people offered the first ripe sheaf (firstfruits) of barley to the LORD as an act of dedicating the harvest to him. On Passover, a marked sheaf of grain was bundled and left standing in the field. On the next day, the first day of Unleavened Bread, the sheaf was cut and prepared for the offering on the third day. On this third day, Yom HaBikkurim, the priest waved the sheaf before the LORD. Counting the days (*omer*) then begins and continues until the day after the seventh Sabbath, the 50th day, which is called *Shavuot* or Pentecost (the next feast on the calendar). Jewish people rarely celebrate Yom HaBikkurim today, but it has great significance for followers of Jesus as the most important day of the year, the day of Jesus' resurrection.
FEAST OF WEEKS or PENTECOST (Shavuot)	**6 SIVAN** *(MAY OR JUNE)*	**Leviticus 23:15-22**	**Feasts of Weeks: Offerings are Given and Commemorates Giving of the Law** Fifty days after Passover, *Shavuot* (Sha-voo-OTE) is celebrated. Also known as Pentecost, Feast of Weeks, the Feast of Harvest, and the Latter Firstfruits, it is the time to present an offering of new grain of the summer wheat harvest to the LORD. It shows joy and thankfulness for the LORD's blessing of harvest. Often called *Matan Torah* (giving of the Law), it is tied to the Ten Commandments because it is believed God gave Moses the Ten Commandments at this time. Historically, children receive treats for memorizing Scripture at Shavuot. The book of Ruth is often read to celebrate the holiday. Pentecost is a popular day for Jewish Confirmation. Shavuot is one of the three pilgrimage feasts when all Jewish males were required to go to Jerusalem to "appear before the LORD." (Deuteronomy 16:16)
FEAST OF TRUMPETS or NEW YEAR (Rosh HaShanah)	**1 TISHRI** *(SEPTEMBER OR OCTOBER)*	**Leviticus 23:23-25**	**Feast of Trumpets: The Beginning of the Civil New Year** *Rosh HaShanah* (Rosh Ha-SHA-nah), the Ten Days of Repentance that follow it, and Yom Kippur make up the High Holy Days. Jewish tradition says that God writes every person's words, deeds, and thoughts in the Book of Life, which he opens and examines on this day. If good deeds outnumber sinful ones for the year, that person's name will be inscribed in the book for another year on Yom Kippur. So during Rosh HaShanah and the Ten Days of Repentance, people can repent of their sins and do good deeds to increase their chances of being inscribed in the Book of Life. Prior to Rosh HaShanah, the *shofar* (ram's horn) is blown to call people to repent and remind them that the holy days are arriving. During the Rosh HaShanah synagogue services, the shofar is blown 100 times.

	YESHUA (JESUS)	FASCINATING FACTS
Passover	Jesus ate the Passover with his disciples, saying that he had eagerly desired to eat this Passover with them before he suffered and that he would not eat it again until the kingdom of God comes. (Luke 22:7-16) After the Passover meal, they sang a hymn and went to the Mount of Olives. (Matthew 26:30) The hymn sung during Passover is the *Hallel* which includes Psalm 118:22: "The stone the builders rejected has become the capstone." Jesus is the capstone that the builders rejected. (Matt. 21:42; 1 Pet. 2:7) Jesus was crucified on Passover Day as the "Lamb of God who takes away the sin of the world." (John 1:29) The Lord's Supper is a remembrance of his sacrifice as the perfect Passover Lamb and the fullfilment of the new covenant between God and man. (Luke 22:20; 1 Cor. 5:7; Eph. 2:11-13) Prophecy of this sacrifice is found in Psalm 22. The Hebrew prophet Isaiah also spoke of the sufferings and sacrifice of the Messiah, and how that sacrifice would be the ultimate atonement for the sins of God's people. (Isaiah 53)	• Jesus' parents traveled to Jerusalem yearly to celebrate Passover. At age 12, Jesus went with them. (Luke 2:41-50) • The Passover lamb must be a perfect male with no spot or blemish. (Exodus 12:5) • The cup of the Lord's Supper is the third cup of the Passover *seder*, the cup of redemption. The bread of the Lord's Supper is the *afikomen.* It is the matzah that is broken, hidden, found, bought for a price, and then eaten to end the meal. *Afikomen* means "I came" in Greek. • A hymn is usually sung at the end of the passover service, as was the case with Jesus and his disciples. (Matthew 26:30)
Unleavened Bread	*Matzot* is plural for *matzah.* Unleavened bread (matzah) is a symbol of Passover. Leaven represents sin. (Luke 12:1; 1 Cor. 5:8) Matzah stands for "without sin" and is a picture of Jesus, the only human without sin. Jesus said that the "bread of God is he who comes down from heaven and gives life to the world" and that he (Jesus) is the "bread of life," the "bread that came down from heaven," "the living bread" which a man may eat and not die. (John 6:32, 35, 41, 48) While leaven is a symbol of sin, the Messiah is "unleavened" or sinless. He conquers the grave with his resurrection because he is not a sinner under the curse of death. Jesus was scourged and pierced at his crucifixion. As the prophet Isaiah proclaims, "By his stripes we are healed." (Isaiah 53:5) All of the festivals instituted by God, including Passover and Unleavened Bread, are "shadows of things to come." (Col. 2:17)	• The only type of bread eaten during the eight days of Passover/ Unleavened Bread is matzah. It is made with flour and water only, not any leaven. It is striped and pierced during baking. • The utensils used must never touch leaven. Bakery goods are made with matzah meal. • On the night before Passover, the father does a final search for any remaining leaven in the house. Traditionally, by candlelight, he sweeps any remaining bread crumbs onto a wooden spoon with a goose feather. When finished, the bread crumbs, the feather, and the spoon are placed in a bag and burned the next morning.
Firstfruits	Yom HaBikkurim is a picture of Jesus' resurrection. Jesus rose on the third day of Passover season, Nisan 16, the day of Firstfruits. That event gave new meaning to this agricultural holiday. The apostle Paul, a Jewish believer and rabbi, wrote, "But Christ has indeed been raised from the dead, the firstfruits of those who have fallen asleep. For as in Adam all die, so in Christ all will be made alive. But each in his own turn: Christ, the firstfruits; then, when he comes, those who belong to him." (1 Cor. 15:20, 22, 23, NIV) Jesus' resurrection is the promise of the future resurrection of believers. (John 5:28, 29) Although most believers in Jesus have never heard of Yom HaBikkurim, they celebrate it as Resurrection Day, or Easter.	Biblical events that happened on this day: • The manna, which God provided from heaven as food for the Israelites while they wandered in the wilderness, stopped after they crossed the Jordan River into the Promised Land. (Josh. 5:10-12) • Queen Esther risked her life to save the Jewish people from annihilation. (Esther 3:12-5:7) • Jesus rose from the dead on the third day. (Luke 24:44-47) • Since the Temple was destroyed in AD 70, firstfruits sacrifices and offerings are no longer offered on this day. Today, Jews use this date to begin the counting of the days (omer). On the 33rd day of counting the omer, a minor rabbinical holiday called Lag B'Omer is celebrated where campfires are built and people roast potatoes and sing songs.
Pentecost	Jesus told his disciples to wait in Jerusalem following his crucifixion, resurrection, and ascension. They were all together in the upper room for Shavuot on the 50th day after the Sabbath of Passover week, thus, the first day of the week. The Holy Spirit filled the house, with a sound like a mighty wind and what appeared to be tongues of fire, and filled the disciples. (Acts 2) The apostle Peter referred to the prophet Joel who said that God would "pour out his Spirit on all flesh." (Joel 2:28-32) Peter also said that the risen and exalted Jesus had poured out the Holy Spirit. (Acts 2:32, 33) The people responded to Peter's message with repentance, and more than 3,000 were baptized. (Acts 2:37-40) The new covenant between God and Israel (Jeremiah 31:31; Hebrews 9:14, 15) is initiated on Shavuot, 50 days after the death of Christ.	• Shavuot is celebrated 50 days after Passover, so it became known as *Pentecost*, which means "50" in Greek. The days from Passover to Shavuot are counted at weekly Sabbath services. • Special foods for this holiday are dairy foods, such as cheesecake and cheese blintzes, because the Law is compared to milk and honey. • Homes and synagogues are decorated with flowers and greenery, which represent the harvest and the Torah as a "tree of life." Observant Jews often spend the night reading and studying the Torah.
Feast of Trumpets	*Rosh HaShanah* is sometimes referred to as the Day of Judgment. Jesus said he has the authority to judge people (John 5:24-27) and the apostle Paul referred to him as the judge of "the living and the dead." (2 Tim. 4:1) God does have a book of life; Revelation 21:27 calls it the "Lamb's book of life." The only way to have one's name inscribed in it is through faith in Jesus as Savior from sin, and then it is permanent. (John 10:27-30) Those whose names are not in the book will be judged and sentenced to hell: "If anyone's name was not found written in the book of life, he was thrown into the lake of fire." (Rev. 20:15) Some people believe the four spring holidays (Passover, Unleavened Bread, Firstfruits, and Feast of Weeks) were fulfilled in Messiah's first coming and that the three autumn holidays (Feast of Trumpets, Day of Atonement, and Feast of Booths) will be fulfilled at his second coming.	• Rosh HaShanah is a serious New Year holiday, not a happy one like January 1. A common custom is sending cards to relatives and friends to wish them a happy, healthy, and prosperous new year. The message includes the greeting *L'shanah tovah tikatevoo*, which means "May you be inscribed [in the Book of Life] for a good year." • It is traditional to eat apple slices dipped in honey. The apples represent provision, and the honey represents sweetness for the coming year. • Many Jewish people attend Rosh HaShanah and Yom Kippur services even if they have not attended synagogue services the rest of the year.

HOLIDAY	DATE OBSERVED	SCRIPTURE BASIS	GENERAL INFORMATION
DAY OF ATONEMENT (Yom Kippur)	**10 TISHRI** *(SEPTEMBER OR OCTOBER)*	**Leviticus 23:26-32**	**Day of Atonement: The Day the High Priest Makes Atonement for Sin** *Yom Kippur* (Yome Ki-POOR), also known as Day of Atonement, is the most solemn holy day of the Jewish people. *Yom* means "day" and *Kippur* means "atonement" or "covering." *Atonement* means the reconciliation of God and man. The ten days between Rosh HaShanah and Yom Kippur are known as the "days of repentance." Yom Kippur is the final day of judgment when God judges the people. In Bible times, the High Priest sacrificed an animal to pay for his sins and the sins of the people. It was a time of fasting and prayer. The shofar (ram's horn) is blown at the end of the evening prayer service for the first time since Rosh HaShanah. When the high priest was finished with the atonement sacrifice, a goat was released into the wilderness. This "scapegoat" carried Israel's sins away, never to return. (Leviticus 16:8-10, 20-22, 29-34)
FEAST OF BOOTHS *or* TABERNACLES (Sukkot)	**15-21 TISHRI** *(SEPTEMBER OR OCTOBER)*	**Leviticus 23:33-43**	**Feast of Booths: Commemorates the 40-Year Wilderness Journey** *Sukkot* (Soo-KOTE or SOO-kote), also known as "Feast of Tabernacles," is a week-long celebration of the fall harvest and a time to build booths (temporary shelters of branches) to remember how the Hebrew people lived under God's care during their forty years in the wilderness. (Nehemiah 8:14-17) The celebration is a reminder of God's faithfulness and protection. Jews continue to celebrate Sukkot by building and dwelling in temporary booths for eight days. The four special plants used to cover the booths are citron, myrtle, palm, and willow. (Leviticus 39:40) Sukkot is one of the three pilgrimage feasts when all Jewish males were required to go to Jerusalem to "appear before the LORD." (Deuteronomy 16:16)
REJOICING IN THE LAW (Simchat Torah)	**22 or 23 TISHRI** *(SEPTEMBER OR OCTOBER)*	**Leviticus 23:36**	**Joy of Torah: Celebrates the Completion of Reading the Torah** The eighth and final day of the celebration of Sukkot was appointed by God as a sacred assembly. Today the final day is known as *Simchat Torah* (SIM-khat TOE-rah or SIM-khat Toe-RAH) meaning "Rejoice in the Torah, God's Word." Starting in the Middle Ages, it is a celebration of the giving and receiving of the *Torah* or the *Pentateuch* (the first five books of the Bible) which is the foundation of Jewish belief and faith. Torah also means "Law" or direction. Followers of Jesus accept the Torah and the other books of the Jewish Scriptures. They believe that "Above all, you must understand that no prophecy of Scripture came about by the prophet's own interpretation. For prophecy never had its origin in the will of man, but men spoke from God as they were carried along by the Holy Spirit." (2 Peter 1:20, 21)
FEAST OF DEDICATION (Hanukkah) (Chanukah)	**25 KISLEV-2 TEVET** *(NOVEMBER OR DECEMBER)*	**John 10:22** Also Book of Maccabees (Apocrypha)	**Feast of Dedication: Commemorates the Purification of the Temple** *Hanukkah* (KHA-noo-kah), the Feast of Dedication, celebrates the Maccabees' victory over the Greeks and the rededication of the Temple in 165 BC after Seleucid king Antiochus Epiphanes defiled it by sacrificing a pig on the altar and pouring the blood on the Scripture scrolls. The Maccabees' victory, a miracle of God's deliverance, is recorded in the books of Maccabees, which are included in the Apocrypha. Hanukkah is also known as the Feast of Lights because of a legendary miraculous provision of oil for the eternal light in the Temple. After cleansing the Temple, the supply of oil to relight the eternal flame (the symbol of God's presence) was only enough for one day. But God performed a great miracle, and the flame burned for the eight days necessary to purify new oil.
FEAST OF LOTS (Purim)	**14 or 15 ADAR** *(FEBRUARY OR MARCH)*	**Book of Esther**	**Feast of Lots: Commemorates the Preservation of the Jewish People** *Purim* (POOR-im) marks the deliverance of the Jews through Jewish Queen Esther in Shushan, Persia (Susa, Iran). Esther was her Persian name, meaning "star." Her Hebrew name was *Hadassah*, which means "myrtle." The annual celebration of Purim is a joyous feast remembering the foiled plot of Haman to kill all the Jews living within King Xerxes's (Ahasuerus's) kingdom. Esther's uncle Mordecai uncovered the plot and warned Esther, who then told the King. The King had Haman executed. Adar 14 and 15 became days of joy and feasting. (Esther 9:18-32) Purim is celebrated on Adar 14 in most cities except those cities surrounded by walls since the time of Joshua. Walled cities celebrate Purim on Adar 15 *(Shushan Purim)*. In Jewish leap years, when there is an extra month of Adar, Purim is always celebrated during the second month.

YESHUA (JESUS)	FASCINATING FACTS

Day of Atonement

The Holy of Holies, in the Temple, was separated from the congregation by a veil from floor to ceiling. It was entered once a year on Yom Kippur, when the High Priest offered the blood sacrifice of atonement on behalf of the people. When Jesus died on the cross, the thick veil was ripped from top to bottom. (Luke 23:44-46)

Christ came as high priest and entered the Holy of Holies (heaven itself) once for all, not by the blood of goats and calves but by his own blood, having obtained eternal redemption. (Hebrews 9:11-28) Believers in Jesus accept his sacrifice on the cross as the final atonement for sin, "being justified freely by his grace through the redemption that is in Christ Jesus." (Romans 3:21-25a)

When Messiah returns, Israel will look on him, whom they pierced, and repent. (Zechariah 12:10) On this day of repentance, Israel will be forgiven and permanently restored. (Isaiah 66:7-14; Romans 11:26)

- After the Temple was destroyed in AD 70, Jewish people could no longer offer the prescribed sacrifices for atonement from sins. They have substituted prayer, good works, and charitable donations hoping to take away the penalty for their sins.
- Yom Kippur is a day of fasting. No work is done on this day, including at home. Many Jewish people spend the day at synagogue, praying for forgiveness of their sins. Immediately after the evening service, they have a "break fast" meal.
- The book of Jonah is read during the afternoon service to remind people of God's forgiveness and mercy.

Feast of Booths

Two ceremonies were part of the last day of Sukkot: 1. People carrying torches marched around the Temple, then set these lights around the walls of the Temple, indicating that Messiah would be a light to the Gentiles. (Isaiah 49:6)

2. A priest carried water from the pool of Siloam to the Temple, symbolizing that when Messiah comes the whole earth will know God "as the waters cover the sea." (Isa. 11:9)

When Jesus attended the Feast of Tabernacles, on the last day of the feast, he said, "If anyone is thirsty, let him come to me and drink. Whoever believes in me, as the Scripture has said, streams of living water will flow from within him." (John 7:37, 38) The next morning while the torches were still burning, he said, "I am the light of the world." (John 8:12)

Sukkot represents the final harvest when all nations will share in the joy and blessings of God's Kingdom. During that time, all believers will celebrate this feast. (Zech. 14:16-19)

- Sukkot is a happy feast when people rejoice in God's forgiveness and material blessings.
- The sukkah, or booth, is a temporary structure built of wood or wood and canvas. The roof is made of branches and leaves, with enough open spaces to see the stars. The sukkah is decorated with fall flowers, leaves, fruits, and vegetables. Many Jewish people erect booths on their lawns or balconies and eat at least one meal a day in them.
- A *lulav*, made up of willow, palm, and myrtle branches, is waved in all four directions (north, south, east, and west) and up and down to symbolize that God's presence is everywhere.

Rejoicing in Law

John 1:1 reads, "In the beginning was the Word, and the Word was with God and the Word was God." John 1:14 reads, "… and the Word became flesh and dwelt (tabernacled) among us." Jesus is the Word which became flesh (incarnated) and dwelt (tabernacled) among us.

The Word of God is a lamp to our feet and a light for our path. (Psalm 119:105) Jesus, the Word made flesh, is also a lamp to our feet and light for our path that leads to salvation. (John 8:12)

We rejoice (*simchat*) in the Torah—the written Torah and the *incarnate Torah*—Jesus. Jesus said that he came to fulfill both the Law and the Prophets. (Matthew 5:17) Torah is the written word; Jesus is the living Word.

- In Israel, Simchat Torah is usually celebrated on 22 Tishri. In other places, it is 23 Tishri.
- In the synagogue, the Torah is divided into portions and read each week in the worship service. During Simchat Torah, men and women in the congregation receive an *aliyah*, which is a chance to read a portion of the Torah from the pulpit. When finished, the congregation celebrates by marching around the sanctuary, carrying the Torah scrolls, singing, and praising God. Then, the reading of the Torah is completed by reading the last chapter of Deuteronomy. The reading of the Torah begins again with Genesis 1 for the next year.

Dedication

Although the history behind Hanukkah is recorded in books that were written in the time between the Hebrew Scriptures and the New Testament, the book of John tells us that it was celebrated in Jesus' day: "Then came the Feast of Dedication at Jerusalem. It was winter, and Jesus was in the temple area walking in Solomon's Colonnade." (John 10:22, 23) The Feast of Dedication is a reminder of those who courageously remain faithful to God in the face of persecution. One of the major themes throughout the New Testament is remaining faithful to Christ, especially during persecution. (Matt. 5:10-12; 1 Cor. 4:12; 2 Cor. 4:9)

The book of Revelation speaks specifically to the persecution believers will face before the return of Christ. (Rev. 2:10; 13:10) Hanukkah is also a reminder that God is faithful and delivers his people not only from the oppression of Antiochus Epiphanes, but also from the oppression of sin and death.

- Hanukkah is primarily a family celebration that centers around the lighting of a nine-candle *menorah*, or candlestick, called a *hanukkiyah*. Each night another candle is lit with the center candle called a *shammash*, or servant candle, until all nine are lit.
- Holiday foods include *latkes* (potato pancakes) and donuts fried in oil. The oil is a reminder of the miracle of the oil.
- Perhaps because Hanukkah falls close to Christmas, it is now traditional to give presents, often one per night after the candles are lit.
- Children play dreydel games with a top that reminds them of the great miracle of God's deliverance from the Greeks. Hanukkah is also called the "Festival of Lights."

Feast of Lots

Purim celebrates the story told in the book of Esther. (Esther 9:18-32) It is a celebration of God's faithful protection of his people.

The Jews of Esther's day were delivered from an irrevocable decree of the Persian king Ahasuerus. God also has an irrevocable decree that all people are sinners and deserve death. (Genesis 2:17; Romans 3:23) However, the Messiah delivers all who believe in him from that irrevocable decree as well. (Isaiah 53; Romans 6:23)

Many have and may continue to persecute believers in Messiah, but Isaiah's prophecy suggests that they will not prevail because "God is with us," or literally because of *Immanuel*. (Isaiah 8:10)

- The word *purim* means "lots" and refers to the lot Haman cast to decide the day for the destruction of the Jewish people. (Esther 3:7)
- God's name is not mentioned in the book of Esther, but his providence and provision are obvious.
- Purim is a happy and noisy holiday. To celebrate, the *megillah* (scroll of the book of Esther) is read in the synagogue. Whenever Haman is mentioned, everyone boos, stamps feet, and shakes noisemakers (called *groggers*). Whenever Mordecai is mentioned, everyone cheers.
- *Hamantashen* is a three-cornered cookie which represents Haman's hat.

JEWISH FEASTS & HOLIDAYS

Gregorian Year	2008	2009	2010	2011	2012	2013	2014	2015
Holiday	(Starts at sundown the previous day)							
Pesach (Passover)	April 20	April 9	March 30	April 19	April 7	March 26	April 15	April 4
HagHaMatzot (Unleavened Bread)	April 21	April 10	March 31	April 20	April 8	March 27	April 16	April 5
Yom HaBikkurim (First Fruits)	April 22	April 11	April 1	April 21	April 9	April 28	April 17	April 6
Shavuot (Pentecost)	June 9	May 29	May 19	June 8	May 27	May 15	June 4	May 24
Jewish Year Starts on Rosh HaShanah	5769	5770	5771	5772	5773	5774	5775	5776
Rosh HaShanah (New Year)	Sept. 30	Sept. 19	Sept. 9	Sept. 29	Sept. 17	Sept. 5	Sept. 25	Sept. 14
Yom Kippur (Day of Atonement)	Oct. 9	Sept. 28	Sept. 18	Oct. 8	Sept. 26	Sept. 14	Oct. 4	Sept. 23
Sukkot (Feast of Booths)	Oct. 14	Oct. 3	Sept. 23	Oct. 13	Oct. 1	Sept. 19	Oct. 9	Sept. 28
Simchat Torah	Oct. 22	Oct. 11	Oct. 1	Oct. 21	Oct. 9	Sept. 27	Oct. 17	Oct. 6
Chanukah (Festival of Lights)	Dec. 22	Dec. 12	Dec. 2	Dec. 21	Dec. 9	Nov. 28	Dec. 17	Dec. 7
Purim (Feast of Lots)	March 21 2008	March 10 2009	Feb. 28 2010	March 20 2011	March 8 2012	Feb. 24 2013	March 16 2014	March 5 2015

The Cycle Pattern in Judges

Israel Disobeys

Israel is at Peace   Israel is Oppressed

Israel is Delivered   Israel Cries Out

God Raises up a Deliverer

Judge	Description	Years Judged
Othniel	After 8 years of oppression from King Cushan of Aram, Othniel went to war and delivered Israel.	40 years
Ehud	After 18 years of oppression from King Eglon of Moab, Ehud killed Eglon, went to war against Moab, and was victorious.	80 years
Shamgar	Shamgar killed 600 of the Philistines with a poking device used to move animals along.	unknown
Deborah	After 20 years of oppression from King Jabin of Canaan, Deborah convinced Barak to attack. Barak was victorious	40 years
Gideon	After 7 years of Midianite oppression, Gideon defeated the Midianites with only 300 men, using trumpets and jars.	40 years
Tola	The son of Puah son of Dodo from the tribe of Issachar. He lived in Ephraim.	23 years
Jair	A man from Gilead who had thirty sons who rode thirty donkeys, and they had thirty towns in Gilead.	22 years
Jephthah	After 18 years of Ammonite oppression, Jephthah delivered Israel after making a vow with the Lord.	6 years
Isban	Isban was from Bethlehem. He had thirty sons and thirty daughters.	7 years
Elon	Elon was from the tribe of Zebulun.	10 years
Abdon	Abdon, son of Hillel, had forty sons and thirty grandsons who rode on seventy donkeys.	8 years
Samson	A Nazarite with superhuman strength. Killed 1000 Philistines with a jawbone. Destroyed a Philistine temple.	20 years

Kings & Prophets

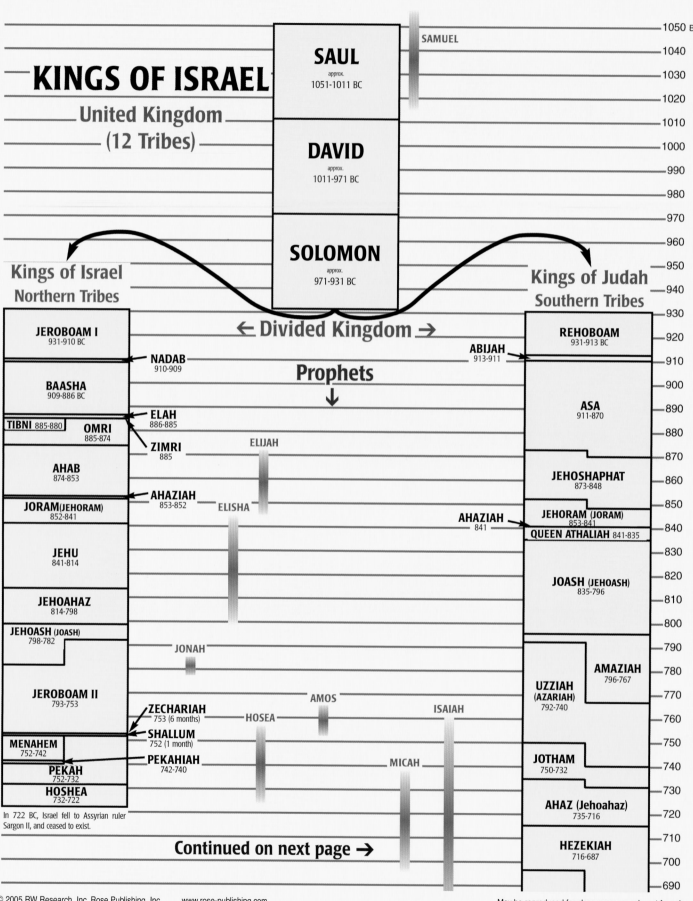

KINGS OF ISRAEL

United Kingdom
(12 Tribes)

SAUL
approx.
1051-1011 BC

DAVID
approx.
1011-971 BC

SOLOMON
approx.
971-931 BC

SAMUEL

Kings of Israel
Northern Tribes

Kings of Judah
Southern Tribes

← **Divided Kingdom** →

Prophets
↓

Kings of Israel (Northern Tribes)	Kings of Judah (Southern Tribes)
JEROBOAM I 931-910 BC	**REHOBOAM** 931-913 BC
NADAB 910-909	**ABIJAH** 913-911
BAASHA 909-886 BC	**ASA** 911-870
ELAH 886-885	
TIBNI 885-880 **OMRI** 885-874	
ZIMRI 885	
AHAB 874-853	**JEHOSHAPHAT** 873-848
JORAM (JEHORAM) 852-841	
AHAZIAH 853-852	**JEHORAM (JORAM)** 853-841
	AHAZIAH 841
	QUEEN ATHALIAH 841-835
JEHU 841-814	**JOASH (JEHOASH)** 835-796
JEHOAHAZ 814-798	
JEHOASH (JOASH) 798-782	
JEROBOAM II 793-753	**AMAZIAH** 796-767
	UZZIAH (AZARIAH) 792-740
ZECHARIAH 753 (6 months)	
SHALLUM 752 (1 month)	**JOTHAM** 750-732
MENAHEM 752-742	
PEKAHIAH 742-740	
PEKAH 752-732	**AHAZ (Jehoahaz)** 735-716
HOSHEA 732-722	
	HEZEKIAH 716-687

ELIJAH

ELISHA

JONAH

AMOS

ISAIAH

ZECHARIAH

HOSEA

MICAH

In 722 BC, Israel fell to Assyrian ruler
Sargon II, and ceased to exist.

Continued on next page →

1050 BC
1040
1030
1020
1010
1000
990
980
970
960
950
940
930
920
910
900
890
880
870
860
850
840
830
820
810
800
790
780
770
760
750
740
730
720
710
700
690

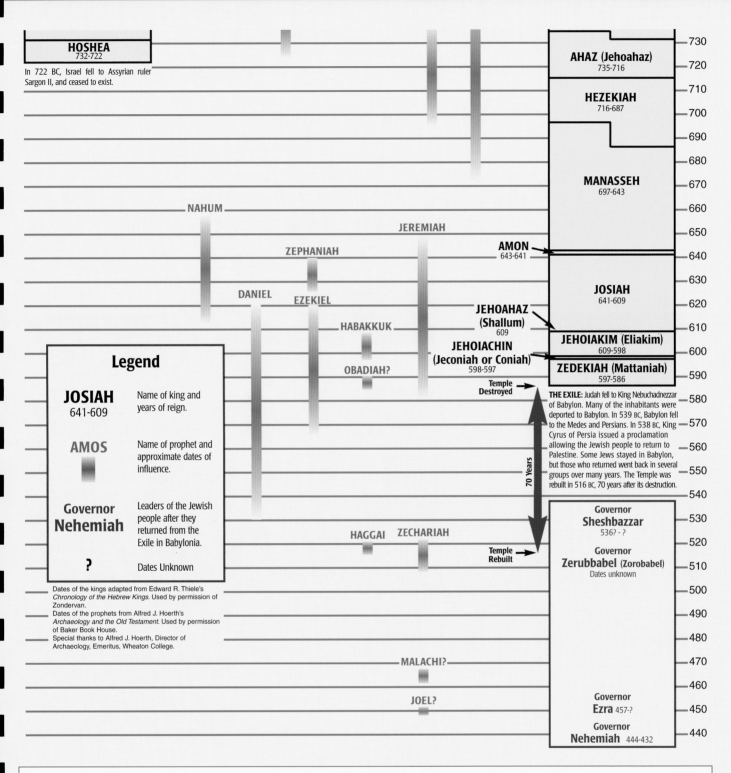

HOSHEA
732-722

In 722 BC, Israel fell to Assyrian ruler Sargon II, and ceased to exist.

AHAZ (Jehoahaz)
735-716 — 730 / 720

HEZEKIAH
716-687 — 710 / 700 / 690

MANASSEH
697-643 — 680 / 670 / 660

NAHUM

JEREMIAH

ZEPHANIAH

AMON
643-641 — 640

DANIEL   EZEKIEL

JOSIAH
641-609 — 630 / 620

JEHOAHAZ (Shallum)
609

HABAKKUK

JEHOIAKIM (Eliakim)
609-598 — 610 / 600

JEHOIACHIN (Jeconiah or Coniah)
598-597

OBADIAH?

ZEDEKIAH (Mattaniah)
597-586 — 590

Temple Destroyed

Legend

JOSIAH
641-609
Name of king and years of reign.

AMOS
Name of prophet and approximate dates of influence.

Governor Nehemiah
Leaders of the Jewish people after they returned from the Exile in Babylonia.

?
Dates Unknown

Dates of the kings adapted from Edward R. Thiele's *Chronology of the Hebrew Kings*. Used by permission of Zondervan.
Dates of the prophets from Alfred J. Hoerth's *Archaeology and the Old Testament*. Used by permission of Baker Book House.
Special thanks to Alfred J. Hoerth, Director of Archaeology, Emeritus, Wheaton College.

THE EXILE: Judah fell to King Nebuchadnezzar of Babylon. Many of the inhabitants were deported to Babylon. In 539 BC, Babylon fell to the Medes and Persians. In 538 BC, King Cyrus of Persia issued a proclamation allowing the Jewish people to return to Palestine. Some Jews stayed in Babylon, but those who returned went back in several groups over many years. The Temple was rebuilt in 516 BC, 70 years after its destruction.

70 Years

— 580 / 570 / 560 / 550 / 540

Governor Sheshbazzar
536? - ? — 530

Governor Zerubbabel (Zorobabel)
Dates unknown — 520 / 510

HAGGAI   ZECHARIAH

Temple Rebuilt

— 500 / 490 / 480

MALACHI? — 470 / 460

JOEL? — 450

Governor Ezra 457-?

Governor Nehemiah 444-432 — 440

Fascinating Facts

Dominant Powers in the Middle East: 900-612 BC - Assyria   612-539 BC - Babylonia   539-330 BC - Medo-Persia

What made a king "good" or "bad"?

The biblical writers were not as interested in a king's abilities as an administrator as they were in the king's desire to follow God's commands. Kings that followed God's law and those who outlawed the altars to foreign gods, the high places, and idol worship were designated as good. Those who did not, were evil. The Bible uses the phrase "He did evil in the eyes (or *sight*) of the Lord," to evaluate the king's reign. In secular history, one of the important kings was Omri of Israel, who conquered the Moabites; but in the Bible this evil king's victories go unmentioned.

The Kings of the United and Divided Kingdoms

United Kingdom
Saul - good ➛ bad
David - good
Solomon - mostly good

Divided Kingdom	
Israel	**Judah**
Jeroboam I ....bad	Rehoboam ....good ➛ bad
Nadab ....bad	Abijah................................bad
Baasha...........................bad	Asa ....good ➛ bad
Elah ....bad	Jehoshaphat ....good
Zimri ....bad	Jehoram ....bad
Tibni..............................bad	Ahaziah ....bad
Omri...............................bad	Queen Athaliah.................bad
Ahab..............................bad	Joash ....good ➛ bad
Ahaziah ....bad	Amaziah...............mostly good
Joram ....bad	Uzziah...............................good
Jehu...............................bad	Jotham ....good
Jehoahaz ....bad	Ahaz.................................bad
Jehoash ....bad	Hezekiah...........................good
Jeroboam II ....bad	Manasseh............bad ➛ good
Zechariah.......................bad	Amon ....bad
Shallum ....bad	Josiah ....good
Menahem........................bad	Jehoahaz ....bad
Pekahiah ....bad	Jehoiakim ....bad
Pekah ....bad	Jehoiachin ....bad
Hoshea ....bad	Zedekiah ....bad

Prophets

Prophet	Prophesied	Date (BC)*	Home/Location
Elijah	To Israel	870-845	Tishbe
Elisha	To Israel	845-800	Abel Meholah
Isaiah	To Judah	760-673	Jerusalem
Jeremiah	To Judah	650-582	Anathoth
Ezekiel	To Exiles in Babylonia	620-570	Babylon
Daniel	In Babylon	620-540	Babylon
Hosea	To Israel	758-725	Israel
Joel	To Judah	450	Jerusalem
Amos	To Israel	765-754	Tekoa
Obadiah	Concerning Edom	590	Jerusalem
Jonah	To Nineveh	781	Gath Hepher
Micah	To Judah	738-698	Moresheth-gath
Nahum	Concerning Nineveh	658-615	Elkosh
Habakkuk	To Judah	608-598	Unknown
Zephaniah	To Judah	640-626	Unknown
Haggai	To Judah	520	Jerusalem
Zechariah	To Judah	522-509	Jerusalem
Malachi	To Judah	465	Jerusalem

Head of Fine Gold — Babylonia (626-539 BC)

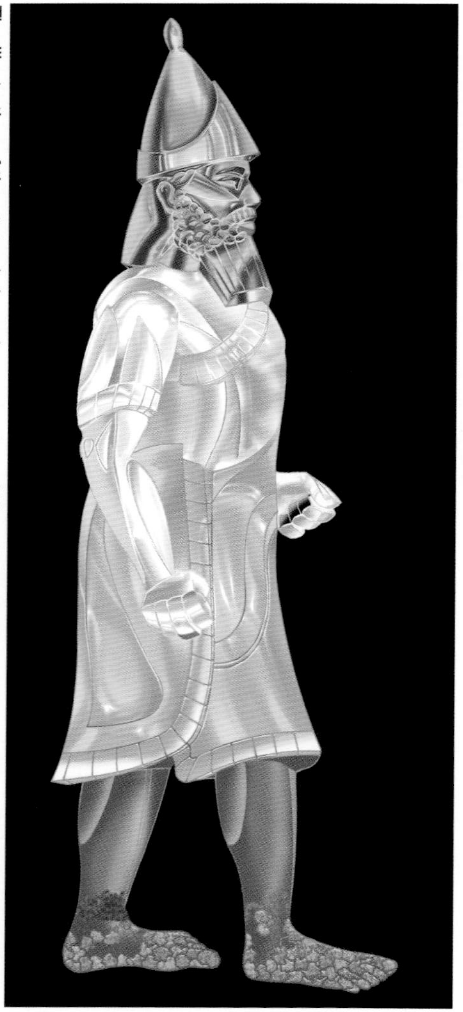

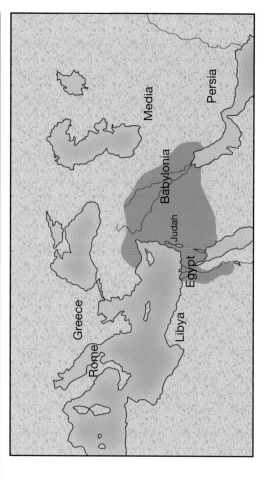

The illustration of the statue is based on a carving of King Nebuchadnezzar's grandson, Nabonidus. It is the most accurate representation of the Babylonian style of art.

Historical and Bible Background of Nebuchadnezzar's Dream

● About 600 years before Jesus was born, Babylonia (Iraq today) was the most powerful and wealthy kingdom in the Middle East.

● King Nebuchadnezzar of Babylon besieged Jerusalem and took Daniel and others captive to Babylon to serve in his court. Nebuchadnezzar also took some of the sacred objects and vessels from the Temple of God back to Babylon.

● One night, Nebuchadnezzar had a dream. The king threatened to kill his advisors if they could not both tell him the dream and interpret it. (Dan. 2:5-11)

● Daniel asked the king for some time to interpret the dream. After Daniel prayed, God revealed the dream and its meaning to him. (Daniel 2:12-23)

● The dream showed a statue with four sections. The head was gold. The chest was silver. The belly and thighs were bronze. The legs were made of iron and the feet were iron mixed with clay. A large rock struck and destroyed the statue and became a huge mountain and filled the whole earth. (Daniel 2:31-35)

● Daniel told King Nebuchadnezzar the dream and interpreted it. (Daniel 2:36-45) The King made Daniel ruler over Babylon.

Head of the Statue
(Daniel 2)

● The head of the statue, made from fine gold, represented the kingdom of Babylonia, which the Lord gave King Nebuchadnezzar to rule.

● The gold symbolized the superior power of Babylonia.

● Eventually Babylonia would be destroyed by an inferior kingdom.

● When King Nebuchadnezzar heard Daniel's interpretation, he said, "Surely your God is the God of gods and the Lord of kings and a revealer of mysteries, for you were able to reveal this mystery."

Vision of Beasts – Lion
(Daniel 7)

● More than 50 years after King Nebuchadnezzar's dream, Daniel had a vision about four great beasts (that were like a lion with eagle's wings, a bear, a leopard, and a terrifying powerful beast).

● The four beasts are four kingdoms. Nebuchadnezzar of the Babylonian kingdom is compared to a lion in Jeremiah 4:7; 50:44, and to an eagle in Ezekiel 17:3,11,12.

● Images of lions with eagle's wings were popular in Babylonia, and can be found on ancient Babylonian architecture and currency. (Daniel 7:4)

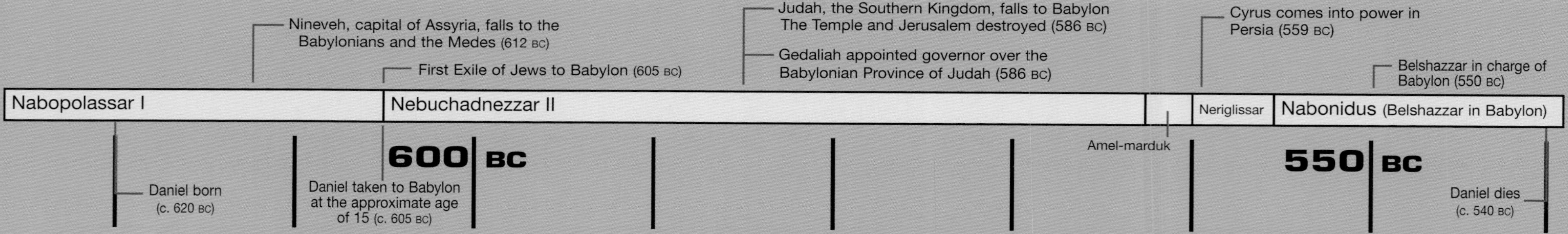

Map labels: Rome, Greece, Media, Persia, Babylonia, Judah, Egypt, Libya

Timeline:

Nabopolassar I | Nebuchadnezzar II | Amel-marduk | Neriglissar | Nabonidus (Belshazzar in Babylon)

600 BC | **550 BC**

- Daniel born (c. 620 BC)
- Daniel taken to Babylon at the approximate age of 15 (c. 605 BC)
- Nineveh, capital of Assyria, falls to the Babylonians and the Medes (612 BC)
- First Exile of Jews to Babylon (605 BC)
- Judah, the Southern Kingdom, falls to Babylon The Temple and Jerusalem destroyed (586 BC)
- Gedaliah appointed governor over the Babylonian Province of Judah (586 BC)
- Cyrus comes into power in Persia (559 BC)
- Belshazzar in charge of Babylon (550 BC)
- Daniel dies (c. 540 BC)

© 2005 RW Research, Inc. Rose Publishing, Inc.   www.rose-publishing.com

Chest and Arms of Silver—Medo-Persia (539-332 BC)

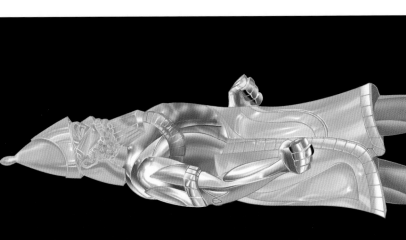

Historical and Bible Background

● In 539 BC, Darius the Mede (from Media) took Babylon without a fight.

● By 538 BC, Mesopotamia and Judah were under Persian rule. Later the Persians gained control of Egypt and Libya.

● King Cyrus and the other kings of the Persian empire developed a policy that allowed all people the freedom to worship their own gods, and live their own ways.

● In 538 BC, Cyrus issued a decree ordering the restoration of the Jewish community. Jews were allowed to return to Jerusalem and rebuild the Temple. (Ezra 1:2-4)

● The Persians paid to rebuild the Temple in Jerusalem. (Ezra 6:8)

● The vessels taken by King Nebuchadnezzar of Babylon were returned to their rightful place in Jerusalem. (Ezra 1:7-11)

● In 457 BC, King Artaxerxes of Persia sent Ezra to Judah for religious reform and spiritual guidance. (Ezra 7:1-6)

● Nehemiah governed Judah from 444-430 BC. While in Judah, Nehemiah rebuilt the walls of Jerusalem.

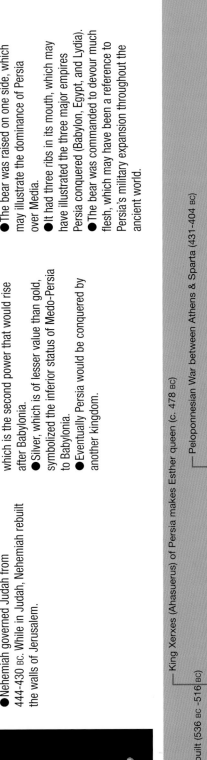

Chest and Arms of Statue
(Daniel 2)

● The chest and arms made of silver represented the kingdom of Medo-Persia, which is the second power that would rise after Babylonia.

● Silver, which is of lesser value than gold, symbolized the inferior status of Medo-Persia to Babylonia.

● Eventually Persia would be conquered by another kingdom.

Vision of Beasts – Bear
(Daniel 7)

● Daniel's vision of the beasts had shown a beast that looked like a bear.

● The bear was raised on one side, which may illustrate the dominance of Persia over Media.

● It had three ribs in its mouth, which may have illustrated the three major empires Persia conquered (Babylon, Egypt, and Lydia).

● The bear was commanded to devour much flesh, which may have been a reference to Persia's military expansion throughout the ancient world.

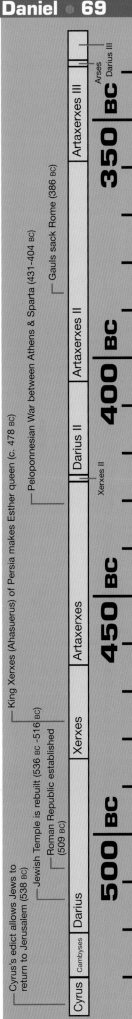

Timeline:

Rulers: Cyrus | Cambyses | Darius | Xerxes | Artaxerxes | Xerxes II, Darius II | Artaxerxes II | Artaxerxes III | Arses, Darius III

- Cyrus's edict allows Jews to return to Jerusalem (538 BC)
- Jewish Temple is rebuilt (536 BC -516 BC)
- Roman Republic established (509 BC)
- King Xerxes (Ahasuerus) of Persia makes Esther queen (c. 478 BC)
- Peloponnesian War between Athens & Sparta (431-404 BC)
- Gauls sack Rome (386 BC)

500 BC — 450 BC — 400 BC — 350 BC

Belly and Thighs of Bronze — Greece (332-63 BC)

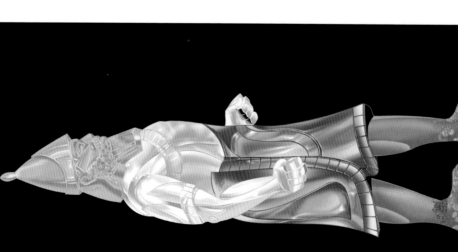

Historical and Bible Background

- In 332 BC, Alexander the Great of Greece conquered the kingdom of Persia, and expanded his kingdom as far east as the Indus river.
- Alexander the Great brought with him rapid Hellenization, the spread of Greek culture, language, and religion into the entire civilized world.
- After Alexander's death in 323 BC, his generals fought over the conquered land.
- After more than 40 years of struggles and warfare (323-280 BC), four major divisions emerged: Egypt (Ptolemies), Syria (Seleucids), Macedonia (Antigonids), and Pergamum (Attalids).
- For over 150 years, the Jews were either under the control of the Ptolemies or the Seleucids.
- From 175-163 BC, the Seleucid ruler Antiochus IV Epiphanes tried to force the Jews to abandon their law and adopt Greek culture. In 167 BC, he desecrated the Jewish Temple by sacrificing a pig on an altar to the Greek god Zeus.
- In response to the desecration of the Temple, a Jewish priest named Judas Maccabeus lead a revolt.
- Maccabeus won, and in 164 BC, the Temple was cleansed and rededicated. This rededication is celebrated every year as Hanukkah.

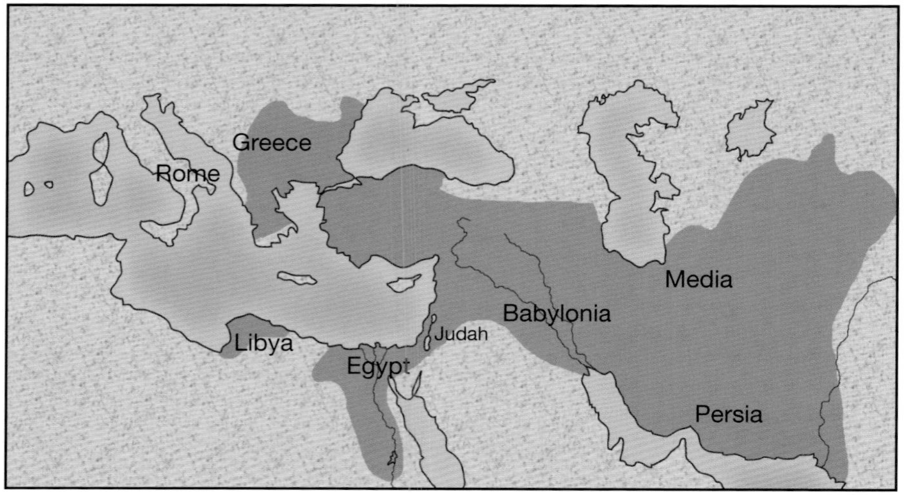

Belly and Thighs of Statue
(Daniel 2)

- The belly and thighs made of bronze represent the kingdom of Greece. This third kingdom would rule over the whole earth.
- Bronze, which is of lesser value than silver, symbolized the inferior status of Greece to that of Persia.
- Eventually Greece would be conquered by another kingdom.

Vision of Beasts – Leopard
(Daniel 7)

- Daniel's vision of the leopard with four heads and four wings may represent the kingdom of Greece.
- The four wings may illustrate the speed of Alexander the Great's conquest.
- The four heads may represent the division of Alexander's kingdom into four provinces after Alexander's death: Egypt under the Ptolemies, Syria under the Seleucids, Macedonia under the Antigonids, and Pergamum under the Attalids.

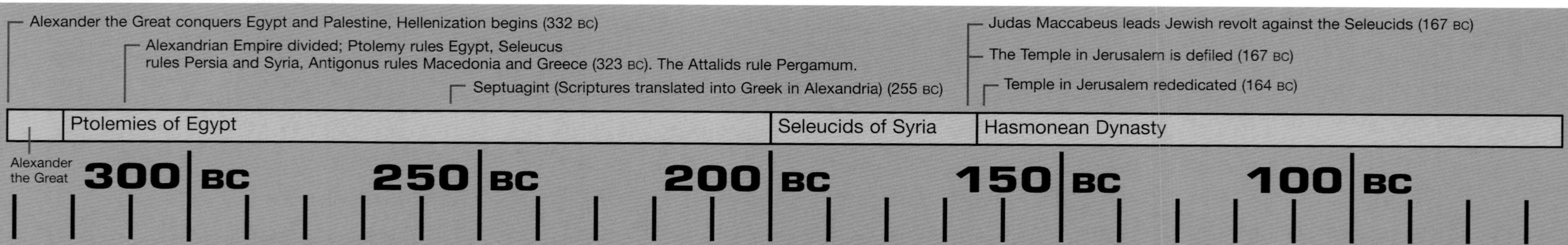

Map labels: Rome, Greece, Libya, Egypt, Judah, Babylonia, Media, Persia

---

Timeline:

- Alexander the Great conquers Egypt and Palestine, Hellenization begins (332 BC)
- Alexandrian Empire divided; Ptolemy rules Egypt, Seleucus rules Persia and Syria, Antigonus rules Macedonia and Greece (323 BC). The Attalids rule Pergamum.
- Septuagint (Scriptures translated into Greek in Alexandria) (255 BC)
- Judas Maccabeus leads Jewish revolt against the Seleucids (167 BC)
- The Temple in Jerusalem is defiled (167 BC)
- Temple in Jerusalem rededicated (164 BC)

Alexander the Great	Ptolemies of Egypt		Seleucids of Syria		Hasmonean Dynasty	
300 BC	**250** BC	**200** BC	**150** BC	**100** BC		

Legs of Iron and Feet of Iron and Clay — Rome

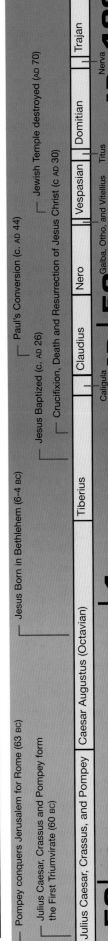

Historical and Bible Background

● Scholars suggest that the fourth kingdom is the Roman empire, however the Bible does not specifically identify this kingdom as Rome.

● In 63 BC, Roman General Pompey conquered Jerusalem.

● On March 15, 44 BC, Julius Caesar was assassinated by Brutus and Cassius, who fled to the East. Two years later, Octavian and Mark Antony defeated Brutus and Cassius at the Battle of Philippi.

● In 37 BC, Herod the Great was appointed king of Judea by Octavian and Mark Antony.

● In 27 BC, Caesar Augustus (Octavian) became the first Roman Emperor.

● During his reign, Herod the Great began to refurbish the Temple in Jerusalem.

● Jesus was born in Bethlehem, c. 6-4 BC.

● In AD 6, Judea became a Roman province ruled by a governor.

● Jesus Christ was crucified by the governor of Judea, Pontius Pilate. Three days after his death, Jesus rose from the dead and was seen by more than 500 people (c. AD 30).

● In AD 70, the Romans destroyed the Jewish temple and Jerusalem.

● Over time, the Roman Empire weakened due to conflict within its borders and invaders attacking from outside.

● The Roman Empire fell in AD 476.

Legs and Feet of Statue
(Daniel 2)

● The legs were made of iron and the feet were a mixture of both iron and clay.

● The legs of iron suggest that this kingdom would be strong as iron and would break, smash and crush things.

● This kingdom would be a divided kingdom, different from the others, both strong and weak, like iron is strong and clay is brittle.

● This kingdom would have a mixture of people who would not be united. (Daniel 2:41-43; 7:23)

Vision of Beasts – Terrifying Beast (Daniel 7)

● Daniel had a vision of a terrifying beast with ten horns and iron teeth.

● The beast's ten horns are ten kings that would rise from this kingdom.

● After them, another man (the "little horn" with eyes and a mouth that boasts) would speak against God and persecute God's people. Three of the first horns (kings) would be uprooted. Eventually the terrifying beast would be thrown into the blazing fire.

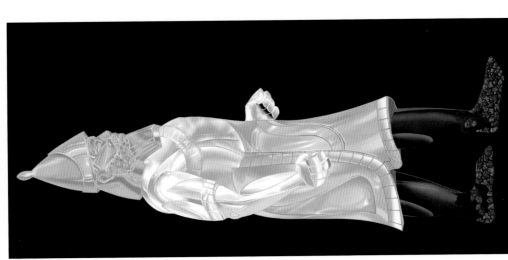

Pompey conquers Jerusalem for Rome (63 BC)

Julius Caesar, Crassus and Pompey form the First Triumvirate (60 BC)

Jesus Born in Bethlehem (6-4 BC)

Jesus Baptized (c. AD 26)

Crucifixion, Death and Resurrection of Jesus Christ (c AD 30)

Paul's Conversion (c. AD 44)

Jewish Temple destroyed (AD 70)

50 BC		AD 1		AD 50					AD 100
Julius Caesar, Crassus, and Pompey	Caesar Augustus (Octavian)		Tiberius	Caligula	Claudius	Nero	Galba, Otho, and Vitellius	Vespasian	Trajan
								Titus	Nerva
								Domitian	

The Statue in the Book of Daniel

The Kingdoms and King Nebuchadnezzar's Dream

NEBUCHADNEZZAR'S DREAM (Daniel 2)	DANIEL'S VISION (Daniel 7)	THE KINGDOMS (Dates Kingdom occupied Judah)
HEAD (FINE GOLD)	LION with eagle's wings	BABYLONIA King Nebuchadnezzar to Belshazzar (605 BC – 539 BC)
CHEST AND ARMS (SILVER)	BEAR raised on one side; three ribs in its mouth	MEDO-PERSIA King Cyrus to Darius III (539 – 332 BC)
BELLY AND THIGHS (BRONZE)	LEOPARD with four wings and four heads	GREECE Alexander the Great and the Four Divisions (332 BC – 63 BC)
LEGS (IRON) & FEET (IRON AND CLAY)	BEAST iron teeth, ten horns; small horn with eyes and mouth	A DIVIDED KINGDOM Many scholars believe this kingdom to be Rome (63 BC through the time of Jesus).
STONE (CUT OUT, NOT BY HUMAN HANDS)	SON OF MAN (Jesus Christ)	THE EVERLASTING KINGDOM OF GOD

Stone Cut Out— Everlasting Kingdom

The Rock (Daniel 2)

• A stone was cut out, not by human hands, and it struck the statue on its feet of iron and clay and broke them in pieces. Then the rest of the statue broke into pieces and what remained was carried away in the wind. Then the stone that struck the statue became a great mountain that filled the whole earth.

• Daniel told the king that God will set up a kingdom that will crush all earthly kingdoms and bring them to an end.

• God's kingdom will never be destroyed and will endure forever.

Vision of Beasts The Son of Man (Daniel 7)

• After seeing the four beasts in a vision, Daniel saw one like a son of man, coming with the clouds of heaven.

• The son of man [Jesus] approached the Ancient of Days [God, the Father] and was led into his presence.

• The son of man was given authority, glory and sovereign power.

• All peoples, nations and men of every language worshiped him.

• His dominion is an everlasting dominion that will not pass away, and his kingdom will never be destroyed.

Bible References & Spiritual Application

• The stone represents God's eternal kingdom that is more powerful than any other kingdom.

• At the time of Daniel, the Temple in Jerusalem was in shambles and the people of Israel were placed in captivity. The defeated captives may have feared that their God was weak and unfaithful.

• Daniel's writing demonstrates that in the midst of despair, God is still present, powerful, and in control. Kingdoms and rulers come and go, but God is ultimately in charge. (Daniel 2:20-21; 7:9-14, 27)

• Despite Babylonia's wealth and power, Daniel emphasized that God's kingdom is eternal and more powerful than any earthly kingdom. (Daniel 2:44)

• The book of Daniel shows that God did not forget his promises. God's promises have been fulfilled in the Son of Man (Daniel 7:13-14), who established an everlasting kingdom on earth. (Daniel 2:44; 7:27)

	Archaeological Find	Description of the Find	Importance of the Find
Genesis	**1. The Sumerian King List, One of History's First Mentions of a Great Flood** The Sumerians established the first civilization in the biblical world. Several clay tablets and prisms containing the list of their kings have been found in the ruins of Mesopotamia.	Surviving copies of the Sumerian king list date to c. 2100 BC. What is striking about the list of Sumerian kings is that the kings are divided into two groups—those who ruled before a great flood and those who ruled after it. Equally striking is that the lengths of reigns (and life spans) of these kings drastically decreased after the flood, as did life spans of people recorded in the Bible.	The king list says, "After the flood had swept over the earth and when kingship was lowered again from heaven . . ." Mention of a flood, hardly necessary in a list of kings, is an argument for the biblical flood described in Genesis 7–8.
Genesis	**2. An Ancient Flood Story** Accounts of a massive flood are found in many cultures around the world. The Gilgamesh Epic (the saga of an ancient Babylonian king, Gilgamesh) includes an expanded flood story on Tablet 11, similar to the flood story in Genesis 6–9. The best known copy of the Epic was found at Nineveh on a series of baked clay tablets.	Tablet 11 (right) of the Gilgamesh Epic tells of a great flood brought on earth by the wrath of gods and includes a hero who is told to build a ship, to take every kind of animal along, and to use birds to check if the water had receded. 	Copies of the Epic and other flood stories have been found in the Near East. The popularity of the flood theme argues for its historicity and supports the flood of Noah's time. *Left: Fragment (6 inches high) of a copy of the Babylonian epic of Gilgamesh dating from the 7th century BC, found at Nineveh.*  *Above: Copied piece from the 15th century BC, found in Megiddo, shows the writing.*
Genesis Nehem.	**3. Ur, Hometown of Abraham** Ur is mentioned four times in the Bible as the hometown of Abraham. It was occupied from the 4th millennium BC. Excavations of Ur (in Iraq today) have continued off and on since the 1800s.	 *The famous Royal Tombs at Ur (c. 2500 BC) reveal gold and silver objects of great beauty.* *Left and right: Part of the "Standard of Ur," from those tombs, made before Abraham, show Sumerian people.*	Finds show that Abraham's ancestral home had been a powerful city-state before it fell. If Ur's decline and fall came during Abraham's time, perhaps archaeology has provided another clue as to why Abraham's father relocated his family to Haran. Genesis 11:31; 15:7; Nehemiah 9:7; Acts 7:2-4.
Genesis	**4. Beni Hasan Tomb Painting** This ancient Egyptian tomb painting, dating close to the time of Abraham, shows a caravan of people from Palestine carrying merchandise for trade in Egypt. They carried eye paint to sell and armed themselves with bows and spears.		Dating to around 1900 BC, this tomb painting, with words and pictures on it, shows how Old Testament people from the time of Abraham and Sarah looked, how they dressed, their hair styles, and even a musical instrument of the day (lyre). The weapons they used (spear, bow and arrow, ax, sword) depict some of the armaments available to Abraham (Gen. 14). *Left: Part of the Beni Hasan tomb painting showing Semitic people from Canaan.*
Exodus Leviticus Deut.	**5. The Law Code of Hammurapi** This black diorite stele (a carved upright stone slab) was commissioned around 1750 BC by Hammurapi (Hammurabi), king of Babylon. It contains about 300 laws. The stele was found, partially defaced, at Susa (in Iran today) where it was taken as loot in the 12th century BC.	On top of the Code of Hammurapi (right), the king is shown in front of a seated deity, Marduk. The king's laws are written on the remainder of the stele for public display. The stele is more than seven feet tall.	Some of the laws, and the way they are written, are remarkably similar to those found in Exodus, Leviticus, and Deuteronomy, indicating that a "common law" existed in the ancient Near East. For example, *lex talionis* ("an eye for an eye") is found in both the law code of Hammurapi and in Exodus 21:24. Unlike Hammurapi's law, the biblical law is between God and His people.
Genesis	**6. Boghazkoy, Hittite Capital** The ancient Hittites' large capital city has been recovered about 90 miles east of Ankara, Turkey. The Hittite's rule extended to Syria and Lebanon. *Right: Warrior god from King's Gate.*	 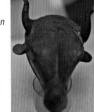 *Hittite artifacts shown at the Museum of Anatolian Civilizations at Ankara, Turkey. Excavations uncovered fortified gateways, temples, and a large archive. The city fell around 1200 BC.*	Although Hittites are mentioned often in the Old Testament, almost nothing was known about them until modern times. One hundred years ago, critics thought the Hittites were an imaginary people made up by the biblical authors. Finding the Hittite's empire forced that claim to be withdrawn and supported the biblical record. The find also helps explain the language, history and literature of people who appear in the Old Testament and ruled in the 2nd millennium BC.
Genesis	**7. Nuzi Tablets** Excavations at the ancient city of Nuzi east of the Tigris River turned up over 20,000 baked clay tablets.	Dating between 1500-1401 BC, many of these tablets, with cuneiform writing on them, reveal customs and stories very similar to those found in Genesis 15-31, such as marriage, adopting an heir, surrogate mothers, and inheritance.	Because culture changed very slowly in the ancient Near East, the tablets help explain some of the common practices and background which are found in earlier biblical events of the patriarchal period (2000-1500 BC).
Genesis	**8. Haran, Home of the Patriarchs** A village of Harran (Haran) exists in Turkey today, and has been found to stand atop the ancient one from the Old Testament period.	Also found near Haran are villages that still bear the names of Abraham's great-grandfather and grandfather, Serug and Nahor, as mentioned in Genesis 11:22-26. Haran was the father of Lot (Genesis 11:27).	The cities of Ur and Haran both had the moon god as their main deity. Terah, father of Abraham, worshiped "other gods" (Joshua 24:2) and moved his family from Ur, in southern Mesopotamia (Iraq today), to Haran in the north (Genesis 11:27-31).

	Archaeological Find	**Description of the Find**	**Importance of the Find**
Genesis Joshua Judges 1 Kings	**9. Shechem** Shechem was strategically placed in the central hill country. It controlled all the roads in the area, but its location made the city vulnerable to attack. Excavations in the city of Shechem reveal a city with walls made of large megalithic stones and the city gate system.	The most important find is a fortress-temple of Baal from the story of Abimelech (Judges 9:46). People could find refuge in the temple from enemies. Before Abimelech, Abraham and Jacob built altars to God in the area of Shechem (Genesis 12, 33) and after the Exodus, the Israelites renewed their covenant with God at Shechem (Joshua 24).	Shechem is important in many biblical stories. It was a city of refuge for anyone who unintentionally caused death (Joshua 20), In the 10th century BC, King Jeroboam I fortified the city and made it the capital of the kingdom of Israel (1 Kings 12:25). The vulnerability of Shechem to attack may be one reason the capital was moved shortly after Jeroboam I died.
Exodus	**10. Pithom and Raamses, Store Cities of the Pharaoh** The location of Raamses is now associated with Qantir (Tell el-Dab'a). Pithom was within the Wadi Tumilat, a natural corridor in and out of Egypt, but its exact location is not yet settled.	Ongoing excavations at Tell el-Dab'a (Raamses) have revealed a prosperous ancient city with many monuments, temples, and buildings. Tell el-Retaba is thought to be the most probable location of Pithom, but sufficient excavation has not been done at the site.	According to Exodus 1, the Hebrews were slaves in the Egyptian cities of Pithom and Raamses before the Exodus. The Egyptians forced the Hebrews to make bricks, both with and without straw (Exodus 1:14a ; 5:7-19).
Exodus 1 Kings	**11. Horned Altars** Excavations have turned up some excellent examples of horned altars. 	Horned altars made of stone have been found at places like Dan and Beersheba. This reconstructed horned altar (left) dates from the 10th century BC and was found at the city of Beersheba. It was most likely a pagan altar. It was obviously made of dressed (cut) stone, a practice prohibited by the Lord in Exodus 20:25.	The Old Testament speaks of horned incense altars at least 20 times. This find shows how horned altars were shaped. The Bible tells how they were used. One was in the Tabernacle. The Lord told Moses to make an acacia-wood horned altar five cubits long, five cubits broad, and three cubits high with the horns of it at the four corners and overlaid with brass (Exodus 27:2; 1 Kings 1:50).
	12. Merneptah (Merenptah) Stele (also called The Israel Stele) The hieroglyphic text of the stele made in Egypt describes the victories of Pharaoh Merneptah around 1230 BC over the Libyans and people of Palestine. The stele stands more than seven feet high.	The Merneptah Stele contains the earliest extrabiblical mention of the name "Israel" thus far known. The Egyptian pharaoh brags of a victory over Israel around 1230 BC.  *Right: Twice the god Amon-Re and Merneptah are depicted in the center, with goddess Mut at left and god Khonsu at right.*	Although this battle between Egypt and Israel is not mentioned in the Old Testament, the stele does show that the Israelites were in fact living in the Promised Land at that time, and that their entrance into the land had already taken place by 1230 BC.
	13. The Oldest Picture of Israelites In Egypt, on a long wall of the great Karnak Temple, is a recently identified scene of the aftermath of a battle between the Egyptians and Israelites dating to about 1209 BC.	 *The drawing (above) of the carved scene shows possibly the Israelites vanquished by the armies of Pharaoh Merneptah. Scene 4 of the Karnak Temple relief, Thebes (Luxor).*	Carved about 200 years after the time of Moses and Joshua, this battle scene is by far the earliest picture of Israelites ever discovered. This same event is also told of on the Merneptah Stele (above). It shows that the Exodus had taken place and the Israelites were living in the Promised Land by 1200 BC.
Joshua	**14. Jericho, Gateway into the Promised Land** The earliest ruins at Jericho date to the Stone Age (Neolithic). A tower (right) found in the Jericho ruins dates back before Abraham's time. The tower is made from stones obtained when the surrounding moat was cut. It was connected to a mudbrick wall.	There is debate over whether Joshua's wall of Jericho has been found. Massive erosion has removed much of the remains of that period, and mud bricks could easily erode away over the centuries. 	The biblical importance of Jericho is underscored by the fact that it is referred to more than 50 times in the Old Testament. Perhaps the most significant references are those in Joshua 6, which tell of the Israelite conquest of the city, their first victory in the Promised Land. Archaeology has shown where the city once stood, and that it guarded the key spot for entering into the Promised Land from the east.
Judges 1 Samuel	**15. The Philistines and the Temple of Rameses III** The earliest known record of the Philistines was carved on the wall of an Egyptian temple at Thebes around 1175-1150 BC.  *Right: Temple of Rameses III at Thebes (Luxor).*	At the Temple of Rameses III, the Philistines are both pictured and listed as being one of several groups of "Sea Peoples" invading the coastal plains from Egypt to Palestine. 	Philistines are mentioned over 200 times in the Old Testament. This temple record shows when the main wave of Philistines tried to invade Egypt. From Samson (Judges 14-16) to David (I Samuel 17), the Israelites battled constantly against the Philistines for control of much of the Promised Land. This record depicts the dress and armor the Philistines might have worn as they interacted with the Israelites. *Left: The Sea Peoples' boat (right side of picture) being defeated by the Egyptians.*
Numb. 1 Kings Jeremiah Hosea	**16. Canaanite Gods and Goddesses** Between 1929-1939 excavators found hundreds of stories about Canaanite gods and goddesses written on clay tablets among the ruins of the ancient city of Ugarit, in modern Syria.	The Old Testament repeatedly refers to gods and goddesses, like Baal and Ashtaroth (Asherah or Astarte), which were worshiped by the Canaanites living among the Israelites in the Promised Land. The prophets of Israel strongly warned God's people not to worship these false gods in Numbers 25, 1 Kings 11, Jeremiah 23, and Hosea 13.	These finds reveal many details about the Canaanite religion, and help us better understand how prevalent idol worship was in Israelite cities and the challenge for the children of Israel to worship the one true God.  *Right: Above: Asherah Below: Astarte Plaque c. 13th-10th century Canaanite period*

	Archaeological Find	Description of the Find	Importance of the Find	
Judges 1 Kings	**17. Dan (Laish), Israel's Northernmost City** Excavations show that the large and well-fortified Canaanite city was destroyed around 1150 BC, after which the city was rebuilt, with Israelite artifacts found thereafter. *Right: The 4000-year-old mud-brick Gate of Dan from the Middle Bronze Age shows gate system construction in the patriarchal period.*	 The city of Dan was originally a Canaanite stronghold that was conquered by the tribe of Dan (Judges 18). Dan has more artifacts of biblical significance than almost any other city found so far.	According to Judges 20:1, Israel's northern boundary was the city of Dan. The book of Judges tells us that the children of Dan destroyed a Canaanite city by sword and fire and built their own city. They named the city Dan and set up graven images. The High Place where Jeroboam I erected a gold calf has been found in Dan (1 Kings 12:28-31).	Zev Radovan
1 Kings 2 Kings 2 Chron. Rev.	**18. Megiddo (Armageddon), City of War** Finds reveal ruins of a strong prosperous Canaanite city under ruins of a heavily fortified Israelite city with a strong city gate. 	Megiddo is on a hill beside a wide plain, a strategic location for many battles. Although Joshua defeated the armies of Megiddo's Canaanite king (Joshua 12:21), the Israelites failed to conquer the city then. Not until the time of David or Solomon, did it come under Israelite control. The gate found at Megiddo was like those associated with Solomon's reign. *Left: The Canaanite bamah (high place) at Megiddo.*	Solomon made Megiddo a fortress city in the 900s BC (1 Kings 4:12; 9:15). Later, in 609 BC, King Josiah of Judah was killed in a battle against the Egyptians on the plain beside Megiddo (2 Kings 23:29, 2 Chronicles 35:22). Revelation 16:16 refers to Megiddo (called Armageddon) as the place where the army of Christ battles the forces of Satan in the end times.	Zev Radovan
Joshua Judges 1 Samuel Jeremiah Amos Zeph. Zech.	**19. Ashkelon, Philistine Seaport** Ongoing excavations (right) since 1985 have discovered the large (about 150 acres) and heavily fortified city of Ashkelon. A small bull figurine was found, illustrating pagan worship.	There is evidence that Ashkelon was a major seaport that traded with other Mediterranean nations. *Right: Ashkelon was one of five major cities of the Philistines (Joshua 13:3 and 1 Samuel 6:17).* 	The Israelites did not conquer Ashkelon (Judges 1:18-19). Nebuchadnezzar destroyed it in 604 BC as predicted by Jeremiah. The prophets Amos, Jeremiah, Zephaniah, and Zechariah all pronounced condemnation upon the city of Ashkelon (Amos 1:6-8, Jeremiah 25:15-20 and 47:5-7, Zephaniah 2:4-7, Zechariah 9:5).	Zev Radovan
Joshua Judges 1 Kings	**20. Gezer, Gift to King Solomon** Archaeologists have excavated the ancient city of Gezer and found clear evidence of Egyptian destruction, as well as a bit of Solomon's defensive walls and the city gate.	Gezer did not become an Israelite city during the conquest and settlement of the Promised Land (Joshua 16:10; Judges 1:29). The Egyptian Pharaoh destroyed the city and its Canaanite inhabitants, then gave it as a wedding gift when Solomon married his daughter (1 Kings 9:15-17).	The wedding gift shows that Egypt was pulling out of Palestine and considered Solomon stronger. Solomon later rebuilt Gezer as an Israelite stronghold. The similarity of Gezer's gateway to those found at Megiddo and Hazor indicates they were all built by Solomon.	
Joshua 1 Samuel 2 Samuel	**21. Shiloh, First Home of the Ark of the Covenant** Archaeology at Shiloh has found an Israelite city from Joshua's time and evidence of subsequent destruction by fire.	According to the Old Testament, Shiloh was an important early sanctuary in the Promised Land. The Tent of Meeting (part of the Tabernacle) and the Ark of the Covenant resided at Shiloh after Joshua's conquest (Joshua 18 and 1 Samuel 1-4).	1 Samuel 4 tells of Israel moving the ark from Shiloh to a battlefield, hoping it would protect them from the Philistines. The Philistines captured the ark in battle. Archaeological evidence indicates that sometime later the Philistines destroyed Shiloh.	
Joshua 1 Samuel 2 Samuel Amos	**22. Ashdod, Where Dagon Fell** Ashdod was one of the five major Philistine cities mentioned in Joshua 13:3 and 1 Samuel 6:17. Archaeological work between 1962-1969 has yielded much new information about Ashdod. No temple of Dagon has been found, but an open area where there had once been a temple has surfaced.	 Archaeologists have found that the Philistine culture had begun to fade away in the city during the 700s BC as Amos prophesied. *Left: "Deity in a Fish-Robe" was often identified as the Philistine god Dagon, 9th century BC, found in Assyria in the 1800s. The true appearance of Dagon is uncertain.*	In 1 Samuel 5 the Philistines brought the Ark of the Covenant to Ashdod after they captured it in battle. After placing the Ark in the temple of Dagon (the chief Philistine god), the statue of Dagon fell and broke into pieces and the people of the city became infested with tumors. They eventually sent the Ark back to Israel. Some three centuries later the prophet Amos received this word from the Lord, "I will cut off the inhabitants from Ashdod . . . and the remnant of the Philistines shall perish . . ." (Amos 1:8).	Arvel Witte
1 Kings 2 Chron. Jeremiah Ezekiel	**23. Shishak's Invasion Record** A record of Pharaoh Shishak's raid of 140 places, including the kingdom of Judah has been found in Egypt carved on a wall in the Karnak Temple of Amun, god of Thebes (Luxor today). The Shishak Relief (Sheshonk I) commemorates his victory over Rehoboam when Solomon's temple was robbed of its riches (probably 925 BC). The relief shows that Egypt raided Israel, not just Judah.	 *Egyptian goddess Mut holds a club and bow, and leads five rows of captives.*  *Right: Shishak grasps a group of captives by the hair and strikes them with his club.*	According to the Old Testament (1 Kings 14 and 2 Chronicles 12), Pharaoh Shishak of Egypt invaded Judah during the fifth year of King Rehoboam's reign. "...Shishak, king of Egypt, came up against Jerusalem, because they had transgressed against the Lord, with twelve hundred chariots, and threescore thousand horsemen; and the people were without number that came with him out of Egypt..." (2 Chronicles 12:2-3). Other verses that refer to Thebes (the city of No) in Egypt are Jeremiah 46:25 and Ezekiel 30:14-16.	Karnak Temple, Carol Witte
1 Samuel 2 Chron.	**24. Beth Shemesh** Excavations now underway at the ancient fortified city of Beth Shemesh (right) have already yielded both Philistine and Israelite artifacts, as well as evidence of its destruction as described in 2 Chronicles 12.		According to 1 Samuel 6:12-15, the Philistines returned the captured Ark of the Covenant to the Israelites at Beth Shemesh. Later, about 940 BC, Pharaoh Shishak of Egypt invaded and destroyed several cities in the foothills region (2 Chron. 12:2-4). Also, discoveries of massive fortifications and a water supply show Solomon's building activity in the city.	Zev Radovan

	Archaeological Find	Description of the Find	Importance of the Find
2 Samuel Jeremiah	**25. Pool at Gibeon** This remarkable pool, dating to before 1000 BC, was found largely intact in Gibeon, six miles north of Jerusalem in excavations around in 1956.	The Pool of Gibeon goes down some 80 feet. The original diggers removed 3000 tons of limestone. A tunnel for the pool runs under the city to an outside spring. This internal water supply was important in case of siege.	2 Samuel 2:13 and Jeremiah 41:12 speak of a great water pool at Gibeon. The find verifies the location of the Pool at Gibeon as mentioned in the Bible and shows the great effort taken to have a secure source of water.
Judges 1 Samuel	**26. Gibeah, King Saul's Capital** Archaeologists have identified Gibeah with the ancient ruins on a hill known today as Tel el-Ful, about three miles north of Jerusalem.	Excavations have shown that the site of Gibeah was inhabited about 1100 BC, the time of King Saul. Saul's fortress-palace was found here. It was small and modest compared with the later palaces of David and Solomon.	Gibeah was the principal town of the tribe of Benjamin (Judges 19:11-14). It was also Saul's home. He eventually made it his capital (1 Sam. 10:26; 11:4; and 15:34). Finding Gibeah so close to Jebusite Jerusalem indicates that Saul never fully controlled the land.
Joshua Judges 1 Samuel	**27. Beth Shean** Archaeology shows that Canaanites, and possibly Philistines, occupied Beth Shean from the time of the Judges until after Saul. Beth Shean was a city within the tribal allotment of Manasseh (Joshua 17:11). However, the Israelites did not conquer Beth Shean (Judges 1:27), and the Philistines eventually took it.	Later King Saul and his armies fought the Philistines on Mt. Gilboa. King Saul and his sons (all but one) died in the battle.	The Philistines hung the bodies of King Saul and his sons from the walls of Beth Shean (1 Sam. 31:10). See the large tell (hill) at left. Some believe that finding Philistine coffins shows that the Philistines occupied the city at or before the time of Saul. *Left: Beth Shean is the large tell in the background. Right: Philistine coffin lid from nearby cemetery.*
2 Samuel 2 Chron.	**28. King David's Jerusalem** The City of David Archaeological Project uncovered much of the buried remains of David's city of Jerusalem between 1978-1985.	Archaeologists have uncovered remains of that city, including evidence of David's conquest and a palace that may have belonged to King David himself. The most important find has been that the Siloam spring was guarded by towers.	According to the Old Testament books of 2 Samuel and 1 Chronicles, King David conquered Jerusalem and made it the capital of Israel. Virtually nothing apart from the Bible was known about the city of that time until excavations were done between 1978-85.
2 Kings	**29. The House of David Inscription (Tel Dan Inscription)** In 1993 and 1994 an archaeologist working at the Old Testament site of the city of Dan found three pieces of an inscribed stone referring to David.	This stone inscribed in Aramaic with the expression "the house of David" (lower left), refers to King David's descendants. Originally part of a victory pillar of a neighboring king of Damascus (possibly Hazael), the stone has been dated to two or three centuries after David's time. It mentions a "king of Israel," possibly Joram son of Ahab, and a king of the "House of David," possibly Ahaziah of Judah.	This Tel Dan inscription is a very important find because it is the first reference to King David found outside of the Bible. *Right: House of David inscription on black basalt stone (detail shown at left).*
Judges 1 Kings	**30. Beersheba, The Southern Boundary of the Promised Land** Excavations between 1969-1976 uncovered the Israelite city of Beersheba with its strong defensive walls and a massive city gate, built after David's time.	Beersheba was found to have a large well, long storehouses, and private residences which date to the 1st millennium BC.	Beersheba eventually became Israel's key fortress city in the south during the period of King Solomon (1 Kings 4:25). Finding the strong walls and gate supports the Bible account of Beersheba after the time of David.
1 Kings 2 Kings 2 Chron. Hosea Amos Micah	**31. Samaria, Capital of the Northern Kingdom of Israel** Few cities are mentioned more times in the Old Testament than Samaria. Excavations have uncovered much of the city and have found it to have been extravagant, prosperous, and strong. *Right: Samarian ivory furniture inlay, 8th cent. BC*	For most of the history of the kingdom of Israel—after the kingdom was split in two following Solomon's rule—Samaria was the third, and last, capital of the Northern Kingdom. The Bible speaks of this well-fortified city built by King Omri and King Ahab.	Although much of the ruins of the Old Testament period were destroyed when King Herod built over and through earlier levels, enough has been found to show that Samaria was extravagant and strong, as described in the Old Testament. See 1 Kings 16:24, 2 Kings 6-22, 2 Chronicles 18, and the prophets Hosea, Amos, and Micah. Amos refers to houses and beds of ivory (Amos 3:15; 6:4).
Joshua 1 Kings	**32. Hazor, Key to Israelite Victory** Archaeology has found evidence of fiery destruction of Hazor, the major city of the north during the Conquest, possibly by the forces of Joshua (Joshua 11).	The rebuilding and fortification by Solomon parallels what he did at Megiddo and Hazor. The distinctive gates were found to be nearly identical to gates of these cities.	Finding that Hazor was about 200 acres, far larger than a normal city in that day, provides reason for the Bible calling it "the head." The city's king, Jabin, rallied the kingdoms in the north against the Israelites. Yet the forces of Joshua prevailed (Joshua 11).
1 Kings 2 Chron.	**33. Ivory Ornaments and Objects** Decorative ivory has been found in several sites in Palestine, including Megiddo and Samaria.	This ivory pomegranate, found in a dealer's shop, possibly an ornament (thought to have been atop a scepter) from Solomon's temple. The inscription says: "Belonging to . . . Holy to the Priest."	According to 1 Kings 10:18 and 2 Chronicles 9:17, King Solomon had a throne made of ivory covered with gold. "The king made a great throne of ivory, and overlaid it with the best gold" (1 Kings 10:18). There is dispute about the authenticity of the inscription.
Genesis Exodus Numb. Joshua 1 Kings 2 Kings Psalms Isaiah	**34. The Gezer Calendar** This small palm-sized limestone tablet bears one of the first examples of Hebrew writing known (971-913 BC).	Found at Gezer, one of King Solomon's fortress cities, this tablet contains a school memorization drill—a short poem about the agricultural seasons in biblical Palestine.	The text gives insight into when certain tasks were done during the agricultural year. It shows literacy in the 10th century BC.

	Archaeological Find	Description of the Find	Importance of the Find
1 Kings 2 Chron.	**35. House of Yahweh Ostracon** This find appears to be a receipt for a donation of three shekels of silver to the House of Yahweh (Solomon's Temple).	This ostracon (writing on a piece of pottery) is 4 inches wide and 3 1/2 inches tall. It is not known where it was found. Some scholars date it between 835 and 796 BC, some 130 years after the Temple was built.	 This extremely important find is the oldest mention of Solomon's Temple that has been found outside the Bible. *Left: House of YHWH ostracon*
1 Kings 2 Kings 2 Chron.	**36. Seals from the Royal Courts of Israel and Judah** Excavations at several sites in modern Israel and antiquity shops have turned up carved semi-precious stones belonging to members of the royal courts of kings in the Old Testament.	Dating from about 900 BC to about 600 BC, these stones were used to press images into pieces of clay that sealed up kings' important documents. One of the most famous seals, found at Megiddo, depicts a lion with the words, "belonging to Shema, servant of Jeroboam." Seals with the names of other kings were found also (See 1 and 2 Kings).	Seals were found for Uzziah (around 760 BC), Hoshea (around 730 BC), and Hezekiah (around 700 BC). The seal at the right says "SHLOMO" (Solomon) in Hebrew.
Genesis 2 Kings	**37. The Moabite Stone** In 1868, a German missionary found a stone slab over three feet tall near Dibon, east of the Dead Sea. Inscribed on the stone were the accomplishments of Mesha, king of Moab around 850 BC. This stone is sometimes called the Mesha Stele.	The ancient Moabites were relatives of the Israelites according to Genesis 19:37. On this stone King Mesha brags of having driven the Israelites out of his land. 2 Kings 3 tells that the king of Moab rebelled against the king of Israel after the death of King Ahab of Israel.	The Moabite stone is one of the earliest finds that mention biblical people. The stone says that King Omri and his son Ahab "humbled" Moab for many years. After Ahab's death, King Mesha said he had "triumphed" over Ahab's family and that Israel had "perished forever." Some scholars say that the stone also contains a reference to the "house of David."
2 Kings	**38. The Black Obelisk of Shalmaneser**  This 6 1/2 foot tall black basalt obelisk (four-sided pillar) reports in pictures and words the conquests of Assyrian King Shalmaneser III, enemy of the Israelites.	The Black Obelisk was discovered in the palace at Nimrud in 1846 and shows the biblical Jehu, king of Israel, kneeling down and bringing tribute to the Assyrian king, Shalmaneser. Dating from 841 BC, this important find is the only picture we have so far of an Israelite king. This is the first mention of tribute paid to Assyria by Israel. King Jehu's reign is mentioned in 2 Kings 9-10, even though the tribute is not. *Right: Part of the inscription (top) reads: "Tribute of Jehu the Israelite."*	
2 Chron.	**39. King Uzziah's Burial Plaque** A stone plaque, found on the grounds of the Russian church on the Mt. of Olives, reads: "Here, the bones of Uzziah, King of Judah, were brought. Do not open."	King Uzziah ruled Judah 792-740 BC, at the time that Amos, Hosea and Isaiah were prophesying. He was 16 years old when he became king and he reigned in Jerusalem for 52 years. As long as he sought the Lord, God gave him success.	According to 2 Chronicles 26, Uzziah sinned against the Lord and was stricken with a leprous disease toward the end of his life, and upon his death was buried in a "field of burial that belonged to the kings."
2 Kings 2 Chron	**40. The Siloam Tunnel Inscription** Two boys discovered this ancient Hebrew inscription carved in stone along the wall of a tunnel as they were wading through the southern end of the tunnel's waters in 1880.	The inscription comes from the days of King Hezekiah (701 BC) who ordered the tunnel to be made so the water from Jerusalem's Gihon Spring could be brought into the city to a man-made reservoir, the Pool of Siloam. This tunnel provided water to Jerusalem during the anticipated siege of King Sennacherib of Assyria.	 The inscription celebrates the completion of this remarkable tunnel as mentioned in 2 Kings 20:20 and 2 Chronicles 32:30. *Above: Siloam Tunnel Inscription found in Hezekiah's Tunnel.*
2 Kings 2 Chron.	**41. The Lachish Reliefs** Among the ruins of the Nineveh palace of Assyrian King Sennacherib were found 62-foot-long reliefs that picture the fall of the Judean fortress of Lachish in 701 BC, over 100 years before the attack on and fall of Judah. *Right: Assyrian troops are shown advancing with stone slingers and archers. Siege towers were wheeled up ramps to batter the city wall.*		These Nineveh palace carvings of the Lachish defeat amplify the biblical record concerning the siege of the kingdom of Judah in the days of King Hezekiah. In 2 Kings 18:13 it says, "Now in the fourteenth year of King Hezekiah did Sennacherib, king of Assyria, come up against all the fenced cities of Judah, and took them." However, before the Assyrians could capture Jerusalem, they were destroyed by "God's angel" and Sennacherib withdrew (2 Kings 20:35; 2 Chronicles 32).
2 Kings 2 Chron. Isaiah	**42. Sennacherib Prism** A 15-inch tall, six-sided baked clay prism from ancient Assyria contains the story of the invasion of the kingdom of Judah by Sennacherib in 701 BC. The prism was found at Nineveh.	King Sennacherib of Assyria is mentioned in 2 Kings 18-19. Isaiah prophesied that God would protect Jerusalem against attack by Sennacherib (Is. 36-37, 2 Chron. 32). While the prism does say that the Assyrians trapped Hezekiah in Jerusalem "like a bird in a cage," like the biblical record, it says nothing of them conquering the city.	The Bible says that God spared Jerusalem. The prism, together with the Lachish reliefs and excavations, adds detail to the biblical account. King Hezekiah prayed to the Lord. Isaiah brought him God's message. That night the Lord smote 185,000 Assyrians, and Sennacherib went back to Nineveh and later was killed by his sons (Isaiah 37:35-38).

	Archaeological Find	Description of the Find	Importance of the Find
1 Chron. Nehem.	**43. The Tomb of the Priestly Hezir Family** In an elaborate tomb complex cut into the wall of Jerusalem's Kidron Valley is a Hebrew inscription identifying the burial cave as belonging to the descendants of Hezir.	The names of three generations of priestly Hezir family members also appear in the inscription, verifying the existence of this priestly family mentioned in 1 Chronicles 24:15 and Nehemiah 10:20.	A list of the Levitical priests during King David's time found in 1 Chronicles 24 includes the name of Hezir. Later, in Nehemiah 10, another priest named Hezir (possibly a descendant of the former Hezir) is listed as one of the priests who signed a covenant to keep God's Law in the restored Temple around 450 BC.
2 Chron. Jeremiah	**44. Carchemish, Where History Changed Course** This city is mentioned only three times in the Bible, but archaeology reveals that it was in a strategic location, desired by the Hittites, Assyrians, and Babylonians.	Carchemish was important in biblical history for one key battle. In 605 BC, the Babylonians defeated the Assyrian and Egyptian armies there. This destroyed the Assyrians and paved the way for the Babylonians to conquer much of the biblical world, including the kingdom of Judah.	In 586 BC, the Babylonians stormed Jerusalem and destroyed the Temple. Jeremiah 46 and 2 Chronicles 35-36 speak of the prophecies and circumstances leading up to the Battle of Carchemish, and the devastating chain of events that followed.
2 Kings Jeremiah	**45. The Lachish Letters** In 1935 an archaeologist unearthed several letters, written about 588 BC, on 21 pottery pieces (ostraca) from among the burned ruins of the ancient city of Lachish of Judah.	 The Lachish messages were desperate pleas by the Judean defenders of the city for military assistance. Apparently the city was conquered by Nebuchadnezzar before the letters could be sent.	The letters show Judah was trying to obtain help from Egypt, relying on man rather than God. One ostracon mentions that no fire signals from another defensive city, Azekah, could be seen. Jeremiah 34:2-7 prophesied the conquest of Judah, destruction of Jerusalem, and exile to Babylon. See 2 Kings 24-25.
Numb. 2 Chron.	**46. Silver Amulets** In 1979, while excavating 6th century BC tombs in Jerusalem, excavators found two small amulets (under two inches long) that looked like necklaces made of silver sheets rolled up like miniature scrolls. They date to about Jehoakim's reign in Judah (2 Chronicles 36).	When unrolled, each of the scrolls was found to have the prayer from Numbers 6:24-26 scratched on it: "The Lord bless thee and keep thee; The Lord make his face shine upon thee, and be gracious unto thee: The Lord lift up his countenance upon thee, and give thee peace." This is the first time God's divine name has been found on an artifact from Jerusalem.	Dating to about 600 BC, these amulets contain the oldest examples of a Scripture passage yet found. 
Genesis Isaiah Jeremiah Daniel	**47. Babylon** The ruins of ancient Babylon, capital of the Babylonian Kingdom, cover 2000-3000 acres in Iraq, 56 miles south of Baghdad. *Right: Reconstruction of the Ishtar Gate, Babylon*	The Ishtar Gate was constructed in about 575 BC by order of King Nebuchadnezzar II on the north side of the city. This reconstruction depicts the Gate's blue glazed tiles with alternating rows of bas-relief dragons and bulls.	The palace of King Nebuchadnezzar, who destroyed Jerusalem in 586 BC and sent the Jews into exile, was the site of Belshazzar's feast in Daniel 5. Jeremiah wrote that the Lord would make Babylon desolate forever (Jeremiah 25:12; 51). The present ruins also echo the prophecy of Isaiah 13:19-20.
2 Chron. Ezra Isaiah	**48. The Cyrus Cylinder** A 9-inch long clay cylinder found at ancient Babylon, dating to 539 BC, tells of King Cyrus of Persia's conquest of Babylon and of his decree to let captives held by Babylon return to their lands and restore their temples.	King Cyrus of Persia (Iran area today) also made a similar decree that the Jews, carried away captive to Babylon, could return to Jerusalem. *Right: Cyrus Cylinder*	Cyrus sent the Jews back to their homeland after many years of exile in Babylon as Isaiah prophesied (2 Chron. 36:23; Ezra 1; Is. 44:28). This "return-home" decree was one of many issued by Cyrus. Though not mentioning Judah, it confirms that this was Cyrus's policy and gives credibility to the biblical record.
Esther Daniel	**49. Susa, Royal City of Queen Esther** Located in modern Iran, Susa's ruins have been excavated by several teams during the last century. The most impressive find has been the remains of the elegant royal palace built mainly by Darius (522-486 BC). The book of Esther is set in Susa later.	 Susa ("Shushan" in Hebrew) was one of three royal cities during the reign of King Cyrus of Persia. Xerxes and Artaxerxes carried on the building of the palace complex. A large number of beautiful artifacts and elaborate stone columns were found at Susa. Daniel saw a vision in Susa (Daniel 8:2, c. 551 BC). *Left: Frieze of life-size Persian royal guard from the palace of Darius the Great (father of Xerxes I) at Susa.*	Queen Esther (c. 478 BC) was married to King Ahasuerus (Xerxes I) and saved the Jews. Artaxerxes sent Ezra and Nehemiah to rebuild Jerusalem (Ez. 7:14-21; Neh. 13:5-8). *Right: Inscribed silver bowl of Artaxerxes I (c. 464-424 BC), son of King Xerxes.* 
	50. The Dead Sea Scrolls The Dead Sea Scrolls are actually hundreds of scrolls and scraps that date between 300 BC and AD 70. The first of them was found in 1947 in caves in the Qumran area near the Dead Sea about seven miles south of Jericho.	Some of the scrolls were found in jars (right). About one-third of the scrolls contain copies of portions of Old Testament books (every book but Esther). These copies are over 1000 years older than most of the manuscripts scholars previously had available for study and translation. 	This is one of the most important finds in history because it shows that the Old Testament was copied very accurately over the centuries. When the scrolls were compared with the oldest Masoretic text, on which most modern translations are based, only insignificant differences were found. Therefore we can be confident that our current translations are faithful to the original.

NEW TESTAMENT CHARTS

The Genealogy of Jesus Christ

The Gospel of Luke

(Luke lists the genealogy from Jesus to Adam)

Adam
Seth
Enosh (Enos)
Kenan (Cainan
Mahalalel (Maleleel)
Jared
Enoch
Methuselah (Mathusala)
Lamech
Noah (Noe)
Shem (Sem)
Arphaxad
Cainan
Shelah (Sala)
Eber (Heber)
Peleg (Phalec)
Reu (Ragau)
Serug (Saruch)
Nahor (Nachor)
Terah (Thara)

The Gospel of Matthew

(Matthew lists the genealogy from Abraham to Jesus)

The Gospel of Matthew	The Gospel of Luke
Abraham	Abraham
Isaac	Isaac
Jacob	Jacob
Judah (Judas) and Tamar (Thamar) ♀	Judah (Juda)
Perez (Phares)	Perez (Phares)
Hezron (Esrom)	Hezron (Esrom)
Ram (Aram)	Ram (Aram)
Amminadab (Aminadab)	Amminadab (Aminadab)
Nahshon (Naasson)	Nahshon (Naasson)
Salmon and Rahab (Rachab) ♀	Salmon
Boaz (Booz) and Ruth ♀	Boaz (Booz)
Obed	Obed
Jesse	Jesse
King David and Uriah's wife (Bathsheba) ♀	David
King Solomon	Nathan
King Rehoboam (Roboam)	Mattatha
King Abijah (Abia)	Menna (Menan)
King Asa	Melea
King Jehoshaphat (Josaphat)	Eliakim
king Jehoram (Joram)	Jonam
King Uzziah (Ozias)	Joseph
King Jotham (Joatham)	Judah (Juda)
King Ahaz (Achaz)	Simeon
King Hezekiah (Ezekias)	Levi
King Manasseh (Manasses)	Matthat
King Amon	Jorim
King Josiah (Josias)	Eliezer
King Jeconiah (Jechonias)	Joshua (Jose)
	Er
	Elmadam (Elmodam)
	Cosam
	Addi
	Melki (Melchi)
	Neri
Shealtiel (Salathiel)	Shealtiel (Salathiel)
Zerubbabel (Zorobabel)	Zerubbabel (Zorobabel)
Abiud	Rhesa
	Joanan (Joanna)
Eliakim	Joda (Juda)
	Josech (Joseph)
Azor	Semein (Semei)
	Mattathias
Zadok (Sadoc)	Maath
	Naggai (Nagge)
Akim (Achim)	Esli
	Nahum (Naum)
Eliud	Amos
	Mattathias
Eleazar	Joseph
	Jannai (Janna)
Matthan	Melki (Melchi)
	Levi
Jacob	Matthat
	Heli (Eli)
Joseph, the husband of Mary ♀	Joseph
JESUS	**JESUS**

Legend

♀ = female

┌─ ─ ─┐
╎   ╎ = names common in both genealogies
└─ ─ ─┘

(Aram) = alternate spellings

Prophecy	Old Testament References	New Testament Fulfillment
Jesus' Birth		
Be of the offspring of the woman; shall bruise the serpent's head	Genesis 3:14, 15 So the LORD God said to the serpent . . . "And I will put enmity between you and the woman, and between your offspring and hers; he will crush your head, and you will strike his heel."	Galatians 4:4 But when the time had fully come, God sent his Son, born of a woman, born under law, Hebrews 2:14 Since the children have flesh and blood, he too shared in their humanity so that by his death he might destroy him who holds the power of death . . . that is, the devil. 1 John 3:8 He who does what is sinful is of the devil, because the devil has been sinning from the beginning. The reason the Son of God appeared was to destroy the devil's work.
All nations shall be blessed through Abraham	Genesis 18:17, 18 Then the LORD said . . . "Abraham will surely become a great and powerful nation, and all nations on earth will be blessed through him." Also Genesis 12:3; 22:18; 26:4; 28:14	Acts 3:25, 26 ". . . He said to Abraham, 'Through your offspring all peoples on earth will be blessed.' When God raised up his servant, he sent him first to you to bless you . . ." Also Matthew 1:1, 17; Galatians 3:16
Be of the tribe of Judah	Genesis 49:8-10 "Judah, your brothers will praise you . . . The sceptre will not depart from Judah, nor the ruler's staff from between his feet, until he comes to whom it belongs and the obedience of the nations is his." Micah 5:2 "But you, Bethlehem Ephratah, though you are small among the clans of Judah, out of you will come for me one who will be ruler over Israel, whose origins are from of old, from ancient times."	Matthew 1:1-3 A record of the genealogy of Jesus Christ the son of David, the son of Abraham . . . Jacob the father of Judah and his brothers, Judah the father of Perez and Zerah . . . Hebrews 7:14 For it is clear that our Lord descended from Judah... Revelation 5:5 Then one of the elders said to me, "Do not weep! See, the Lion of the tribe of Judah, the Root of David, has triumphed. He is able to open the scroll and its seven seals."
Be born in the town of Bethlehem of Judea (Judah)	Micah 5:2-5 "But you, Bethlehem Ephratah, though you are small among the clans of Judah, out of you will come for me one who will be ruler over Israel, whose origins are from of old, from ancient times." . . .	Matthew 2:1-6 After Jesus was born in Bethlehem in Judea, during the time of King Herod, Magi from the east came to Jerusalem and asked, "Where is the one who has been born king of the Jews? . . ."
Be born a king of the line of David	Isaiah 9:7 . . . He will reign on David's throne and over his kingdom . . . Also 2 Samuel 7:12, 13; Jeremiah 23:5; 30:9	Matthew 1:1 A record of the genealogy of Jesus Christ the son of David, the son of Abraham . . . Also Luke 1:32; Acts 13:22, 23
A child to be born	Isaiah 9:6 For to us a child is born . . . he will be called Wonderful Counselor, Mighty God . . .	Luke 2:11 Today in the town of David a Saviour has been born to you; he is Christ the Lord.
Be born of a virgin	Isaiah 7:13, 14 Then Isaiah said, "Hear now, you house of David! Is it not enough to try the patience of men? Will you try the patience of my God also? Therefore the Lord himself will give you a sign: The virgin will be with child and will give birth to a son, and will call him Immanuel (God with us)."	Matthew 1:18-23 . . . His mother Mary was pledged to be married to Joseph, but before they came together, she was found to be with child through the Holy Spirit. Luke 1:26-35 . . . God sent the angel . . . to a virgin pledged to be married to a man named Joseph, a descendant of David. The virgin's name was Mary. . . .
Kings shall bring him gifts, fall down before him	Psalm 72:10, 11 The kings of Tarshish and of distant shores will bring tribute to him; the kings of Sheba and Seba will present him gifts. All kings will bow down to him and all nations will serve him.	Matthew 2:1-11 After Jesus was born in Bethlehem in Judea, during the time of King Herod, Magi from the east came to Jerusalem . . . On coming to the house, they saw the child with his mother Mary, and they bowed down and worshipped him. Then they opened their treasures and presented him with gifts of gold and of incense and of myrrh.
Be born of the seed of Abraham	Genesis 17:7, 8; 26:3, 4	Matthew 1:1, 17; Galatians 3:16, 29; Hebrews 2:16
Be born of the seed of Isaac	Genesis 17:19; 21:12; 26:2-4	Matthew 1:2, 17; Romans 9:7; Hebrews 11:17-19
Be of the seed of Jacob; a star out of Jacob	Genesis 28:13, 14; Numbers 24:17, 19	Matthew 1:2; Luke 1:33; 3:23-38
Be a firstborn son, sanctified	Exodus 13:2; Numbers 3:13; 8:17	Luke 2:7, 23
Be a rod out of the stem of Jesse	Isaiah 11:1, 2	Matthew 1:6; Acts 13:22, 23
Massacre of children	Jeremiah 31:15	Matthew 2:16-18
Have eternal existence	Micah 5:2	John 1:1, 4; 8:58; Colossians 1:15-19

Color Key
- Prophecies more than 1,200 years before Jesus' birth are highlighted in green.
- Prophecies more than 800 years before Jesus' birth are highlighted in yellow.
- Prophecies more than 500 years before Jesus' birth are highlighted in blue.

Prophecy	Old Testament References	New Testament Fulfillment
Jesus' Life and Ministry		
Be called out of Egypt	Hosea 11:1 "When Israel was a child, I loved him, and out of Egypt I called my son. . . ."	Matthew 2:13-15, 19-21 . . . So he . . . took the child and his mother during the night and left for Egypt . . .
Be rejected by his brethren	Psalm 69:8 I am a stranger to my brothers, an alien to my own mother's sons . . .	John 7:3-5 Jesus' brothers said to him, "You ought to leave here . . . so that your disciples may see the miracles you do. . . ." For even his own brothers did not believe in him.
Rulers take council against him	Psalm 2:1, 2 Why do the nations conspire and the peoples plot in vain? The kings of the earth take their stand and the rulers gather together against the LORD and against his Anointed One.	Matthew 12:14 But the Pharisees went out and plotted how they might kill Jesus. Matthew 26:3, 4 Then the chief priests and the elders . . . plotted to arrest Jesus in some sly way and kill him. Matthew 26:47 . . . Judas . . . arrived. With him was a large crowd armed with swords and clubs, sent from the chief priests and the elders of the people. See also Luke 23:11, 12
Be rejected as capstone	Psalm 118:22, 23 The stone the builders rejected has become the capstone; the LORD has done this, and it is marvellous in our eyes.	Matthew 21:42 Jesus said to them, "Have you never read in the Scriptures: "'The stone the builders rejected has become the capstone . . .'"
Was to enter the Temple	Malachi 3:1 ". . . Then suddenly the Lord you are seeking will come to his temple; the messenger of the covenant, whom you desire, will come . . ." Haggai 2:7, 9	Matthew 21:12-16 Jesus entered the temple area and drove out all who were buying and selling there. . . . See also Mark 11:11; Luke 2:25-47; Luke 19:45-47
Call those who were not his people	Isaiah 55:4, 5 . . . Surely you will summon nations you know not, and nations that do not know you will hasten to you . . . Also Hosea 2:23	Romans 9:23-26 . . . even us, whom he also called, not only from the Jews but also from the Gentiles? . . .
The King comes to Jerusalem riding on a donkey	Zechariah 9:9 . . . See, your king comes to you, righteous and having salvation, gentle and riding on a donkey, on a colt, the foal of a donkey.	Mark 11:1-10 . . . When they brought the colt to Jesus and threw their cloaks over it, he sat on it. . . . Also Matthew 21:1-5; Luke 19:28-38; John 12:14, 15
Be a "stone of stumbling" to the Jews	Isaiah 8:14 . . . and he will be a sanctuary; but for both houses of Israel he will be a stone that causes men to stumble and a rock that makes them fall. And for the people of Jerusalem he will be a trap and a snare.	Romans 9:31-33 . . . Israel. . . stumbled over the "stumbling-stone." As it is written: "See, I lay in Zion a stone that causes men to stumble and a rock that makes them fall, and the one who trusts in him will never be put to shame." 1 Peter 2:7, 8 . . . They stumble because they disobey the message—which is also what they were destined for.
Upon his coming, the deaf hear, the blind see	Isaiah 29:18 In that day the deaf will hear the words of the scroll, and out of gloom and darkness the eyes of the blind will see. Isaiah 35:5 Then will the eyes of the blind be opened and the ears of the deaf unstopped.	Matthew 11:5 The blind receive sight, the lame walk, those who have leprosy are cured, the deaf hear, the dead are raised, and the good news is preached to the poor. Also John 9:39; Luke 7:19-22; Mark 7:37
Fulfill promises to Jews, be a light to the Gentiles	Isaiah 42:6 ". . . I will keep you and will make you to be a covenant for the people and a light for the Gentiles . . ." Isaiah 49:6 ". . . I will also make you a light for the Gentiles, that you may bring my salvation to the ends of the earth."	Luke 2:25-32 ". . . a light for revelation to the Gentiles and for glory to your people Israel." Acts 26:23 ". . . that the Christ would suffer and, as the first to rise from the dead, would proclaim light to his own people and to the Gentiles."
A new everlasting covenant	Jeremiah 31:31-34 ". . . I will make a new covenant with the house of Israel and with the house of Judah. It will not be like the covenant I made with their forefathers . . . I will put my law in their minds and write it on their hearts. . . ." Also Jeremiah 32:37-40; 50:5	Luke 22:15-20 . . . "This cup is the new covenant in my blood . . ." Hebrews 10:15-20 . . . "This is the covenant I will make with them after that time . . ." a new and living way opened for us . . . Also Matthew 26:27-29; Mark 14:22-24; Luke 22:15-20; 1 Corinthians 11:25; Hebrews 8:8-12
Be a prophet like Moses, speaking God's words	Deuteronomy 18:15, 18, 19	Matthew 21:11; Luke 7:16; 24:19; John 6:14; 7:40; Acts 3:18-22
Be hated without reason	Psalm 35:19; 69:4	John 15:24, 25

Color Key	Prophecies more than 1,200 years before Jesus' birth are highlighted in green.
	Prophecies more than 800 years before Jesus' birth are highlighted in yellow.
	Prophecies more than 500 years before Jesus' birth are highlighted in blue.

Prophecy	Old Testament References	New Testament Fulfillment
Jesus' Life and Ministry		
Come to do the will of God	Psalm 40:7, 8	Matthew 26:39; Hebrews 10:5-9
Anointed by God	Psalm 45:6, 7	Hebrews 1:8, 9
Have great zeal for God's house	Psalm 69:9	John 2:17
Care for the poor and needy	Psalm 72:12-14	Luke 7:22
Speak in parables with hidden meaning	Psalm 78:2	Matthew 13:10-16; 34, 35; Luke 8:10
Will pray for His enemies	Psalm 109:4	Matthew 5:44; Luke 23:34
Be a priest after the order of Melchizedek	Psalm 110:4	Hebrews 5:1-6; 6:20; 7:15-17
People's hearts are hardened	Isaiah 6:9, 10	Matt. 13:13-15; John 12:37-40; Acts 28:24-27
His ministry in Zebulun, Naphtali, and Galilee	Isaiah 9:1, 2	Matthew 4:12-16
The government is on his shoulders	Isaiah 9:6	Matthew 28:18; 1 Corinthians 15:24, 25
Someone will prepare for the coming of the Lord	Isaiah 40:3-5	Matthew 3:3; Mark 1:3; Luke 3:3-5; John 1:23
The Spirit of the Lord rests upon him	Isaiah 11:2; 42:1; 61:1, 2	Matt. 3:16; Mark 1:10; Luke 3:22; 4:18; John 1:32; 3:34; Acts 10:38
Be a healer and savior, do miracles	Isaiah 35:4-6	Matthew 9:30; 11:4-6; 12:22; 20:34; 21:14; Mark 7:32-35; John 9:1-7; 11:47
Be a Shepherd who tends his sheep	Isaiah 40:10, 11	John 10:11; Hebrews 13:20; 1 Peter 2:25
Be a Servant of God	Isaiah 42:1-4	Matthew 12:16-21
The Redeemer to come out of Zion	Isaiah 59:16-20	Romans 11:26, 27
Nations shall walk in the light of the Lord	Isaiah 60:1-3	Matthew 4:16; Luke 2:32; John 12:46
Anointed to preach liberty to the captives	Isaiah 61:1-2a	Luke 4:16-21; Acts 10:38
His Spirit poured out upon people	Joel 2:28-32	Acts 2:16-23
David's house shall be restored	Amos 9:11, 12	Acts 15:16-18
God shall dwell among His people	Zechariah 2:10-13	John 1:14; Revelation 21:3
A new priesthood established	Zechariah 3:8	1 Peter 2:5, 9; Revelation 1:6, 5:10
Messenger sent to prepare the way before Him	Malachi 3:1	Matthew 11:10; Mark 1:2-4, 7; Luke 7:27, 28
Prophet sent before the day of the Lord	Malachi 4:5, 6	Matthew 11:13, 14; Mark 9:11-13; Luke 1:17; 7:27, 28

Color Key	Prophecies more than **1200 years** before Jesus' birth are highlighted in green.
	Prophecies more than **800 years** before Jesus' birth are highlighted in yellow.
	Prophecies more than **500 years** before Jesus' birth are highlighted in blue.

Prophecy	Old Testament References	New Testament Fulfillment
Jesus' Death and Resurrection		
Be Passover sacrifice with no bone broken	Exodus 12:46 It must be eaten inside one house; take none of the meat outside the house. Do not break any of the bones. Numbers 9:12 They must not leave any of it till morning or break any of its bones. When they celebrate the Passover, they must follow all the regulations. Also Psalm 34:20	John 19:31-36 . . . But when they came to Jesus and found that he was already dead, they did not break his legs. . . .These things happened so that the scripture would be fulfilled: "Not one of his bones will be broken."
Be hung upon a tree as a curse for us	Deuteronomy 21:23 . . . Be sure to bury him that same day, because anyone who is hung on a tree is under God's curse. You must not desecrate the land the LORD your God is giving you as an inheritance.	Galatians 3:13 Christ redeemed us from the curse of the law by becoming a curse for us, for it is written: "Cursed is everyone who is hung on a tree."
Be thirsty during his execution	Psalm 22:15 My strength is dried up like a potsherd, and my tongue sticks to the roof of my mouth; you lay me in the dust of death..	John 19:28 Later, knowing that all was now completed, and so that the Scripture would be fulfilled, Jesus said, "I am thirsty."
Be accused by false witnesses	Psalm 27:12 Do not hand me over to the desire of my foes, for false witnesses rise up against me, breathing out violence. Psalm 35:11 Ruthless witnesses come forward; they question me on things I know nothing about.	Matthew 26:60 . . . many false witnesses came forward. . . . Mark 14:55-61 . . . Then some stood up and gave this false testimony against him. . . .
Be struck on the head	Micah 5:1. . . They will strike Israel's ruler on the cheek with a rod.	Matthew 27:30 They spat on him, and took the staff and struck him on the head again and again.
Have hands and feet pierced	Psalm 22:16 Dogs have surrounded me; a band of evil men has encircled me, they have pierced my hands and my feet. Zechariah 12:10 ". . .They will look on me, the one they have pierced, and they will mourn for him as . . . for a firstborn son.	Matthew 27:35 . . . they had crucified him . . . Also John 19:18, 34-37 John 20:25-29 . . . "Unless I see the nail marks in his hands . . . and put my hand into his side, I will not believe it.". . . Then he said ". . . Reach out your hand and put it into my side." . . .
Have soldiers cast lots for his coat	Psalm 22:18 They divide my garments among them and cast lots for my clothing.	John 19:23, 24 . . . This garment was seamless . . . "Let's not tear it," they said to one another. "Let's decide by lot who will get it." Also Matthew 27:35; Mark 15:24; Luke 23:34
Be given gall and vinegar (sour wine)	Psalm 69:20-22 . . . They put gall in my food and gave me vinegar for my thirst. . . .	Matthew 27:34 There they offered Jesus wine to drink, mixed with gall; but after tasting it, he refused to drink it. Also Matthew 27:48; Mark 15:23; 15:36; Luke 23:36; John 19:29
Be beaten and spat upon	Isaiah 50:6 I offered my back to those who beat me, my cheeks to those who pulled out my beard; I did not hide my face from mocking and spitting.	Matthew 26:67 Then they spat in his face and struck him with their fists. Others slapped him. Matthew 27:26-30 . . . They spat on him, and took the staff and struck him on the head again and again. Also Mark 14:65; 15:15-19; Luke 22:63-65; John 19:1
Be betrayed by a friend	Psalm 41:9 Even my close friend, whom I trusted, he who shared my bread, has lifted up his heel against me. Psalm 55:12-14 If an enemy were insulting me, I could endure it; if a foe were raising himself against me, I could hide from him. But it is you, a man like myself, my companion, my close friend, with whom I once enjoyed sweet fellowship as we walked with the throng at the house of God.	Matthew 26:14-16 Then one of the Twelve . . . the one called Judas Iscariot . . . went to the chief priests and asked, "What are you willing to give me if I hand him over to you?" . . . Matthew 26:23 Jesus replied, "The one who has dipped his hand into the bowl with me will betray me." Also Matthew 26:47-50; Luke 22:19-23, 48; John 13:18-30; 18:2-5
Be despised and rejected	Isaiah 53:2, 3 . . . He was despised and rejected by men, . . . Like one from whom men hide their faces he was despised, and we esteemed him not.	Luke 17:25 But first he must suffer many things and be rejected by this generation. Luke 23:18 . . . "Away with this man! Release Barabbas to us!" Also Matthew 26:67; John 1:11
Be accused and afflicted, but did not open his mouth	Isaiah 53:7 He was oppressed and afflicted, yet he did not open his mouth; he was led like a lamb to the slaughter, and as a sheep before her shearers is silent, so he did not open his mouth.	Matthew 27:12 When he was accused by the chief priests and the elders, he gave no answer. Luke 23:9 He plied him with many questions, but Jesus gave him no answer. Also Matthew 26:62, 63; 27:14; Mark 14:61; 15:5; John 19:9
Commit his spirit into God's hand	Psalm 31:5 Into your hands I commit my spirit; redeem me, O LORD, the God of truth.	Luke 23:46 Jesus called out with a loud voice, "Father, into your hands I commit my spirit." When he had said this, he breathed his last.

Color Key	Prophecies more than **1200** years before Jesus' birth are highlighted in green.
	Prophecies more than **800** years before Jesus' birth are highlighted in yellow.
	Prophecies more than **500** years before Jesus' birth are highlighted in blue.

Prophecy	Old Testament References	New Testament Fulfillment
Jesus' Death and Resurrection		
Be buried with the rich	Isaiah 53:9 He was assigned a grave with the wicked, and with the rich in his death, though he had done no violence, nor was any deceit in his mouth.	Matthew 27:57-60 . . . there came a rich man from Arimathea, named Joseph, who had himself become a disciple of Jesus. . . . he asked for Jesus' body, . . . and placed it in his own new tomb. . . .
Be numbered (crucified) with transgressors	Isaiah 53:12 . . . he poured out his life unto death, and was numbered with the transgressors . . .	Matthew 27:38 Two robbers were crucified with him, . . . Also Mark 15:27, 28; Luke 22:37; 23:32, 33
The 30 pieces of silver buy the potter's field	Zechariah 11:12, 13 . . . So they paid me thirty pieces of silver. . . . I took the thirty pieces of silver and threw them into the house of the LORD to the potter.	Matthew 27:3, 6-10 . . . Judas . . . returned the thirty silver coins to the chief priests and the elders . . . they decided to use the money to buy the potter's field . . .
Be sold for thirty pieces of silver	Zechariah 11:12	Matthew 26:14, 15
Be Passover male lamb, without blemish, slain, with blood applied as protection from judgment	Exodus 12:1-11, Isaiah 53:7	John 1:29-36; 1 Corinthians 5:7, 8; 1 Peter 1:18, 19; Revelation 5:6-13; 7:14; 21:22-27; 22:1-4
Be lifted up, just as Moses lifted up a serpent	Numbers 21:8, 9	John 3:14, 15
Be raised from the dead	Psalm 16:8-11	Luke 24:6-8; John 20; Acts 1:3; 2:32; 13:34-37; 2 Timothy 2:8
Conquer death through his resurrection	Psalm 16:8-11; 49:15; 86:13	Acts 2:24-36; 13:30-39; 1 Corinthians 15:3, 4
Feel forsaken by God	Psalm 22:1	Matthew 27:46; Mark 15:34
Be mocked and insulted by many	Psalm 22:7, 8, 17	Matthew 27:31, 39-43; Mark 15:29-32; Luke 23:35-39
Friends stand afar off	Psalm 38:11; 88:18	Matthew 26:56-58; 27:55; Mark 15:40; Luke 23:49
Ascend on high	Psalm 68:18	Luke 24:51; Acts 1:9; Ephesians 4:8
Reproaches of others fall on him	Psalm 69:9	Romans 15:3
Another to succeed Judas	Psalm 109:7, 8	Acts 1:16-20
Be a Son who is given	Isaiah 9:6	John 3:16; Romans 8:32
Swallow up death in victory	Isaiah 25:8	1 Corinthians 15:54-57
Be mistreated, hardly recognized	Isaiah 52:14	Hebrews 5:8; 1 Peter 2:21
Bare our griefs and carry our sorrows	Isaiah 53:4, 5	Matthew 8:17; Rom. 5:6-8
Be wounded for our transgressions	Isaiah 53:5	1 Corinthians 15:3; 2 Corinthians 5:21; 1 Peter 3:18
Be led as a lamb to the slaughter	Isaiah 53:7	John 1:29, 36; Acts 8:28-35; 1 Peter 1:19; Revelation 5:6
Be sinless and without guile	Isaiah 53:9	1 Peter 2:22
Make intercession for the transgressors	Isaiah 53:12	Luke 23:34; "Father, forgive them for they know not what they do."
Be made into an offering for sin	Isaiah 53:10, 11	Acts 10:43; 13:38, 39; Romans 3:21-26; 4:5-8; Ephesians 1:7; 1 Peter 2:21-25; 1 John 2:2
Be "cut off" at a specific time after Jerusalem wall is rebuilt, before the Temple is destroyed	Daniel 9:24-26; Zechariah 9:9	Matt. 21:1-5; 1:15; 24:1, 2 Luke 19:37, 38; John 12:13-15
His body would be pierced	Zechariah 12:10	John 19:34-37
Shepherd smitten, sheep scattered (deserted by his followers)	Zechariah 13:6, 7	Matthew 26:31, 56; Mark 14:27; John 16:32

Color Key	Prophecies more than **1200** years before Jesus' birth are highlighted in green.
	Prophecies more than **800** years before Jesus' birth are highlighted in yellow.
	Prophecies more than **500** years before Jesus' birth are highlighted in blue.

Prophecy	Old Testament References	New Testament Fulfillment
Jesus' Titles and Attributes		
"I Am" (Jehovah)	Exodus 3:13-15	John 8:24; 13:19
A Prophet like Moses	Deuteronomy 18:18, 19	John 1:21; 6:14; Acts 3:22, 23; Hebrews 3:1-6
The throne of David established forever	2 Samuel 7:12, 13, 16, 25, 26; Psalm 89:3, 4, 36, 37; Isaiah 9:7 1 Chronicles 17:11-14, 23-27;	Luke 1:32, 33; Acts 2:29-36; 2 Timothy 2:8; Hebrews 1:8
The promised Redeemer	Job 19:25-27; Psalm 130:7, 8; Isaiah 59:20	Galatians 4:4, 5; Titus 2:13, 14
The Son of God	Psalm 2:7	Matt. 3:17; 8:29; 16:16; Mark 1:11; Luke 1:32, 35; Acts 13:33; Hebrews 1:5; 5:5; 2 Peter 1:17
Delights to do God's will	Psalm 40:8	John 4:34; 6:38
A King known for righteousness, anointed	Psalm 45:1-7	Hebrews 1:8, 9
Seed of David	Psalm 89:3, 4	John 7:42; Acts 13:22, 23
The firstborn over all creation	Psalm 89:27	Romans 8:29; Colossians 1:15
Never changing, everlasting	Psalm 102:24-27	Hebrews 1:10-12; 13:8
David's son; David's Lord at God's right hand	Psalm 110:1	Matthew 22:41-45; Mark 12:35-37; 16:19; Acts 7:56; Romans 1:3; Ephesians 1:20; Hebrews 1:3
A Priest according to the order of Melchizedek	Psalm 110:4	Hebrews 5:5, 6, 10; 6:20; 7:1-22
The Chief Cornerstone	Psalm 118:22, 23	Matthew 21:42; Mark 12:10, 11; Luke 20:17; Acts 4:10-12; Ephesians 2:20; 1 Peter 2:4-7
The way of repentance for all nations	Isaiah 2:2-4	Luke 24:47
Immanuel, God with us	Isaiah 7:14; 8:8, 10	Matt. 1:21-23; John 1:14; 14:8-11; Colossians 2:9
A stone of stumbling, a rock of offense	Isaiah 8:14, 15	Matt. 21:42-44; Romans 9:32, 33; 1 Peter 2:6-8
The light which has shone out of darkness	Isaiah 9:1, 2	Matthew 4:14-16; Luke 1:7, 9; 2:32; John 1:4, 5
Prince of Peace	Isaiah 9:6	John 14:27; Acts 10:36; Romans 5:1; Ephesians 2:14; Col. 1:20
Full of wisdom, power and righteousness	Isaiah 11:1-10	Acts 10:38; 1 Corinthians 1:30; Ephesians 1:17; Colossians 2:2, 3
The key of the house of David is upon his shoulder	Isaiah 22:21-25	Revelation 3:7
The stone in Zion, a sure foundation	Isaiah 28:16	Romans 9:33; 1 Peter 2:6
God's elect Servant, in whom he delights	Isaiah 42:1-4	Matthew 12:17-21; Philippians 2:7
Spirit of the LORD shall rest on him	Isaiah 61:1	Matthew 3:16; Luke 4:18
The Righteous Branch	Jeremiah 23:5, 6; 33:15, 16	Romans 3:22; 1 Cor.1:30; 2 Cor. 5:21; Philippians 3:9
The Good Shepherd	Ezekiel 34:23, 24; 37:24	John 10:11; Hebrews 13:20; 1 Peter 2:25
The enthroned High Priest	Zechariah 6:12, 13	Hebrews 7:11-28; 8:1, 2
Sun of Righteousness; the Dayspring; our Light	Malachi 4:2, 3	Luke 1:78; Ephesians 5:14; 2 Peter 1:19; John 8:12; Revelation 2:28; 22:16

Color Key	Prophecies more than **1200** years before Jesus' birth are highlighted in green.
	Prophecies more than **800** years before Jesus' birth are highlighted in yellow.
	Prophecies more than **500** years before Jesus' birth are highlighted in blue.

Events in the Life of Jesus

Event	Matthew	Mark	Luke	John
Birth in Bethlehem	1:18-25		2:1-20	
Childhood	2:1-23		2:21-52	
Baptism/Ministry Begins	3:13-17	1:9-11	3:21-23	1:19-34
Performs First Miracle				2:1-11
Calls Disciples	4:18-22; 9:9; 10	1:16-20; 2:13, 14; 3:13-19; 16:13-17	5:1-11, 27, 28; 6:13-16; 9:1-6	1:38-51
Heals and Forgives Sin	9:1-8	2:1-12	5:17-26	
Sermon on the Mount	5:1–8:1		6:17-49	
Calms the Storm	8:23-27	4:35-41	8:22-25	
Feeds the 5000	14:13-21	6:32-44	9:10-17	6:1-13
Walks on Water	14:22-33	6:45-51		6:16-21
Transfiguration	17:1-8	9:2-8	9:28-36	
Heals the Blind	9:27-31; 12:22, 23; 20:29-34	8:22-26; 10:46-52	18:35-43	9:1-41
Parable of Good Samaritan			10:25-37	
Parable of Prodigal Son			15:11-32	
Raises Lazarus				11:38-44
Heals 10 Lepers			17:11-19	
Blesses Children	19:13-15	10:13-16	18:15-17	
Palm Sunday	21:1-11	11:1-10	19:29-40	12:12-15
Clears the Temple	21:12, 13	11:15-17	19:45, 46	2:14-17
Last Supper	26:17-29	14:12-25	22:7-20	
Betrayed	26:47-56	14:43-52	22:47-53	18:2-12
Suffers	27:26-34	15:16-24	22:63-65	19:1-17
Dies on the Cross	27:35-50	15:25-37	23:33-46	19:18-30
Rises from the Dead	28:1-8	16:1-8	24:1-12	20:1-10
Appears to Others	28:9, 10, 16-20	16:9-18	24:13-50	20:11-31; 21:1-14
Ascends to Heaven		16:19	24:51-53	

Miracles of Jesus

Miracle	Matthew	Mark	Luke	John
Healing				
Man With Leprosy	8:1-4	1:40-45	5:12-15	
Centurion's Servant	8:5-13		7:1-10	
Peter's Mother-in-law	8:14-15	1:29-31	4:38,39	
Cast Out Demons	8:28-34	5:1-20	8:26-39	
Paralyzed Man	9:1-8	2:1-12	5:17-26	
Woman with Hemorrhage	9:20-22	5:25-34	8:43-48	
Two Blind Men	9:27-31			
Mute, Demon-Possessed Man	9:32, 33		11:14	
Man with Shriveled Hand	12:9-13	3:1-5	6:6-10	
Blind, Mute, Possessed Man	12:22, 23			
Canaanite Woman's Daughter	15:21-28	7:24-30		
Boy with a Demon	17:14-21	9:14-29	9:37-42	
Blind (Bartimaeus)	20:29-34	10:46-52	18:35-43	
Deaf Mute		7:31-37		
Possessed Man in Synagogue		1:21-28	4:31-37	
Blind Man at Bethsaida		8:22-26		
Crippled Woman			13:10-17	
Man with Dropsy			14:1-4	
Ten Lepers			17:11-19	
High Priest's Servant			22:49-51	
Official's Son				4:46-54
Sick Man at Pool of Bethesda				5:1-15
Man Born Blind				9:1-41
Power Over Nature				
Calming the Storm	8:23-27	4:35-41	8:22-25	
Feeding the 5000	14:13-21	6:32-44	9:10-17	6:1-13
Walking on Water	14:22-33	6:45-51		6:16-21
Feeding the 4,000	15:29-38	8:1-9		
Coin in Fish	17:24-27			
Fig Tree Withered	21:18-22	11:12-14, 20-25		
Large Catch of Fish			5:4-11	
Water Turned to Wine				2:1-11
Another Large Catch of Fish				21:1-11
Raising the Dead				
Jairus's Daughter	9:18, 19, 23-26	5:21-24, 35-43	8:40-42, 49-56	
Widow's Son			7:11-17	
Lazarus				11:1-44

Parables of Jesus

Parable	Matthew	Mark	Luke
Lamp Under a Bowl	5:14-16	4:21, 22	8:16, 17; 11:33-36
Wise and Foolish Builders	7:24-27		6:46-49
New Cloth on an Old Garment	9:16	2:21	5:36
New Wine in Old Wineskins	9:17	2:22	5:37, 38
Sower and the Seeds	13:3-8, 18-23	4:3-8, 13-20	8:5-8, 11-15
Weeds in the Field	13:24-30, 36-43		
Mustard Seed	13:31, 32	4:30-32	13:18, 19
Yeast	13:33		13:20, 21
Hidden Treasure	13:44		
Valuable Pearl	13:45, 46		
Net of Good and Bad Fish	13:47-50		
Owner of a House	13:52		
Lost Sheep	18:12-14		15:4-7
Unmerciful Servant	18:23-35		
Workers in the Vineyard	20:1-16		
Two Sons	21:28-32		
Evil Tenants	21:33-44	12:1-11	20:9-18
Wedding Banquet	22:2-14		14:16-24
Fig Tree	24:32-35	13:28-31	21:29-33
Faithful vs. Wicked Servant	24:45-51		12:42-48
Ten Virgins	25:1-13		
Talents	25:14-30		19:12-27
Sheep and Goats	25:31-46		
Growing Seed		4:26-29	
Watchful Servants		13:32-37	12:35-40
Money Lender			7:41-43
Good Samaritan			10:30-37
Friend in Need			11:5-8
Rich Fool			12:16-21
Unfruitful Fig Tree			13:6-9
Lowest Seat at the Feast			14:7-14
Cost of Discipleship			14:28-33
Lost Coin			15:8-10
Prodigal Son			15:11-32
Shrewd Manager			16:1-13
Rich Man and Lazarus			16:19-31
Master and His Servant			17:7-10
Persistent Widow			18:2-8
Pharisee and Tax Collector			18:9-14

The Beatitudes

Blessed are the poor in spirit: for theirs is the kingdom of heaven.

Blessed are they that mourn: for they shall be comforted.

Blessed are the meek: for they shall inherit the earth.

Blessed are they which do hunger and thirst after righteousness:
for they shall be filled.

Blessed are the merciful: for they shall obtain mercy.

Blessed are the pure in heart: for they shall see God.

Blessed are the peacemakers: for they shall be called the children of God.

Blessed are they which are persecuted for righteousness' sake:
for theirs is the kingdom of heaven.

Blessed are ye, when men shall revile you, and persecute you, and
shall say all manner of evil against you falsely, for my sake.

Rejoice, and be exceeding glad: for great is your reward in heaven.

Matthew 5:3-12, The Holy Bible

What Do the Beatitudes Mean?

Jesus surprised His disciples by telling them what kind of people would be blessed by God. His list of traits are called Beatitudes, meaning "to bless" or "to make happy."

Poor of Spirit
This word was taken from a Greek word meaning "to crouch." It can mean lowly, afflicted, helpless, powerless to solve a problem, lacking wealth and education, or begging. Is there a problem or situation in your life that is beyond your control? Are you reduced to begging God for help? God promises to help the poor of spirit.

Mourn
This word means "to wail." This is deeper than sadness; it is despond and despair. Do you know anyone who is crushed with the disappointments of life? God promises to comfort.

Meek
Meekness means humility, a gentleness of spirit, or a mild disposition. A meek person is one who trusts God and accepts today's circumstances as God's best for them, even if

situations in their lives are painful, frightening, frustrating, or annoying. Two of the most powerful people in the Bible, Jesus and Moses, were considered "meek." (Numbers 12:3, Matthew 11:29, 21:5)

Hunger and thirst after righteousness
These people eagerly desire (or crave) righteousness. Righteousness is holy and upright living, conforming to God's standard.

Merciful
These people are kind, even to those who treat them without respect. They forgive. God is kind to us, even though sometimes we treat Him and His commands without respect. Isaiah 55:7 says, "Let the wicked forsake his way and the evil man his thoughts. Let him turn to the LORD, and He will have mercy on him, and to our God, for He will freely pardon." Is there someone you need to pardon? If we refuse to forgive, God will not forgive us.

Pure of Heart
This person approaches life with innocence and blamelessness. Psalm 73:1 says, "Surely God is good…to those who are pure in heart."

Peacemakers
These are people who want peace. They do not stir up fights or arguments. They do not look for reasons to complain or to say bad things about others. James 3:18 says, "Peacemakers who sow in peace, raise a harvest of righteousness."

Persecuted for righteousness
These people are teased, harassed, harmed or bothered by others because they choose to do what is right. Jesus said, "No servant is greater than his master. If they persecuted Me, they will persecute you also." He said, "Rejoice in that day and leap for joy, because great is your reward in heaven." You will have a great reward when you suffer for the Lord. (Luke 6:23; John 15:20)

The Twelve Disciples

Peter

Philip

James

James

Bartholomew

Thaddaeus

John

Matthew

Simon the Zealot

Andrew

Thomas

Judas Iscariot

Who Are the Twelve Disciples?

THEIR BACKGROUNDS
- They were twelve Jewish men whom Jesus called to follow him during his 3-year ministry on earth.
- The twelve disciples were from the Galilee region in the north except for Judas Iscariot, who was from Judea in the south.
- Their occupations ranged from fisherman to tax collectors and revolutionaries.
- Some were married. (Mark 1:29-31; 1 Cor. 9:3-6)
- Some were well-versed in Scripture. (John 1:46)

THEIR PURPOSE
- After being baptized by John the Baptist and spending 40 days in the wilderness, Jesus started teaching and many people started following him.
- After a night of prayer and meditation, Jesus chose twelve men out of all those who were following him.
- These twelve men would be Jesus' main focus of instruction.
- These disciples were selected to let the world know of God's love, that God sent Jesus to redeem the world. (see John 17:23)

THEIR MISSION
- These are the twelve men who, for the most part, would prove to be valuable companions to Jesus.
- Their instruction and conversations would become the teachings, knowledge, and instruction for the church that would later grow and spread.
- Jesus knew their personalities, both strong and weak.
- Jesus knew that these men would disappoint him, desert him, deny him, and betray him.
- Jesus knew that these men, once filled with the Holy Spirit, would be the first witnesses of the Gospel, carrying God's message of redemption to Judea, Samaria, and the ends of the earth.
- The twelve tribes of Israel were blessed in order to be a blessing to all nations. In a similar way, these twelve men, along with all disciples of Jesus who follow their lead, were to bless all nations. (Galatians 3:8) Followers of Christ are commanded to go out and make disciples of all nations, baptizing them in the name of the Father, The Son, and the Holy Spirit.

Being a Disciple of Christ

BEGINNING THE JOURNEY: COUNT THE COST
- Jesus said that whoever wants to follow him, that person must deny himself and take up his cross. He said that if one wants to save his life he will lose it, but if he loses his life for Jesus and for the gospel he will save it.
- When Simon Peter, James and John encountered Jesus, they pulled their boats up on shore, left everything and followed him.

FOLLOWING CHRIST TOGETHER: FELLOWSHIP
- Jesus prayed that his followers would be brought to complete unity.
- The followers of Jesus were not to give up meeting together and were to encourage one another.

SERVING CHRIST AND OTHERS
- Jesus said that whoever wants to become great among his disciples must be a servant, just as Jesus himself did not come to be served, but to serve, and "to give his life a ransom for many."

FAILURES AND FORGIVENESS
- When Jesus was arrested all the disciples deserted him and fled, and Peter denied knowing him because he feared for his life.
- Later Jesus said that the disciples would receive power when the Holy Spirit came to them and that they would share the good news in Jerusalem, and in all Judea and Samaria, and all over the earth.

IN THE POWER OF THE SPIRIT
- Jesus promised the disciples that he would send the Holy Spirit to them, and that the Holy Spirit would guide them and provide them with gifts that would help them carry out their mission.
- Paul wrote to the Corinthian church informing them that there is only one Spirit, but different kinds of gifts. There is only one God, but several kinds of good works.

(Mark 8:34, 35; Luke 5:11b; John 17:23a; Hebrews 10:25; Matthew 20:26-28; Matthew 26:56b; Mark 14:71, 72; Acts 1:8; John 16:5-16; 1 Corinthians 12:4-12)

Peter

James, son of Zebedee

	Peter	**James, son of Zebedee**
Other Names	• Simeon bar Jona (Simon, son of Jona) • Cephas ("rock" or "stone") • Simon Peter • Simon	• Son of Zebedee • Boanerges (Son of Thunder) • "James the Elder" • "James the Great"
General Information	• Son of Jona and born in Bethsaida.(John 1:42-44) • Lived in Capernaum. (Matthew 8:5-14) • Fisherman. (Matthew 4:18) • Brother of Andrew. (Matthew 4:18) • Partner with James and John.(Luke 5:10) • Married. (Matthew 8:14) • One of the pillars of the Jerusalem church. (Galatians 2:9) • Boldly preached, healed, and ministered to Jews and Gentiles after Pentecost. (Acts 2–12) • Imprisoned by Herod for preaching and rescued by an angel of the Lord. (Acts 12:3-19) • Wrote 1 Peter and 2 Peter.	• Son of Zebedee. (Matthew 4:21) • Son of Salome. (Matthew 27:56; Mark 16:1) • Fisherman with his father and his brother. (Matthew 4:18-22) • Brother of John. (Matthew 4:21) • Partner with Peter. (Luke 5:10) • Put to death by the sword by Herod Agrippa I. The only one of the twelve disciples who died for his faith that was recorded in Scripture. (Acts 12:2)
Personality & Character	• Impulsive (Matthew 14:28), yet cowardly. (Matthew 14:30; 26:69-74) • Hot tempered (John 18:10), yet tenderhearted. (Matthew 26:75) • Insightful (Matthew 16:16), yet dense. (Matthew 16:21-23) • Courageous and solid after Pentecost. (Acts 5:27-30)	• Vengeful and fiery. (Luke 9:54) • Selfish and conceited. (Mark 10:35-37) • Committed to Christ and courageous to the end. (Acts12:2)
Encounters with Jesus	• Was called to be a fisher of men. (Matthew 4:19) Left everything to follow Jesus. (Luke 5:11) • One of the three disciples in the core group of disciples. (Mark 5:37; 9:2; 13:3; 14:33) • Simon said Jesus is the Christ, Son of the living God. Jesus names him Peter (rock) and said, "Upon this rock I will build my church, and the gates of Hell will not prevail against it." (Matthew 16:16-19) • Was reprimanded because he refused to accept that Jesus had to die. (Matthew 16:23) • Witnessed Jesus' Transfiguration (where Jesus' divinity was revealed). (Mark 9:2-8) • Was sent to prepare the upper room for the Last Supper. (Luke 22:8) • Jesus predicted that Peter would deny knowing him three times. (Luke 22:31-34) • Was with Jesus in the Garden of Gethsemane. (Matthew 26:36-46) • Jesus instructed Peter after his resurrection. (John 21:15-19)	• Was called to be a fisher of men. (Matthew 4:19) Left everything to follow Jesus. (Luke 5:11) • One of the three disciples in the core group of disciples. (Mark 5:37; 9:2; 13:3; 14:33) • Jesus named him and John "Sons of Thunder." (Mark 3:17) • Was rebuked with his brother John for requesting God to rain fire on a Samaritan village. (Luke 9:54, 55) • Witnessed Jesus' Transfiguration (where Jesus' divinity was revealed). (Mark 9:2-8) • Jesus responded to James's and John's request to sit at his right and left in the Kingdom. (Mark 10:35-43) • Was with Jesus in the Garden of Gethsemane. (Matthew 26:36-46) • Witnessed the miraculous catch of fish on the Sea of Galilee after Jesus' resurrection. (John 21:2-7)
Key Lesson	God can forgive sins and strengthen the faith of those who love him.	Stand firm in the face of persecution.
Stories	Papias (second-century Christian) recorded that Mark served as Peter's scribe and wrote the Gospel of Mark based on Peter's testimony. According to some stories, Peter asked to be crucified upside down. Peter may have been crucified during the reign of Nero in Rome. Symbols for Peter are sometimes keys, representing the keys to the kingdom of heaven. (Matthew 16:19)	Some claim he was the first bishop in Spain. Symbols of James sometimes include the bishop's hat and the sword, which is in reference to his martyrdom.

John

- Son of Zebedee
- Boanerges (Son of Thunder)
- "The Evangelist"
- "The Revealer"
- "The Beloved Disciple" (The disciple whom Jesus loved)

- Son of Zebedee. (Matthew 4:21)
- Son of Salome. (Matthew 27:56; Mark 16:1)
- Fisherman with his father and his brother. (Matthew 4:18-22)
- Brother of James. (Matthew 4:21)
- Partner with Peter. (Luke 5:10)
- One of the pillars of the Jerusalem church. (Galatians 2:9)
- Healed and preached. (Acts 3–4; 8)
- Exiled to the island of Patmos. (Revelation 1:1, 9)
- Wrote the Gospel of John, 1, 2, and 3 John, and Revelation.

- Vengeful and fiery. (Luke 9:54)
- Judgmental. (Mark 9:38)
- Selfish. (Mark 10:35-37)
- Bold, loving and compassionate after Pentecost. (Acts 4:13; 1 John 4)

- One of the three disciples in the core group of disciples. (Mark 5:37; 9:2; 13:3; 14:33)
- Suggested that driving out demons could only be performed by those who follow Jesus and his disciples. (Mark 9:38)
- Witnessed Jesus' Transfiguration (where Jesus' divinity was revealed). (Mark 9:2-8)
- Was sent to prepare the upper room for the Last Supper. (Luke 22:8)
- Reclined next to Jesus during the Last Supper. (John 13:23)
- Was given the responsibility at the cross to take care of Mary, Jesus' mother. (John 19:26, 27)
- Ran ahead of Peter to see Jesus' empty tomb and expressed faith by "seeing and believing." (John 20:2-8)
- Witnessed the miraculous catch of fish on the Sea of Galilee after Jesus' resurrection. (John 21:2-7)

God's love, evident in Jesus Christ, saves, transforms, and unites all believers.

Some stories suggest that John was released from exile on the island of Patmos and returned to Ephesus (Turkey today).
Stories suggest that John died in Ephesus around ad 100.
Symbols of John sometimes include the eagle (Revelation 4:7) and a book.

Andrew

- "Protokletos" (First Called)

- Son of Jona. (John 1:42)
- Born in Bethsaida. (John 1:44)
- Lived in Capernaum with Peter. (Mark 1:29)
- Fisherman. (Matthew. 4:18)
- Brother of Simon Peter. (Matthew 4:18)
- Disciple of John the Baptist.(John 1:35-40)
- Listed as one of Christ's twelve disciples. (Matthew 10:2-4; Mark 3:16-19; Luke 6:14-16)
- The name Andrew derives from Greek, meaning "manly."

- Enthusiastic about Christ. (John 1:35-42)
- Inquisitive. (John 1:35-38)
- Resourceful. (John 6:8, 9)

- First to follow Jesus. (John 1:35-40)
- Called to be a fisher of men. (Matthew 4:19)
- Sent out on a mission to the Jews to preach "the kingdom of heaven is at hand," heal the sick, cleanse the lepers, raise the dead, and cast out demons. (Matthew 10:5-8)
- Informed Jesus that several Greeks wanted to see him. (John 12:20-22)
- Told Jesus of the boy with five loaves of bread and two fish. (John 6:8, 9)
- Was present when Jesus appeared to the disciples after the Resurrection. (John 20:19-25)
- Was present for the Great Commission when Jesus sent his disciples to all nations. (Matthew 28:16-20)
- Witnessed Jesus being taken up into heaven. (Acts 1:8, 9)

Go out and eagerly share the good news about Jesus Christ.

Some suggest that Andrew preached in Greece, Asia Minor, and Russia.
A seventh-century story suggests that Andrew was crucified on an X-shaped cross by a Roman proconsul.
The symbol for Andrew is sometimes the X-shaped cross.

Philip

- None

- Born in Bethsaida.(John 1:44)
- Well versed in Scripture. (John 1:45, 46)
- Listed as one of Christ's twelve disciples. (Matthew 10:2-4; Mark 3:16-19; Luke 6:14-16)
- The disciple Philip is often confused with Philip the evangelist found in Acts.
- The name Philip derives from Greek, meaning "he who loves horses."
- Philip probably spoke Greek. (John 12:20, 21)

- Practical. (John 6:7)
- Helpful. (John 12:20, 21)
- Literal and confused. (John 14:8)

- The third disciple Jesus called. (John 1:43)
- Brought Nathanael (Bartholomew) to Jesus. (John 1:45, 46)
- Jesus tested him regarding the feeding of the multitude. (John 6:5-7)
- Informed Jesus that several Greeks wanted to see him. (John 12:20-22)
- Asked Jesus to show him the Father. (John 14:8, 9)
- Was present at the Last Supper. (Matthew 26:20)

All the knowledge in the world does not compare to the truth found in Jesus.

Tradition suggests that Philip lived and preached in Scythia (Ukraine today).
Some stories suggest that Philip was crucified on a tall cross at Hierapolis of Phrygia (Turkey today).
Symbols for Philip sometimes include loaves of bread (John 6:5-7) and a tall cross.

Bartholomew

Matthew

Thomas

	Bartholomew	**Matthew**	**Thomas**
Other Names	• Nathanael	• Levi • Levi the son of Alphaeus	• Didymus (Twin) • Judas Thomas • "Doubting Thomas"
General Information	• Born and/or raised in Cana of Galilee. (John 21:2) • Well versed in the Hebrew Scriptures. (John 1:46) • Listed as one of Christ's twelve disciples. (Matthew 10:2-4; Acts 1:13) • The name Bartholomew derives from Greek, meaning "son of Tolmai." • The name Nathanael derives from the Hebrew, meaning "God has given."	• Son of Alphaeus. (Mark 2:14) • From Capernaum. (Mark 2:1-17) • Tax collector in Galilee. (Matthew 9:9) • Possible brother of James son of Alphaeus. (Mark 3:18) • Listed as one of Christ's twelve disciples. (Matthew 10:2-4; Acts 1:13) • Wrote the Gospel of Matthew • The name Matthew derives from Hebrew, meaning "gift of God."	• He was a twin. (John 20:24) • Listed as one of Christ's twelve disciples. (Matthew 10:2-4; Mark 3:16-19; Luke 6:14-16)
Personality & Character	• Skeptical. (John 1:46) • Honest. (John 1:47) • Faithful. (John 1:49)	• Penitent. (Matthew 9:9; 10:2) • Hospitable. (Matthew 9:10)	• Inquisitive. (John 14:5) • Doubtful. (John 20:24, 25) • Courageous. (John 11:16) • Faithful. (John 20:24-29)
Encounters with Jesus	• Jesus told Nathanael that he was an honest Israelite and informed him that he saw him sitting under the fig tree. (John 1:47, 48) • Nathanael said that Jesus was the "Son of God" and "King of Israel." (John 1:49) • Jesus enlightened Nathanael with what to expect (John 1:50, 51) • Witnessed the miraculous catch of fish and ate breakfast with Jesus after his resurrection. (John 21:2-7)	• Matthew left his tax collector booth to follow Jesus. (Matthew 9:9) • Matthew invited Jesus over to dine with him and his corrupt friends. (Matthew 9:10) • Sent out on a mission to the Jews to preach "the kingdom of heaven is at hand," heal the sick, cleanse the lepers, raise the dead, and cast out demons. (Matthew 10:5-8) • Was present at the Last Supper (Matthew 26:20)	• Courageously encouraged disciples to go to Bethany. (John 11:16) • Asked Jesus how to know where Jesus was going. (John 14:5) • Doubted Jesus' resurrection saying he would have to touch his wounds in order to believe. (John 20:25) • Affirmed that Jesus was Lord and God. (John 20:28) • Witnessed the miraculous catch of fish and ate breakfast with Jesus after his resurrection. (John 21:2-7)
Key Lesson	Believers are called to test all things with Scripture and remain true to its principles.	Jesus Christ is for everyone, even sinners and outcasts.	Jesus can overcome doubts and lead believers to faithfulness.
Stories	Some suggest that Bartholomew ministered to Asia Minor and India and the Armenian church claims Bartholomew as their founder. Tradition suggests that Bartholomew was flayed alive in Armenia. The symbol for Bartholomew is sometimes a blade.	Some stories suggest that Matthew ministered to Persia, Macedonia, Syria, Parthia, Media, and Ethiopia bringing the good news to kings. Some stories suggest that Matthew died a martyr. The symbol for Matthew is sometimes a bag of coins in reference to his occupation as a tax collector before he encountered Jesus.	Stories suggest that Thomas traveled to India and founded the Christian church there. Some suggest Thomas was killed by a spear for his faith, and was buried in India. Some say Thomas was a carpenter. Symbols for Thomas include the spearhead and the T-square.

James, son of Alphaeus

Thaddaeus

Simon the Zealot

Judas Iscariot

James, son of Alphaeus	Thaddaeus	Simon the Zealot	Judas Iscariot
• James the son of Alphaeus • "James the Younger" • "James the Less"	• Jude • Judas the son of James • Lebbaeus	• Simon the Cananaean	• "Judas the Betrayer" • Judas the son of Simon
• Son of Alphaeus. (Mark 3:18) • Possible brother of Matthew (Levi) the tax collector, also the son of Alphaeus. (Mark 2:14) • Listed as one of Christ's twelve disciples. (Matt. 10:3; Acts 1:13) • James the son of Alphaeus is often confused with James the brother of Jesus (who wrote the book of James) or James the brother of Joseph.	• Son of James. (Luke 6:16) • Listed as one of Christ's twelve disciples. (Matthew 10:2-4; Acts 1:13) • The Aramaic meaning of both Thaddaeus and Lebbaeus is the same, "beloved" or "dear to the heart." • The name "Judas" derives from the Hebrew name Judah, meaning "praise." • Jude is sometimes confused with Judas the brother of Jesus, Judas Barsabbas, and Judas Iscariot.	• Was a Zealot. (Matthew 10:4; Mark 3:18; Luke 6:15; Acts 1:13) • Listed as one of Christ's twelve disciples. (Matthew 10:2-4; Acts 1:13) • The name Simon derives from the Hebrew name Shimon, meaning "hearing." • The word "Cananaean" derives from an Aramaic word meaning "zealous one."	• Judas was the treasurer for the group of disciples; was a thief. (John 12:5, 6; 13:29) • Judas betrayed Jesus, felt remorse, threw the blood money in the temple and hanged himself. The chief priest used the money to purchase the potter's field, fulfilling prophecy. (Matthew 27:3-10) • Judas purchased the Field of Blood and fell headlong and "burst open…" (Acts 1:18-20) • Judas was replaced by Matthias who was added to the eleven apostles. (Acts 1:26)
• Unknown.	• Inquisitive. (John 14:22) • Confused. (John 14:22)	• Patriotic. (Matthew 10:4) • Loyal. (Mark 3:18) • Passionate. (Luke 6:15) • Sacrificial. (Acts 1:13)	• Greedy. (Matthew 26:14-16) • Deceitful. (Matthew 26:25) • Treacherous. (Matthew 26:47-50) • Remorseful. (Matthew 27:3-5)
• Selected as one of Christ's twelve disciples. (Matthew 10:2-4; Luke 6:14-16) • Sent out on a mission to the Jews to preach "the kingdom of heaven is at hand," heal the sick, cleanse the lepers, raise the dead, and cast out demons. (Matthew 10:5-8) • Was present at the Last Supper. (Matthew 26:20) • Was present when Jesus appeared to the disciples after the Resurrection. (John 20:19-25)	• Selected as one of Christ's twelve disciples. (Matthew 10:2-4; Acts 1:13) • Sent out on a mission to the Jews to preach "the kingdom of heaven is at hand," heal the sick, cleanse the lepers, raise the dead, and cast out demons. (Matthew 10:5-8) • Asked Jesus how he would reveal himself to his followers and not to the world. (John 14:22) • Was present at the Last Supper. (Matthew 26:20)	• Selected as one of Christ's twelve disciples. (Matthew 10:2-4; Acts 1:13) • Sent out on a mission to the Jews to preach "the kingdom of heaven is at hand," heal the sick, cleanse the lepers, raise the dead, and cast out demons. (Matthew 10:5-8) • Was present at the Last Supper. (Matthew 26:20) • Was present for the Great Commission and Jesus' Ascension into heaven. (Matthew 28:16)	• Selected as one of Christ's twelve disciples. (Matthew 10:4; Luke 6:15) • Jesus referred to Judas as the devil. (John 6:70, 71) • Criticized Mary for anointing Jesus with expensive perfume. (John 12:4-8) • Conversed with Jesus during the Last Supper. (Matthew 26:23-25; John 13:27, 28) • The devil entered his heart at the Last Supper. (John 13:2) • Betrayed Jesus for 30 pieces of silver. (Matthew 26:14-16; 47-51)
All followers of Jesus can still accomplish the work of God without being in the limelight.	Jesus will reveal his truths to believers who follow him.	One should be willing to sacrifice his or her politics to follow Jesus.	Not all who claim to follow Jesus are faithful to him and his goals.
Some suggest that James, son of Alphaeus, belonged to the revolutionary group known as the Zealots. Some say that James was arrested by the Jews, thrown off the Temple, and then beaten to death by a club.	Some suggest that Thaddaeus belonged to the revolutionary group, the Zealots. Some scholars believe that Thaddaeus authored the book of Jude, although most believe the author is Judas, the brother of Jesus. The symbol for Thaddaeus is sometimes a gold ship with silver sails before a red horizon, which is a reference to the ship he took on missionary journeys.	One story suggests that Simon was the bridegroom at the wedding in Cana. Some stories suggest that Simon was a missionary to Persia. The symbol for Simon is sometimes a book resting on a fish, which is a reference to Simon fishing for people.	Judas was possibly from Kerioth in Judea. Some scholars suggest that Judas was a member of the Zealot sect known as the Sicarii, who were dagger-bearing assassins.

Other Disciples in the New Testament

Other Followers of Jesus ▼	Apostles, Evangelists and Teachers ▼	Important Leaders ▼
Cleopas: Follower of Jesus who spoke with Jesus on the road to Emmaus. (Luke 24:18)	**Apollos:** Missionary. (Acts 18:18-27; 1 Corinthians 1:12; 3:4-6, 22; 4:6; 16:12; Titus 3:13)	**Ananias:** Disciple and healer. (Acts 9:11)
James: Brother of Jesus, leader of Jerusalem church, and author of James. (Matt. 13:55, 56; Acts 12:17)	**Aquila:** Teacher and missionary. (Acts 18; Romans 16:3; 1 Corinthians 16:19; 2 Timothy 4:19)	**Archippus:** Leader of house church. (Colossians 4:17; Philemon 2)
Joanna: Follower of Jesus. (Luke 8:3; 24:10)	**Barnabas:** Missionary, apostle, and partner with Paul. (Acts 4:36; 9–15; 1 Cor. 9:6; Gal. 2:1, 9, 13; Col. 4:10)	**Aristarchus:** Missionary and fellow prisoner with Paul. (Acts19:29; 20:4; 27:2; Col. 4:10; Philemon 24)
Joseph of Arimathea: Follower of Jesus. (Matthew 27:57; John 19:38)	**Junia:** Apostle. (Romans 16:7)	**Epaphras:** Preacher, fellow worker and prisoner with Paul. (Colossians 1:7; 4;12; Philemon 23)
Joseph Barsabbas: Follower of Jesus. (Acts 1:23)	**Luke:** Physician, worker, and prisoner with Paul, and author of Luke. (Colossians 4:14; 2 Timothy 4:11)	**Epaphroditus:** Fellow worker with Paul. (Philippians 2:25; 4:18)
Judas (Jude): Brother of Jesus and author of the book of Jude. (Matthew 13:54, 55; Mark 6:3; Jude 1)	**Mark (John Mark):** Missionary, cousin to Barnabas, and author of the Gospel Mark. (Acts 12; 1 Peter 5:13)	**Judas Barsabbas:** Prophet. (Acts 15:22-35)
Lazarus: Friend and follower of Jesus. (John 11–12)	**Paul (Saul):** Apostle, missionary, and author of Romans to Philemon. (Acts to Philemon; 2 Peter 3:15)	**Lucius of Cyrene:** Prophet and teacher in the church at Antioch. (Acts 13:1)
Mary, the mother of James and Joseph: Follower of Jesus. (Matthew 27:55; 28:5, 7)	**Philip the Evangelist:** Deacon and missionary. (Acts 6:5; 8)	**Manaen**: Prophet and teacher of the church in Antioch. (Acts 13:1)
Mary of Bethany: Friend and follower of Jesus. (Luke 10:38-42; John 11–12)	**Priscilla:** Teacher and missionary. (Acts 18; Rom. 16:3; 1 Cor. 16:19; 2 Tim. 4:19)	**Mnason**: An early disciple. (Acts 21:16)
Mary Magdalene: Follower of Jesus. (Matthew 27, 28; Mark 15, 16; Luke 8:2; 24:10; John 20)	**Silas:** Missionary. (Acts 15–18; 2 Corinthians 1:19; 1 Thessalonians 1:1; 2 Thessalonians 1:1; 1 Peter 5:12)	**Philemon:** Leader of a house church. (Philemon 1)
Matthias: Follower who replaced Judas Iscariot. (Acts 1:15-26)	**Stephen:** Deacon, missionary, preacher, and martyr. (Acts 6–8; 11:19; 22:20)	**Phoebe:** Deacon and helper of Paul. (Romans 16:1, 2)
Salome: Follower of Jesus. (Mark 15:40)	**Timothy:** Pastor and teacher. (Acts 16–20; Rom. 16:21; 1 Cor. 4:17; Philippians 2:19-22; 1 and 2 Timothy)	**Simeon (Niger):** Prophet and teacher in the church at Antioch. (Acts 13:1)
Susanna: Follower of Jesus. (Luke 8:3)	**Titus:** Pastor and teacher. (2 Corinthians 2:13; 7:6; 8:6-23; 12:18; Galatians. 2:1-3; Titus 1:4, 5)	**Tychicus:** Pastor and fellow worker with Paul. (Ephesians 6:21; Colossians 4:7)

Evidence for the Resurrection

The Bible teaches that Jesus is the Son of God, and that he was crucified and died for the forgiveness of sin, was resurrected from the dead, and lives today.

Over the centuries, skeptics have developed several objections to the resurrection of Jesus and have proposed several alternative theories about what actually happened to the body of Jesus Christ. Many believe that Jesus' resurrection is too difficult to prove beyond a reasonable doubt. Here is evidence to answer those doubts.

Skeptics' Theories

Answers

Skeptics' Theories	Answers
OBJECTION 1: Jesus Was a Mythological Figure	Evidence for Jesus Christ comes from many written documents from the first century, including 39 ancient sources in addition to the New Testament and early church leaders. An early statement of faith was probably written 8-20 years after the death of Jesus. The creed states that Jesus "was buried, and that he rose again the third day according to the scriptures." (1 Corinthians 15:3-8) Most critical historians agree that documents take more than 20 years to become corrupted by mythological development.
OBJECTION 2: Jesus Was Just a Man	Evidence supports that Jesus was all he claimed to be. For over three years, Jesus performed many miracles and signs such as controlling the weather, walking on water, giving sight to the blind, healing the lame and diseased, casting out demons, and raising people from the dead. These miracles convinced people of his day that Jesus was all he claimed to be. More than one hundred prophecies found in the Old Testament were fulfilled in Jesus Christ. Jesus predicted he would suffer, die, and rise again, months before his crucifixion. C.S. Lewis wrote in *Mere Christianity* that Jesus could not only be a good man. Because of Jesus' teachings, he could only be the Son of God, a liar, or a madman.
OBJECTION 3: Jesus' Followers Made It All Up	Evidence suggests that such a deception is highly unlikely. People will not knowingly die for a lie. The disciples were not fearless liars who wanted to fool the world. After the crucifixion, the disciples fled in fear for their lives. However, once they saw, touched, and spoke with the risen Lord, their lives were transformed. Furthermore, all of Jesus' followers doubted the resurrection until Jesus physically appeared to them; then they believed.
OBJECTION 4: The Witnesses Were Unreliable	All four gospels agree that the first eyewitnesses to the proof of Jesus' resurrection were women. On the surface, this does not seem like a major proof for the resurrection. The significance of these eyewitnesses lies in understanding the role of woman in first century Judea. During the time of Jesus, a woman's testimony was considered worthless. In fact, a woman was not allowed to serve as a witness in court. If early believers wanted to fabricate the resurrection, they would have come up with witnesses who had political and religious influence in their community, not women who weren't even considered reliable witnesses. The greatest weapon against these early eyewitnesses would have been to produce the body of Jesus. The silence of those who opposed Christianity while Jesus' followers preached about the empty tomb only confirmed the fact that the tomb really was empty and its vacancy could not be explained otherwise.
OBJECTION 5: The Resurrection Is Not Important	The physical resurrection of Jesus Christ is important only if it is true. If Jesus did not rise from the grave, then the unbeliever is no worse or better off than before. However, if Jesus did rise from the dead, then it is reasonable to believe that everything Jesus claimed is true. If what Jesus claimed is true, then he died for the sins of the world and one receives eternal life by believing in Jesus.

Evidence for the Resurrection

Skeptics' Theories   ## Answers

THEORY 1: The Eyewitnesses Hallucinated	It is very unlikely, if not impossible for more than 500 people to have the same hallucination. Those who saw Jesus after his death did not expect to see him and were surprised by his being there. Psychiatrists agree that hallucinations require expectation. A psychiatric study performed in 1975 suggests that the content of the hallucination "reflects the efforts [of the one experiencing the hallucination] to master anxiety to fulfill various wishes and needs."
THEORY 2: Jesus Did Not Die on the Cross	If Jesus did not die, the Roman soldiers would have failed in their duties. Jesus had to survive massive blood loss, torture, and a stab wound in his side, and roll the stone away (which normally would take several men to accomplish). Witnesses saw that when Jesus was stabbed in the side, water mixed with blood poured out, medically indicating that Jesus had already died. According to studies of first century tombs, the tomb was likely sealed by a 2,000-pound rolling stone that fit in a sloping track, which would have been impossible for a sole individual to move from the inside of the tomb.
THEORY 3: Jesus' Body Was Stolen	The enemies of Jesus took several steps to prevent the disciples from stealing the body, such as sealing the stone and providing a guard of soldiers to watch the tomb. The soldiers at the tomb would not sleep for fear of death. During the crucifixion, the disciples were cowards who had abandoned Jesus. One disciple denied that he knew Jesus to a young servant girl. The disciples did not understand his purposes, nor the importance of the resurrection. These men did not have the courage to pass by the guard at the tomb, silently move the extremely large stone, rob the grave, and leave undetected.
THEORY 4: Everyone Went to the Wrong Tomb	The women observed where Jesus' body was laid only a few days earlier. After hearing the report from the women, Peter and John ran to the tomb without directions from the women. It is unlikely that Peter and John would make the same mistake as the women. If Jesus' body were still in its correct tomb, his enemies could have produced the body immediately. Even if everyone went to the wrong tomb, Joseph of Arimathea, the owner of the tomb, would have corrected them.

On Pentecost, 50 days after the resurrection of Jesus, Peter addressed the crowd and specifically pointed out:

- Everyone there knew that Jesus of Nazareth was a man accredited by God by miracles and signs. (Acts 2:22)
- Everyone there knew that Jesus was crucified, and that his death was by God's set purpose. (Acts 2:23)
- Everyone there knew that David spoke about the resurrection of Jesus nearly 1000 years before. (Acts 2:24-31)
- Everyone there was a witness to the fact that Jesus was raised to life. (Acts 2:32)

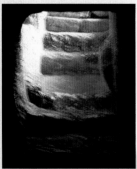

Biblical Descriptions of Heaven

A Throne of God. (Deuteronomy 26:15; Psalm 11:4; Isaiah 66:1)

A reward. (Matthew 5:12)

A place safe from theft and destruction. (Matthew 6:20)

A place of rejoicing. (Luke 15:7)

A place where there will be no marrying or giving in marriage. (Matthew 22:29, 30)

A house with many rooms. (John 14:2)

A home of righteousness. (2 Peter 3:13)

A garden paradise. (Revelation 2:7)

A place that doesn't experience hunger, thirst, tears, hot sun, or scorching heat. (Revelation 7:16, 17)

A place of victory and playing harps. (Revelation 15:2)

A holy city. (Revelation 21:2)

A place where God dwells with us. (Revelation 21:3)

A place that doesn't experience sadness, death, or pain. (Revelation 21:4)

A place of brilliance like that of a very precious jewels. The walls are made of jasper and the city made of pure gold, as pure as glass. The foundations of the city walls are decorated with precious stones. The twelve gates are each made from one single pearl. (Revelation 21:11, 18, 19-21)

A place that is lit by the glory of God. (Revelation 21:23)

A place with no night. (Revelation 21:25)

A place where no impure thing or person exists. (Revelation 21:27)

A place of life and healing. (Revelation 22:1-3)

A place where God reigns forever. (Rev. 22:5)

Biblical Descriptions of Hell

A place of weeping and gnashing of teeth. (Matthew 25:30)

A place of outer darkness. (Matthew 22:13)

A place of torments. (Luke 16:23)

A place of sorrows. (2 Samuel 22:5-7)

A place of everlasting destruction. (2 Thessalonians 1:9)

A place where people are tormented with fire and brimstone. (Revelation 21:8)

A place of worms that don't die. (Mark 9:43)

A place where fire is not quenched. (Mark 9:43)

A place where there is no rest. (Revelation 14:11)

A place that will ultimately be a lake of fire. (Revelation 20:14)

A place of hopeless of unsatisfied desires. (Luke 16:24)

A furnace of fire. (Matthew 13:42, 50)

A place of separation. (Matthew 13:49)

A place filled with the cowardly, the unbelieving, the vile, the murderers, the sexually immoral, those who practice magic arts, the idolaters, and all liars. (Revelation 21:8)

A place shut out from the presence of the Lord and the majesty of his power. (2 Thessalonians 1:9)

A place where fallen angels dwell. (2 Peter 2:4; Jude 1:16)

100 WELL-KNOWN EVENTS FROM ACTS TO REVELATION

Event 1	The Final Words of Jesus (Acts 1:4-8)
Event 2	The Ascension of Jesus (Acts 1:5-12)
Event 3	The Prayer Meeting and Election in the Upper Room (Acts 1:13-26)
Event 4	Pentecost (Acts 2:1-13)
Event 5	Peter's First Sermon (Acts 2:14-36)
Event 6	The First Great Harvest of Souls (Acts 2:37-47)
Event 7	Healing of the Lame Man at the Gate Beautiful (Acts 3:1-11)
Event 8	Peter's Second Sermon (Acts 3:12-26)
Event 9	First Persecution and Second Great Harvest of Souls (Acts 4:1-4)
Event 10	Peter's Defenses Before the Sanhedrin (Acts 4:5-22)
Event 11	The Excitement and Testimony of the Early Church (Acts 4:23-37)
Event 12	Divine Judgment Upon Ananias and Sapphira (Acts 5:1-11)
Event 13	The First Set of Miracles Performed by the Apostles (Acts 5:12-16)
Event 14	The Second Persecution and Second Defense by the Apostles (Acts 5:17-32)
Event 15	Gamaliel's Wise Advice (Acts 5:33-42)
Event 16	Election of the First Seven Deacons (Acts 6:1-7)
Event 17	Ministry of Stephen (Acts 6:8-15)
Event 18	Stephen's Message to the Sanhedrin (Acts 7:1-53)
Event 19	The Martyrdom of Stephen (Acts 7:54-60)
Event 20	Persecution of the Church by Saul (Acts 9:1-4)
Event 21	Philip's Revival in Samaria and Simon's Condemnation (Acts 8:5-25)
Event 22	Conversion of the Ethiopian Eunuch (Acts 8:26-40)
Event 23	Conversion of Saul (Acts 9:1-19)
Event 24	The Early Ministry of Saul (Acts 9:20-31)
Event 25	Paul Recounts His Struggle Over the Flesh as a New Believer (Romans 7:7-25)
Event 26	The Healing of Aeneas (Acts 9:32-35)
Event 27	The Raising of Dorcas (Acts 9:36-43)
Event 28	Peter's Sheet Vision at Joppa (Acts 10:1-22)
Event 29	Conversion of Cornelius (Acts 10:23-48)
Event 30	The Ministry of Barnabas at the Antioch Church (Acts 11:19-26)
Event 31	The Martyrdom of James and Release of Peter (Acts 12:1-19)
Event 32	Herod Agrippa Struck Dead for Blasphemy (Acts 12:20-25)
Event 33	The First Missionary Journey (Acts 13:1-5)

Event 34	Ministry of Barnabas and Saul in Cyprus (Acts 13:6-12)
Event 35	Desertion of John Mark (Acts 13:13)
Event 36	Paul's First Recorded Sermon (Acts 13:14-43)
Event 37	Paul Turns to the Gentiles (Acts 13:44-52)
Event 38	Paul Heals a Crippled Man at Lystra (Acts 14:6-18)
Event 39	Paul is Stoned at Lystra (Acts 14:19, 20)
Event 40	Paul is Caught Up Into the Third Heaven (2 Corinthians 12:2-10)
Event 41	Paul Writes Galatians Following His First Missionary Journey (Galatians 1:1-5)
Event 42	Paul Rebukes Peter (Galatians 2:11-14)
Event 43	The Council at Jerusalem (Acts 15:1-22)
Event 44	The Second Missionary Journey (Acts 15:36-16:5)
Event 45	Paul's Macedonian Vision (Acts 16:6-10)
Event 46	Conversion of Lydia at Philippi (Acts 16:13-15)
Event 47	Conversion of a Demonic Girl at Philippi (Acts 16:16-24)
Event 48	Conversion of the Jailer at Philippi (Acts 16:25-34)
Event 49	Founding of the Church at Thessalonica (Acts 17:1-9)
Event 50	Paul and Silas at Berea (Acts 17:10-15)
Event 51	Paul's Sermon on Mars Hill (Acts 17:16-34)
Event 52	Founding of the Church at Corinth (Acts 18:1-17)
Event 53	Paul Writes 1 and 2 Thessalonians During His 2nd Missionary Journey (1 Thes. 1:1-10; 2 Thes. 1:1-14)
Event 54	The Third Missionary Journey (Acts 18:22, 23)
Event 55	The Ministry of Apollos (Acts 18:24-28)
Event 56	Baptism of John the Baptist's Twelve Disciples (Acts 19:1-7)
Event 57	Paul's Extended Ministry in Ephesus (Acts 19:8-41)
Event 58	Paul Raises Eutychus from the Dead at Troas (Acts 20:6-12)
Event 59	Paul Addresses the Ephesian Elders at Miletus (Acts 20:17-38)
Event 60	Paul is Warned Not to Go to Jerusalem (Acts 21:4-14)
Event 61	Paul Writes 1 and 2 Corinthians, and Romans During His Third Missionary Journey (Romans 1:1-8)
Event 62	Paul Expresses His Great Sorrow Over Israel's Blindness (Romans 10:1-3)
Event 63	Paul Condemns the Fornicator in the Corinthian Church (1 Corinthians 5:1-8)
Event 64	Paul Recalls His Terrible Sufferings (2 Corinthians 11:24-28)
Event 65	Paul's Thorn in the Flesh Given Him by Satan (2 Corinthians 12:2-10)
Event 66	Paul Takes a Jewish Vow in Jerusalem (Acts 21:17-26)
Event 67	Paul is Seized in the Temple and Rescued by the Roman Soldiers (Acts 21:27-40)

Event 68	Paul Addresses an Angry Jewish Mob (Acts 22:1-21)
Event 69	Paul is Again Rescued by the Roman Soldiers (Acts 22:22-30)
Event 70	Paul Addresses the Sadducees and Pharisees (Acts 23:1-9)
Event 71	Paul is Taken to Caesarea to Escape a Plot to Kill Him (Acts 23:10-24)
Event 72	Paul's Defense Before Felix (Acts 24:10-26)
Event 73	Paul Appeals His Case to Caesar (Acts 25:10-12)
Event 74	Paul's Defense Before Festus and King Agrippa (Acts 26:1-32)
Event 75	Paul's Terrible Ocean Storm En Route to Rome (Acts 27:14-44)
Event 76	Paul on the Isle of Melita (Acts 28:1-10)
Event 77	Paul Writes the Four Prison Epistles in Rome (Eph. 1:1, 2; Col. 1:1-8; Philemon 1:1-3; Philippians 1:1-6)
Event 78	Paul Asks Philemon to Forgive Onesimus (Philemon 10-19)
Event 79	Paul Writes 1 Timothy and Titus Prior to His Second Roman Imprisonment (1 Timothy 1:1-3; Titus 1:1-5)
Event 80	Paul is Rearrested and Writes 2 Timothy Just Prior to His Martyrdom (2 Timothy 1:1-6; 4:6-8)
Event 81	Paul Asks for Timothy and John Mark to Visit Him in Prison (2 Timothy 4:9-11)
Event 82	James Writes His Epistle (James 1:1)
Event 83	Matthew Writes His Gospel Account (Matthew 1:1)
Event 84	Mark Writes His Gospel Account (Mark 1:1-4a)
Event 85	Luke Writes His Gospel Account (Luke 1:1-4)
Event 86	John Writes His Gospel Account (John 1:1-5)
Event 87	Luke Writes the Book of Acts (Acts 1:1, 2)
Event 88	The Author of Hebrews Writes His Epistle (Hebrews 1:1-12)
Event 89	Peter Writes First and Second Peter (1 Peter 1:1, 2; 2 Peter 1:1, 2)
Event 90	John Writes His Three Epistles (1 John 1:1, 2; 2 John 12:1, 2; 3 John 1:1-4)
Event 91	Jude Writes His Epistle (Jude 1:1-4)
Event 92	John Writes the Book of Revelation (Revelation 1:4-8)
Event 93	John is Banished to the Isle of Patmos (Revelation 1:9)
Event 94	John Sees the Ascended Christ (Revelation 1:10-18)
Event 95	John Receives Christ's Message to the Seven Churches (Revelation 1:19, 20)
Event 96	John Hears the Creation and Redemption Songs of Praise (Revelation 4:11; 5:9)
Event 97	John Views the Coming Great Tribulation (Revelation 6:12-17)
Event 98	John Sees the Glorious Second Coming of Christ (Revelation 19:6-9; 11-21)
Event 99	John Attempts to Worship an Angel on Two Separate Occasions But is Rebuked Each Time (Rev. 19:10; 22:8, 9)
Event 100	John Describes the Glorious New Millennium, Final Defeat of Satan, the Great White Throne Judgment; and the New Jerusalem (Rev. 20:1-15; 21:1-11)

1 Corinthians 13

What Love is	How to Love	Scripture
Patient	Be willing to wait for God's perfect timing. Have self-restraint. Control your impulses.	Isaiah 40:31 Romans 15:1 James 1:4
Kind	Ask, "What would this person like?" "What does she need?" Speak softly and be caring	Proverbs 25:11 Isaiah 58:6,7 Ephesians 4:32
Does not envy	Be content with what you have. List your blessings. Be happy for other's good.	1 Corinthians 3:3 Exodus 20:17 Philippians 4:11,12
Does not boast	Be humble. Don't brag. Give credit to others.	Psalm 49:6,7 Psalm 34:2 Philippians 3:1-8
Not proud	Don't think you are better than other people. Be modest. Don't be arrogant or overbearing.	1 Corinthians 8:1 Philippians 2:2-8 John 13:14,15
Not rude	Be courteous and kind. Be gracious. Use good manners.	Numbers 12:3 1 Peter 4:9 1 Peter 5:5
Not self-seeking	Think of others first. Give someone else first choice. Don't be greedy and selfish.	1 Corinthians 10:24 Acts 20:35 John 15:13
Not easily angered	Think the best of people. Don't jump to conclusions. Ask questions and listen.	Matthew 5:22 Romans 15:2 James 1:19
Keeps no record of wrongs	Forgive the "wrongs." Remember the "rights." What did Jesus do?	Galatians 6:1 Matthew 6:12 John 8:11
Does not delight in evil	Don't watch or read evil things. Turn away from gossip. Don't gloat when others fall.	Matthew 5:29 Proverbs 11:13 Galatians 6:1
Rejoices with the truth	Be happy about good things. Spread good news. Tell the truth to yourself and others.	Philippians 1:18 Isaiah 60:1 Ephesians 4:25
Always protects	Protect the helpless and weak. Protect yourself against temptation. Defend the name of Jesus.	James 1:27 Proverbs 4:14,15 1 Peter 3:15
Always trusts	Trust is believing God's promises. Pray about everything and trust Him. Believe that all things work for good.	Isaiah 14:24 Philippians 4:6 Romans 8:28
Always hopes	Never give up. Remember God doesn't give up on you. Expect good things from God.	Ephesians 6:13 Romans 5:10 1 John 3:3
Always perseveres	Be persistent. Keep on praying. If God is for you, who can be against you? Be faithful to God and others.	James 5:16 Romans 8:31 1 Peter 4:8
Never fails	Love never fails. God's love never fails. Pray for a loving heart like His.	1 Corinthians 13:13 John 15:9 John 13:35

THE ARMOR OF GOD

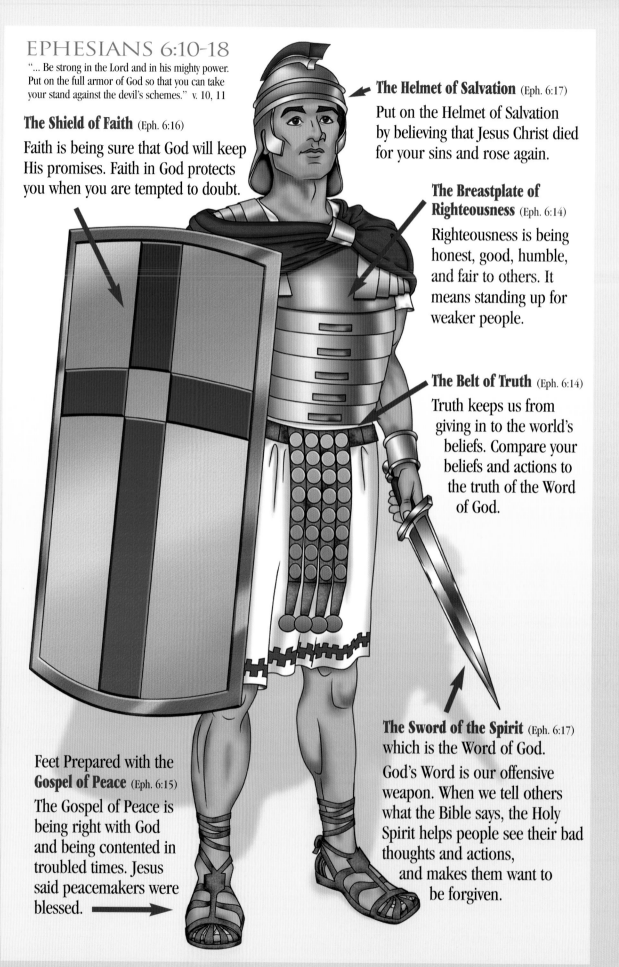

EPHESIANS 6:10-18

"... Be strong in the Lord and in his mighty power. Put on the full armor of God so that you can take your stand against the devil's schemes." v. 10, 11

The Shield of Faith (Eph. 6:16)

Faith is being sure that God will keep His promises. Faith in God protects you when you are tempted to doubt.

The Helmet of Salvation (Eph. 6:17)

Put on the Helmet of Salvation by believing that Jesus Christ died for your sins and rose again.

The Breastplate of Righteousness (Eph. 6:14)

Righteousness is being honest, good, humble, and fair to others. It means standing up for weaker people.

The Belt of Truth (Eph. 6:14)

Truth keeps us from giving in to the world's beliefs. Compare your beliefs and actions to the truth of the Word of God.

The Sword of the Spirit (Eph. 6:17) which is the Word of God.

God's Word is our offensive weapon. When we tell others what the Bible says, the Holy Spirit helps people see their bad thoughts and actions, and makes them want to be forgiven.

Feet Prepared with the Gospel of Peace (Eph. 6:15)

The Gospel of Peace is being right with God and being contented in troubled times. Jesus said peacemakers were blessed.

THE FRUIT OF THE SPIRIT

Fruit of the Spirit (Galatians 5:22-23)	Descriptive Definition	Other Scriptures	Greek Definition
Love	Love is not based on emotions or feelings. It is a decision to be committed to the well being of others without any conditions or circumstances.	John 15:12-14	**Agape:** Love which seeks the highest good of others.
Joy	Joy is not based on financial success, good health, or popularity. By obeying God's will, fellowship, ministering to others, and sharing the Gospel, believers will experience joy.	1 Peter 1:8, 9	**Chara:** Gladness, delight, a special presence of God.
Peace	Peace is a state of assurance, lack of fear, and sense of contentment. It is fellowship, harmony, and unity between individuals. Peace is freedom from worry, disturbance, and oppressive thoughts.	Philippians 4:7	**Eirene:** Peace between individuals, harmony, unity.
Patience	Patience is a slowness in avenging wrongs. It is the quality of restraint that prevents believers from speaking or acting hastily in the face of disagreement, opposition, or persecution.	1 Thessalonians 5:14,15	**Makrothumia:** Longsuffering, bearing trials without complaint.
Kindness	Kindness is an eagerness to put others at ease. It is a sweet and attractive temperament that shows friendly regard.	Proverbs 11:16,17	**Chrestotes:** Merciful, easy to bear. Morally good and upright.
Goodness	Goodness is the selfless desire to be open hearted and generous to others above what they deserve.	Titus 3:8	**Agathosune:** Useful, generous.
Faithfulness	Faithfulness is firm devotion to God, loyalty to friends, and dependability to carry out responsibilities. Faith is the conviction that even now God is working and acting on one's behalf.	Revelation 2:10b	**Pistis:** Trust, conviction.
Gentleness	Gentleness is a humble non-threatening demeanor that derives from a position of strength and authority, and is useful in calming another's anger. Gentleness is not a quality that is weak and passive.	1 Peter 3:15	**Prautes:** Humble, meek.
Self-Control	Self-control is to restrain one's emotions, actions, and desires, and to be in harmony with the will of God. Self-control is doing God's will, not living for one's self.	Titus 2:11,12	**Egkrateia:** Being in control of one's self.

© 2005 RW Research, Inc. Rose Publishing, Inc.   www.rose-publishing.com

ACTS OF THE SINFUL NATURE
(Galatians 5:19-21 and Colossians 3:5-9)

Sexual Immorality	Factions
Impurity	Envy
Debauchery	Drunkenness
Idolatry	Orgies
Witchcraft	Lust
Hatred	Evil Desires
Discord	Greed
Jealousy	Anger
Fits of Rage	Malice
Selfish Ambition	Slander
Dissensions	Deceit

Background Information on the Seven Cities

Ephesus: The City of Change
Ephesus was colonized by the Greeks no earlier than 1200 BC and was located near the Aegean Sea, providing a major harbor and caravan gateway for trade to all of Asia Minor and beyond. By the first century, Ephesus was already an established city, predominant in the Roman Province of Asia Minor and home to the Roman governor. Besides becoming a city of great wealth, it was noted for the Celsus library, established in the second century. The Ephesians worshiped Diana, the Roman goddess of nature and fertility, identified with the Greek goddess Artemis. At the present day, Ephesus has all the appearance of an inland city, caused by natural changes in the coastline. Paul founded the church at Ephesus.

Smyrna: The City of Life
Smyrna, a thriving seaport city now called Izmir, is about 35 miles north of Ephesus. Founded as a Greek colony more than 1,000 years before Christ, it paralleled Ephesus in wealth, beauty and commerce. Proud of being the city of the poet Homer, it was filled with the pagan temples of Apollo, Asclepia, Aphrodite, Cybele, Emperor Tiberius, and Zeus. Although it was a free city, it gave full allegiance to the Roman Empire which ordered Polycarp, the Bishop of Smyrna, to be burned at the stake in Rome. The temple of Athena, dating back to the seventh century BC was the most important building of that period. It was famous for its superb school of medicine. Although the origin of the city is not mentioned in the Bible, the church in Smyrna was probably founded by believers from Ephesus.

Pergamum: The City of Authority
Pergamum, founded no later than 399 BC, became the capital city of the Roman province in Asia giving the traveler the impression of a royal city, the home of authority. Located about 60 miles north of Smyrna and 15 miles from the Aegean Sea, Pergamum was a center of learning, medicine, and religious books. The library, rivaling the Alexandrian library, drew many princes, priests, and scholars. Noted for marble carving, it excelled the other six cities in architectural beauty. They worshiped Zeus Olympus, the savior-god; Athena, patron goddess of Athens; the Roman Emperor, as god; Dionysus, god of vegetation; and Asclepius, god of healing. The animal cult worship of the god-Serpent and the god-Bull were also practiced. Some scholars believe that Gaius, addressed by John in the book of 3 John, was the first Bishop of Pergamum.

Thyatira: Weakness Made Strong
Thyatira, a small town about 35 miles southeast of Pergamum, was founded by the general Seleucid Nicator under Alexander the Great in about 300 BC. Military garrisons greatly strengthened the city which was noted for commerce and guilds such as tanners, coppersmiths, potters, and purple dyers. Objects of worship included the Emperor, the Thyatiran war hero, Tyrimnos, and trade guild gods, e.g., bronzesmiths worshiped the goddess of war, Pallas Athena. How the church was established is unknown, but "Lydia, a seller of purple, of the city of Thyatira," came to the Lord under Paul's ministry in Philippi (Acts 16:14, 15).

Sardis: The City of Death
The city of Sardis was founded in about 1200 BC and became the capital of the Lydian kingdom located 30 miles southeast of Thyatira. It stood on a lofty plateau above the Hermus valley. Sardis was twice defeated, once by King Cyrus of Persia (359 BC), and again by Antiochus III of Syria (218 BC). The wealth of the Lydian kings arose from trade and the commerce with the East. An impressive acropolis housed a temple dedicated to the goddess Artemis. Goddesses Artemis and Cybele were commemorated on local coins. Two hundred years after Christ's birth, Sardis lay in decay. Today Sardis is a small village called Sart. When and how the church there was started are unknown.

Philadelphia: The Missionary City
The city of Philadelphia, founded by King Attalus of Pergamum (140 BC), was located in the Hermus River valley about 28 miles southeast of Sardis. An earthquake destroyed the city in AD 17; however, it was rebuilt by Emperor Tiberius. Famous for its grape industry, Philadelphia was also noted for textiles and leather goods. It became a strong fortress city and was called the "Gateway to the East." Although Dionysis was the major pagan god, people also worshiped sun and serpent gods. Philadelphia, the last of the Byzantine cities, was finally captured by the Turks in 1390. Christians lived there until the early 1900s. When and how the church was established there is not known, but it prospered for many centuries.

Laodicea: The City of Compromise
The city of Laodicea was located on a fertile plain overlooking the Lycus River about 50 miles southeast of Philadelphia. Laodicea, which became the capital of ancient Phrygia, was established by Antiochus II (261-246 BC) and named in honor of his sister-wife Laodice before their divorce in 253 BC. Located on a major trade route running from Ephesus to Syria, Laodicea accumulated great wealth. It was known for banking and the manufacture of expensive cloth made from soft black wool. Its medical school became famous for the development of an ear salve made of spice and Phrygian powder. Zeus Azeus and Men Karou were the main Phrygian gods. Cicero lived in Laodicea in 50 BC. Laodicea was so wealthy that when a massive earthquake destroyed the city in AD 60, it refused aid from Rome and rebuilt at its own expense. Most scholars believe that Epaphras started the church there (Colossians 1:7; 4:12, 13). Paul was aware of their spiritual struggles (Colossians 2:1).

"He who has an ear, let him hear what the Spirit says to the churches…"				
To the Church	**Your Strengths**	**Your Faults**	**Instruction**	**Promise**
Loveless **Ephesus** (Rev. 2:1-7)	Hard work Patient endurance Reject evil Persevere	You have forsaken your first love	Repent and do the works as you did at first	You will eat from the tree of life
Suffering **Smyrna** (Rev. 2:8-11)	Endure your suffering and poverty, yet you are rich	None	Remain faithful even when facing prison, persecution, or death	I will give you the crown of life You will not be hurt by the second death
Worldly **Pergamum** (Pergamos) (Rev. 2:12-17)	Loyalty to Christ Refuse to deny Him	Tolerates cults, heresies, idolatry, and immorality	Repent	Hidden manna and a stone with a new name on it
Wrong Doctrine **Thyatira** (Rev. 2:18-29)	Deeds, love, faith, service Patient endurance Constant improvement	Tolerates cult idolatry and immorality	Judgment coming Repent Hold fast until I come	I will give you authority over the nations and gift of the morning star
Spiritually Dead **Sardis** (Rev. 3:1-6)	Some have kept the faith	Church is dead	Wake up, repent Turn to Jesus again Strengthen what little remains	Faithful will walk with Jesus and not be blotted out of the book of life
Spiritually Alive **Philadelphia** (Rev. 3:7-13)	Kept my word Have not denied my name	None	I have placed before you an open door I will keep you from the hour of trial	I will make you a pillar in the temple of my God
Complacent **Laodicea** (Rev. 3:14-22)	None	Neither hot nor cold You rely on riches but don't realize your wretched condition	Turn from indifference and repent	I will invite those who overcome to sit with me on my throne

Locations of the Seven Churches

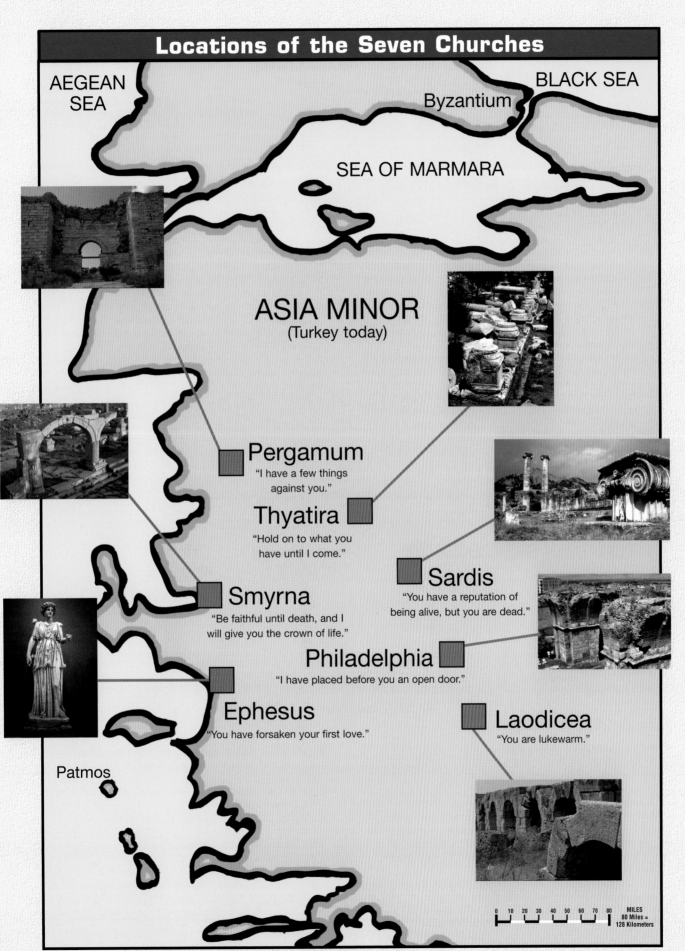

AEGEAN SEA

BLACK SEA

Byzantium

SEA OF MARMARA

ASIA MINOR
(Turkey today)

Pergamum
"I have a few things against you."

Thyatira
"Hold on to what you have until I come."

Smyrna
"Be faithful until death, and I will give you the crown of life."

Sardis
"You have a reputation of being alive, but you are dead."

Philadelphia
"I have placed before you an open door."

Ephesus
"You have forsaken your first love."

Laodicea
"You are lukewarm."

Patmos

MILES
80 Miles =
128 Kilometers
0 10 20 30 40 50 60 70 80

HISTORIC PREMILLENNIALISM

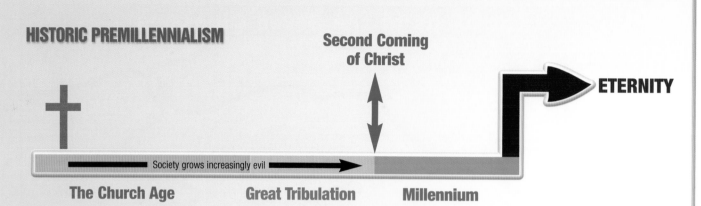

What is historic premillennialism?

Historic premillennialism is the belief that the Second Coming of Christ will precede the millennium and that the church has replaced the nation of Israel as God's covenant people. Also known as "covenant premillennialism," historic premillennialism treats the millennium as a literal future event. Most historic premillennialists believe that Christians will remain on the earth during the great tribulation. The tribulation will purify the churches by rooting out false believers. According to historic premillennialists . . .

- God's promises of land and blessings to Abraham and his offspring were conditional promises, based on obedience. Israel's persistent disobedience negated God's covenant with them.
- God has maintained a covenant of grace throughout the Old and New Testaments with all who trusted in Him. These believers—embodied today in the church—are the true Israel (see Romans 9:6-8; Galatians 6:16).
- Most references to "Israel" in Revelation refer symbolically to the church.

What Scriptures seem to support historic premillennialism?

- The revealing of the Antichrist precedes Christ's return—2 Thess. 2:3, 4.
- The tribulation will root out false members from the churches—Rev. 2:22, 23;
- The saints are on earth during the tribulation—Revelation 13:7
- God's promises to Abraham and his offspring were conditional—Gen. 22:18; 2 Chronicles 33:8; Isaiah 1:19, 20; Jeremiah 7:6, 7.
- The New Testament frequently uses "Israel" and "the twelve tribes" to refer to Christians—Romans 9:6-8; James 1:1.

When has historic premillennialism been popular? Historic premillennialism seems to have been the earliest view of the end-times among post-apostolic Christians. Many early church fathers—including Lactantius (AD 240-320), Irenaeus (AD 130-200), Justin Martyr (AD 100-165), and probably Papias (AD 60-130), a disciple of the apostle John—embraced historic premillennialism. Modern supporters include scholars such as John Warwick Montgomery, George R. Beasley-Murray, David Dockery, Robert Gundry, and George E. Ladd.

DISPENSATIONAL PREMILLENNIALISM

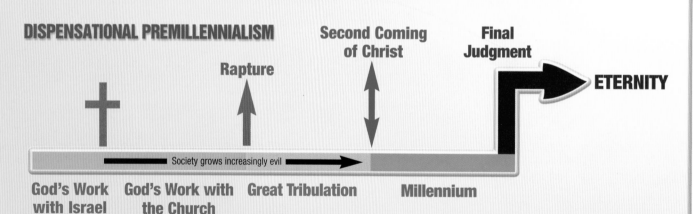

What is dispensational premillennialism?

Dispensational premillennialism is the belief that the Second Coming of Christ will precede the millennium and that God will still give the nation of Israel the land described in Genesis 15:18.
Dispensational premillennialism treats the millennium as a literal, future event. Most dispensational premillennialists are pre-tribulationists; they understand Rev. 4:1, 2 to refer to "the rapture," when Christ removes Christians from the earth before the great tribulation begins. Some dispensational premillennialists, known as mid-tribulationists, believe the rapture will occur during the great tribulation. According to the dispensational premillennialists . . .

- God's promises to Abraham and his offspring were unconditional; therefore, the Jews will still receive the land described in Genesis 15:18.
- During the great tribulation, many Jews will turn to Jesus Christ.
- All references to Israel in Revelation refer to the nation of Israel.

What Scriptures seem to support dispensational premillennialism?

- God's promises to Abraham and his offspring were unconditional— Genesis 15:7-21.
- God will keep Christians from the outpouring of His wrath during the tribulation —I Thessalonians 5:9; Revelation 3:10.
- The church is not specifically mentioned between Revelation 4 and 19.

When has dispensational premillennialism been popular? This view emerged in the 1800's among the Plymouth Brethren. Dispensational premillennialism increased in popularity in the late 1800's and has remained widespread throughout the 20th century. Proponents have included J. Nelson Darby, C.I. Scofield, Harry A. Ironside, Gleason Archer, Donald G. Barnhouse, Hal Lindsey, Chuck Smith, John MacArthur, Charles Ryrie, Charles Stanley, Norman L. Geisler, and Tim LaHaye.

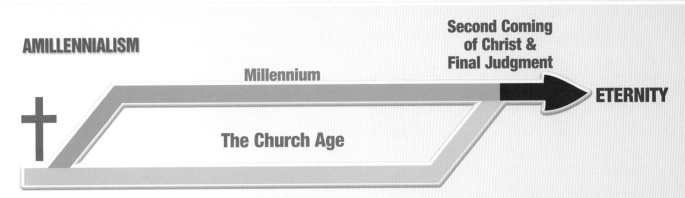

AMILLENNIALISM

Millennium

Second Coming of Christ & Final Judgment

ETERNITY

The Church Age

Tribulation

What is amillennialism?

Amillennialism is the belief that the millennium is the spiritual reign of Jesus in the hearts of his followers. Revelation 19:11-21 portrays Christ's triumph over Satan through His death and resurrection. This triumph restrained the power of Satan on the earth (Revelation 20:1-3). The "first resurrection" in Revelation 20:5 is not a physical restoration from the dead; it is the spiritual resurrection that is also known as regeneration. When Christ returns, He will immediately defeat the powers of evil, resurrect the saved and the unsaved, judge them, and deliver them to their eternal destinies.

According to amillennialists . . .

- The great tribulation represents calamities and persecutions that have occurred throughout church history.
- Most references to "Israel" in Revelation are symbolic references to the people of God on earth (compare Romans 9:6-8; Galatians 6:16).
- In apocalyptic literature, numbers represent concepts, not literal statistics. For example, six symbolizes incompleteness, seven represents completeness, ten indicates something that is extreme but limited, twelve represents the perfection of God's people, and one thousand symbolizes a great amount or long period of time.

What Scriptures seem to support amillennialism?

- The Bible frequently uses the number 1,000 figuratively—Psalms 50:10; 90:4; 105:8; 2 Peter 3:8.
- The first resurrection (Rev. 20:4) could refer to the spiritual resurrection (the regeneration or new birth) of persons who trust Christ—Rom. 11:13-15; Ephesians 2:1-4.
- The Second Coming of Christ and the resurrection of the saved and the unsaved will occur at the same time—Daniel 12:2, 3; John 5:28, 29.
- The saints are on earth during the tribulation—Revelation 13:7.

When has amillennialism been popular? Amillennialism became popular in the fifth century. Amillennialism has remained widespread throughout church history. Prominent amillennialists include the Protestant reformers Martin Luther and John Calvin, as well as evangelical theologians such as E.Y. Mullins, Abraham Kuyper, G.C. Berkouwer, Herschel Hobbs, Stanley Grenz, and J. I. Packer. Many students of church history believe that the church father Augustine of Hippo was the first amillennialist.

POSTMILLENNIALISM

Second Coming of Christ & Final Judgment

ETERNITY

Society gradually improves

The Church Age

Tribulation

Millennium

What is postmillennialism?

Postmillennialism is the belief that the Second Coming of Christ will occur after the millennium. The millennial reign described in Revelation 20:1-6 represents a long time period when, through the preaching of the gospel, most of the world will submit to Jesus Christ. During this time, Satan will have no power over the earth, and evil regimes will collapse (see Rev. 19:19–20:3). A period of great tribulation may precede the millennium. According to postmillennialists . . .

- During the millennium, Christ will rule the earth through His Spirit and through His church; He will not, however, be physically present on the earth.
- The resurrection depicted in Revelation 20:4 represents the spiritual regeneration of people who trust Jesus Christ.
- The Second Coming of Christ, the final conflict between good and evil, the defeat of Satan, the physical resurrection of all people, and the final judgment will occur together, immediately after the millennium (Rev. 20:7-15).

What Scriptures seem to support postmillennialism?

- Every ethnic group will receive the gospel before the Second Coming—Matthew 24:14; Mark 13:10.
- The first resurrection (Rev. 20:4) could refer to the spiritual resurrection (the regeneration or new birth) of persons who trust Christ—Romans 11:13-15; Ephesians 2:1-4.
- The Second Coming of Christ and the resurrection of all people, saved and unsaved, will occur at the same time—Dan. 12:2, 3; John 5:28, 29.

When has postmillennialism been popular? The earliest postmillennialist writer was Joachim of Fiore (AD 1135-1202). Postmillennialism became popular in the 19th century, partly because of that era's optimism about the future. Prominent postmillennialists include early church leaders such as Eusebius and Athanasius; preachers such as Jonathan Edwards and Charles Haddon Spurgeon; and theologians such as B. B. Warfield, Augustus H. Strong, Charles Hodge, R.L. Dabney, Loraine Boettner, and R.C. Sproul.

Four Views of the End Times Glossary

666 Number of the beast, recorded in Revelation 13:18. Neither Greek nor Hebrew had a written system of numbers. Instead, each letter of the alphabet indicated a different number. Many scholars have noted that, in Hebrew, the number of Emperor Nero's name is 666. (Nero reigned AD 54-68. He was the first emperor to persecute Christians.) Perhaps the best approach to the number is to remember that *six* is a symbol of incompleteness; 666 would, therefore, indicate absolute imperfection.

144,000 Group of believers who endure the great tribulation (Revelation 7:14). Some students believe that these persons are literally 144,000 Jews—12,000 from each tribe—who trust in Jesus Christ (see Revelation 7:4-9).[1] Others point out that, after the Assyrians conquered Israel (722 BC), ten of the tribes ceased to exist. Furthermore, in the New Testament, "Israel" and "twelve tribes" frequently refer to Christians (Rom. 9:6-8; Gal. 6:16; James 1:1; see also Matt. 19:28; Luke 22:30). So, this group could symbolize the church on earth. In this case, the number would symbolize the people of God (12) multiplied by the people of God (12) multiplied by greatness (1,000)—in other words, the full number of God's people who endure to the end.[2]

antichrist (From Greek, *antichristos,* in place of Christ) Anyone who denies the apostle's teachings about Jesus Christ (1 John 2:18-22; 4:3; 2 John 1:7). Specifically, the antichrist is a Satanic counterfeit of Jesus Christ, described as "lawless" (2 Thessalonians 2:3-8) and as a "beast" (Revelation 13:1-18; 17:3-17). The antichrist may be a specific person who rises to power during the tribulation. Or, the antichrist may be a symbol of the false teachers and leaders who will arise when the end of the age draws near.

apocalyptic literature (From Greek, *apokalypsis,* revealing) Jewish genre of writing, structured around visions that figuratively pointed to hidden truths for the purpose of assuring God's people of the goodness of God's plans during periods of persecution.

Armageddon (From Hebrew, *Har-Megiddon,* Mount Megiddo) The city of Megiddo was located between the Plain of Jezreel and the western coast of Israel. Deborah, Gideon, Saul, Ahaziah, and Josiah fought decisive battles near Megiddo. So, the valley of Megiddo became the symbol of a point of decisive conflict. Based on the reference to "Armageddon" in Revelation 16:16, some students believe that a literal battle will occur near Megiddo. Others, however, point out that there is no such place as *Mount* Megiddo; Megiddo lies in a broad plain.[3] These students understand the reference to Armageddon as a symbol of the ultimate conflict between good and evil.

Church age The time period from the beginning of the church (about AD 30) until Jesus Christ returns for everyone who has trusted in Him, as promised in John 14.

eschatology (From Greek, *eschatos,* final) Study of the Bible's teachings about events leading to Christ's second coming.

final judgement The event described in Revelation 20:11-15, when God resurrects all people, judges them, and delivers them to their eternal destinies.

first coming of Christ The earthly life and ministry of Jesus Christ, about 4 BC-AD 30.

mark of the beast Indication of a person's allegiance to antichrist (Rev. 13:16, 17). The people of God receive a similar mark, indicating their allegiance to Christ (Revelation 7:3; 9:4; 14:1; 22:4). Some premillennialists believe that the mark of the beast will be an actual mark, required by the the antichrist. Other interpreters of Revelation understand the mark as a reference to a person's deeds ("hand") and beliefs ("forehead"). "Hand" and "forehead" carry this meaning in Exodus 13:9, 16.

millennium (From Latin, *mille,* thousand) Christ's reign on earth, described in Revelation 20:4-6. Premillennialists believe that the millennium is a future event and that Christ will return *before* (pre-) the millennium. Amillennialists treat the millennium as a symbol of Christ's present reign among His people. Postmillennialists believe that Christ will return *after* (post-) the millennium.

rapture (From Latin, *raptus,* carry away) Event described in 1 Thessalonians 4:15-17, when Christ will return for His people. Dispensational premillennialists say the rapture and the second coming of Christ are two events. They place the rapture *before* the tribulation and the second coming *after* the tribulation. Historic premillennialists say that the rapture and second coming are one event.

second coming The bodily return of Jesus Christ to earth, to reign as king.

tribulation, great Time-period when severe calamities besiege the world and persons who remain faithful to Christ will suffer intense persecution (see Revelation 7:14). Amillennialists and many postmillennialists treat the tribulation as a symbol of the calamities and persecutions that have occurred throughout church history. Premillennialists place the tribulation at the end of time. Some premillennialists believe the tribulation will last exactly seven years. Other premillennialists view the seven years as a symbol of the completeness of God's dealings with the world.

---

[1] Hal Lindsey, *There's A New World Coming* (Santa Ana: Vision, 1973) 112-125; J. Vernon McGee, *Revelation Chapters 6-13* in *Thru the Bible Commentary* (Nashville: Nelson, 1991) 64-69.
[2] George E. Ladd, *A Commentary on the Revelation of John* (Grand Rapids: Eerdmans, 1972) 117; Herschel Hobbs, "Amillennialism," in *Revelation: Three Viewpoints* (Nashville: Broadman, 1977) 99.
[3] Bruce M. Metzger, *Breaking the Code* (Nashville: Abingdon, 1993) 84; Leon Morris, *The Revelation of St. John* (Grand Rapids: Eerdmans, 1984) 200; Robert H. Mounce, *The Book of Revelation* (Grand Rapids: Eerdmans, 1977) 302.

Archaeological Find	Description of the Find	Importance of the Find
The Life and Ministry of Jesus		

Matt.
Mark
Luke
John

1. The Church of the Nativity in Bethlehem

Archaeology has shown that the use of caves as animal stables in the Holy Land has been a common practice from very ancient times. Ancient records show that for at least two centuries before a church was built, Christians had marked this particular cave as the place of Jesus' birth.

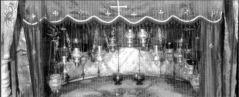

Since AD 326 a building known as the Church of the Nativity has stood over a cave at what was the ancient outskirts of Bethlehem.

Matthew 2:1-8, Luke 2:4-15, and John 7:42 all identify Bethlehem as the place of Jesus' birth. Because Joseph and Mary could find no room at the village inn and the newborn Jesus was laid in a manger (animal feedbox), it has been assumed that the birth took place in a stable. The niche at left marks the place that Christians throughout history identified as Jesus' birthplace. Archaeology and tradition combine in this instance to lend both accuracy and insight to the Gospel accounts.

John McRay

2. Nazareth, Hometown of Jesus

Today Nazareth is a bustling Arab-Jewish city built atop and around the ancient village, located in the southern hills of lower Galilee.

The modern Church of the Annunciation (left) stands over an ancient church building. Excavations in the church and around its grounds have turned up silos, olive oil presses, foundations of houses, and many artifacts from Christ's time. The nearby Church of St. Gabriel stands over the city's ancient well, and the well is still fed by fresh spring water.

Left: Church of the Annunciation

Little would be known about the town where Mary received the angelic news that she would give birth to Christ, and where Jesus grew up, if it were not for the Christian holy places and archaeology. Matthew 2:23, 4:13, Mark 1:9, and Luke 1:26-28 give the New Testament accounts of the events connected with Nazareth. John 1:46 also mentions Nazareth.

Gretchen Goldsmith

3. Bethsaida, City of Woe

Much of the ancient harbor city of Bethsaida has been recovered since 1987 after several seasons of archaeological work. It has finally been placed accurately on Biblical maps for the first time.

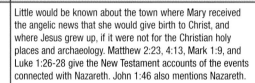

Bethsaida was the birthplace of Peter, Andrew, and Philip, and is mentioned in the Gospels more than any other city except Capernaum and Jerusalem. Jesus pronounced a "woe" (condemnation) upon the city in Matthew 11:21 and Luke 10:13. It was destroyed around AD 66-68, and was never rebuilt. Mark 8:22 and John 1:44 also mention Bethsaida.

John McRay

John

4. Cana, Site of a Wedding Feast

Archaeological investigations show that the ruins at Khirbet Qana are a village during the time of Christ. Its ruins are located about nine miles north of Nazareth.

The Gospel of John (John 2:1-11) records the miracle of Jesus turning water into wine during a wedding celebration in the village of Cana.

Right: Cana ruins at Khirbet Qana date to the time of Christ

John McRay

Matt.
Mark
Luke

5. The House Church at Capernaum

While excavating an early church building at Capernaum in 1968, archaeologists found that the building had been placed over a house from the time of Jesus.

Right: Words were found scratched on the walls of the house indicating that the early Christians believed the house had been that of the apostle Simon Peter.

Matthew 8:14, Mark 1:29, and Luke 4:38 all speak of Peter's house and Jesus' visits there. This probably is the reason Christians began to worship at this site.

Gretchen Goldsmith

Matt.
Mark
Luke
John

6. The Synagogue at Capernaum

Archaeologists have restored a synagogue that stood there some 350 years after Jesus' time. However, recently it was discovered that this synagogue was built over the foundation of the synagogue from Jesus' time, confirming that this is the place where important Bible events took place.

Capernaum served as Jesus' headquarters during his ministry in Galilee. According to Mark 1:21-28, 3:1-6, Luke 4:31-37, and John 6:59, Jesus both taught and healed people in the synagogue there.

Left: A newer synagogue at Capernaum was built on the foundation of the black basalt synagogue of Jesus' time (shown at right).

Gretchen Goldsmith

Matt.
Mark
Luke

7. Gergesa, Where Christ Cast Out Demons

The location of Gergesa has remained a mystery until recently. In 1970 Israeli archaeologist Vasilios Tzaferis investigated ruins of a Byzantine church from AD 585 uncovered during road construction along the east side of the Sea of Galilee.

The excavations turned up an ancient church building, monastery, and chapels. A mosaic-paved chapel had been built at the foot of a steep slope, leading Dr. Tzaferis to conclude that the ancient Christians had built the entire complex here to preserve an early tradition that this was where the miracle occurred in which swine ran off a cliff into the sea.

In Matthew 8:28-34 Christ casts demons out of two men into a herd of swine that ran down a steep place into the Sea of Galilee. Two other possible locations were thought to be Gadara or Gerasa (Mark 5:1-13; Luke 8:26-39) but both are located far from the Sea of Galilee or any steep place. The ruins of the El-Kursi monastery probably mark the location of Gergesa.

John

8. Jacob's Well Near Sychar

The well can be found today beside what archaeologists have identified as the ancient north-south road near Mount Gerizim, in the eastern part of Nablus.

Today the well is still fed by an underground stream, and an unfinished church building covers it.

John 4:1-42 tells the story of Jesus' encounter with a Samaritan woman at Jacob's well. Since ancient times Christian pilgrims have come to the well and have written about it.

Archaeological Find	Description of the Find	Importance of the Find
The Life and Ministry of Jesus		

9. Jericho, Where Jesus Met Zacchaeus

Most of the ruins of Herod the Great's winter palace at Jericho reveal that it was built in the finest Roman style. Jericho is where Herod the Great built many grand buildings at great public expense.

The Jericho of Jesus' day lay a few miles south of the Old Testament city. Jericho was connected to Jerusalem by means of a 17-mile-long road that ran through a steep valley. Among the structures discovered there were Herod the Great's winter palace and a hippodrome (stadium for horse races and other spectacles).

Herod the Great was king when Jesus was born (Matthew 2:1-12). Jericho was the city where Jesus encountered Zacchaeus, a tax collector (Luke 19:2-10). Jericho is also the setting of Jesus' story of "The Good Samaritan" (Luke 10:30-37).

---

10. The Pool of Bethesda in Jerusalem

Site of Jesus' healing of a paralyzed man (John 5:2-11), much of the remains of this pool have been unearthed since 1956.

At right are the ruins of what was the Pool of Bethesda. Portions of the five porticos (roofs supported by columns) mentioned in the Gospel story have been found and can be seen by visitors today.

John 5:2 (NIV) says, "Now there is in Jerusalem near the Sheep Gate a pool, which in Aramaic is called Bethesda and which is surrounded by five covered colonnades."

---

11. Bethany, Where Jesus Raised Lazarus

A village grew around the first century AD tombs that once comprised Bethany's cemetery. Since early Christian times one tomb has been said to be that of Lazarus.

By the AD 300s a church had been built over the tomb of Lazarus, with steps leading down into the tomb. Today visitors can still visit that ancient tomb and reflect on the great miracle Jesus performed there.

The village of Bethany is mentioned 13 times in the New Testament. Located on the east side of the Mount of Olives, only a short distance from Jerusalem, it was a favorite stopover for Jesus and the disciples when they came to Jerusalem. It was from Bethany's cemetery that Jesus raised Lazarus (John 11).

---

12. The Pontius Pilate Inscription

In 1961 archaeologists working at the ruins of Caesarea Maritima, in Israel, found a stone slab bearing the name of Pontius Pilate, who was involved in the trial of Jesus.

Right: Portion of the stone, bearing Pilate's name, which commemorated his dedication of a temple to Emperor Tiberius.

This is the oldest appearance of Pilate's name to be found, and it actually dates to the time of Jesus.
Luke 3:1 says: "Now in the fifteenth year of the reign of Tiberias Caesar, Pontius Pilate being governor of Judea, and Herod being tetrarch of Galilee…"

---

13. Caiaphas's Family Tomb

In 1990 builders accidentally uncovered a first century AD burial cave south of Jerusalem. Later, archaeologists investigated, and found several stone boxes (called ossuaries) that contained human bones.

Left: The ossuary of Caiaphas, the priest who brought Jesus to trial. Ossuaries were used to store the bones of several generations of family members.

Inside the stone boxes were the bones of two infants, a child, a teenager, a woman, and a man. One box had the name "Caiaphas" on it. The man's bones may be those of Caiaphas, the priest who brought Jesus to trial, mentioned in Matthew 26:57 and John 18:13, 14.

---

14. Crucifixion Evidence

In 1968, the bones of a young man who had been crucified during New Testament times were found in the Jerusalem area. The bones were found in a stone box bearing the name "Yehohanan."

A 7-inch long nail was still embedded in the heel bone.

This find shows gruesome evidence of how the Romans crucified persons such as Jesus. Luke 23:33 NIV says, "When they came to the place called the Skull, there they crucified him [Jesus], along with the criminals—one on his right, the other on his left."

---

15. Rolling Stone Tombs

At several places in modern Israel there are examples of the type of tomb in which Jesus' body was placed after the Crucifixion. Mostly cut into the sides of hills, each used a large circular stone to cover the entrance.

Inside tombs is a central room, called an antechamber, and as many as six to eight burial shafts. Later, as the bodies decayed, the bones would be removed from each shaft and placed in a covered stone box (called an ossuary) in the central room. The photograph at right was taken from inside the tomb, looking out past the rolling stone and up the steps.

At right is a tomb with a rolling stone entrance. The curved edge of the stone is on the right. Tombs were mostly cut into the sides of hills and used a large circular stone to roll in front of the entrance. Matt. 27:60; 28:2; Mk. 15:46; 16:3, 4; Luke 24:2.

---

16. Jesus' Burial Place, the Tomb of Joseph of Arimathea

Two different places in Jerusalem have been pointed out as the site of the tomb from which Jesus arose. Most archaeologists believe that the Church of the Holy Sepulchre, built around AD 340, stands over the site of the tomb.

Archaeology in and around the Church of the Holy Sepulchre has revealed a rock quarry from the end of the Old Testament era. Tombs had been cut into the quarry wall during the first century AD. The other proposed site for the tomb is the Garden Tomb, or "Gordon's Calvary."

Archaeology in the Garden Tomb area has turned up tombs of the type used during Old Testament times, with some having been reused between AD 400-600. Evidence from both locations may shed new light on the search for this all-important Christian site. Matthew 27:57-60, Mark 15:45-46, Luke 23:50-53, and John 19:38-42 refer to the tomb of Joseph of Arimathea.

Archaeological Find	Description of the Find	Importance of the Find
Palestine and Trans-Jordan		
17. Megiddo (Church Inscription) In 2005, a prayer hall was discovered outside of the Megiddo Prison. The floor of the prayer hall features a detailed mosaic floor with inscriptions that consecrate the church to "God Jesus Christ."	*Right: This inscription on the mosaic floors consecrates the church to God Jesus Christ. The name of Jesus is identified as being sacred by a line place above it.* 	The Bible teaches and the Christian Church has always upheld that Jesus is God (John 1:1-5, 20:28; Hebrews 1:6-8). This find verifies that the Christian Church recognized the divinity of Jesus as early as the third century.
18. Herodium, King Herod's Palace While failing to find Herod's tomb itself, excavations near Bethlehem have revealed much of one of his luxurious palaces.	An ancient non-biblical writer, Josephus, wrote that Herod was buried at his 45-acre palace, called Herodium, about two miles southeast of Bethlehem.	Matthew 2:19, 20 tells of the death of King Herod while the young child Jesus was in Egypt. Matthew 2:1-16 and Luke 1:5 also refer to Herod.
19. The Madaba Mosaic Map This mosaic map of the Holy Land was made about AD 560 to serve as the decorative floor of an early church located near the Dead Sea in modern Jordan.	 *Left: Portion of Madaba mosaic map*	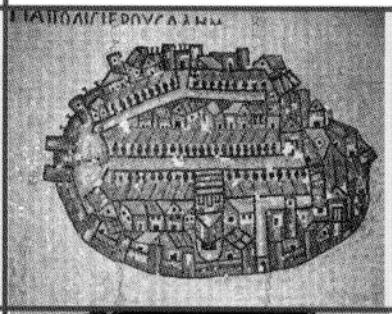  This oldest map of the Holy Land yet found shows the locations of dozens of places where important Biblical events occurred. *Left: Madaba mosaic map*
20. The Galilee Boat When drought caused the waters of the Sea of Galilee to recede in 1986, residents of a village on the northwest shore found a boat buried in the mud. Later it was removed and restored.	Coins and pottery found with the boat date to New Testament times. The only such boat ever found, it shows what the boats used by Jesus and the disciples were like.	 *Left: The prow of a boat similar to those used by Jesus and his disciples. (Matthew 8:23; Mark 1; 3–6; 8; Luke 5; 8; John 6:22)*
21. Tiberias, Capital City on the Sea of Galilee The modern city of Tiberias stands today over much of the ancient one. However, excavations in 1973-74 revealed two large round stone towers on either side of the main gate dating to the city of Jesus' time.	Herod Antipas (one of Herod the Great's sons) founded Tiberias in AD 18 as the capital of Galilee. He was involved in Jesus' trial.  *Left: Synagogue floor preserved in Tiberias.*	Although Tiberias is mentioned only once in Scripture (John 6:23), it was an important city of the area where Jesus probably carried out much of his ministry.
22. Caesarea Philippi Excavations since 1990 have recovered much of the city of Caesarea Philippi from Jesus' day.	A large palace was found which matches Josephus's descriptions of that of Herod Agrippa II, a descendant of Herod the Great. Herod Agrippa II was the governor of Galilee before whom Paul gave a defense of his faith (see Acts 26:2-29).	According to Matthew 16:13-20 and Mark 8:27-30 Jesus and the disciples were near this city when Jesus asked them who people were saying he was. Peter said, "You are the Christ."
23. Caesarea on the Sea Since the 1950s excavations have turned up most of Herod's harbor, as well as city streets, a theater, the marketplace, shops, aqueducts, temples, and private dwellings.	 Excavations of Caesarea illustrate how important this city was in Jesus' and Paul's day. *Caesarea's amphitheater*	Caesarea is where the Apostle Peter first won Gentile converts (Acts 10), and was the site of his imprisonment (Acts 23–26). It was also the home of the Roman governors, such as Pontius Pilate. The city began as Herod's dream and grew into Roman Palestine's major port and governmental center. King Herod Agrippa I was smitten of God in this amphitheater (Acts 12:23).
24. Megiddo (Armageddon), City of War Archaeology validates the biblical references by revealing a Canaanite city, under the ruins of a heavily fortified Israelite city with a strong city gate.	*Right: The Bamah of Megiddo (round object right of center)*	Because of its strategic location on a hill beside a wide plain, Megiddo witnessed many battles during the Old Testament period. Revelation 16:16 refers to Megiddo (then called Armageddon) as the place where Christ's faithful people battle the forces of Satan in the end times.
25. Sepphoris, Metropolis of Galilee Extensive excavations at Sepphoris have revealed that it was a sizable city built on a Roman plan.	Among the excavated ruins are a large theater, temples, public buildings, and a lavish palace with beautiful mosaics. Although Sepphoris was located only about three miles from Nazareth, it is mentioned nowhere in the New Testament.	Because Sepphoris was very near Nazareth, it is possible that Joseph and the young Jesus could have worked on building projects there. It was also the chief residence of Herod Antipas, who played a role in Jesus' trial in Jerusalem.
26. The Ten Cities of the Decapolis Archaeologists have located almost all ten cities (only the identification of Tell el-Ashari, in Jordan, with Dion remains indefinite). Enough archaeological work has been done to confirm that these were important and wealthy cities in Jesus' day.	 *Left: Beth Shean, also known as Sythopolis, one of the Decapolis. (Deca = 10; polis = city)*	Two of the Gospels (Matthew 4:25; Mark 5:20; 7:31) speak of the spread of Jesus' message among the people of the Decapolis, a league of ten cities where Greek language and culture flourished. One ancient writer lists them as Damascus, Abila, Scythopolis, Hippos, Raphana, Gadara, Pella, Dion, Philadelphia, and Gerasa. For many years the locations of only about half of the cities were known.

Side labels (left margin):
Matt. Luke (18)
Matt. Mark Luke John (20)
John (21)
Matt. Mark Acts (22)
Acts (23)
Rev. (24)
Matt. Mark (26)

Photo credits (right margin): Zev Radovan; Gretchen Goldsmith; Zev Radovan; John McRay; Gretchen Goldsmith; Larry McKinney; Gretchen Goldsmith

Archaeological Find	Description of the Find	Importance of the Find

Jerusalem and the Temple of Jesus' Day

	Archaeological Find	Description of the Find	Importance of the Find
Matt. Mark John	**27. Herod's Palace and Pilate's Praetorium in Jerusalem** Since about AD 1100, some pavement north of the Temple Mount has been pointed out as the Praetorium, but archaeologists have found that it dates to about a century after Jesus' and Paul's time.	More recently, archaeologists have identified some Herodian walls, foundations and pavement near the present Jaffa Gate that conform to ancient descriptions of the Praetorium. These remnants can be found today in the vicinity of the Armenian Orthodox Seminary and what is called "the Citadel," or "David's Tower."	Eight passages in the New Testament refer to a place in Jerusalem called in Greek "the Praetorium." In those passages "Praetorium" has been translated as, "the palace courtyard," "the headquarters," "the governor's headquarters," "Pilate's headquarters," "Herod's headquarters," and "the place of the imperial guard." It is where Jesus was brought before Pontius Pilate (Matthew 27:27; Mark 15:16; John 18:28-33).
Matt. Mark Luke	**28. The Jerusalem Temple of Jesus' Day (Herod's Temple)** Beginning in 1968 excavations commenced in the area of the south retaining wall of the Temple Mount in Jerusalem.	The work has uncovered much of this part of the Temple as it was in Jesus' day, including the southern gates and steps leading up to them. At right is the only step on the Temple Mount believed to be from Jesus' day. 	It is unknown which entrance to the Temple Mount Jesus and the disciples used in Matthew 21, Mark 11, Luke 19-21, and John 2,5, and 7. Luke 1:9 mentions the priest's custom of burning incense when he went into the Temple of the Lord.
	29. "Place of Trumpeting," Temple Inscription from Jesus' Day In 1969 excavators removing debris from the southwest corner of the retaining wall of the ancient Temple in Jerusalem found a rectangular capstone from one of the Temple towers.	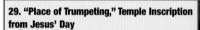	The "place of trumpeting" on the stone refers to the place where the priests blew trumpets announcing the beginnings of holy festivals (Psalm 81:3 and Joel 2:15). This rare find brings to life the Temple rituals of Jesus' day. *Left: The Hebrew words carved into this Temple tower capstone say, "…to the place of the trumpeting."*
	30. A Temple Sundial Relic from Jesus' Day During excavations around Jerusalem's Temple Mount in 1972, excavators found a limestone sundial in a pile of debris left by the Roman army when they destroyed the Temple in AD 70.	Archaeologists discovered that the notches cut into the face of the sundial were carefully calibrated to tell the time and seasons based on the sun's movement in Jerusalem. Carved on its back is a seven-branched menorah (candelabra), like the large one in the Temple. The pile of debris bears testimony to the Roman destruction of the Temple.	Jesus said in Mark 13:2, regarding the Temple, "Not one stone will be left upon another that will not be thrown down" (Matt. 24:2; Luke 21:6). The calibrations on the sundial speak to the importance of correctly measuring both time and the seasons in the priests' performance of the Temple rituals.
Acts Eph.	**31. Fragments of a Warning to Gentiles from the Temple of Jesus' Day** In 1871 a stone slab containing Greek writing surfaced in Jerusalem. In 1938 another slab similar to it was found just north of the Temple Mount. Both translate, "No gentile may enter within this Temple barrier! Anyone caught will be responsible for his own death."	 *Left: Stone slab with Greek writing gives warning that Gentiles should not enter the Temple. (In Acts 21:27-29 the Jews accused Paul of bringing Greeks into the Temple.)*	According to Josephus, a Jewish writer of the first century, these warnings were hung on a low wall that divided the public square of the Temple from the sacred inner courtyard that was accessible only to Jews. These rare finds from the Temple of Jesus' day shed light on the Temple regulations, and enrich our understanding of the importance of Ephesians 2:14, "For he [Jesus] is our peace, who has made us both one, and has broken down the dividing wall of hostility."
Mark Luke Hebrews	**32. The Holy of Holies in the Temple of Jesus' Day** Archaeologist and leading authority on the Temple, Leen Ritmeyer, has now found what appear to be the foundations of the walls of the Holy of Holies (the most sacred portion) of the ancient Temple.	*The Temple was completely destroyed by the Romans in AD 70. Six centuries later the Muslims built a shrine called the Dome of the Rock on the vacant Temple Mount (right). Many scholars conclude that the exact location of the Temple can no longer be found. However, in the bedrock beneath the Dome of the Rock, trenches were discovered, cut into the rock. Photo shot from above.*	The trenches conform precisely to the dimensions of the walls of the Holy of Holies, as described in ancient Jewish writings. Finding the trenches that match the dimensions of the walls of the Holy of Holies could well provide the location of the events recorded in Mark 15:38 and Luke 23:45 (the veil of the Temple was torn in two from top to bottom when Jesus died). The Holy of Holies is mentioned in Hebrews 6:19, 9:3-11, 10:20.
Mark Luke	**33. The Arch of Titus** Carved in relief on the triumphal Arch of Titus, in the ancient Forum (public square) of Rome, is a scene of Roman soldiers on parade carrying the sacred items looted from the Temple in Jerusalem in AD 70. These items included the Table of the Showbread, the Menorah (Golden Lampstand), and a scroll of God's Law.		Between Christ's resurrection and the time when Christianity was spreading throughout the Mediterranean world, a cataclysmic event occurred—the Roman army, under General Titus, invaded Jerusalem. On the ninth of Av (a Jewish calendar month corresponding to June) in AD 70, the army destroyed both the city and the Temple, carrying away the sacred Temple items. In the ancient Forum in the city of Rome there still stands a triumphal archway commemorating the victory of Titus and his army. See Mark 13:2; Luke 2:16.

Archaeological Find	Description of the Find	Importance of the Find
The Ministry of Paul		

The Ministry of Paul

34. Damascus, City of Saul's Conversion

Located in Syria, modern Damascus covers most of the ancient city today. Limited excavations have revealed some of the city's Roman gates, arches, and even the remains of "the street called Straight," where Saul stayed during his sojourn in the city (Acts 9:11).

Acts

Though first mentioned in the Bible in Genesis 14:15, Damascus is important also in the New Testament as the site of the conversion and early witness of Saul (Paul), as recorded in Acts 9:1-25. This reference reveals that Saul stayed at a home located on the main east-west road, near the heart of the city.

Left: Straight Street in modern Damascus.

35. The Politarch Inscriptions

Thirty-two inscriptions have been found that have the term "politarchs" ("city authorities"), and nineteen of them come from Thessalonica. At least three inscriptions date from Paul's time.

Because the Greek term "politarchs" could not be found in existing ancient literature outside of the New Testament, some critics argued that Luke must have been mistaken in his use of the term in Acts 17:6. That passage speaks of some believers at Thessalonica being dragged by a mob before the "politarchs." At least three inscriptions date from Paul's time, showing that Luke was quite correct in this detail.

36. The Areopagus at Athens

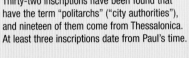

Archaeological investigations have located two terraces linked by steps on the hill. The upper terrace has a long rock-cut bench designed for seating many persons. Since early Christian times, a hill in the heart of Athens, immediately west of the Acropolis, has been referred to as the Areopagus.

Left: Areopagus (Mars Hill) in Athens, Greece

Acts 17:19-34 gives the account of Paul's presentation of the Gospel before the Athenian administrative council, known as the Areopagus. The term "Areopagus" is Greek for "Hill of Ares (or Mars)." The council seems to have taken its name from the place where they met.

37. The Gallio Inscription

Archaeologists found a stone inscription at Delphi, in Greece, that mentions a Roman governor (proconsul) named Gallio of the province of Achaia.

This inscription contains a Roman date, corresponding to 52 AD. The name "Gallio" is highlighted.

Gallio is the same governor referred to in Acts 18:12. The date on this inscription allows Bible scholars to know almost exactly when the Apostle Paul was ministering to early Christians in Corinth.

38. The Bema at Corinth

One of the most important New Testament archaeological finds from Corinth is the city's "Bema," a platform where officials addressed the public.

Left: Wall at right is the platform on which the Bema was built. Spectators stood about 7.5 feet below on stone pavement.

In AD 51 the Apostle Paul was brought before the Roman governor Gallio at this platform in Corinth (Acts 18:12-17). The Bema was discovered in 1935. The identity of the Bema is certain because of seven pieces of an inscription found nearby.

39. Ephesus, Jewel of Asia Minor

Archaeology has recovered much of the city of Ephesus from Paul's day. The temple of Artemis, one of the seven wonders of the ancient world, has been located. Also found was the theater where Paul's companions were dragged during a riot of silversmiths resulting from Paul's preaching (Acts 19:23-41).

This large city was the place the Apostle Paul stayed the longest during his missionary journeys (Acts 18:19-21 and 19:1-41). The letter to the Ephesians was written to the believers at Ephesus by Paul.

Right: A statue of Diana (Artemis), the goddess worshiped by the Ephesians and mentioned in Acts 19.

40. The Erastus Inscription

Romans

In 1929 archaeologists found a paving stone near the theater of Corinth in Greece that contains Erastus's name, and notes that he was indeed a Roman public official there.

Writing from Corinth, the Apostle Paul passed along greetings from several Corinthian believers, including Erastus, the city treasurer or chamberlain (Romans 16:23). This find, with seven inch high letters, verifies Erastus's existence as a public official in Corinth just as the Bible says.

Right: Erastus's name on paving stone. Foot at top shows size.

Early Christianity in the Mediterranean World

41. Thessalonica, Capital of Macedonia

Acts
1 Thes.
2 Thes.

Located about 115 miles southwest of Philippi, along the ancient Roman highway known as the Via Egnatia, lies the city of Thessalonica. The Via Egnatia was an important east-west Roman highway that passed through this area.

Archaeological remains include the remnants of several early church buildings, a Roman triumphal arch, and some of the city's ancient walls. Little is seen here from the time of Paul because modern Salonika, the second largest city in Greece, covers the buried remains of Roman Thessalonica.

According to Acts 17:1-10 Paul visited here, preaching three times in the synagogue. He was subsequently expelled from the city. Still, he persisted in planting a church, and eventually wrote two epistles to the Christians there. Thessalonica went on to become an important center of early Christianity, with several churches.

Archaeological Find	Description of the Find	Importance of the Find

Early Christianity in the Mediterranean World

Acts

42. Antioch, Important Center of Early Christianity

Artifacts found in Antioch (in Turkey today) reveal that the city had a population that was diverse racially and ethnically. It was an important crossroad in the immense Roman highway system. It grew to be second only to Jerusalem as a large center of Christianity.

Excavations have shown that Antioch was a large Roman city in Paul's day covered today by the Turkish city of Antakya.

Acts 11 and 14 recount the work of Paul and Barnabas in Antioch helping to build a Christian community made up of people from a wide variety of backgrounds. These finds help to explain why the establishment of the strong body of believers at Antioch played such a vital role in the future spread of Christianity throughout the entire Mediterranean region.

Left: Modern Antakya, Turkey

Acts Phil.

43. Philippi, Where Paul First Preached in Europe

Among the ruins at Philippi are numerous carved shrines to various Greco-Roman and eastern gods and goddesses. On top of the city's acropolis (highest hill) are the remains of ramparts (defensive walls) and a theater.

Left: Excavated area of the Roman forum in Philippi.

Located in northeast Greece, Philippi is where Paul preached his first sermon on European soil, and won a convert in Lydia, "a seller of purple" (see Acts 16:12-14). Paul wrote a letter to the Philippians.

Right: The Via Egnatia, an important east-west Roman highway that passed through this significant early seat of Christianity.

Acts

44. "God Fearers" Inscriptions

At the ancient sites of Aphrodisias and Miletus in modern Turkey, scholars have discovered two interesting inscriptions carved in marble.

Each inscription contains the term "theosebeis" ("God Fearers") with reference to a group identified by outsiders as being a part of the Jews.

This term is much the same as what is found in Acts 13:16 and Acts 17 where the meaning has puzzled scholars for a long time. The inscriptions show that the God Fearers likely were non-Jews who believed in the God of Israel.

Rev.

45. Seven Churches of Revelation

Archaeological excavations have now been carried out at all seven ancient cities, and the work at Ephesus, Smyrna, Pergamum, and Sardis in particular has been very extensive.

Little remains of Smyrna from the New Testament period. Today the city of Izmir in Turkey covers Smyrna's remains.

In Revelation 1:11 John is instructed by the Lord to send messages to seven churches in the Roman province of Asia, located in western Turkey today. Revelation 2 and 3 contain the messages addressed to the churches at Ephesus, Smyrna, Pergamum, Thyatira, Sardis, Philadelphia, and Laodicea.

Ancient Manuscripts

46. The Dead Sea Scrolls

These finds, including both entire ancient scrolls and scraps of them, were found mostly in caves along the northwest shore of the Dead Sea. In 1947 shepherds found the first seven scrolls stuffed in ancient pottery jars in a cave.

Practically all of the Dead Sea scrolls are written in Hebrew and Aramaic. Among them are the oldest copies yet found of almost all of the books of the Old Testament. They date from between about 300 BC to AD 70. Also of special significance are the non-biblical documents, which reveal much about the varied nature of Judaism during the time between the Old and New Testament periods.

Right: One of the eleven caves in the Qumran area, about seven miles south of Jericho, where the scrolls were found. These scrolls were important for shedding light on the Bible.

47. Earliest New Testament Copy

In 1920 a British traveler in Egypt acquired a small fragment of papyrus (a paperlike substance made from woven reed stalks). Later, scholars discovered that the writing on it was from the Gospel of John.

Left: An illustration of the oldest New Testament fragment yet found. The words on it are from John 18:31-33, 37-38. Since the discovery of the Dead Sea Scrolls some scholars believe the original (autograph) may have been written as early as the AD 40s. It was part of a codex dated AD 125. It is known as the John Rylands Papyrus and is in the John Rylands Library in Manchester, England.

Because no originals of the Biblical books have survived, scholars have relied on the finds of ancient copies to piece together the text of the Bible. The papyrus codex was likely copied within a generation of the original book of John itself.

48. Oldest Copy of John's Gospel

In 1956 the world learned of the existence of a copy of the Gospel of John that had been penned in Greek on papyrus AD 150-200.

Hailed as the oldest remaining copy of the majority of John's Gospel, about two-thirds of the text has survived the ravages of time. Swiss industrialist M. Martin Bodmer purchased it in Egypt, and later gave it to a museum.

This early copy has proved invaluable to Bible scholars and translators for helping to reconstruct the most accurate Greek text possible of the Gospel of John.

49. The Oldest Complete Copy of the New Testament

In 1844 New Testament scholar Konstantin von Tischendorf discovered the oldest surviving copy of the New Testament. He found it among the books belonging to a monastery that has stood at the foot of Mount Sinai since ancient times.

Known today as Codex Sinaiticus, this Bible was written on parchment around AD 350. This text is also known by the name "'Aleph," the Hebrew letter "A." The other early key Greek text is Codex Vaticanus, also known as "B."

Right: Drawing of parchment codex made from fine quality skins of sheep or goats.

Codex Sinaiticus has proved vital to scholars and translators in verifying the accuracy with which the New Testament has been reproduced across the ages. When new Bible versions refer to "most reliable texts," they are referring to "A" and "B."

50. Greco-Roman References to Jesus

Flavius Josephus, Jewish historian, wrote Antiquities (AD 93), which mentions both Jesus and his brothers. Tacitus wrote Annals between AD 115-117, which mentions Jesus' execution by Pilate.

Antiquities states, "About this time arose Jesus, a wise man. For he was a doer of marvelous deeds, and a teacher of men who gladly receive the truth. And when Pilate,...had condemned him to the cross, those who had loved him at first did not cease to do so. And even to this day the race of Christians, who are named from him, has not died out."

Tacitus's Annals state, "Christus, from whom the name [Christians] had its origin, suffered the extreme penalty during the reign of Tiberias at the hand of one of our procurators, Pontius Pilate, and a deadly superstition, thus checked for the moment, again broke out not only in Judaea, the first source of the evil, but also in the City..."

MAPS

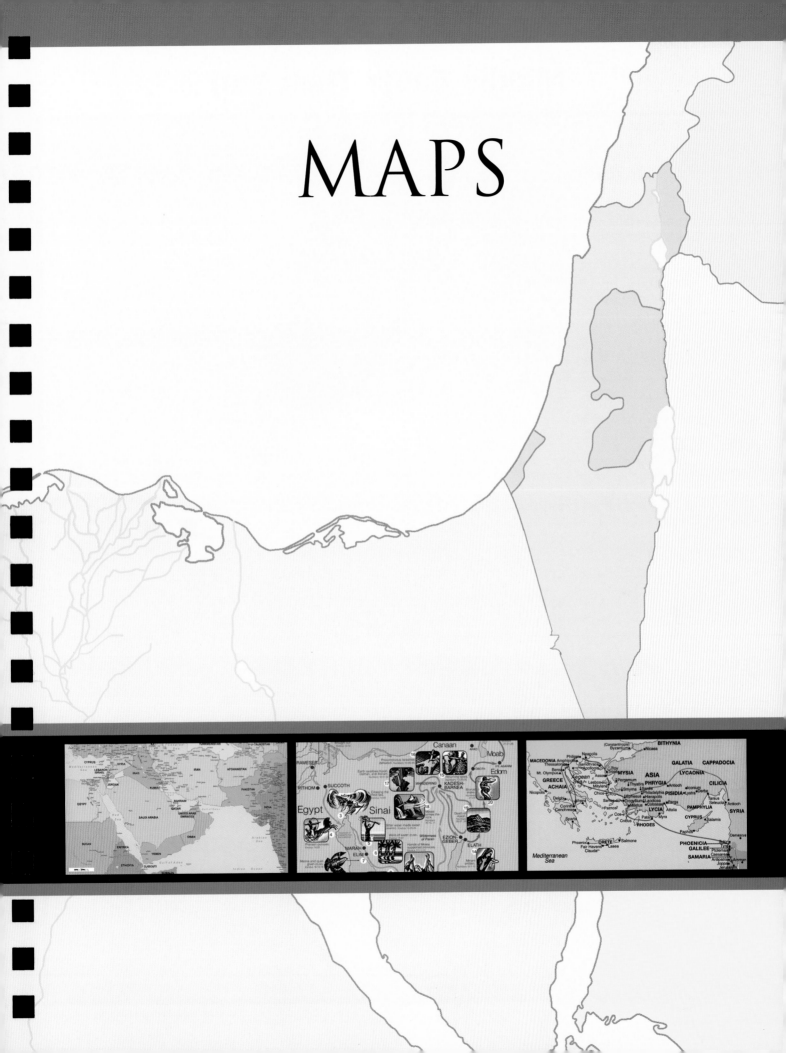

Middle East: Then (BC)

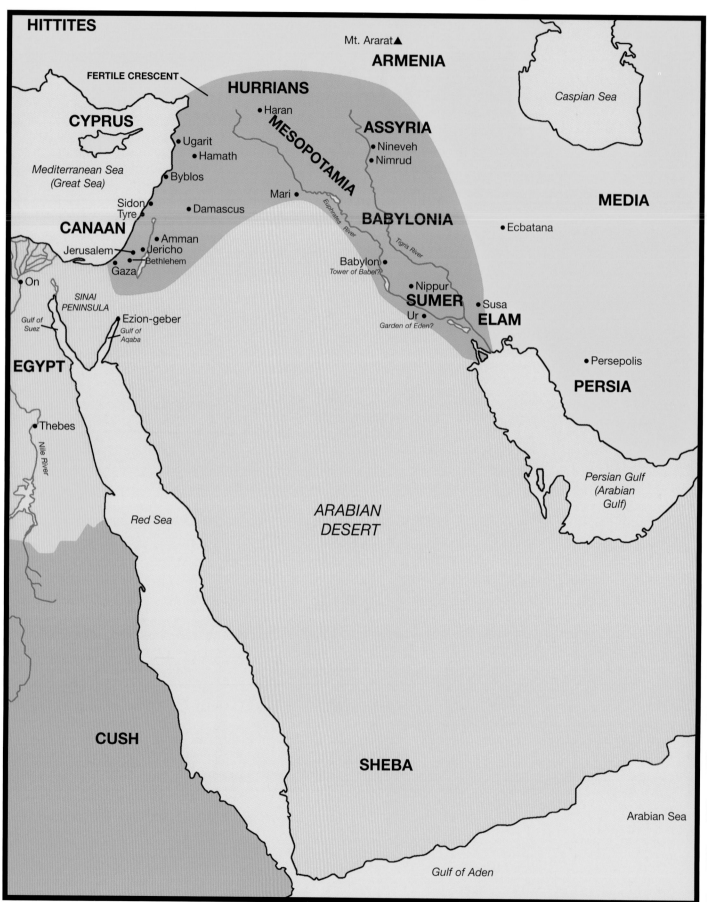

HITTITES

Mt. Ararat▲

ARMENIA

FERTILE CRESCENT

HURRIANS

Caspian Sea

CYPRUS

•Haran

ASSYRIA

•Ugarit

•Nineveh

•Hamath

•Nimrud

MESOPOTAMIA

Mediterranean Sea
(Great Sea)

•Byblos

MEDIA

Mari•

Sidon•

•Damascus

Euphrates River

Tyre•

BABYLONIA

•Ecbatana

CANAAN

•Amman

Tigris River

Jerusalem—

•Jericho

Babylon

Bethlehem

Tower of Babel?

Gaza

•Nippur

SUMER

•Susa

•On

Ur•

ELAM

SINAI
PENINSULA

Garden of Eden?

Ezion-geber

•Persepolis

Gulf of
Suez

Gulf of
Aqaba

PERSIA

EGYPT

•Thebes

Nile River

Persian Gulf
(Arabian
Gulf)

Red Sea

ARABIAN
DESERT

CUSH

SHEBA

Arabian Sea

Gulf of Aden

Middle East: Now

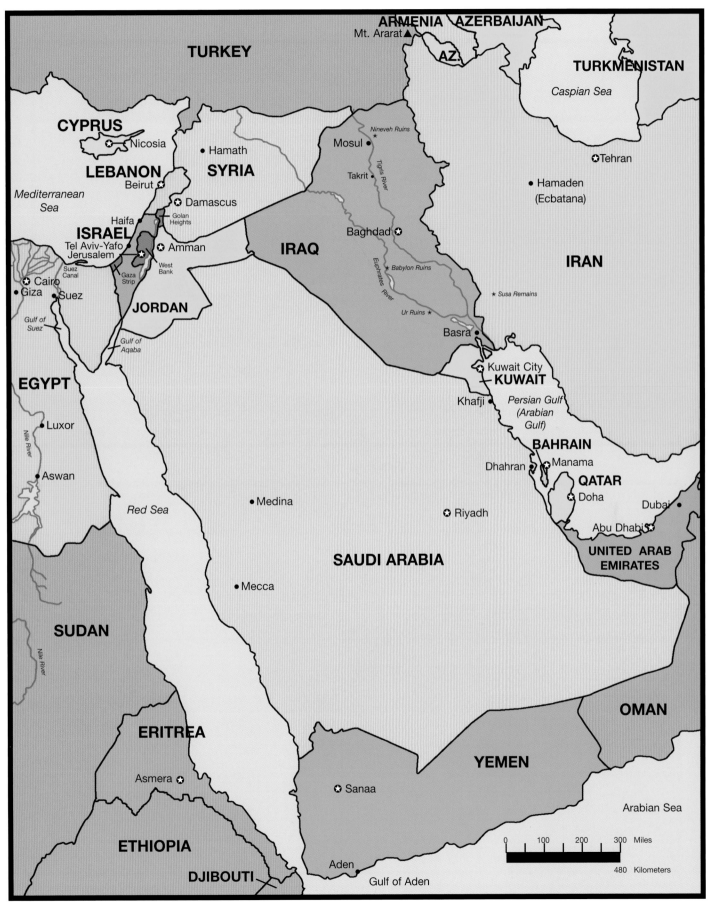

Middle East: Expansion by Assyrian Rulers

Ashurnasirpal II 875 BC

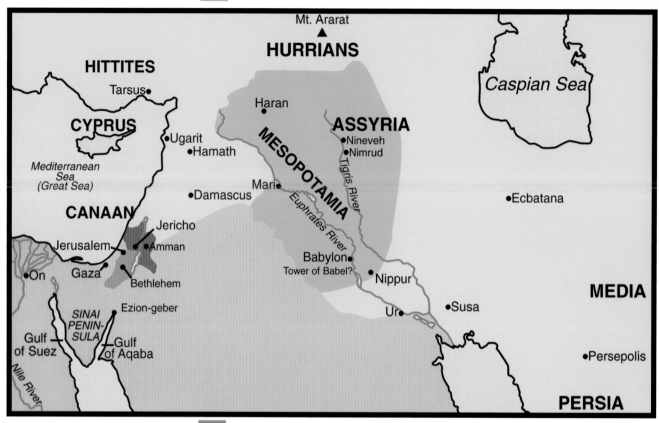

Shalmaneser III 850 BC

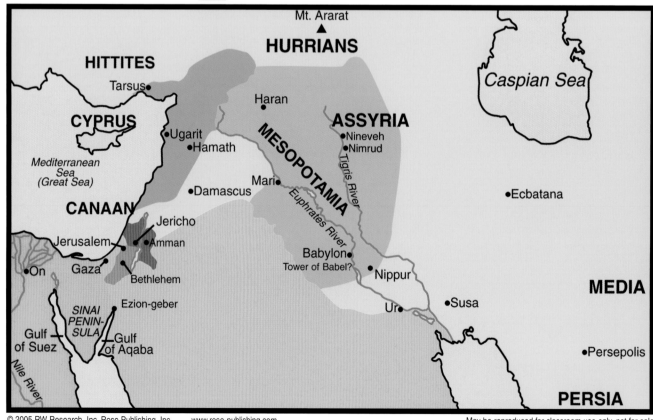

Middle East: Expansion by Assyrian Rulers

Sargon II 720 BC and Sennacherib 700 BC

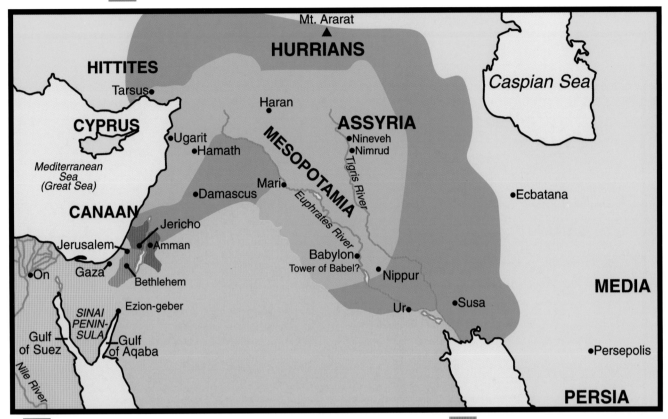

Esarhaddon 675 BC and Ashurbanipal 650 BC   Jerusalem (not under Assyrian control)

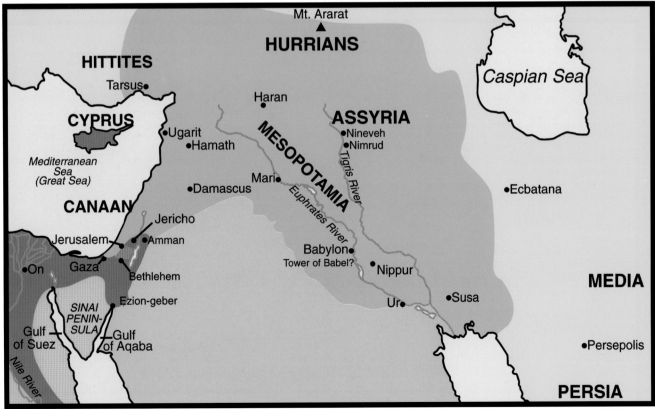

Middle East: Babylonian and Persian Empires

	Babylonian Kingdom		Lydian Kingdom		Scythians
	Median Kingdom		Arabian Desert		

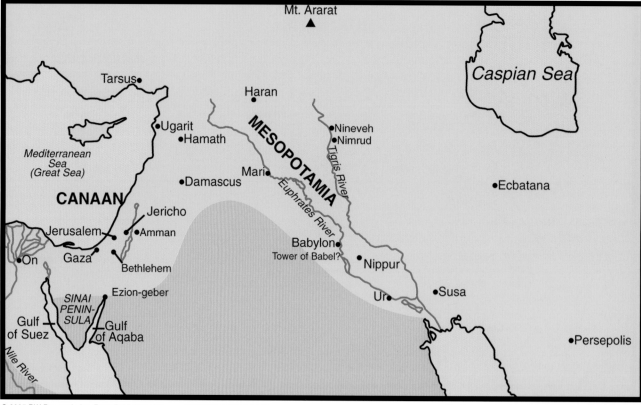

Babylonian Empire

Mt. Ararat ▲

Caspian Sea

Tarsus•

Haran•

CYPRUS

•Ugarit
•Hamath

MESOPOTAMIA

•Nineveh
•Nimrud

Mediterranean
Sea
(Great Sea)

Mari•

BABYLONIA

•Ecbatana

•Damascus

Tigris River

CANAAN

Euphrates River

Jericho
Jerusalem•
•Amman

Babylon•
Tower of Babel?

•On   Gaza

•Nippur

MEDIA

Bethlehem

SUMER

•Susa

Ezion-geber

Ur•

ELAM

SINAI
PENIN-
SULA

•Persepolis

Gulf
of Suez

Gulf
of Aqaba

Nile River

PERSIA

	Persian Empire		Arabian Desert

Persian Empire

Mt. Ararat ▲

Caspian Sea

Tarsus•

Haran•

•Ugarit
•Hamath

MESOPOTAMIA

•Nineveh
•Nimrud

Mediterranean
Sea
(Great Sea)

Mari•

Tigris River

•Damascus

•Ecbatana

CANAAN

Euphrates River

Jericho
Jerusalem•
•Amman

Babylon•
Tower of Babel?

•On   Gaza

•Nippur

Bethlehem

Ezion-geber

•Susa

Ur•

SINAI
PENIN-
SULA

Gulf
of Suez

Gulf
of Aqaba

•Persepolis

Nile River

Middle East: Fascinating Facts and Figures

- The Garden of Eden may have been in Iraq near the Tigris and Euphrates Rivers

- Noah's ark may have landed on Mount Ararat in Turkey. Some people think it landed in the general area of the mountains of northern Iraq. See Genesis 6-8.

- The "Tower of Babel" may have been near Babylon. Ancient Babylon was in Iraq. It is believed that different languages started at the Tower of Babel. See Genesis 11.

- Abraham lived in Ur which was the capital of the ancient kingdom of Sumer in Mesopotamia. Ruins of Ur are still in Iraq near the Euphrates River. See Genesis 11.

- God called Abraham to leave his father's home in Ur and go to a new land. The new land was Canaan, much of which is now called Israel. See Genesis 12.

- God promised Abraham and Sarah a son, Isaac, whose children would become a great nation. He made a covenant (solemn agreement) to be their God and to give them the land of Canaan. In return, they were to worship and obey Him. See Genesis 15.

- God passed the blessing and inheritance from Abraham to Isaac to Jacob (Israel) and to Jacob's twelve sons. Jacob's twelve sons were the start of the twelve tribes of Israel. See Genesis 12, 26, 28. (Also Genesis 15, 17, 21, 22, 25, 27, 32, 35, 48, 49.)

- Joseph did not have a tribe. Instead, his two sons—Manasseh and Ephraim—were "adopted" by Jacob and given the inheritance which was land for two tribes. The tribe of Levi was not given an area of land, but was spread throughout the other tribes.

- The Arabs came from Abraham's other son, Ishmael, of Hagar and from his sons of Keturah. Abraham loved Ishmael, but sent him and his mother away. God promised to make Ishmael a great nation, too, and gave him an inheritance outside the Promised Land of Canaan. See Genesis 16, 17, 21, and 25.

- God trained Abraham and his family to trust and obey Him through many problems. They were in slavery in Egypt about 400 years. God sent plagues on Egypt so Pharaoh would let His people go. Moses led the children of Israel through 40 years of wandering in the desert, much of the time on the Sinai Peninsula. See Exodus.

- Moses wrote out the laws and a song for the Israelite people and gave them a blessing. See Deuteronomy 31-33. Before Moses died, he saw the Promised Land from Mt. Nebo.

- Joshua led Israel into the Promised Land. God told them to conquer the land, drive out the Canaanites, destroy the idols, and worship only God. See Joshua.

- Joshua divided the land among the twelve Israelite tribes according to God's directions. He urged them to keep trusting God and to obey His commands. See Joshua 24.

- Daniel was "kidnapped" as a teenager and was taken to Iraq (Babylon) as a POW.

- Jonah went to northern Iraq (Nineveh).

The Middle East and Central Asia

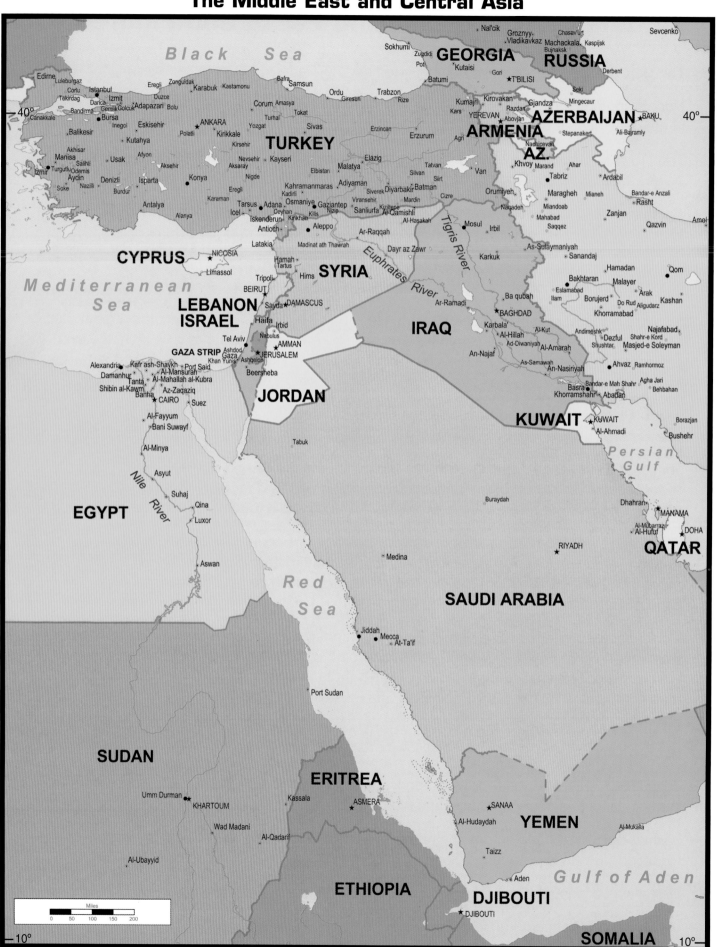

The Middle East and Central Asia

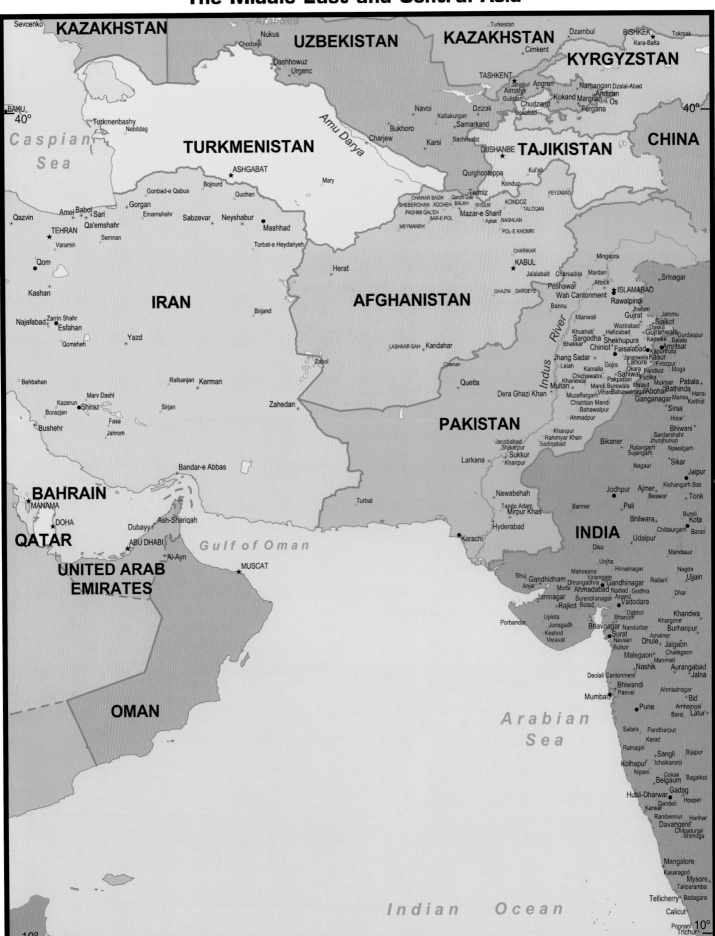

Holy Land: Then—Twelve Tribes

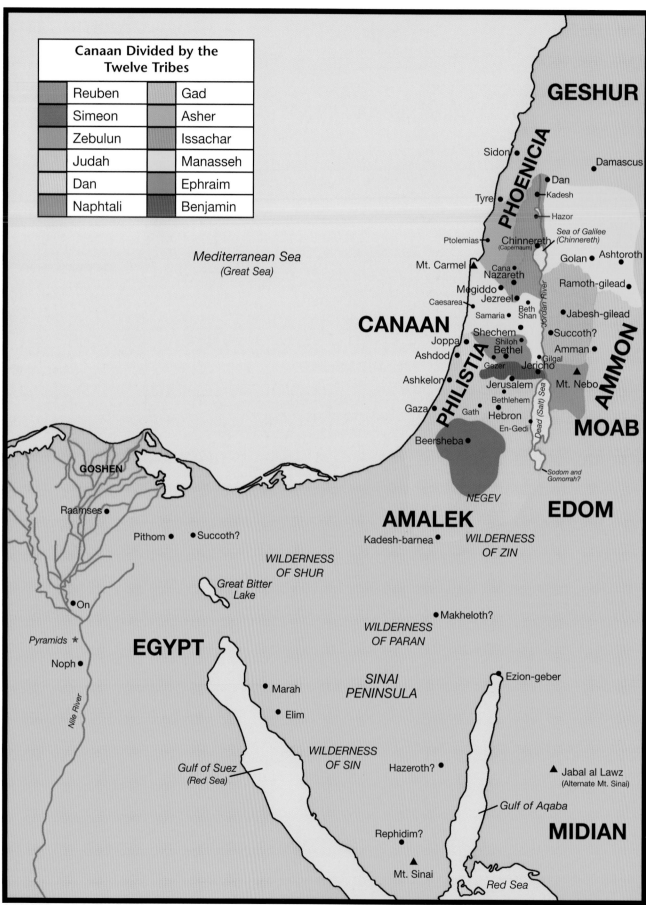

Canaan Divided by the Twelve Tribes

Reuben	Gad
Simeon	Asher
Zebulun	Issachar
Judah	Manasseh
Dan	Ephraim
Naphtali	Benjamin

GESHUR

Mediterranean Sea
(Great Sea)

PHOENICIA

Sidon

Damascus

Dan
Kadesh

Tyre

Hazor

Ptolemais
Chinnereth
(Capernaum)

Sea of Galilee
(Chinnereth)

Mt. Carmel
Cana
Nazareth

Golan
Ashtoroth

Megiddo
Jezreel

Ramoth-gilead

Caesarea

Jordan River

Samaria
Beth
Shan

Jabesh-gilead

CANAAN

Shechem

Succoth?

Joppa
Shiloh
Bethel

Amman

AMMON

Ashdod

Gilgal

Gezer
Jericho

Philistia

Ashkelon

Jerusalem
Mt. Nebo

MOAB

Bethlehem

Gaza
Gath
Hebron

Dead (Salt) Sea

Beersheba
En-Gedi

Sodom and
Gomorrah?

GOSHEN

NEGEV

EDOM

Raamses

AMALEK

Pithom
Succoth?
Kadesh-barnea

WILDERNESS
OF ZIN

WILDERNESS
OF SHUR

Great Bitter
Lake

On

Makheloth?

WILDERNESS
OF PARAN

Pyramids

EGYPT

Noph

SINAI
PENINSULA

Ezion-geber

Marah

Elim

Nile River

WILDERNESS
OF SIN

Hazeroth?

Jabal al Lawz
(Alternate Mt. Sinai)

Gulf of Suez
(Red Sea)

Gulf of Aqaba

MIDIAN

Rephidim?

Mt. Sinai

Red Sea

Holy Land: Now

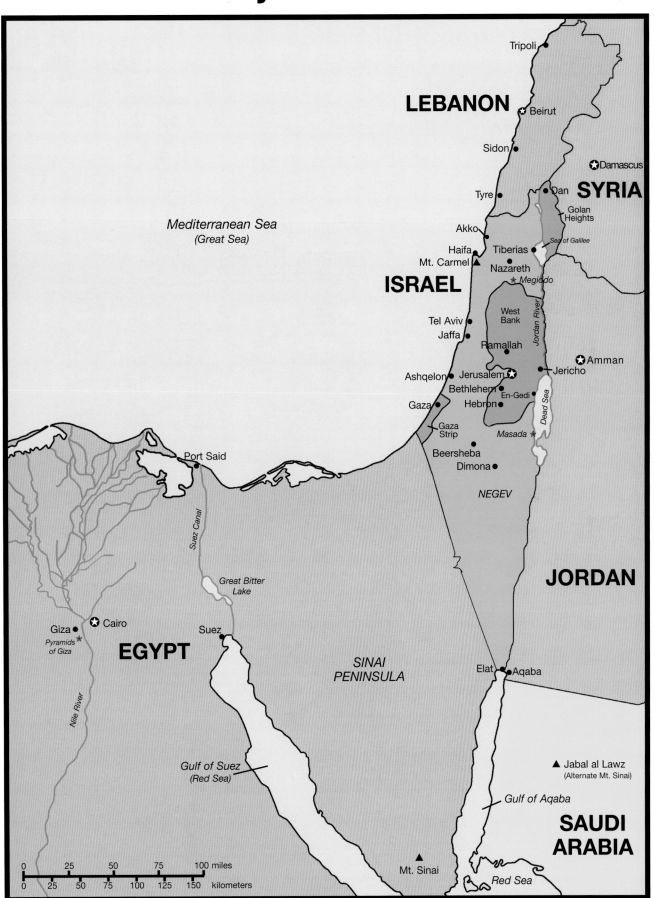

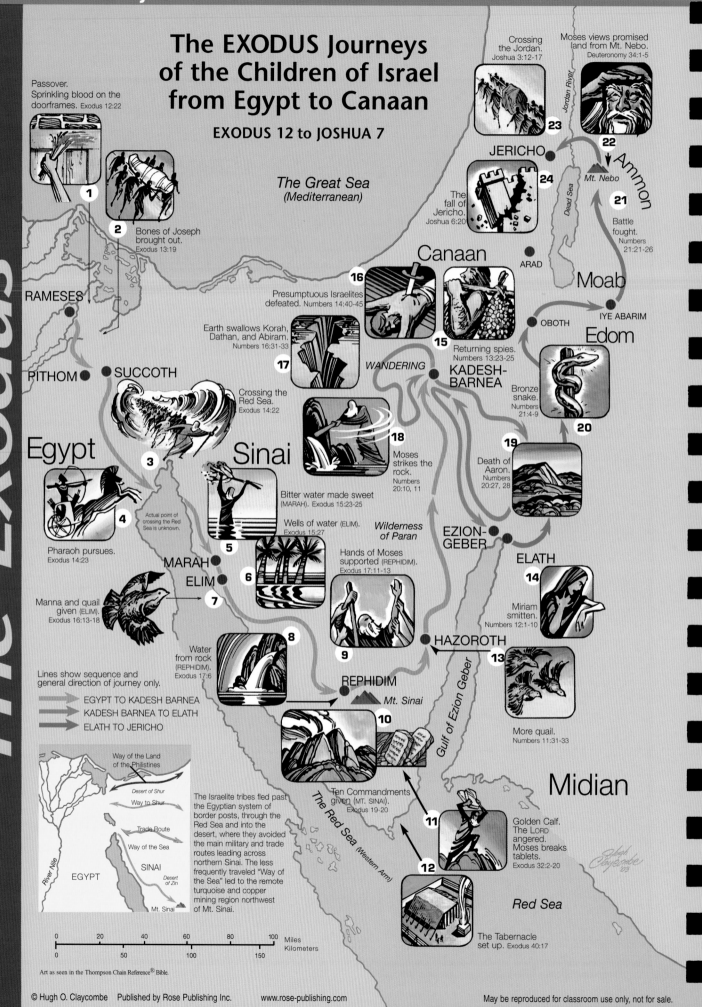

The EXODUS Journeys of the Children of Israel from Egypt to Canaan

EXODUS 12 to JOSHUA 7

The Exodus

1 Passover. Sprinkling blood on the doorframes. Exodus 12:22

2 Bones of Joseph brought out. Exodus 13:19

23 Crossing the Jordan. Joshua 3:12-17

Moses views promised land from Mt. Nebo. Deuteronomy 34:1-5

22 *Mt. Nebo*

21 Battle fought. Numbers 21:21-26

JERICHO

24 The fall of Jericho. Joshua 6:20

The Great Sea (Mediterranean)

Ammon

Jordan River

Dead Sea

Moab

Canaan

ARAD

16 Presumptuous Israelites defeated. Numbers 14:40-45

Earth swallows Korah, Dathan, and Abiram. Numbers 16:31-33

17

WANDERING

15 Returning spies. Numbers 13:23-25

KADESH-BARNEA

OBOTH

IYE ABARIM

Edom

20 Bronze snake. Numbers 21:4-9

RAMESES

PITHOM

SUCCOTH

Egypt

3 Crossing the Red Sea. Exodus 14:22

Actual point of crossing the Red Sea is unknown.

Sinai

18 Moses strikes the rock. Numbers 20:10, 11

19 Death of Aaron. Numbers 20:27, 28

4 Pharaoh pursues. Exodus 14:23

5 Bitter water made sweet (MARAH). Exodus 15:23-25

6 Wells of water (ELIM). Exodus 15:27

Wilderness of Paran

EZION-GEBER

14 Miriam smitten. Numbers 12:1-10

ELATH

MARAH

ELIM

7 Manna and quail given (ELIM). Exodus 16:13-18

8 Water from rock (REPHIDIM). Exodus 17:6

9 Hands of Moses supported (REPHIDIM). Exodus 17:11-13

HAZOROTH

13 More quail. Numbers 11:31-33

Gulf of Ezion Geber

Lines show sequence and general direction of journey only.

➡ EGYPT TO KADESH BARNEA
➡ KADESH BARNEA TO ELATH
➡ ELATH TO JERICHO

REPHIDIM

▲ *Mt. Sinai*

10 Ten Commandments given (MT. SINAI). Exodus 19-20

Midian

11

12 Golden Calf. The LORD angered. Moses breaks tablets. Exodus 32:2-20

The Red Sea (Western Arm)

Red Sea

The Tabernacle set up. Exodus 40:17

Way of the Land of the Philistines

Desert of Shur

Way to Shur

Trade Route

Way of the Sea

River Nile

EGYPT

SINAI

Desert of Zin

Mt. Sinai

The Israelite tribes fled past the Egyptian system of border posts, through the Red Sea and into the desert, where they avoided the main military and trade routes leading across northern Sinai. The less frequently traveled "Way of the Sea" led to the remote turquoise and copper mining region northwest of Mt. Sinai.

0	20	40	60	80	100	Miles
0	50		100		150	Kilometers

Art as seen in the Thompson Chain Reference® Bible.

Time Line of the Exodus

c. 1897 BC–1404 BC (Low Date: c. 1741 BC–1248 BC)

Joseph
c. 1897 BC–1884 BC
(c. 1741 BC–1728 BC)

Joseph is sold into slavery in Egypt by his brothers. He later becomes an official "over all the land of Egypt."

Moses' Birth
c. 1525 BC (c. 1369 BC)

Moses is born to a Hebrew slave. He's placed in a basket to avoid being killed by Pharaoh, the king of Egypt, when he's rescued by royalty and raised as a prince of Egypt.

The Red Sea
c. 1446 BC (c. 1290 BC)

The people of Israel pass safely through the Red Sea. Pharaoh, the Egyptian army, and 600 chariots are covered by the sea as they pursue the Israelites.

Mt. Sinai
c. 1446 BC–1445 BC
(c. 1290 BC–1289 BC)

After providing food for the Israelites, God gives Moses and the people his law as well as instructions for the Tabernacle on Mt. Sinai. When returning from the top of the mountain, Moses is angered that people are worshiping a golden calf.

Moses' Death
c. 1405 BC (c. 1249 BC)

Moses climbs to the top of Mt. Nebo where God shows him the Promised Land. He may not enter because he disregarded God's instructions and struck the rock at Meribah. Moses dies on Mt. Nebo at the age of 120.

The Promised Land
c. 1404 BC (c. 1248 BC)

Israel enters the Promised Land under the leadership of Joshua, son of Nun. The people cross through the Jordan River on dry ground with the Ark of the Covenant before them. Once across, the children of Israel begin their conquest of the Promised Land by destroying Jericho.

Israel in Egypt
c. 1876 BC (1720 BC)

Jacob, who is also called Israel, moves his entire family to Egypt to be with Joseph. After some time, Israel's descendants (the Israelites) become slaves in Egypt. Their slavery lasts for several centuries.

Ten Plagues
c. 1446 BC (1290 BC)

God sends ten plagues on Egypt leading to Israel's release by Pharaoh and the beginning of the Exodus. The tenth plague is the death of every "first born" in Egypt. The Passover feast celebrates Israel's deliverance from death when the LORD "passes over" their homes because door posts have the blood of a perfect lamb on them.

Joseph's Bones
c. 1446 BC (1290 BC)

Joseph's bones are carried out of Egypt. An oath had been made to Joseph, that when God comes to lead Israel to the Promised Land, they need to carry Joseph's bones out with them.

Spies Report
c. 1444 BC (1288 BC)

Spies return from scouting the Promised Land. The people doubt God's promise and fear the people of Canaan. Only two spies give an encouraging report. Israel is punished with 40 years of wandering in the wilderness before they can enter the Promised Land.

Timeline dates:
- 1850 BC (1694 BC)
- 1650 BC (1494 BC)
- 1450 BC (1294 BC)
- 1440 BC (1284 BC)
- 1430 BC (1274 BC)
- 1420 BC (1264 BC)
- 1410 BC (1254 BC)
- 1400 BC (1244 BC)

Key People

Moses
Moses led the children of Israel out of Egypt and through the wilderness. Moses was the key figure during the Exodus. He received the Law from God on Mt. Sinai, and is known as the author of the Torah, the first five books of the Old Testament.

Aaron
Aaron was Moses' older brother and spokesperson. Aaron was the first High Priest and all High Priests after him had to be a descendant of Aaron. Aaron died on Mt. Hor at age 123.

Miriam
Miriam was Moses' older sister. She was the first woman called a prophetess in Scripture. Miriam was an important leader during the Exodus. Like Aaron, she was successful when she supported Moses, but failed when she went against him. She died at Kadesh, just before entering the Promised Land.

Joshua, son of Nun
Joshua was the leader of the military during the Exodus and was one of the two spies to give an encouraging report from Canaan. He lead the Israelites into the Promised Land after Moses died. Joshua died and was buried at Timnath Serah in the hill country of Ephraim after conquering the lands of Canaan for Israel.

Pharaoh
Pharaoh was a king of Egypt and was considered to be a god to the Egyptians. God hardened Pharaoh's heart so He could prove to Pharaoh, Egypt, and the Israelites that He is the true God.

Some scholars date the Exodus around 1290 BC (low date) and others date it about 156 years earlier 1446 BC (high date).

The Holy Land: United Kingdom

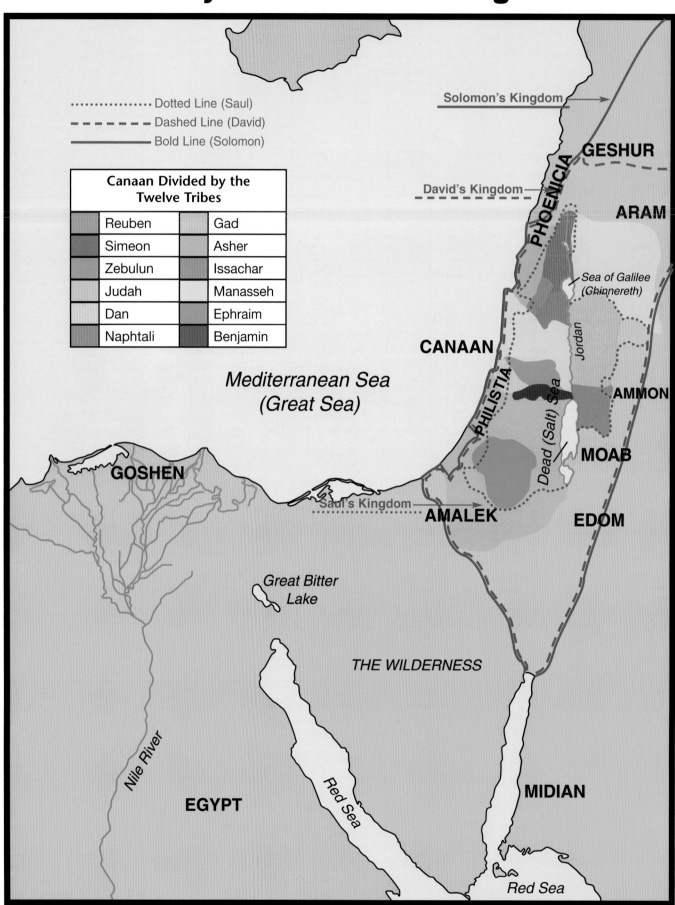

Dotted Line (Saul)
Dashed Line (David)
Bold Line (Solomon)

Canaan Divided by the Twelve Tribes	
Reuben	Gad
Simeon	Asher
Zebulun	Issachar
Judah	Manasseh
Dan	Ephraim
Naphtali	Benjamin

Solomon's Kingdom

GESHUR

PHOENICIA

David's Kingdom

ARAM

Sea of Galilee (Chinnereth)

Jordan

CANAAN

PHILISTIA

Dead (Salt) Sea

AMMON

Mediterranean Sea (Great Sea)

MOAB

GOSHEN

Saul's Kingdom

AMALEK

EDOM

Great Bitter Lake

THE WILDERNESS

Nile River

Red Sea

EGYPT

MIDIAN

Red Sea

The Holy Land: Divided Kingdom

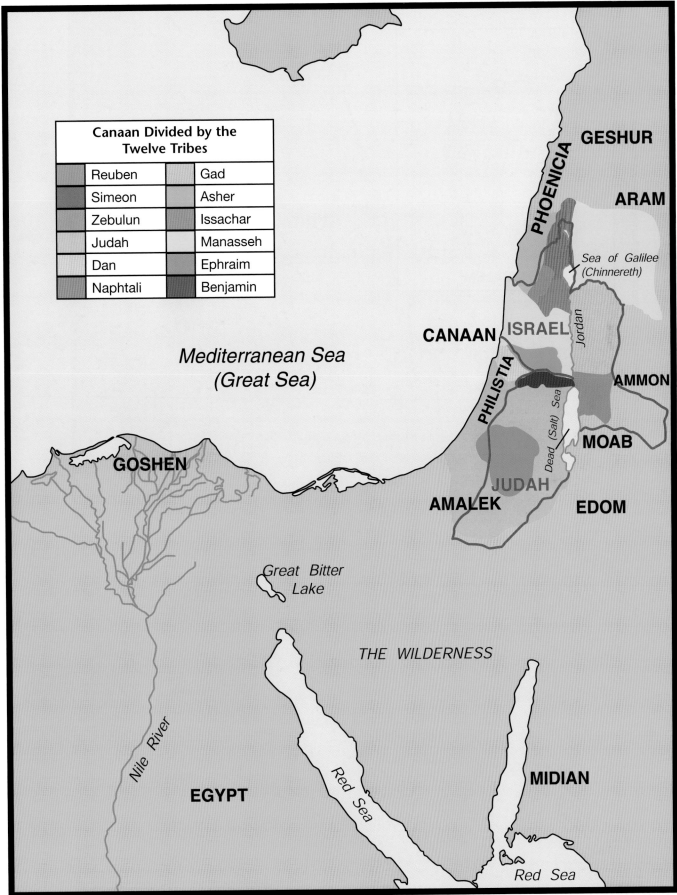

Canaan Divided by the Twelve Tribes

	Reuben		Gad
	Simeon		Asher
	Zebulun		Issachar
	Judah		Manasseh
	Dan		Ephraim
	Naphtali		Benjamin

GESHUR

PHOENICIA

ARAM

Sea of Galilee (Chinnereth)

CANAAN

ISRAEL

Jordan

Mediterranean Sea (Great Sea)

PHILISTIA

AMMON

Dead (Salt) Sea

MOAB

GOSHEN

JUDAH

AMALEK

EDOM

Great Bitter Lake

THE WILDERNESS

Nile River

Red Sea

MIDIAN

EGYPT

Red Sea

Where Jesus Walked: Then

Where Jesus Walked: Now

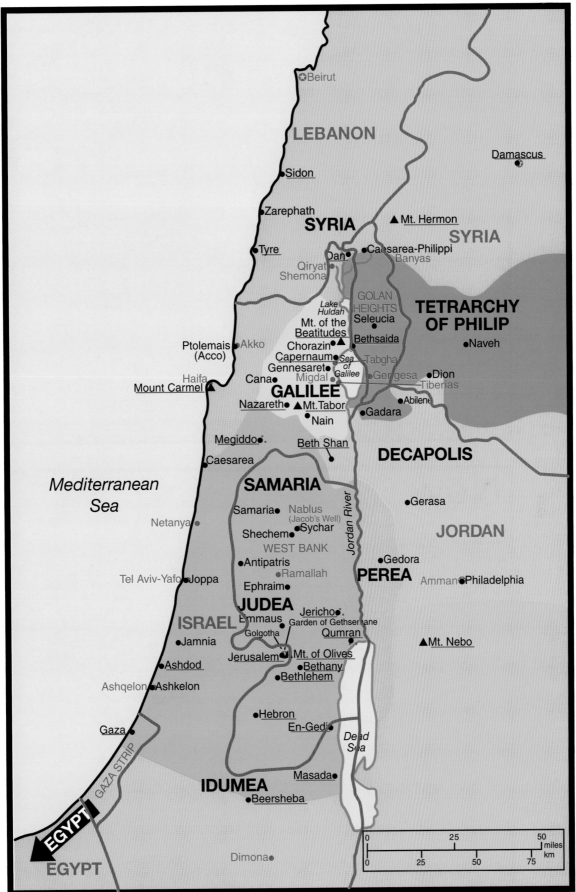

Beirut

LEBANON

Damascus

Sidon

Zarephath

SYRIA

Mt. Hermon

SYRIA

Tyre

Dan

Caesarea-Philippi
Banyas

Qiryat
Shemona

GOLAN
HEIGHTS

TETRARCHY
OF PHILIP

Lake
Huldah

Mt. of the
Beatitudes

Seleucia

Bethsaida

Naveh

Ptolemais
(Acco)

Akko

Chorazin

Capernaum

Sea
of
Galilee

Tabgha

Gennesaret

Migdal

Gergesa

Dion

Haifa

Cana

GALILEE

Tiberias

Mount Carmel

Nazareth

Mt. Tabor

Abilene

Nain

Gadara

Megiddo

Beth Shan

DECAPOLIS

Caesarea

Mediterranean
Sea

SAMARIA

Gerasa

Samaria

Nablus
(Jacob's Well)

Jordan River

JORDAN

Netanya

Shechem

Sychar

WEST BANK

Gedora

Tel Aviv-Yafo

Joppa

Antipatris

Ramallah

PEREA

Amman

Philadelphia

Ephraim

JUDEA

Jericho

ISRAEL

Emmaus

Garden of Gethsemane

Golgotha

Qumran

Mt. Nebo

Jamnia

Jerusalem

Mt. of Olives

Ashdod

Bethany

Bethlehem

Ashqelon

Ashkelon

Hebron

Gaza

En-Gedi

Dead
Sea

GAZA STRIP

Masada

IDUMEA

Beersheba

EGYPT

| 0 | 25 | 50 |
| | | miles |

EGYPT

Dimona

| 0 | 25 | 50 | 75 |
| | | | km |

Paul's Journeys: Then and Now

Where Did it Happen?

Jesus Christ Appears and Speaks to Paul
Acts 9:1-22

Paul Escapes From Damascus in Basket
Acts 9:19-25

Paul Speaks of Jesus to Jews in Synagogues
Acts 9,13,14,17,18,19

Businesswoman is First Convert in Europe
Acts 16:12-15

Violent Earthquake Demolishes Prison
Acts 16:12, 22-34

Athens–Paul Tells All About "Unknown God"
Acts 17:16-34

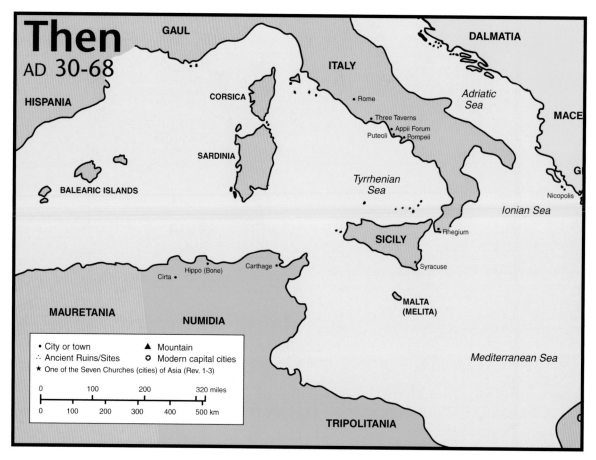

Then
AD 30-68

GAUL
DALMATIA
ITALY
HISPANIA
CORSICA
Rome
Three Taverns
Appii Forum
Puteoli • Pompeii
Adriatic Sea
MACE
SARDINIA
Tyrrhenian Sea
Nicopolis
Ionian Sea
BALEARIC ISLANDS
G
Rhegium
SICILY
Syracuse
Cirta • Hippo (Bone) Carthage
MAURETANIA NUMIDIA
MALTA (MELITA)
Mediterranean Sea

• City or town ▲ Mountain
∴ Ancient Ruins/Sites ✡ Modern capital cities
★ One of the Seven Churches (cities) of Asia (Rev. 1-3)

0   100   200   320 miles
0   100 200 300 400 500 km

TRIPOLITANIA

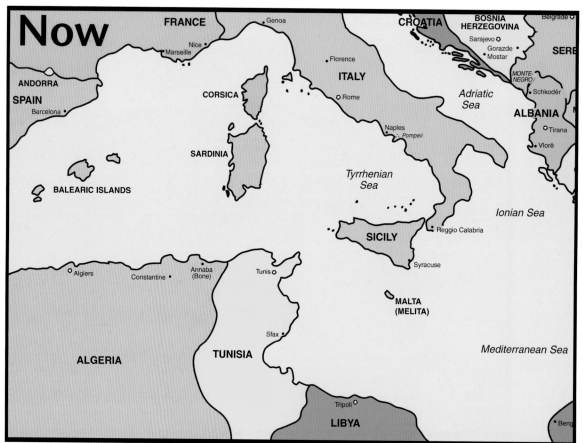

Now
FRANCE
Genoa
CROATIA
BOSNIA HERZEGOVINA
Belgrade
Nice
Marseille
Sarajevo
Gorazde
Mostar
SER
ANDORRA
SPAIN
Barcelona
Florence
ITALY
Rome
Adriatic Sea
MONTE-NEGRO
Schkodër
ALBANIA
CORSICA
Naples
Pompeii
Tirana
Vlorë
SARDINIA
Tyrrhenian Sea
Ionian Sea
BALEARIC ISLANDS
Reggio Calabria
SICILY
Syracuse
Algiers
Constantine
Annaba (Bone)
Tunis
MALTA (MELITA)
ALGERIA
Sfax
TUNISIA
Mediterranean Sea
Tripoli
LIBYA
Beng

Paul's Journeys: Then and Now

Then AD 30-68

MATIA
THRACE
Black Sea
MACEDONIA
Philippi • Neapolis
Amphipolis •
Thessalonica •
Apollonia •
Berea •
Samothrace
Mt. Olympus ▲
GREECE
Nicopolis
ACHAIA
Delphi
Ionian Sea
Corinth
Cenchreae •
Sparta •
Athens •
Aegean Sea
Assos
Lesbos
Mitylene
Chios
Samos •
Patmos •
*Troy
Troas
MYSIA
Pergamum *
★ Thyatira
★ Sardis
★ Smyrna ★ Philadelphia
★ Ephesus • Hierapolis
Trogyllium • Laodicea
Miletus • Colossae
Cos
Cnidus
ASIA
PHRYGIA
GALATIA
• Antioch
PISIDIA LYCAONIA
• Iconium
Lystra •
• Derbe
CAPPADOCIA
CILICIA
• Tarsus
PONTUS
BITHYNIA
• Nicaea
(Constantinople)
Byzantium
Attalia • Perga
LYCIA PAMPHYLIA
Patara • Myra
RHODES
• Antioch
Seleucia
SYRIA
CRETE
Phoenix •
Clauda • Fair Lasea
Havens
Salmone
Mediterranean Sea
Cyrene •
CYRENAICA
LIBYA
Salamis
Paphos •
CYPRUS
PHOENICIA — Damascus
Sidon
Tyre
Ptolemais
GALILEE Caesarea
SAMARIA Antipatris
Joppa
Jerusalem •
JUDEA • Gaza
Alexandria •
EGYPT
Amman •
ARABIA →

Now

OSNIA
EGOVINA
Belgrade ✪
Bucharest ✪
ROMANIA
evo ✪
Gorazde •
Mostar •
SERBIA
MONTE-
NEGRO /
• Shkodër
ALBANIA
✪ Tirana
• Vlorë
MACEDONIA
✪ Skopje
✪ Sofia
BULGARIA
• Plovdiv
Istanbul
(Constantinople)
• Zonguldak
Black Sea
tic
Ionian Sea
GREECE
Thessaloniki
Mt. Olympus ▲
Philippi ruins
Samothrace
Aegean Sea
Lesbos
Chios
Korinthos •
Athens •
Sparti •
Samos •
Patmos •
Ilion (Troy)
Troas
Bergama
Pergamum ruins
∴ *Sardis ruins*
• Izmir (Smyrna)
∴ *Ephesus ruins*
Miletus ruins
Cos
Cnidus
• Bursa
• Balikesir
Eskisehir •
∴ Antioch
∴ *Colossae
ruins*
Lystra ∴
✪ Ankara
TURKEY
ASIA MINOR
• Konya (Iconium)
• Adana
• Tarsus
Iskenderun
Antalya •
∴ *Perga ruins*
Mersin •
Antakya •
RHODES
CRETE
Kale (Myra)
SYRIA
CYPRUS
Nicosia ✪
LEBANON
Tripoli •
Beirut •
Damascus •
Sidon •
Tyre •
Acre •
Haifa •
ISRAEL
Tel Aviv-Yafo •
Jerusalem •
Amman •
Mediterranean Sea
Cyrene •
• Benghazi LIBYA
Alexandria •
EGYPT
Port Said •
Gaza •
JORDAN

Where Did it Happen?

Idol Sales Drop; Silversmiths Riot
Acts 19:23-41

Young Man Sleeps; Falls, Dies, is Revived
Acts 20:6-12

Paul Witnesses to Felix, Festus and King Agrippa
Acts 24, 25, 26

Paul Survives 14-Day Storm and Shipwreck
Acts 27-28

Malta–Poisonous Snake Strikes Paul
Acts 28:1-6

Paul Under Guard: Writes and Preaches
Acts 28:16-30

Paul's First Journey

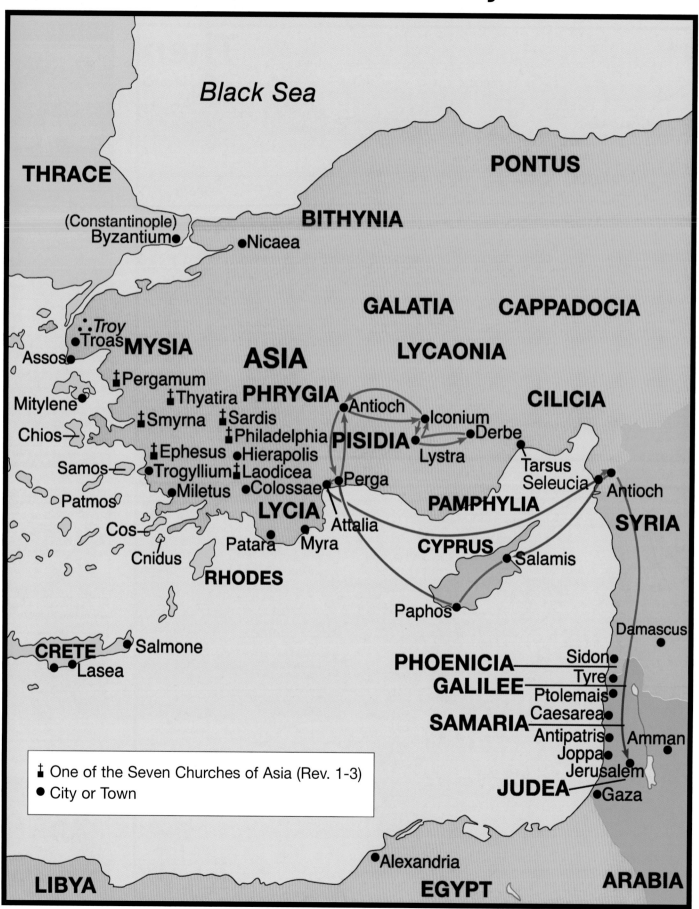

Black Sea

THRACE

PONTUS

BITHYNIA

(Constantinople)
Byzantium •Nicaea

GALATIA   CAPPADOCIA

LYCAONIA

∴Troy
•Troas MYSIA   ASIA
Assos•
‡Pergamum   CILICIA
Mitylene•   ‡Thyatira   PHRYGIA   •Antioch
Chios→   ‡Smyrna   ‡Sardis   •Iconium
                  ‡Philadelphia PISIDIA   •Derbe
Samos→ ‡Ephesus •Hierapolis   •Tarsus
        •Trogyllium ‡Laodicea Lystra   Seleucia•
Patmos •Miletus •Colossae   •Perga   •Antioch
        LYCIA   PAMPHYLIA   SYRIA
Cos→   •Attalia
    Patara •Myra   CYPRUS
Cnidus
RHODES   •Salamis
                                    •Damascus
CRETE •Salmone
   •Lasea   PHOENICIA   Sidon•
             GALILEE   Tyre•
                            Ptolemais•
             SAMARIA   Caesarea•
                            Antipatris• •Amman
                            Joppa•
                            Jerusalem
             JUDEA   •Gaza

‡ One of the Seven Churches of Asia (Rev. 1-3)
• City or Town

•Alexandria
LIBYA   EGYPT   ARABIA

Paul's Second Journey

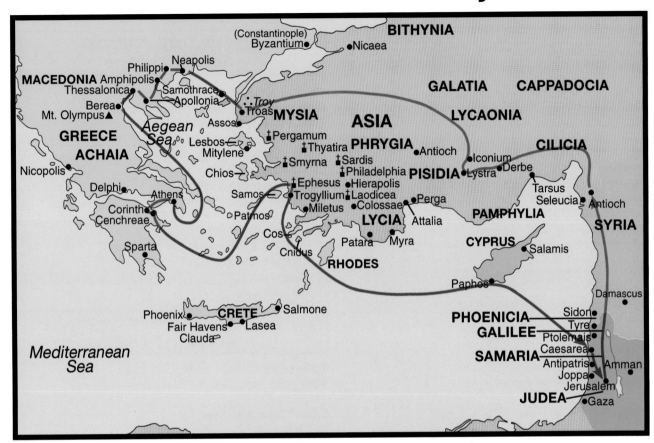

Paul's Third Journey

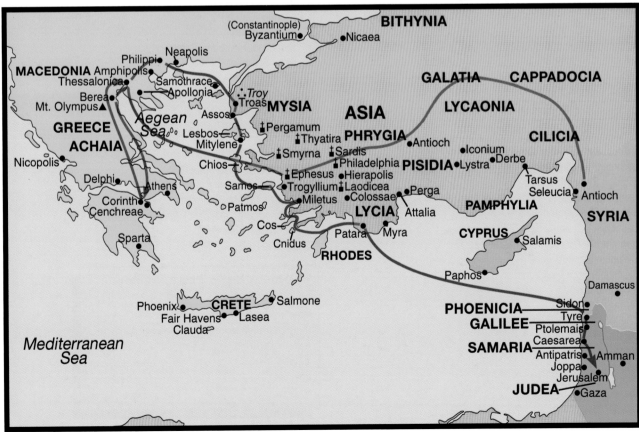

Paul's Travels and Missionary Journeys

Paul's Early Travels
Acts 9-12

- ❑ To Damascus to persecute Christians (Conversion) *Acts 9*
- ❑ Stays in Damascus *Acts 9*
- ❑ Arabia *Galatians 1:17*
- ❑ Leaves Damascus *Acts 9:25*
- ❑ Jerusalem *Acts 9:26*
- ❑ Caesarea and Tarsus *Acts 9:30, Galatians 1:21*
- ❑ In Antioch for a year *Acts 11:26*
- ❑ To Judea/Jerusalem for famine relief *Acts 11:30*
- ❑ Antioch (Syria) *Acts 12:25*

Paul's First Journey
Acts 13:1-14:28

Traveled with: Barnabas, John Mark
Main route: Cyprus and Turkey
Cities/Places: 1400 miles
- ❑ Antioch (Syria today)
- ❑ Seleucia
- ❑ Salamis and Paphos (on Cyprus)
- ❑ Perga
- ❑ **ANTIOCH of Pisidia** (Turkey today)
- ❑ Iconium
- ❑ Lystra and Derbe
- ❑ Lystra
- ❑ Iconium and Antioch (Turkey)
- ❑ Perga (via Pisida and Pamphylia)
- ❑ Attalia
- ❑ Antioch (Syria)
- ❑ Jerusalem (via Phoenicia and Samaria) *Acts 15*

Paul's Second Journey
Acts 15:36-18:22

Traveled with: Silas, Timothy, Priscilla and Aquilla, Luke
Main route: Syria, Turkey, Greece, Jerusalem
Cities/Places: 2800 miles
- ❑ Through Syria and Cilicia
- ❑ Derbe and Lystra
- ❑ Through Phrygia and Galatia
- ❑ (past Mysia) Troas
- ❑ Samothracia (Samothrace) and Neapolis
- ❑ Philippi in Macedonia
- ❑ Amphipolis and Apollonia
- ❑ Thessalonica
- ❑ Berea (Beroea)
- ❑ Athens (Mars Hill—"Aeropagus")
- ❑ **CORINTH**
- ❑ Cenchrea (Cenchreae)
- ❑ Ephesus
- ❑ Caesarea (in Syria)
- ❑ "Went up" to Jerusalem
- ❑ Antioch (Syria)

Paul's Third Journey
Acts 18:23-21:16

Traveled with: Timothy, Luke, and others
Main route: Turkey, Greece, Lebanon, Israel
Cities/Places: 2700 miles
- ❑ Through Galatia and Phrygia
- ❑ **EPHESUS**
- ❑ Through Macedonia
- ❑ Through Greece (Achaia)
- ❑ Philippi in Macedonia and Troas
- ❑ Assos, Mitylene; near Chios, Samos, (Trogyllium), Miletus
- ❑ Cos, through Rhodes, Patara
- ❑ Tyre and Ptolemais
- ❑ Caesarea
- ❑ Jerusalem

Paul's Journey to Rome
Acts 21:17-28:31

Traveled with: Roman guards, Luke, others
Main route: Israel, Lebanon, Turkey, Crete, Malta, Sicily, Italy
Cities/Places: 2250 miles
- ❑ Jerusalem
- ❑ Antipatris and Caesarea
- ❑ Sidon, Myra, Cnidus
- ❑ Fair Havens (Crete)
- ❑ Clauda (Cauda)
- ❑ Malta (Melita)
- ❑ Syracuse, Rhegium, Puteoli
- ❑ Appii Forum and Three Taverns
- ❑ **ROME**

Other Travels Before Paul's Death

Cities/Places (order unknown):
- ❑ Macedonia *1 Timothy 1:3*
- ❑ Troas and Miletus *2 Timothy 4:13, 20*
- ❑ Crete *Titus 1:5*
- ❑ Planned to go to Spain *Romans 15:28*
- ❑ Nicopolis *Titus 3:12*
- ❑ Back to Rome *2 Timothy 1*

How to Remember Paul's Journeys

Paul was a PACER in a race!

(A pacer takes the lead or sets an example.)

P - PAUL ("I have run the race; I have kept the faith.")

A - ANTIOCH of Pisidia	First Journey
C - CORINTH area	Second Journey
E - EPHESUS area	Third Journey
R - ROME	Fourth Journey

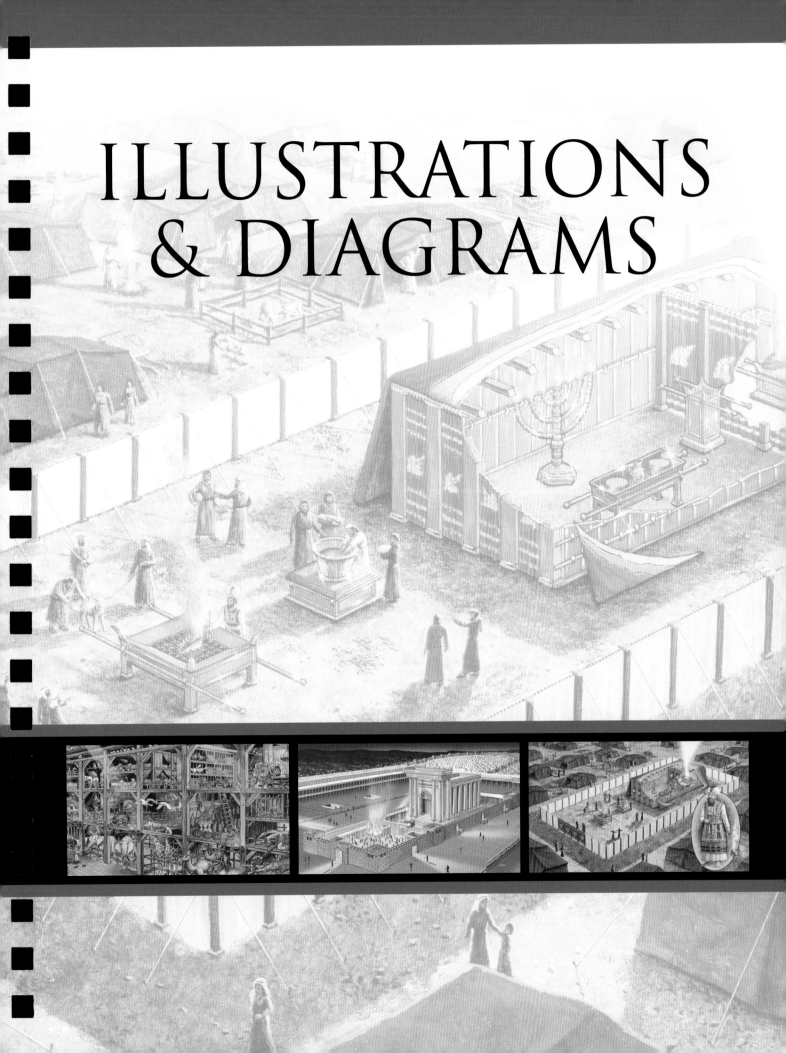

ILLUSTRATIONS & DIAGRAMS

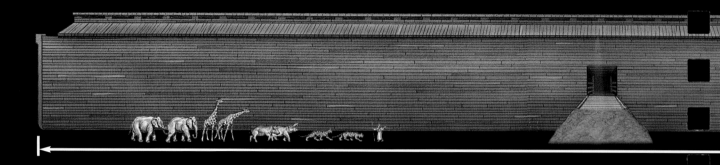

NOAH'S ARK

◄ **About 100 to 120 Years**
God Grieves Over Corrupt Earth; Tells Noah to Build an Ark

God is sorrowful about the great wickedness and violence in all the people on the earth, and sees their evil thoughts. He tells Noah, who is righteous and "walked with God," that He will destroy the people and the earth with a flood. God gives Noah plans to build an ark and be saved. Noah does everything God tells him to do.

Building the ark took about 100 years when Noah was about the ages of 500 to 600. Gen. 6:3-22; 5:32; 7:6

─ 7 Days ─
God Shuts Door of Ark
God tells Noah and the animals to go into the ark. After seven days, God shuts them in.

Genesis 7:7, 10, 16

─ 40 Days ─
The Flood Begins
Underground waters burst forth and rain falls 40 days and nights covering the ground. Noah, his three sons, and their wives are safe in the ark along with every kind of animal and bird. Genesis 7:11

─ 110 Days ─
Water Covers All The Earth
After the rain ends, the water covers all the land and mountains. The ark floats safely high above the ground. Even the highest mountains are under more than 20 feet (nearly 7 meters) of flood waters. Nothing is left alive anywhere on earth, except for Noah and those in the ark. The water covers the earth for 150 days. God sends a wind across the waters and the waters recede. Genesis 7:17–8:1

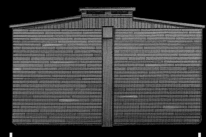

45 ft. (13.5 m)

450 feet (138 meters)

75 feet (23 meters)

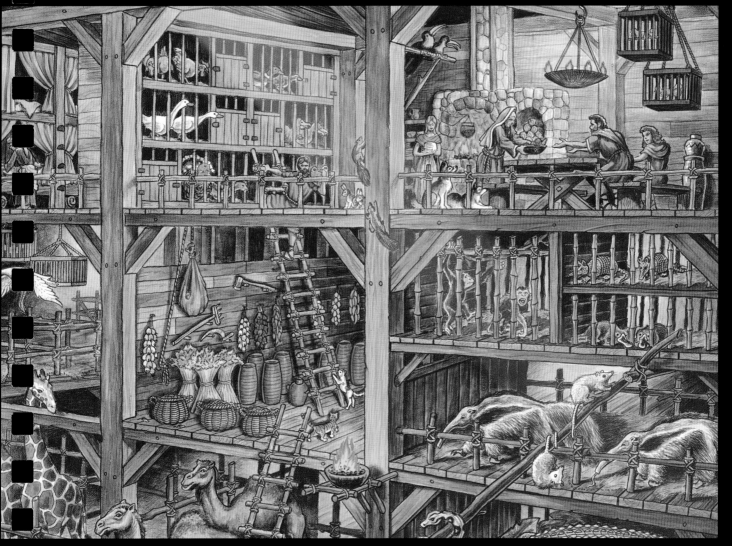

74 Days
The Water Goes Down and The Ark Rests
God does not forget Noah, his family, and the animals in the ark. He makes the water go down. On the 17th day of the seventh month of the year, the ark rests in the Ararat mountains, five months from the start of the flood. Genesis 8:1-4

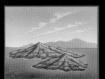

40 Days
Mountain Tops Are Seen
The water lowers. The mountain tops can be seen on the first day of the 10th month, two and a half months later. After 40 days, Noah checks the water. Genesis 8:5, 6

28 Days
Noah Sends Out Birds
Noah sends a raven out of a window. Then he sends a dove every seven days. At last it brings an olive leaf; and finally it doesn't return. Genesis 8:6-12

22 Days
601 Years Old
Noah was 600 years old when the rain began. Now he is age 601 on the first day of the year. Noah wonders if the land is dry. Genesis 7:11; 8:13

57 Days
Noah Opens the Roof
Noah opens the ark roof and sees that the earth is almost dry. By the 27th day of the second month, the earth is completely dry. God tells Noah that they can leave the ark and the animals can go, reproduce, and live all over the earth. Genesis 8:13-19

A New Start
Noah builds an altar and offers animal and bird sacrifices pleasing to the LORD. The rainbow is a sign of God's promise to never again destroy all creatures with a flood. Genesis. 8:20-9:17

THE TABERNACLE

Tribe of
Reuben
(South)

Tribes of
Simeon
(South)

Tribes of
Gad
(South)

12

12

The families of
Kohath
(Numbers 3)

13.b

13.a

13.c

1.g

11.a

11.d

11.b

15

11.c

14

The families
of
Moses
Aaron
Nadab
Eleazar
Ithamar

Tribes of
Issachar
(East)

Tribes of
Judah
(East)

Tribes of
Zebulun
(East)

16

Tribe of
Ephraim
(West)

Tribe of
Manasseh
(West)

Tribe of
Benjamin
(West)

The families of
Gershonites
(Numbers 3)

1.c
1.b
1.a
3
8
7
10
1.d
6
9
1.f
4
5
1.e
1.h

2.g
2.h
2.f
2.d
2.e
2.c
2.b
2.a
2.i

The families of
Merarites
(Numbers 3)

Tribes of
Dan
(North)

Tribes of
Asher
(North)

Tribes of
Naphtali
(North)

Key to the Tabernacle

1 The Tabernacle (Enlarged to show detail)
(Exodus 26:1-37) (The new holy temple – Ephesians 2:19-22)
30 cubits long x 10 cubits wide x 10 cubits high (45 ft x 15 ft x 15 ft
or 13.8 m x 4.6 m x 4.6 m)
The general appearance of the Tabernacle was that of a rectangular box.
It was divided into two sections—the Holy Place and the Most Holy Place
(Holy of Holies).
  a. Goats' hair covering with linen beneath (Ex. 25:4; 26:7)
  b. Ram skin covering dyed red (Ex. 25:5; 26:14)
  c. Badger, porpoise, or sea cow skin covering (Ex. 25:5)
  d. Boards (48 boards, Ex. 26:15-25)
  e. Sockets (100 total, 96 silver sockets for the boards, four under the
     pillars of the veil)
  f. Bars (Ex. 26:26-29)
  g. Pillars, hooks (Ex. 26:32, 37; 36:36, 38)
  h. Curtains at the entrance (Ex. 26:1-6)

2 The High Priest and His Holy Garments
(Exodus 28:1-43; 39:1-31) (A great high priest – Hebrews 4:14, 15)
  a. Embroidered coat (Ex. 28:4; Ps. 132:9)
  b. Robe with golden bells and pomegranates (Ex. 28:34)
  c. Ephod and girdle (Ex. 28:4)
  d. Breastplate and the Urim and Thummim (Ex. 28:30)
  e. Stones in the breastplate (12 tribes of Israel) (Ex. 28:17-21)
  f. Shoulder stones of onyx (Ex. 28:9-12; 39:6, 7)
  g. Mitre (Ex. 28:4, 39)
  h. Turban or Holy Plate or crown (diadem) of gold inscribed,
     "Holy to the Lord" (Ex. 28:36; 29:6)
  i. The Censer of burning coals (Lev. 16:12, 13; Heb. 9:4)

3 The Holy Place
(Exodus 26:33, Hebrews 9:2, 6)
10 cubits wide x 20 cubits long (15 ft x 30 ft or 4.6 m x 9.2 m)
The priests entered into the Holy Place daily to minister to the Lord.
The table of showbread stood on the right, the seven-branched golden
candlestick (lampstand) stood on the left, and the altar of incense stood
in the Holy Place right in front of the veiled Holy of Holies.

4 The Golden Lampstand (Candlestick)
(Exodus 25:31-40)
The lampstand or candlestick was made of pure, hammered gold, one
solid piece. It had a central shaft with six branches, three on each side,
making it a seven-branched lampstand. Each branch had knobs, flowers,
and an almond-shaped bowl to hold pure olive oil. It was part of the
priests' ministry to keep the lamp burning perpetually.

5 The Table of Showbread (Shewbread)
(Exodus 25:23-30; Hebrews 9:2)
2 cubits long x 1 cubit wide x 1$\frac{1}{2}$ cubits high (36 in x 18 in x 27 in
or 92 cm x 46 cm x 69 cm)
The table of showbread was made of shittim (acacia) wood. It was
overlaid with gold and had a crown or frame of gold around it that was
as wide as a man's hand. A ring of gold was put on each of the four
legs, to put the carrying poles through. The carrying poles were made
of shittim wood overlaid with gold. Also made of pure gold were the
dishes, pans, pitchers and bowls. Twelve loaves of bread were placed
on the table, six in a row. Fresh bread was placed there every Sabbath.

6 The Altar of Incense
(Exodus 30:1-10; Hebrews 9:2)
1 cubit long x 1 cubit wide x 2 cubits high (1$\frac{1}{2}$ ft x 1$\frac{1}{2}$ ft x 3 ft
or 46 cm x 46 cm x 92 cm)
The altar of incense was made from shittim (acacia) wood. Its four
corners each had a horn made from one piece. Its top, sides, and horns
were overlaid with gold, with a crown or molding all around the top.
Aaron, the High Priest, burned incense upon it every morning and
evening. Once a year, on the Day of Atonement, the horns of the
altar were sprinkled with the blood of the sin offering.

7 The Veil
(Exodus 26:31-33; Hebrews 10:19, 20)
A woven veil of blue, purple, and scarlet thread, with designs of
cherubim embroidered on it, was hung on four pillars of acacia wood
overlaid with gold. Four gold hooks were put in four sockets of silver.
The veil was hung from these, and was a divider between the
Holy Place and the Most Holy Place.

8 The Most Holy Place (Holy of Holies)
(Exodus 26:33, 34, Hebrews 9:3)
10 cubits long x 10 cubits wide (15 ft x 15 ft or 4.6 m x 4.6 m)
Also called the Holy of Holies, here resided the Ark of the Covenant. It
was exactly one-half the length of the Holy Place. The shekinah glory of
God rested upon the lid of the Ark (Mercy Seat). The high priest entered
the Most Holy Place once a year, on the Day of Atonement, to sprinkle
blood on the Mercy Seat to atone for his sins and the people's sins.

9 The Ark of the Covenant
(Exodus 25:10-16; Hebrews 9:4)
2$\frac{1}{2}$ cubits long x 1$\frac{1}{2}$ cubits wide x 1$\frac{1}{2}$ cubits high (45 in x 27 in x 27 in
or 115 cm x 69 cm x 69 cm)
The Ark was made of acacia wood. It was overlaid with gold, inside and
out. A gold crown or molding was set around the edge of the top. Four
gold rings, one in each leg were placed for the carrying poles. The poles
were acacia wood overlaid with gold. The Mercy Seat was set on top of
the Ark.

10 The Mercy Seat
(Exodus 25:17-22; Hebrews 9:5)
2$\frac{1}{2}$ cubits long x 1$\frac{1}{2}$ cubits wide (45 in x 27 in or 115 cm x 69 cm)
The Mercy Seat was made of pure gold. It had a winged cherub on
each side, facing each other with wings outstretched above them,
towards each other. The Mercy Seat was beaten or hammered from
one solid piece of gold. It was placed above the Ark.

11 The Gate of the Court
(Exodus 27:16; 38:18, 19; John 10:9)
20 cubits wide x 5 cubits high (30 ft x 7$\frac{1}{2}$ ft or 9.2 m x 2.3 m)
The entrance to the court was made with:
  a. Hanging curtains (blue, purple, scarlet, white) (Ex. 27:16; 38:18)
  b. Four pillars of brass (Ex. 27:14-16; 38:14, 15)
  c. Sockets of bronze (brass) (Ex. 27:14-16)
  d. Hooks and fillets (clasps) of silver (tops of pillars) (Ex. 27:10, 11)

12 The Offerings
(Hebrews 8:3; 9:11-14, 18-22; 10:1-4)
  • Burnt offering (bull, sheep, goats or birds) (Leviticus 1:1-17)
  • Grain offering (Leviticus 2:1-16)
  • Peace offering (goat or lamb) (Lev. 3:1-17)
  • Sin offering (bull or lamb) (Lev. 4:1-35)
  • Trespass offering (female of the flock, lamb, goat kid, or bird or
    grain) (Lev. 5 & 6)

13 The Court Fence (Not shown to scale)
(Exodus 27:9-18; 38:9-17; 40:33)
100 cubits long x 50 cubits wide x 5 cubits high (150 ft x 75 ft x 7$\frac{1}{2}$ ft
or 46 m x 23 m x 2.3 m)
The court fence was the outer border of the Tabernacle site. It consisted
of the following:
  a. Linen curtains (white) (Ex. 27:9, 11, 15, 16; Rev. 19:8)
  b. Pillars, sockets, hooks, and fillets (tops and rods) (Ex. 27:11,17)
  c. Pins of bronze (brass) (Ex. 27:19; 38:20)

14 The Brazen Altar
(Exodus 27:1-8, 40:6, 10, 29)
5 cubits long x 5 cubits wide x 3 cubits high (7$\frac{1}{2}$ ft x 7$\frac{1}{2}$ ft x 4$\frac{1}{2}$ ft
or 23 m x 23 m x 1.38 m)
The brazen altar was made of shittim (acacia) wood. It was square and
covered with bronze (brass). The four corners had horns overlaid with
bronze. Also there were pans to receive ashes, shovels, basins,
fleshhooks (forks), and fire pans, all of bronze. A bronze grate with
a bronze ring in each corner was put under the brazen altar.
Staves (carrying poles) were made of shittim wood covered with bronze
to carry the altar.

15 Laver of Bronze
(Exodus 30:17-21; 40:7, 30-32; Ephesians 5:26; Hebrews 10:22)
A large basin of brass, in which the Aaron and his sons washed their
hands and feet, was placed between the brazen altar and the
Tabernacle. The Lord said if they did not wash when they came near
the brazen altar to minister, they would die.

16 The Cloud and the Pillar of Fire
(Exodus 25:8, 22; 29:43; 40:34-38)
The Lord manifested His presence with a cloud by day and a pillar of fire
by night. It would rest above the Tabernacle, directly above the Mercy
Seat. When the cloud or pillar of fire moved, the children of Israel
followed it. Wherever it stopped, they camped there until it moved again.

The Tabernacle

The new religious observances taught by Moses in the desert centered on rituals connected with the tabernacle, and amplified Israel's sense of of separateness, purity, and oneness under the Lordship of Yahweh.

A few desert shrines have been found in Sinai, notably at Serabit el-Khadem and at Timnah in the Negev, and show marked Egyptian influence.

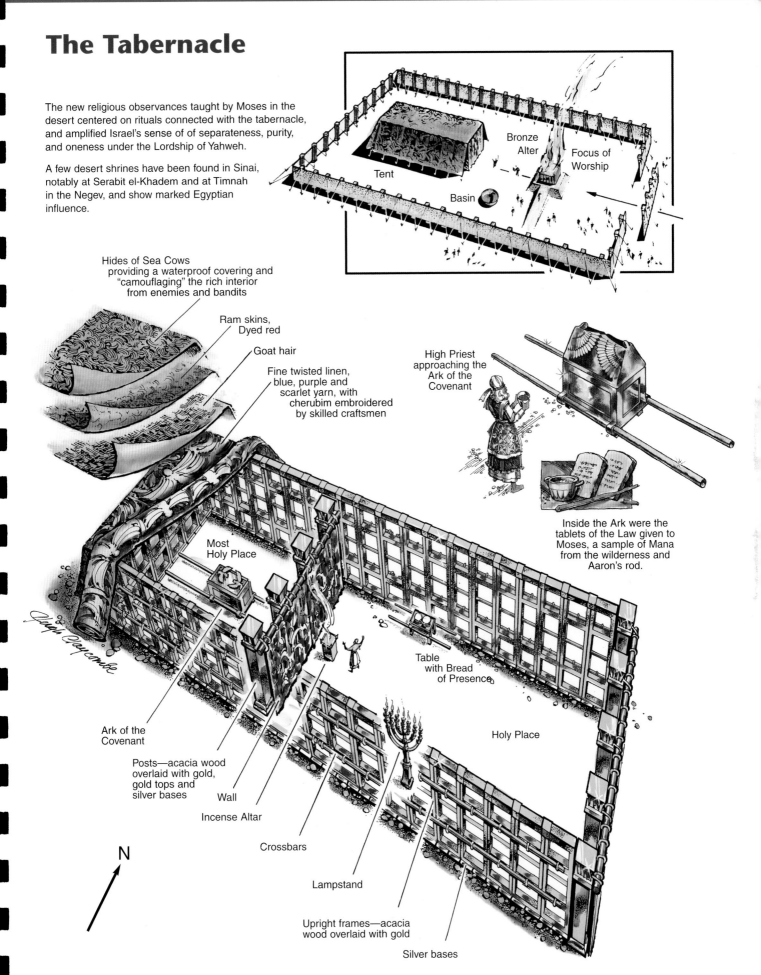

Tent

Bronze Alter

Focus of Worship

Basin

Hides of Sea Cows providing a waterproof covering and "camouflaging" the rich interior from enemies and bandits

Ram skins, Dyed red

Goat hair

Fine twisted linen, blue, purple and scarlet yarn, with cherubim embroidered by skilled craftsmen

High Priest approaching the Ark of the Covenant

Inside the Ark were the tablets of the Law given to Moses, a sample of Mana from the wilderness and Aaron's rod.

Most Holy Place

Table with Bread of Presence

Ark of the Covenant

Holy Place

Posts—acacia wood overlaid with gold, gold tops and silver bases

Wall

Incense Altar

Crossbars

N

Lampstand

Upright frames—acacia wood overlaid with gold

Silver bases

The Tabernacle: Pattern of Worship

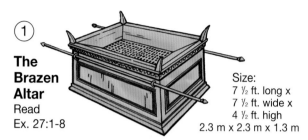

① **The Brazen Altar**
Read Ex. 27:1-8

Size:
7 ½ ft. long x
7 ½ ft. wide x
4 ½ ft. high
2.3 m x 2.3 m x 1.3 m

God wanted to dwell among his people. How does a holy God dwell among sinful people? First God required the people to sacrifice a perfect animal for their sins (Lev. 17:11). The blood of the animal was important to justify the people before God. Only the finest animal—a perfect one—was good enough. Sacrifices needed to be offered on a regular basis (Heb. 9:25).

The person bringing the offering would put his hand on the head of the lamb while it was killed. This symbolically put the person's sins onto the animal, and the animal died in his place.
To think about:
• Jesus is our perfect sacrifice and shed his blood for our sins. (See John 1:29; Rev. 13:8; Hebrews 10:10; Romans 4:25.) Jesus was not only the perfect sacrifice, but his sacrifice covered all sin—past and future. No more sacrifices are required.
• In Romans 12:1, we are told to present our bodies as a living sacrifice. What does this mean to you?

② **The Laver of Brass**
Read Ex. 30:18 & Ex. 38:8

Size:
None
indicated

The next step was for the priests only. In fact, the rest of the work was performed by the priests on behalf of the people.

After making the sacrifice, the priest washed himself at the brass laver. This washing purified the priest and prepared him to enter the Tabernacle. In Exodus 30:20, God says they must wash so that they do not die when they enter the Tabernacle.

The brazen laver was made from brass mirrors donated by the women. The Bible does not describe the laver completely, but perhaps it had a shiny mirrored surface which would help the priest wash thoroughly and to remind him that the Lord sees past the outward appearance, straight into the heart.
To think about:
• Even though we Christians have accepted Jesus' sacrificial death on our behalf, we too need to be cleansed.
Read 1 John 1:8, 9. How would Jesus' disciples understand this verse?

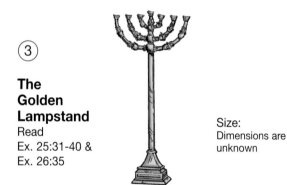

③ **The Golden Lampstand**
Read Ex. 25:31-40 & Ex. 26:35

Size:
Dimensions are unknown

From the laver, the priest passed through a veil into the Holy Place. The room he entered had three objects: a golden lampstand on the south, a table on the north and an altar of incense to the west just before the veil to the most holy place, the Holy of Holies.

The unique lampstand was beaten from a single piece of gold. It was not pieced together. Scripture tells us it was fueled by oil, not wax. It had lamps at the top of each branch, not candles.

Its purpose was to provide light in this otherwise dark room. Trimming the lamp wicks to keep them burning brightly was an important job for the priest.
To think about:
• Jesus called himself the light of the world in many places in the Bible. See John 12:46.
• Christians are called to be lights. See Acts 13:47. How are we lights?

Size:
3 ft. long x
1 ½ ft. wide x
2 ¼ ft. high
92 cm x 46 cm x 69 cm

④ **The Table of Showbread**
(pronounced show-bread)
Read Ex. 25:23-30

On the Table of Showbread, Aaron and his sons placed twelve loaves of bread made from fine flour. These twelve loaves represented the twelve tribes of Israel. The table with the loaves was a continual remainder of the everlasting promises, the covenant between God and the Children of Israel, and a memorial of God's provision of food. The bread was eaten by Aaron and his sons and was replaced every week on the Sabbath.
To think about:
• Jesus called himself the "Bread of Life." See John 6:35 and 6:51. He said that those who came to him would never hunger again. Physical bread—even the special bread of the Tabernacle—is consumed. But the spiritual Bread of Life, Jesus, gives eternal life.
• Hebrews 8:6, 7 and Heb. 10:16 tell of a better covenant through Jesus, one superior to the Old Testament covenant to Israel. The law would be written on people's hearts, not on tablets of stone.

The Tabernacle: Pattern of Worship

⑤

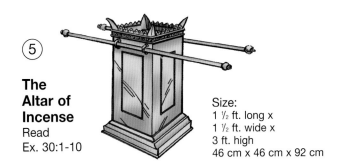

The Altar of Incense
Read
Ex. 30:1-10

Size:
1 ½ ft. long x
1 ½ ft. wide x
3 ft. high
46 cm x 46 cm x 92 cm

The Lord required that special incense be burned constantly on the altar of incense. It was a special sweet incense, a mixture of spices to be used only for the Tabernacle. See Ex. 30:35-37. God specifically required this recipe. None other was to be burned on the altar. It was a matter of life and death, as Lev. 10:1, 2 clearly shows us, when two of Aaron's sons offered a "strange fire" before the Lord and were struck dead. In the New Testament (Luke 1:5-13), the priest Zacharias was in the Holy Place when an angel appeared near the Table of Incense. Zacharias fell down with fear. The angel announced that God had heard Zacharias's prayers and he and his wife would have a son (John the Baptist).

To think about:
• Incense represents the prayers of the faithful. There are several references to this in the book of Revelation (5:8; 8:3, 4).
• Are our prayers a sweet incense toward God?

⑥

The Veil
Read
Ex. 26:33
Ex. 30:10

Size:
At least 15 ft.
(4.6 m) wide

The Veil separated the holy place from the most holy place where the Ark of the Covenant was kept. It was a barrier between God and man. Once a year Aaron would enter the most holy place (Holy of Holies) through this veil. The veil was a heavy woven cloth stretching for ten cubits (15 feet or 4.6 meters). There was no separation in the middle. The high priest had to go around the side to enter the most holy place.

Later when the Temple was constructed, it followed a similar design. The veil of the Temple was torn from top to bottom when Jesus died. This symbolizes the ability of every believer, not just a high priest, to approach God through the death of Jesus.

To think about:
• For hundreds of years, the Israelites needed a human high priest to represent them before God. Read 1 Timothy 2:5; Hebrews 8:1; Hebrews 9:11, and Hebrews 10:11, 12. Name a few ways in which Jesus is a better high priest than Aaron.

⑦

The Ark of the Covenant and the Mercy Seat
Read Ex. 25:10, 14-16;
Ex. 25:22; Heb. 9

Size:
3¾ ft. long x 2¼ ft. wide x 2¼ ft. high
1.15 m x 69 cm x 69 cm

The central focus of the entire Tabernacle was the most holy place where God spoke to the high priest above the Mercy Seat—the area where the winged cherubim face each other.

Annually the high priest would sprinkle blood on the Mercy Seat to atone for the sins of all the people.

God's purpose and desire is to dwell among his people and to commune with them. The layout of the Tabernacle, along with the steps of sacrifice, cleansing, and remembering God's promises are all designed to bring sinful mankind to a loving and holy God.

To think about:
• Christianity is not a religion in which man reaches to know God. It is God who approaches his creatures and makes it possible for them to know him. (John 6:44; Eph. 2:8, 9)
• Our efforts to be "good people" are not enough to approach God. Jesus alone is the Way to God. (John 14:6; Heb. 10:19-23)

Israelites Communed with God through the Tabernacle	Christians Commune with God through Jesus
1. Brazen Altar for sacrifices	Christ's sacrifice
2. Laver of Brass for washing	Cleansing through confession
3. Candlestick/Lampstand	Enlighted by the Holy Spirit
4. Table of Showbread	Fed by the Living Word
5. Altar of Incense	Prayer, communication, intercession
6-7. Through the Veil into the Most Holy Place	Entering God's presence boldly through Christ.
8. Priests and the garments	Service to God and others.

Why is The Tabernacle Important Today?
1. Today, we are God's dwelling place. 1 Cor. 6:19
2. God's holy presence is among us. Exodus 40:34-38
3. As believers, we are part of a priesthood. 1 Peter 2:5, 9; Rev. 5:10; Rev. 20:6, and Hebrews 4:16.
4. The Tabernacle shows a pattern of worship prescribed by God. Hebrews 10:19-25

The Garments of the High Priest

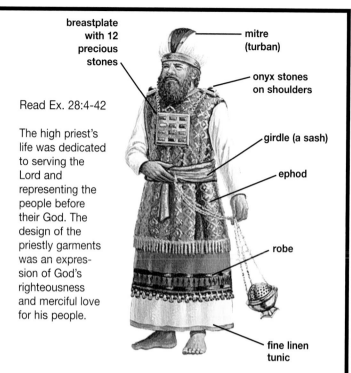

breastplate with 12 precious stones

mitre (turban)

onyx stones on shoulders

girdle (a sash)

ephod

robe

fine linen tunic

• The priest dressed first in a tunic and mitre (a turban) of fine linen.
• The mitre had a gold plate (or crown) inscribed with the words "HOLINESS TO THE LORD" just over the priest's forehead. The Hebrew words can also be translated "Set Apart as Holy to the Lord." This was worn in the Lord's presence so that the people's sacrifices would always be acceptable to God.
• The priest wore a blue robe with the ephod (a vest or waist coat) with stones on each shoulder bearing the names of the sons of Israel.
• Over the ephod, the priest wore a gold breastplate that was set with twelve precious stones carved with the names of the twelve tribes of Israel. This was worn over his heart and was to continually remind the Lord of his people (v. 29).
• The Urim and Thummim were kept in the priest's pocket over his heart as objects used to determine the Lord's will for his people.

To think about:

Our service to God is to be holy and set apart. As we pray for others and bring their names and burdens to God, we remember that God loves his children with deep affection. (Read Jer. 31:3.)

Christ is our example as high priest: he is righteous and merciful. He was willing to sacrifice his life for us and now lives to intercede for us. (Read Matt. 20:25-28 and Heb. 7:25.)

Read Ex. 28:4-42

The high priest's life was dedicated to serving the Lord and representing the people before their God. The design of the priestly garments was an expression of God's righteousness and merciful love for his people.

The Tabernacle

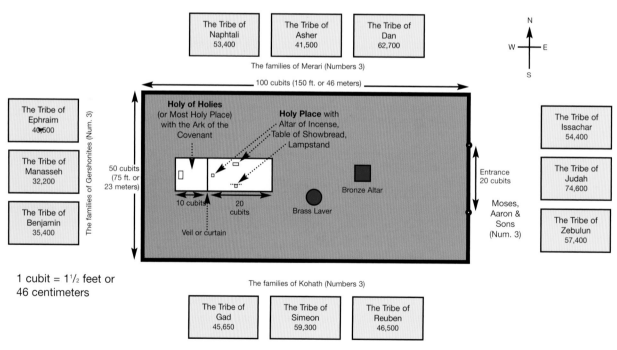

N
W — E
S

The Tribe of Naphtali 53,400

The Tribe of Asher 41,500

The Tribe of Dan 62,700

The families of Merari (Numbers 3)

100 cubits (150 ft. or 46 meters)

The Tribe of Ephraim 40,500

The Tribe of Manasseh 32,200

The Tribe of Benjamin 35,400

The families of Gershonites (Num. 3)

50 cubits (75 ft. or 23 meters)

Holy of Holies (or Most Holy Place) with the Ark of the Covenant

Holy Place with Altar of Incense, Table of Showbread, Lampstand

10 cubits
20 cubits

Veil or curtain

Brass Laver

Bronze Altar

Entrance 20 cubits

Moses, Aaron & Sons (Num. 3)

The Tribe of Issachar 54,400

The Tribe of Judah 74,600

The Tribe of Zebulun 57,400

1 cubit = 1½ feet or 46 centimeters

The families of Kohath (Numbers 3)

The Tribe of Gad 45,650

The Tribe of Simeon 59,300

The Tribe of Reuben 46,500

What is the Tabernacle?

The Tabernacle was a moveable "tent of meeting" that God commanded Moses to build. (Read Exodus 25:1, 2 and 25:8, 9.) God wanted to dwell among his people, the Israelites. He wanted to have fellowship with them and be able to communicate with them (Ex. 25:22).

The Tabernacle and its courtyard were constructed according to a pattern set by God, not by Moses. We study the Tabernacle to understand the steps that the Lord laid out for a sinful people to approach a holy God. The Tabernacle became the place that God dwelt with his people for 400 years: from the Exodus until the time of King Solomon, when the Temple was built.

The Tabernacle was in the center of the Israelite camp. The 12 Tribes of Israel were encamped around it. The figures in the boxes refer to the number of males age 20 or over in each tribe. The total would be 603,550.

Fascinating Facts About the Tabernacle

• There are 50 chapters in the Bible that discuss the Tabernacle.
• The Tabernacle would have fit in half of a football or soccer field.
• The Tabernacle of the Old Testament was a "shadow" of things in heaven. Hebrews 8:1-5 tells us that the real Tabernacle is in heaven. This is where Jesus Himself is our high priest (Heb. 8:2).
• The Tabernacle was built using many expensive materials: gold, silver, bronze, precious woods, and rare cloth. In modern terms the cost would exceed $1 million. Offerings from the Israelites paid for the materials. (Ex. 35:22-36:3)
• The Israelites were so generous they gave more than was needed. Moses had to command them to stop giving. (Ex. 36:6)

Sacrifices in the Tabernacle

Sacrifice	Meaning Today
Sin Offering and Guilt Offering (Leviticus 4–6; Numbers 15:1-12) Sin offerings and guilt offerings focused on paying for sin. The sin offerings atoned for sins against God. The guilt offerings addressed sins against others, and included paying damages with interest. Various animals were offered, depending on the person's position and income. Priests and leaders, as examples to others, had to offer larger sacrifices for sin, while the poor offered what they could afford. Blood was sprinkled on the altar, the parts of the animals were burned, often with wine poured on them (drink offering). Other parts were roasted for the priests. Since the priests were full-time Tabernacle workers, sacrificed animals were their main source of food.	**Christ's Offering:** Isaiah 53:10; Matthew 20:28; 2 Corinthians 5:21 **Paying for Damages:** Matthew 5:23, 24; Luke 19:1-10 **Poor:** Luke 2:2-24; 21:1-4 **Leaders as Examples:** 1 Timothy 3:1-7; 5:19, 20 **Providing for Christian Workers:** Philippians 4:18; 1 Corinthians 9:13, 14; 1 Timothy 5:17, 18
Burnt Offering (Leviticus 1) This sacrifice represented complete dedication and surrender to God. The animal, usually an unblemished male, bears the worshipper's sins, and dies in his/her place. After the blood was sprinkled on the altar, the animal was completely burned up. None of it was roasted for eating.	**Surrender:** Psalm 51:16, 17; Matthew 26:39; Romans 12:1 **Dedication:** Philippians 2:17; 2 Timothy 4:6, 7
 **Grain (Meal) Offering** (Leviticus 2) This offering was given to God in thankfulness. The people brought fine flour, unleavened cakes, or roasted grain to the priests. The priests burned a symbolic handful at the altar, and could partake of the rest. There was very little ceremony involved. 	**Giving:** Matthew 26:6-10; 2 Corinthians 9:7-11 **Praise:** Psalm 100; Hebrews 13:15, 16 **Thankfulness:** Psalm 147; Philippians 4:6
 **Fellowship (Peace) Offering** (Leviticus 2; 7:11-21) This offering symbolized fellowship and peace with God through shed blood. After some meat was ceremonially waved and given to the priests, worshippers and their guests could share in the feast as a meal with God.	**God's Peace:** Colossians 1:20; Acts 10:36 **God's Feast:** Luke 14:15-24; 1 Corinthians 11:17-26; Jude 1:12; Revelation 3:20

THE ARK OF THE COVENANT

The Ark of the Covenant and the Mercy Seat

2¼ feet (69 cm)

← 3¾ feet (114 cm) →

← 2¼ feet (69 cm) →

The carrying poles were fifteen feet long. They are not drawn to scale.

The Ark of the Covenant was the place where God met and talked with Moses (Exodus 25:22). It was made of acacia wood and covered with gold.

The Tabernacle (the "tent of meeting") was built to house the Ark of the Covenant. The Ark was the first item of furniture constructed after God told Moses to build the Tabernacle (Exodus 25:10-22).

The Ark of the Covenant was intended to be the central focus of the Most Holy Place in the Tabernacle and later the Temple (Exodus 40:1-21). The Ark of the Covenant rested in the Most Holy Place and both were separated from the rest of the Holy Place by a thick curtain (veil) according to Exodus 26:31-33. The heavy veil in the Temple was torn from top to bottom at the moment of Jesus' death (Matthew 27:50-51). The torn veil symbolizes the free access believers have through Christ to the presence of God. (Hebrews 6:19-20; 10:19-20)

God set apart the tribe of Levi to carry the Ark and stand before Him, to serve Him, and to bless His Name (Deuteronomy 10:8). Only the High Priest was allowed to enter the Holy of Holies once a year (Leviticus 16) on Yom Kippur, the Day of Atonement, to sacrifice and to sprinkle blood on the Mercy Seat (the top of the Ark of the Covenant where the winged cherubim face each other) to atone for the sins of the people (Exodus 37:6-9).

2 Samuel 6:2 and Psalm 99:1 say that God dwells between the cherubim.

The Journey of the Ark of the Covenant from Mt. Sinai

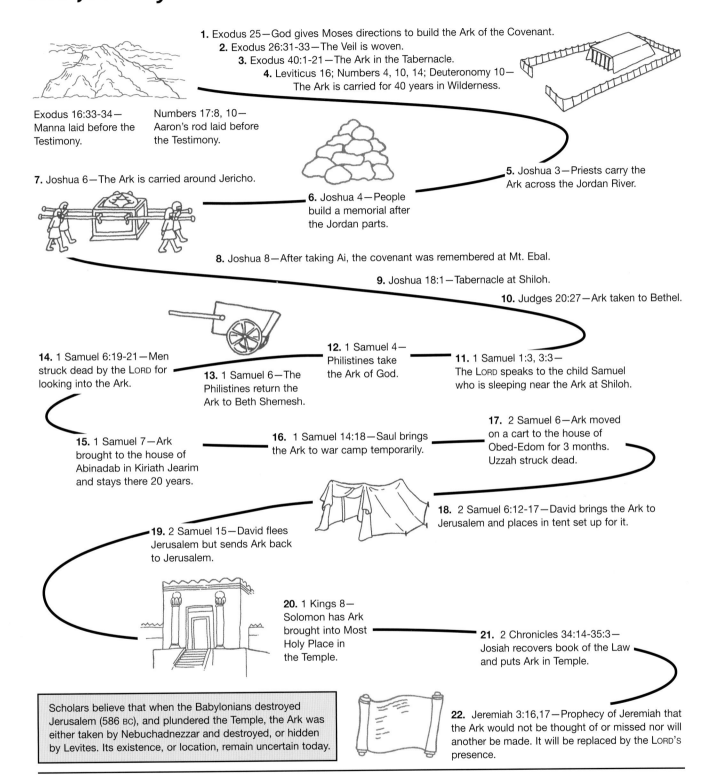

1. Exodus 25—God gives Moses directions to build the Ark of the Covenant.
2. Exodus 26:31-33—The Veil is woven.
3. Exodus 40:1-21—The Ark in the Tabernacle.
4. Leviticus 16; Numbers 4, 10, 14; Deuteronomy 10—The Ark is carried for 40 years in Wilderness.

Exodus 16:33-34—Manna laid before the Testimony.

Numbers 17:8, 10—Aaron's rod laid before the Testimony.

7. Joshua 6—The Ark is carried around Jericho.

6. Joshua 4—People build a memorial after the Jordan parts.

5. Joshua 3—Priests carry the Ark across the Jordan River.

8. Joshua 8—After taking Ai, the covenant was remembered at Mt. Ebal.

9. Joshua 18:1—Tabernacle at Shiloh.

10. Judges 20:27—Ark taken to Bethel.

14. 1 Samuel 6:19-21—Men struck dead by the LORD for looking into the Ark.

13. 1 Samuel 6—The Philistines return the Ark to Beth Shemesh.

12. 1 Samuel 4—Philistines take the Ark of God.

11. 1 Samuel 1:3, 3:3—The LORD speaks to the child Samuel who is sleeping near the Ark at Shiloh.

15. 1 Samuel 7—Ark brought to the house of Abinadab in Kiriath Jearim and stays there 20 years.

16. 1 Samuel 14:18—Saul brings the Ark to war camp temporarily.

17. 2 Samuel 6—Ark moved on a cart to the house of Obed-Edom for 3 months. Uzzah struck dead.

19. 2 Samuel 15—David flees Jerusalem but sends Ark back to Jerusalem.

18. 2 Samuel 6:12-17—David brings the Ark to Jerusalem and places in tent set up for it.

20. 1 Kings 8—Solomon has Ark brought into Most Holy Place in the Temple.

21. 2 Chronicles 34:14-35:3—Josiah recovers book of the Law and puts Ark in Temple.

Scholars believe that when the Babylonians destroyed Jerusalem (586 BC), and plundered the Temple, the Ark was either taken by Nebuchadnezzar and destroyed, or hidden by Levites. Its existence, or location, remain uncertain today.

22. Jeremiah 3:16,17—Prophecy of Jeremiah that the Ark would not be thought of or missed nor will another be made. It will be replaced by the LORD'S presence.

Hebrews 9:7, 11, 12—But only the high priest entered the inner room, and that only once a year, and never without blood, which he offered [by sprinkling on the Ark] for himself and for the sins the people had committed in ignorance. When Christ came as high priest of the good things that are already here, he went through the greater and more perfect tabernacle that is not man-made, that is to say, not a part of this creation. He did not enter by means of the blood of goats and calves; but he entered the Most Holy Place once for all by his own blood, having obtained eternal redemption.

Revelation 11:19— Then God's temple in heaven was opened, and within his temple was seen the ark of his covenant. And there came flashes of lightning, rumblings, peals of thunder, an earthquake and a great hailstorm.

SOLOMON'S TEMPLE

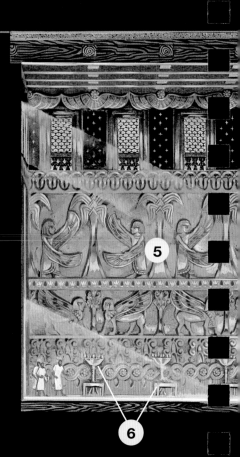

The Temple is shown here with the north wall removed.   East is at the left; west is to the right.

BRONZE ALTAR
Fires transformed
sacrifice to ash.

THE SEA held
17,500 gallons
(66 kiloliters)for
ceremonial washing.
(1 Kings 7:23)

BRONZE PILLARS "Jachin"
and "Boaz" supported
the roof of the **PORTICO**.

HOLY PLACE

LAMPSTANDS, TABLES
for bread of the presence.

BIBLICAL SOURCES—
1 Ki. 6-8, 1 Ch. 28, 29;
2 Ch. 2-5 Interior dimensions
(in Royal Cubits)—Length:
102.5 ft. (31.5 meters);
Width: 34.2 ft. (10.5 m);
Height: 5 stories (15.75 m).
(In common cubits)—90 ft.
(27 m) by 30 ft. (9 m);
4½ stories high (13.5 m).

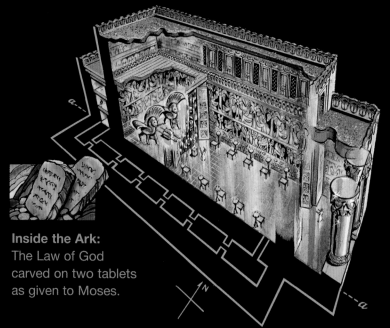

ARK OF THE COVENANT—Beneath wings of
guarding cherubim was this gold-covered chest
carried from the wilderness of Sinai.
Its lid was regarded as the very throne of God;
upon it the High Priest placed life (blood)
and from here God poured forth His mercy.

Inside the Ark:
The Law of God
carved on two tablets
as given to Moses.

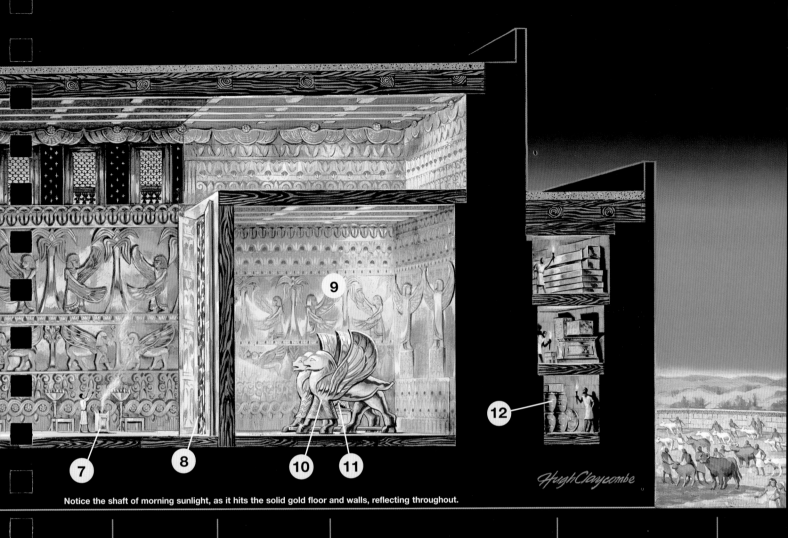

Notice the shaft of morning sunlight, as it hits the solid gold floor and walls, reflecting throughout.

HughClaycombe

INCENSE ALTAR for time of prayer.

BARRIER TAPESTRY "veil" or "curtain" with blue, purple, crimson design on linen.

CHERUBIM Massive sculptures touched each other wingtip to wingtip and wall to wall.

BEDROCK upon which the Temple rested was once a threshing floor honorably purchased by Solomon's father, David. (2 Samuel 24:24)

STORE ROOMS or "Treasuries" 3 stories high surrounded Temple on sides and rear, and contained the king's wealth.

ART FORMS—"On the walls…he (Solomon) carved cherubim, palm trees," "so he overlaid the whole interior with gold." (1 Kings 6) These were not objects of worship but only for God. Cherubim were winged spiritual beings guarding sacred objects. Scripture says the Temple was decorated with various colors, turquoise, and marble, inlaid and painted possibly similar to other ancient temples.

Living creatures being led to the Temple for sacrifice. Their blood would bear away the sin of a repenting and praying people temporarily.

SACRIFICE—Creature killed and its blood (life) drained away into vessels, placed on horns and base of altar then (daily) before Barrier Tapestry. Other portions were eaten or burned.

THE TEMPLE CONSTRUCTION began in 966 BC, took seven years to build, and was destroyed by the Babylonians in 586 BC. Solomon relied on the architects of King Hiram of Tyre. Therefore, his temple was an expression of the Syrian "long room plan" of that region and period of history.

a------   ------a

THE TEMPLE TOUR

The Temple in the Bible was built in 960 BC by King Solomon. To understand the Temple's purpose, it is important to know that God made the world and established the rules. God told Adam that the result of sin was death, Adam disobeyed, and sin, death, and disease entered the world. In spite of this, God loved his people and had mercy.

Before Jesus' death and resurrection, God provided a way to atone for sin so that people could be in His holy presence. God allowed the blood of a perfect animal to temporarily take the place of the sinner's life. This blood sacrifice took away sin and made the sinner right with God temporarily.

God loved the world so much that He sent His son Jesus to atone, or take away, a believer's sin once and for all. The blood of Jesus Christ was the final sacrifice needed. (Genesis 2:17; 4:3-7; Leviticus 1; 16:1, 2; Isaiah 59:2; Romans 3:23; Hebrews 10:26-31)

Here are steps to peace with God during the time of the temple ("Then") and today ("Now").

1 BRAZEN ALTAR (Bronze Altar)
Then God required the people to regularly sacrifice a perfect animal (lambs, goats, doves, bulls) for their sins. The blood of the animal justified the people before God and restored their relationship with Him.
Now Jesus is our perfect sacrifice. He led a sinless life and willingly died for our sins to make us right with God for all time. No more sacrifices are required. (Lev.17:11; Heb. 9:25; John 1:29; Rev. 13:8; Hebrews 10:10; Rom. 4:25)

2 SACRIFICE
Then The person bringing the offering put his hand on the head of the animal while it was killed, symbolically putting his sins onto the animal. The animal died in his place.
Now Jesus is the Lamb of God, just as bulls or lambs were sacrificed. We are told to present our bodies as a living sacrifice acceptable to God, holy, not conformed to the world, and with a renewed mind. (John 1:29; Romans 12:1, 2)

We are to offer God another kind of sacrifice: praising His name, doing good, and sharing with others. (Hebrews 13:15, 16)

3 "THE SEA" (Bronze Basin)
Then Priests washed themselves at the basin, purifying themselves before entering the Temple. It was about 15 ft. (4.6 m) across and held more than 10,000 gallons (38,000 liters) of water. It stood on 12 bronze oxen.
Now Believers in Christ are saved and cleansed by the blood of Jesus.
Even though we have accepted Jesus' sacrificial death on our behalf, we too need to be cleansed, spiritually. If we confess our sins, God will forgive and cleanse us. (Exodus 30:18; 38:8; 1 Kings 7:23-26; 1 John 1:7-10)

4 BRASS PILLARS (Bronze Pillars)
Then The pillars, called "Jachin" on the right and "Boaz" on the left, supported the roof of the portico. They were 27 feet (9 m) high.
Now Those who are faithful to Jesus through trials will be made "a pillar" in the Temple of God. (Revelation 3:12)

5 HOLY PLACE
Then Only priests were allowed to enter the Holy Place. They did this daily.
Now Believers in Jesus have been made holy through Jesus' sacrifice and can go directly to God. (Ex.29–30; Heb. 9–10)

6 GOLDEN LAMPSTANDS AND TABLES OF SHOWBREAD
Then Ten gold lampstands and ten tables for bread were made for the Temple. (1 Kings 7:49; 2 Chron. 4:7, 8, 19, 20)
Now Christ is the light of the world and the bread of life. (John 9:5; 6:48-51)

7 GOLDEN INCENSE ALTAR
Then Prayers were offered at the gold Altar of Incense where special sweet incense required by God was burned.
Now The prayers of God's people are a sweet incense to God. (1 Kings 6:22; 2 Chronicles 4:19; Exodus 30:35-37; Rev. 5:8)

8 THE VEIL
(Curtain, and doors of olive wood)
Then The veil separated the Holy Place from the Most Holy Place where the Ark of the Covenant rested, separating a holy

God from sinful people. Once a year only the High Priest entered here.
Now Believers in Jesus may enter God's presence through prayer because they are made acceptable to God by the blood of Jesus, the great High Priest. When Jesus died, the Temple veil tore in two from top to bottom. (2 Chronicles 3:14; 1 Kings 6:31-35; Exodus 25–26; Matt. 27:51; Heb. 10:19-22)

9 MOST HOLY PLACE
Then The Most Holy Place was God's throne room where He would meet and give His commands, between the two cherubim, on the Mercy Seat over the Ark of the Covenant. The high priest sprinkled blood on the Mercy Seat on the Day of Atonement to atone for the sins of the people for that year.
Now believers can come boldly before God's throne of grace. (Hebrews 14:16)

10 CHERUBIM
Then Massive olive-wood sculptures of cherubim, winged creatures, represented the guardians of God's divine presence. These cherubim were overlaid with gold and they touched each other, wingtip to wingtip and wall to wall. When God banished man from the Garden of Eden, he placed cherubim and a flaming sword to guard the way to the tree of life. (1 Kings 6:19-29; Genesis 3:24)
Now Believers can have eternal life in God's presence through faith in Jesus Christ. (John 3:16; John 17)

11 ARK OF THE COVENANT
Then The Ark was a carved wooden box overlaid with gold. Inside was the Law of God (the Ten Commandments) inscribed on two tablets of stone. Its lid, the Mercy Seat, represented the meeting place between God and man (Ex.25:10-22).
Now God wants to commune with us today. He made it possible to know Him through Jesus. (Jn. 14:6; Heb. 9:4; 10:22)

12 STOREROOMS (Treasuries)
Then Three-story rooms contained the treasures of God's Temple and the dedicated gifts. These treasures were plundered several times.
Now We are commanded by Jesus to not lay up treasures for ourselves on earth, but to lay up treasures in heaven. (1 Chronicles 28:11, 12; Matthew 6:19-21)

JESUS & THE TEMPLE

Birth

• About forty days after his birth Jesus' parents brought him into the Temple to be presented to the Lord, as required in the Law. They would have offered a sacrifice of a pair of doves or two young pigeons. (Luke 2:22-24; Leviticus 12:3-8)

• The Holy Spirit revealed to Simeon, a righteous and devout man, that he would see the Lord's Christ before he died. Moved by the Spirit, he came into the Temple and took the baby Jesus in his arms and praised God, saying, "My eyes have seen your salvation . . . a light for revelation to the Gentiles and for glory to your people Israel." (Luke 2:25-33)

• An elderly prophetess Anna, who was worshiping, fasting and praying in the Temple night and day, gave thanks to God and spoke about the child to all who were looking forward to the redemption of Jerusalem. (Luke 2:36-38)

From Thirty Years Old

• Jesus was about 30 years old when he began his ministry. After he was baptized, he was tempted by the devil for 40 days. The devil led him to the highest point of the Temple and dared him to throw himself down since he was the Son of God.

© 2004 Hugh Claycombe

Jesus said, "It is written, you must not put the Lord your God to the test." The devil left for awhile. (Matthew 3:16, 17; 4:1-7; Luke 4:1-13 Deuteronomy 6:16)

• Jesus taught in the Temple often. (Matthew 12; 21; 24; 26:55; Mark 11–15; Luke 18–21; Luke 22:53; John 2–10; 18:20)

• Jesus drove out all those buying and selling in the Temple. He said that His house was a house of prayer, but they had made it a den of thieves. (Matthew 21:12, 13; Mark 11:15-17; Luke 19:45, 46; John 2:14, 15)

• Jesus healed blind and sick people in the Temple. (Matthew 21:14)

• Jesus told parables in the Temple. (Matthew 21:23-46; 22:1-14; Mark 12:1-11)

Twelve Years Old

• When Jesus was 12 years old, his family went to the Passover feast in Jerusalem. Three days after it ended, his parents found him in the Temple courts, sitting among the teachers, listening and answering questions. All who heard him were astonished at his understanding and answers. He said he had to be doing his Father's business. (Luke 2:41-50)

• Jesus watched people give money in the Temple. He commented on the widow who gave all she had. (Mark 12:41; Luke 21)

• Jesus said that He was greater than the Temple. (Matthew 12:6)

• He said, "Destroy this Temple, and I will raise it in three days," referring to his death and resurrection. (John 2:19-22; 22:21)

HEROD'S TEMPLE

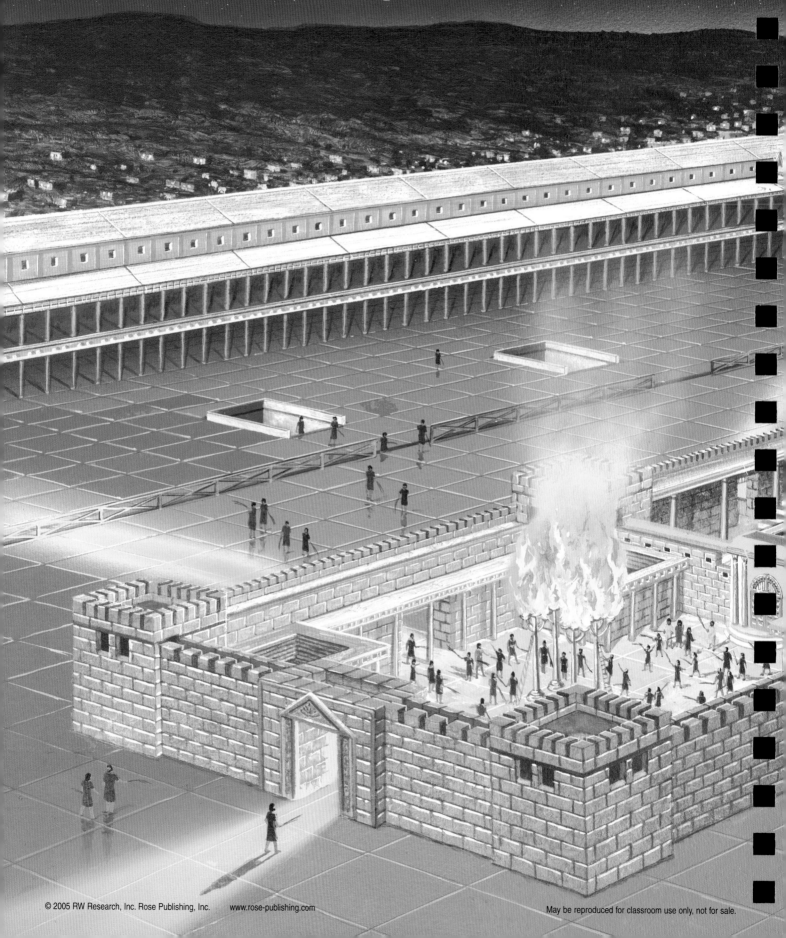

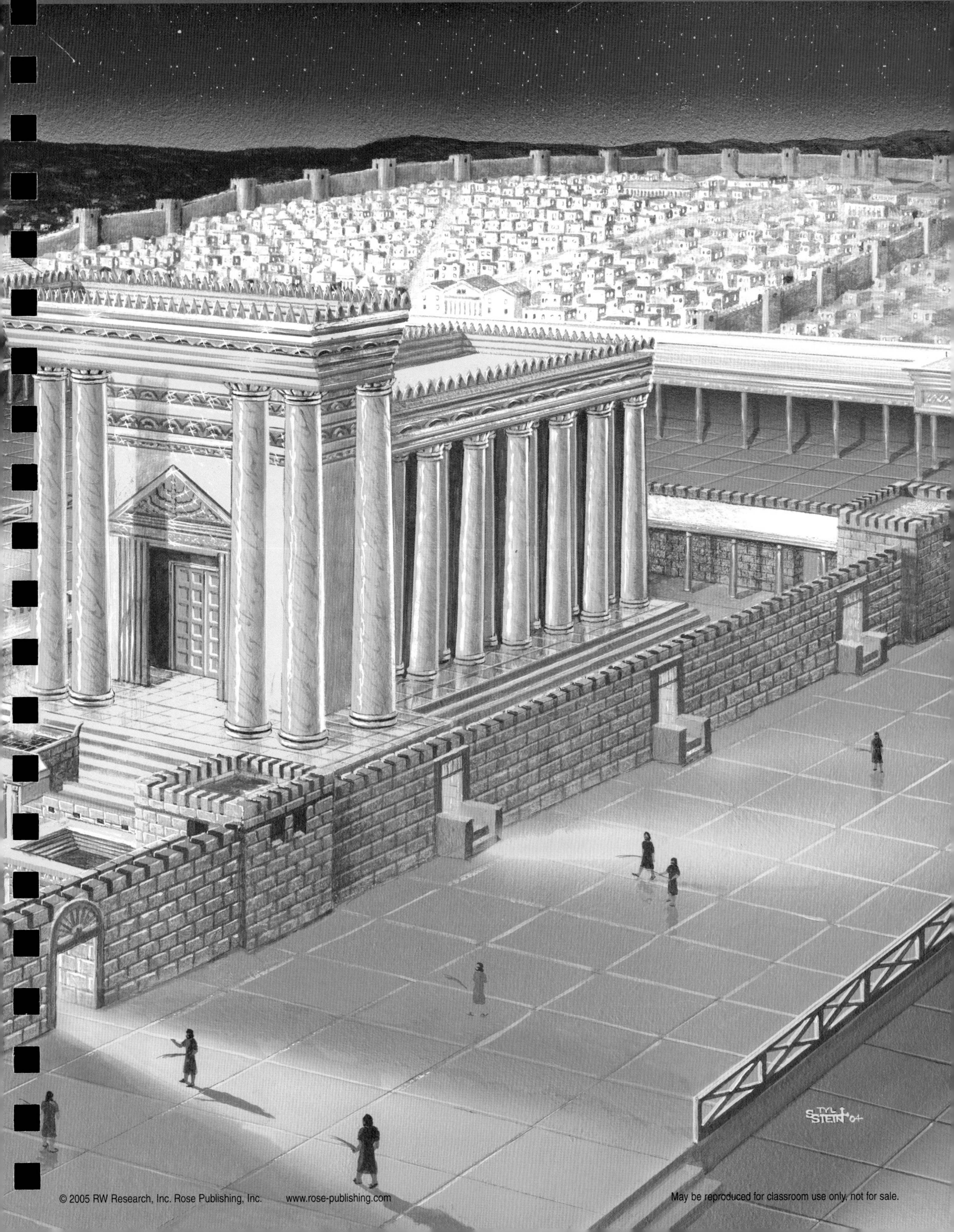
STYLSTEIN '04

Herod's Temple – 20 BC–AD 70
Aerial view showing outer courts

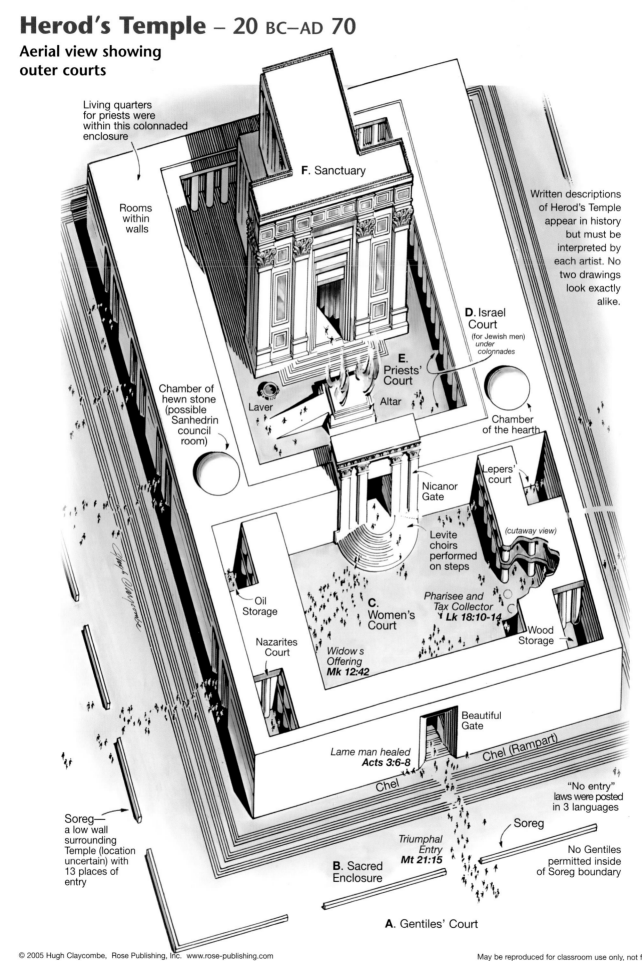

Living quarters for priests were within this colonnaded enclosure

Rooms within walls

Chamber of hewn stone (possible Sanhedrin council room)

F. Sanctuary

Written descriptions of Herod's Temple appear in history but must be interpreted by each artist. No two drawings look exactly alike.

D. Israel Court
(for Jewish men) *under colonnades*

E. Priests' Court

Laver

Altar

Chamber of the hearth

Nicanor Gate

Lepers' court

(cutaway view)

Levite choirs performed on steps

Oil Storage

C. Women's Court

Nazarites Court

Pharisee and Tax Collector **Lk 18:10-14**

Wood Storage

Widow s Offering **Mk 12:42**

Beautiful Gate

Lame man healed **Acts 3:6-8**

Chel (Rampart)

Chel

"No entry" laws were posted in 3 languages

Soreg— a low wall surrounding Temple (location uncertain) with 13 places of entry

Triumphal Entry **Mt 21:15**

Soreg

No Gentiles permitted inside of Soreg boundary

B. Sacred Enclosure

A. Gentiles' Court

Herod's Temple – 20 BC–AD 70

Begun in 20 BC, Herod's new structure towered 15 stories high, following the floor dimensions of the former temples in the Holy Place and the Most Holy Place. The high sanctuary shown here in a cutaway view was built on the site of the former temples of Solomon and Zerubbabel, and was completed in just 18 months.

The outer courts surrounding the temple mount were not completed until AD 64. The entire structure was demolished by the Romans in AD 70.

Dimensions of rooms, steps, doorways, cornices and exterior measurements are mentioned in history (Josephus and the Mishnah) but are subject to interpretation, and all drawings vary.

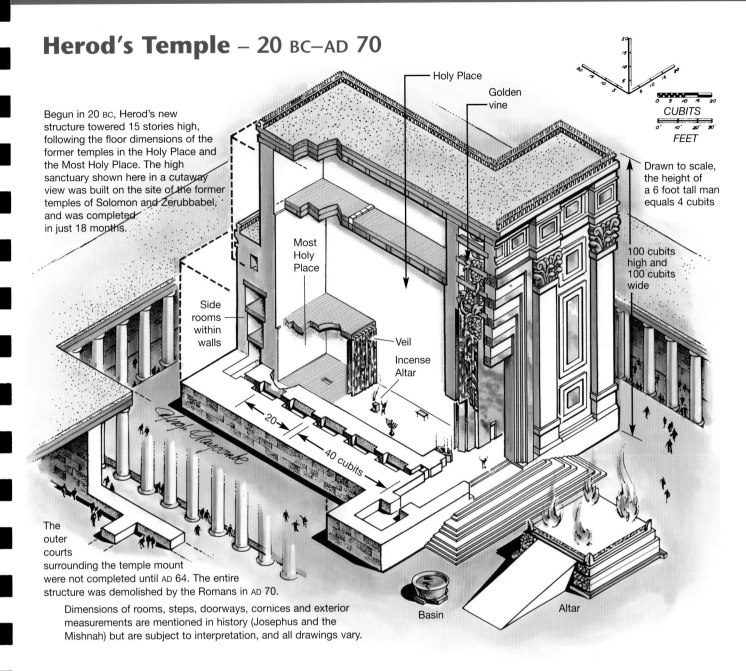

Holy Place

Golden vine

CUBITS

FEET

Drawn to scale, the height of a 6 foot tall man equals 4 cubits

100 cubits high and 100 cubits wide

Most Holy Place

Side rooms within walls

Veil

Incense Altar

20

40 cubits

Basin

Altar

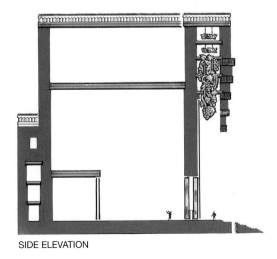

SIDE ELEVATION

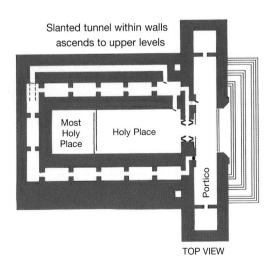

Slanted tunnel within walls ascends to upper levels

Most Holy Place

Holy Place

Portico

TOP VIEW

Jerusalem, the Mount of Olives and Bethany

Walking with Jesus Each Day

2. Clearing of the Temple MONDAY
Mt 21:10–17;
Mk 11:15–18;
Lk 19:45–48

The next day he returned to the Temple and found the court of the Gentiles full of traders and money changers making large profits as they gave out Jewish coins in exchange for "pagan" money. Jesus drove them out and overturned their tables.

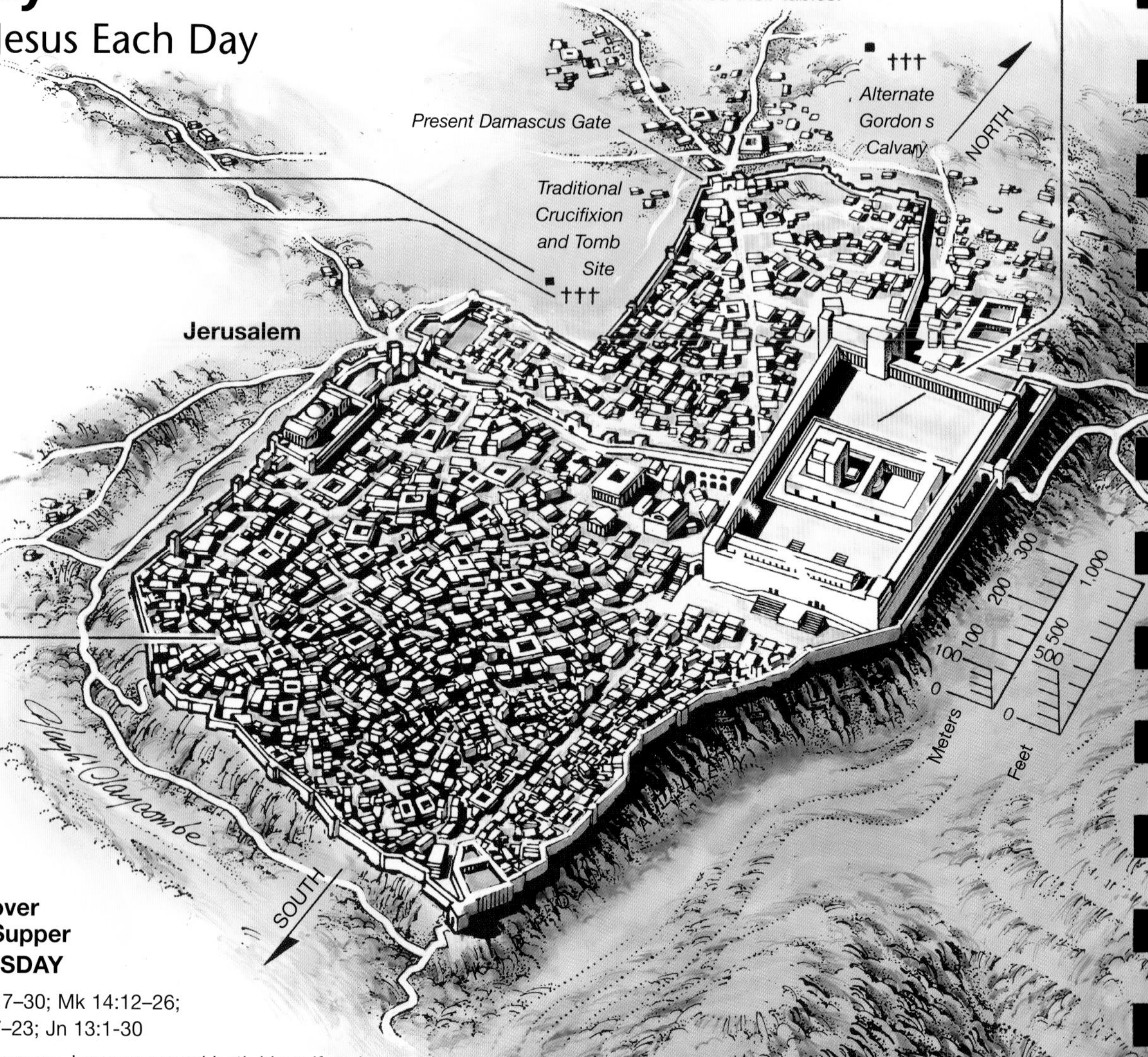

†††
Alternate Gordon's Calvary

Present Damascus Gate

Traditional Crucifixion and Tomb Site
†††

Jerusalem

NORTH

SOUTH

Meters
Feet
0 100 200 300
0 500 1,000

5. Passover Last Supper THURSDAY

Mt 26:17–30; Mk 14:12–26;
Lk 22:7–23; Jn 13:1-30

In an upper room Jesus prepared both himself and his disciples for his death. He gave the Passover meal a new meaning. The loaf of bread and cup of wine represented his body soon to be sacrificed and his blood soon to be shed. And so he instituted the "Lord's Supper." After singing a hymn they went to the Garden of Gethsemane, where Jesus prayed in agony, knowing what lay ahead of him.

6. Crucifixion FRIDAY Mt 27:1–66; Mk 15:1–47; Lk 22:66–23:56; Jn 18:28–19:37
Following betrayal, arrest, desertion, false trials, denial, condemnation, beatings, and mockery, Jesus was required to carry his cross to "The Place of the Skull," where he was crucified with two other prisoners.

7. In the tomb FRIDAY afternoon, SATURDAY, SUNDAY morning
Jesus' body was placed in the tomb before 6:00 PM Friday night, when the Sabbath began and all work stopped, and it lay in the tomb throughout the Sabbath.

8. Resurrection SUNDAY Mt 28:1–13; Mk 16:1–20; Lk 24:1–49; Jn 20:1–31
Early in the morning, women went to the tomb and found that the stone closing the tomb's entrance had been rolled back. An angel told them Jesus was alive. Jesus appeared to Mary Magdalene in the garden, to Peter, to the two disciples on the road to Emmaus, and later that day to all the disciples but Thomas. His resurrection was established as a fact.

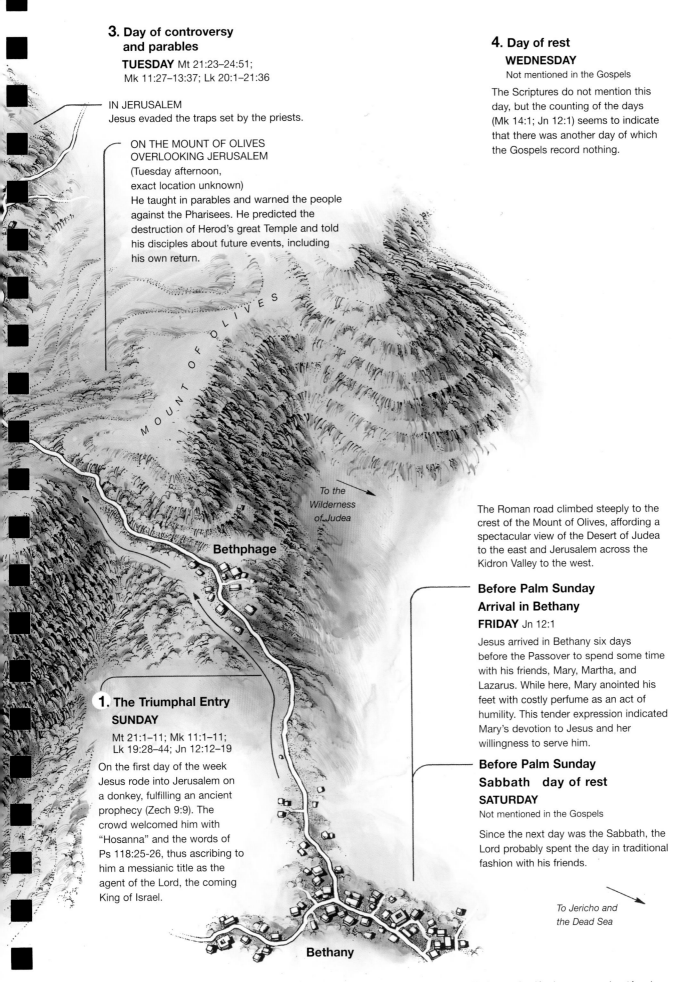

3. Day of controversy and parables

TUESDAY Mt 21:23–24:51;
Mk 11:27–13:37; Lk 20:1–21:36

IN JERUSALEM
Jesus evaded the traps set by the priests.

ON THE MOUNT OF OLIVES
OVERLOOKING JERUSALEM
(Tuesday afternoon,
exact location unknown)
He taught in parables and warned the people
against the Pharisees. He predicted the
destruction of Herod's great Temple and told
his disciples about future events, including
his own return.

M O U N T   O F   O L I V E S

To the
Wilderness
of Judea

Bethphage

1. The Triumphal Entry

SUNDAY

Mt 21:1–11; Mk 11:1–11;
Lk 19:28–44; Jn 12:12–19

On the first day of the week
Jesus rode into Jerusalem on
a donkey, fulfilling an ancient
prophecy (Zech 9:9). The
crowd welcomed him with
"Hosanna" and the words of
Ps 118:25-26, thus ascribing to
him a messianic title as the
agent of the Lord, the coming
King of Israel.

Bethany

4. Day of rest

WEDNESDAY

Not mentioned in the Gospels

The Scriptures do not mention this
day, but the counting of the days
(Mk 14:1; Jn 12:1) seems to indicate
that there was another day of which
the Gospels record nothing.

The Roman road climbed steeply to the
crest of the Mount of Olives, affording a
spectacular view of the Desert of Judea
to the east and Jerusalem across the
Kidron Valley to the west.

Before Palm Sunday
Arrival in Bethany

FRIDAY Jn 12:1

Jesus arrived in Bethany six days
before the Passover to spend some time
with his friends, Mary, Martha, and
Lazarus. While here, Mary anointed his
feet with costly perfume as an act of
humility. This tender expression indicated
Mary's devotion to Jesus and her
willingness to serve him.

Before Palm Sunday
Sabbath   day of rest

SATURDAY

Not mentioned in the Gospels

Since the next day was the Sabbath, the
Lord probably spent the day in traditional
fashion with his friends.

To Jericho and
the Dead Sea

Jesus' Hours on the Cross

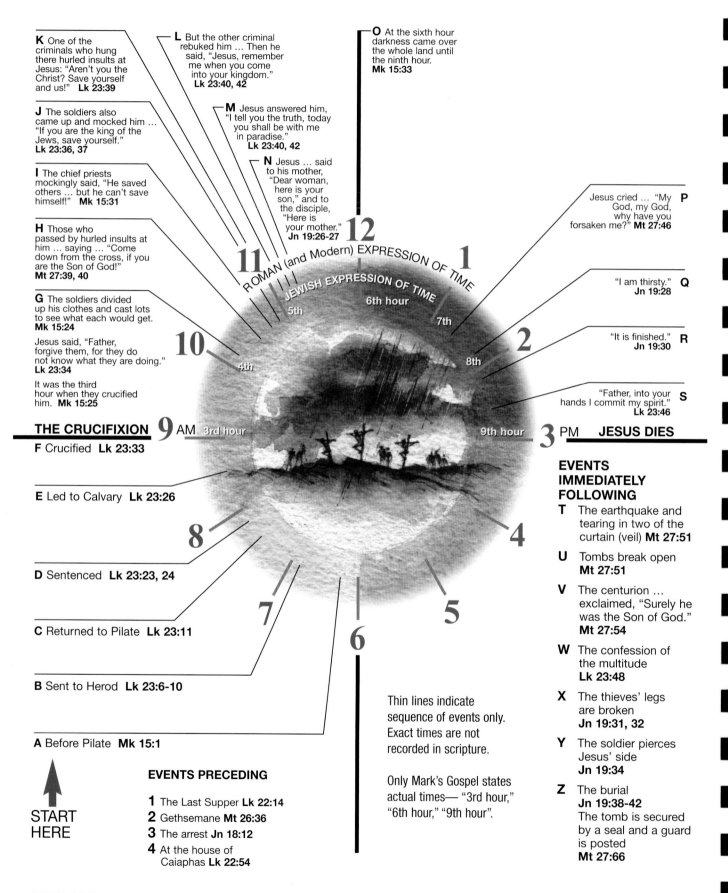

K One of the criminals who hung there hurled insults at Jesus: "Aren't you the Christ? Save yourself and us!" **Lk 23:39**

J The soldiers also came up and mocked him ... "If you are the king of the Jews, save yourself." **Lk 23:36, 37**

I The chief priests mockingly said, "He saved others ... but he can't save himself!" **Mk 15:31**

H Those who passed by hurled insults at him ... saying ... "Come down from the cross, if you are the Son of God!" **Mt 27:39, 40**

G The soldiers divided up his clothes and cast lots to see what each would get. **Mk 15:24**

Jesus said, "Father, forgive them, for they do not know what they are doing." **Lk 23:34**

It was the third hour when they crucified him. **Mk 15:25**

THE CRUCIFIXION

F Crucified **Lk 23:33**

E Led to Calvary **Lk 23:26**

D Sentenced **Lk 23:23, 24**

C Returned to Pilate **Lk 23:11**

B Sent to Herod **Lk 23:6-10**

A Before Pilate **Mk 15:1**

L But the other criminal rebuked him ... Then he said, "Jesus, remember me when you come into your kingdom." **Lk 23:40, 42**

M Jesus answered him, "I tell you the truth, today you shall be with me in paradise." **Lk 23:40, 42**

N Jesus ... said to his mother, "Dear woman, here is your son," and to the disciple, "Here is your mother." **Jn 19:26-27**

O At the sixth hour darkness came over the whole land until the ninth hour. **Mk 15:33**

ROMAN (and Modern) EXPRESSION OF TIME

JEWISH EXPRESSION OF TIME

5th hour · 6th hour · 7th

4th · 8th

3rd hour · 9th hour

9 AM · **3** PM · **JESUS DIES**

P Jesus cried ... "My God, my God, why have you forsaken me?" **Mt 27:46**

Q "I am thirsty." **Jn 19:28**

R "It is finished." **Jn 19:30**

S "Father, into your hands I commit my spirit." **Lk 23:46**

EVENTS IMMEDIATELY FOLLOWING

T The earthquake and tearing in two of the curtain (veil) **Mt 27:51**

U Tombs break open **Mt 27:51**

V The centurion ... exclaimed, "Surely he was the Son of God." **Mt 27:54**

W The confession of the multitude **Lk 23:48**

X The thieves' legs are broken **Jn 19:31, 32**

Y The soldier pierces Jesus' side **Jn 19:34**

Z The burial **Jn 19:38-42** The tomb is secured by a seal and a guard is posted **Mt 27:66**

START HERE

EVENTS PRECEDING

1 The Last Supper **Lk 22:14**
2 Gethsemane **Mt 26:36**
3 The arrest **Jn 18:12**
4 At the house of Caiaphas **Lk 22:54**

Thin lines indicate sequence of events only. Exact times are not recorded in scripture.

Only Mark's Gospel states actual times— "3rd hour," "6th hour," "9th hour".

CHRISTIANITY, CULTS & RELIGIONS

Biblical Christianity

Key Person or Founder, Date, Location

Jesus Christ. Founded about AD 30–33, in the Judean province of Palestine (Israel today), under the Roman Empire. Followers of Jesus Christ became known as Christians.

Key Writings

The Bible, written originally in Hebrew and Aramaic (Old Testament), and Greek (New Testament).

Who is God?

The one God is Triune (one God in three Persons, not three gods): Father, Son, and Holy Spirit. Often the title "God" designates the first Person, God the Father. God is a spiritual being without a physical body. He is personal and involved with people. He created the universe out of nothing. He is eternal, changeless, holy, loving, and perfect.

Who is Jesus?

Jesus is God, the second Person of the Trinity. As God the Son, He has always existed and was never created. He is fully God and fully man (the two natures joined, not mixed). As the second Person of the Trinity, He is coequal with God the Father and the Holy Spirit. In becoming man, He was begotten through the Holy Spirit and born of the virgin Mary. Jesus is the only way to the Father, salvation, and eternal life. He died on a cross according to God's plan, as full sacrifice and payment for our sins. He rose from the dead on the third day, spiritually and physically immortal. For the next 40 days He was seen by more than 500 eyewitnesses. His wounds were touched and He ate meals. He physically ascended to Heaven. Jesus will come again visibly and physically at the end of the world to establish God's kingdom and judge the world.

Who is the Holy Spirit?

The Holy Spirit is God, the third Person of the Trinity. The Holy Spirit is a person, not a force or energy field. He comforts, grieves, reproves, convicts, guides, teaches, and fills Christians. He is not the Father, nor is he the Son, Jesus Christ.

How to Be Saved

Salvation is by God's grace, not by an individual's good works. Salvation must be received by faith. People must believe in their hearts that Jesus died for their sins and physically rose again, which is the assurance of forgiveness and resurrection of the body. This is God's loving plan to forgive sinful people.

What Happens After Death

Believers go to be with Jesus. After death, all people await the final Judgment. Both saved and lost people will be resurrected. Those who are saved will live with Jesus in Heaven. Those who are lost will suffer the torment of eternal separation from God (Hell). Jesus' bodily resurrection guarantees believers that they, too, will be resurrected and receive new immortal bodies.

Other Facts, Beliefs, or Practices

Group worship, usually in churches. No secret rites. Baptism and Lord's Supper (Communion). Active voluntary missionary efforts. Aid to those in need: the poor, widows, orphans, and downtrodden. Christians believe that Jesus is the Jewish Messiah promised to Israel in the Old Testament (Tanakh). Jesus said His followers would be known by their love for one another.

Jehovah's Witnesses
(Watchtower Bible & Tract Society)

Mormonism
(Latter-day Saints)

Unification Church

Founder

Jehovah's Witnesses: Charles Taze Russell (1852–1916), later Joseph F. Rutherford (1869–1942). Began 1879 in Pennsylvania. Headquarters in Brooklyn, New York.

Mormonism: Joseph Smith, Jr. (1805–1844), founded the Church of Jesus Christ of Latter-day Saints (LDS) in 1830 in New York. Headquarters in Salt Lake City, Utah.

Unification Church: Sun Myung Moon (b. 1920). Founded "Holy Spirit Association for the Unification of World Christianity" 1954 in South Korea. Current headquarters in New York City.

Writings

Jehovah's Witnesses: All current Watchtower publications, including the Bible (*New World Translation* only), *Reasoning from the Scriptures, You Can Live Forever in Paradise on Earth. Watchtower* and *Awake!* magazines.

Mormonism: The *Book of Mormon; Doctrine and Covenants; Pearl of Great Price;* the Bible (King James Version only or Smith's "Inspired Version"); authoritative teachings of Mormon prophets and other LDS "general authorities."

Unification Church: *Divine Principle* by Sun Myung Moon, considered the "Completed Testament." *Outline of the Principle, Level 4,* and the Bible. (The Bible is "not the truth itself, but a textbook teaching the truth.")

God

Jehovah's Witnesses: One-person God, called Jehovah. No Trinity. Jesus is the first thing Jehovah created.

Mormonism: God the Father was once a man, but "progressed" to godhood. He has a physical body, as does his wife (Heavenly Mother). No Trinity. Father, Son, and Holy Ghost are three separate gods. Worthy men may one day become gods themselves.

Unification Church: God is both positive and negative. God created the universe out of himself; the universe is God's "body." God does not know the future, is suffering, and needs man (Sun Myung Moon) to make Him happy. No Trinity.

Jesus

Jehovah's Witnesses: Jesus is not God. Before he lived on earth, he was Michael, the archangel. Jehovah made the universe through him. On earth he was a man who lived a perfect life. After dying on a stake (not a cross), he was resurrected as a spirit; his body was destroyed. Jesus is not coming again; he "returned" invisibly in 1914 in spirit. Very soon, he and the angels will destroy all non-Jehovah's Witnesses.

Mormonism: Jesus is a separate god from the Father (Elohim). He was created as a spirit child by the Father and Mother in Heaven, and is the "elder brother" of all men and spirit beings. His body was created through sexual union between Elohim and Mary. Jesus was married. His death on the cross does not provide full atonement for all sin, but does provide everyone with resurrection.

Unification Church: Jesus was a perfect man, not God. He is the son of Zechariah, not born of a virgin. His mission was to unite the Jews behind him, find a perfect bride, and begin a perfect family. The mission failed. Jesus did not resurrect physically. The second coming of Christ is fulfilled in Sun Myung Moon, who is superior to Jesus and will finish Jesus' mission.

Holy Spirit

Jehovah's Witnesses: Impersonal "holy spirit" is not God, but rather an invisible, active force from Jehovah.

Mormonism: The "holy spirit" is different from the "Holy Ghost." The "holy spirit" is not God, but is an influence or electricity-like emanation from God (or "light of Christ").

Unification Church: The Holy Spirit is a feminine spirit who works with Jesus in the spirit world to lead people to Sun Myung Moon.

Salvation

Jehovah's Witnesses: Be baptized as Jehovah's Witnesses. Most followers must earn everlasting life on earth by "door-to-door work." Salvation in heaven is limited to 144,000 "anointed ones." This number is already reached.

Mormonism: Resurrected by grace, but saved (exalted to godhood) by works, including faithfulness to church leaders, Mormon baptism, tithing, ordination, marriage, and secret temple rituals. No eternal life without Mormon membership.

Unification Church: Obedience to and acceptance of the True Parents (Moon and his wife) eliminate sin and result in perfection. Those married by Moon and his wife drink a special holy wine containing 21 ingredients (including the True Parents' blood).

Death

Jehovah's Witnesses: The 144,000 live as spirits in heaven. The rest of the righteous, "the great crowd," live on earth, and must obey God perfectly for 1,000 years or be annihilated.

Mormonism: Eventually nearly everyone goes to one of three separate heavenly "kingdoms," with some achieving godhood. Apostates and murderers go to "outer darkness."

Unification Church: After death one goes to the spirit world. There is no resurrection. Members advance by convincing others to follow Sun Myung Moon. Everyone will be saved, even Satan.

Other Beliefs

Jehovah's Witnesses: Known as the Watchtower Bible and Tract Society. Meet in "Kingdom Halls" instead of churches. Active members encouraged to distribute literature door-to-door. Once a year, Lord's Evening Meal (communion); only "anointed" ones may partake. Do not observe holidays or birthdays. Forbidden to vote, salute the flag, work in the military, or accept blood transfusions.

Mormonism: No alcohol, tobacco, coffee, or tea. Baptism on behalf of the dead. Two-year missionary commitment encouraged. Door-to-door proselytizing. Secret temple rituals available only to members in good standing. Extensive social network. People of African ancestry were not granted full access to Mormon priesthood and privileges until 1978.

Unification Church: Also known as "Family Federation for World Peace and Unification." Mass marriages, based on different racial backgrounds, arranged and performed by Moon. Members believe that Jesus bows down to Sun Myung Moon and that Moon is the King of Kings, Lord of Lords, and the Lamb of God. Contact with spirits of the dead accepted.

Christian Science

Founder

Mary Baker Eddy (1821–1910). Founded 1875 in Massachusetts. Current headquarters in Boston, Massachusetts.

Writings

Science and Health, With Key to the Scriptures; Miscellaneous Writings; Manual of the Mother Church; and other books by Mrs. Eddy. The Bible (not as reliable). Christian Science Journal, Christian Science Sentinel, and other official periodicals.

God

According to Mrs. Eddy, God is an impersonal Principle of life, truth, love, intelligence, and spirit. God is all that truly exists; matter is an illusion.

Jesus

Jesus was not the Christ, but a man who displayed the Christ idea. ("Christ" means perfection, not a person.) Jesus was not God, and God can never become man or flesh. He did not suffer and could not suffer for sins. He did not die on the cross. He was not resurrected physically. He will not literally come back.

Holy Spirit

Holy spirit is defined as the teaching of Christian Science. Impersonal power.

Salvation

Humanity is already eternally saved. Sin, evil, sickness, and death are not real.

Death

Death is not real. Heaven and hell are states of mind. The way to reach heaven is by attaining harmony (oneness with God).

Other Beliefs

Members use Christian Science "practitioners" (authorized professional healers who "treat" supposed illnesses for a fee) instead of doctors. Healing comes through realizing one cannot really be sick or hurt and that the body cannot be ill, suffer pain, or die (matter is an illusion). Attracts followers by claims of miraculous healing. Publishes Christian Science Monitor newspaper.

Unity School of Christianity

Founder

Charles (1854–1948) and Myrtle (1845–1931) Fillmore. Founded 1889 in Kansas City, Missouri. Headquarters in Unity Village, Missouri.

Writings

Unity magazine. Lessons in Truth, Metaphysical Bible Dictionary, the Bible (not as reliable, interpreted with "hidden" meanings).

God

Invisible impersonal power. "God" is interchangeable with "Principle," "Law," "Being," "Mind," "Spirit." God is in everything, much as the soul is in the body. No Trinity. The spirit is reality; matter is not.

Jesus

Jesus was a man and not the Christ. Instead, he was a man who had "Christ Consciousness." "Christ" is a state of perfection in every person. Jesus had lived many times before and was in search of his own salvation. Jesus did not die as a sacrifice for anyone's sins. Jesus did not rise physically and will never return to earth in physical form.

Holy Spirit

The Holy Spirit is the law of God in action, "the executive power of both Father and Son." A "definite" thought in the mind of man.

Salvation

By recognizing that each person is as much a Son of God as Jesus is. There is no evil, no devil, no sin, no poverty, and no old age. A person is reincarnated until he learns these truths and becomes "perfect."

Death

Death is a result of wrong thinking. One moves to a different body (reincarnation) until enlightenment. No literal heaven or hell.

Other Beliefs

Worship services in Unity churches. Counseling and prayer ministry ("Silent Unity") by phone and mail. It is reported that Unity receives millions of prayer requests annually. Unity devotionals, such as Daily Word, are used by members of other religious groups and churches. Millions of pieces of literature are printed each year.

Scientology

Founder

Founded by L. Ron Hubbard (1911–1986). Founded 1954 in California. Current headquarters in Los Angeles, California.

Writings

Dianetics: The Modern Science of Mental Health and others by Hubbard. The Way to Happiness.

God

Does not define God or Supreme Being, but rejects biblical description of God. Everyone is a "thetan," an immortal spirit with unlimited powers over its own universe, but not all are aware of this.

Jesus

Jesus is rarely mentioned in Scientology. Jesus was not the Creator, nor was he an "operating thetan" (in control of supernatural powers, cleared from mental defects). Jesus did not die for sins.

Holy Spirit

The Holy Spirit is not part of this belief.

Salvation

No sin or need to repent. Salvation is freedom from reincarnation. One must work with an "auditor" on his "engrams" (hang-ups) to achieve the state of "clear," then progress up the "bridge to total freedom."

Death

Hell is a myth. People who get clear of engrams become operating thetans.

Other Beliefs

Members observe birth of Hubbard and anniversary of publication of Dianetics. Controversy follows the group worldwide. Time magazine and Reader's Digest have published damaging exposés. Organizations related to Scientology include Narconon, Criminon, Way to Happiness Foundation, WISE, Hubbard College of Administration, Applied Scholastics.

Wicca

Founder
No one person. Roots in 19th-century Britain. Partly inspired by Margaret Murray (1862–1963) and organized by Gerald Gardner (1884–1964) in the 1930s to 1950s.

Writings
No holy books; however, many groups use *The Book of Shadows*, first compiled by Gardner and later expanded by him and by other leaders. Other popular works include *A Witches' Bible* and *The Spiral Dance*.

God
The supreme being is called the Goddess, sometimes the Goddess and God, or goddess and horned god ("Lord and Lady"). The Goddess can be a symbol, the impersonal force in everything, or a personal being. Wiccans can be pantheists, polytheists, or both.

Jesus
Jesus is either rejected altogether or sometimes considered a spiritual teacher who taught love and compassion.

Holy Spirit
The Holy Spirit is not part of this belief. However, some Wiccans may refer to "Spirit" as a kind of divine energy.

Salvation
Wiccans do not believe that humanity is sinful or needs saving. It is important for Wiccans to honor and work for the preservation of nature (which they equate with the Goddess).

Death
The body replenishes the earth, which is the Goddess's wish. Some Wiccans are agnostic about life after death, others believe in reincarnation. Some believe in a wonderful place called Summerland.

Other Beliefs
Wiccans practice divination and spell-casting, with most rituals performed in a circle. Many Wiccans are part of a coven (local assembly), though many are "solitary." Covens meet for ritual and seasonal holidays, including the eight major holidays (such as Vernal Equinox, Summer Solstice, and Beltane). Wicca is an occultic "nature religion," not Satanism.

New Age

Founder
Based on Eastern mysticism, Hinduism, and paganism. Popularized in part by actress Shirley MacLaine (b. 1934) in the 1980s and 1990s. Beliefs vary.

Writings
No holy book. Use selected Bible passages; *I Ching;* Hindu, Buddhist, and Taoist writings; and Native American beliefs. Writings on astrology, mysticism, and magic.

God
Everything and everyone is God. God is an impersonal force or principle, not a person. People have unlimited inner power and need to discover it.

Jesus
Jesus is not the one true God. He is not a savior, but a spiritual model, and guru, and is now an "ascended master." He was a New Ager who tapped into divine power in the same way that anyone can. Many believe he went east to India or Tibet and learned mystical truths. He did not rise physically, but "rose" into a higher spiritual realm.

Holy Spirit
Sometimes a psychic force. Man is divine and can experience psychic phenomena such as contacting unearthly beings.

Salvation
Need to offset bad karma with good karma. Can tap into supernatural power through meditation, self-awareness, and "spirit guides." Use terms such as "reborn" for this new self-awareness.

Death
Human reincarnations occur until person reaches oneness with God. No eternal life as a resurrected person. No literal heaven or hell.

Other Beliefs
Can include yoga, meditation, visualization, astrology, channeling, hypnosis, trances, and tarot card readings. Use of crystals to get in harmony with God (Energy), for psychic healing, for contact with spirits, and for developing higher consciousness or other psychic powers. Strive for world unity and peace. Emphasis on holistic health.

Islam

Founder
Muhammad (570–632) is the final "seal" of many prophets sent by Allah (God). The Islamic calendar began in AD 622, when Muhammad fled Mecca. Main sects: Sunni, Shi'ite.

Writings
Qur'an (Koran) was revealed to Muhammad by the angel Gabriel. The biblical Law of Moses, Psalms of David, and Gospel of Jesus (the *Injil*) are accepted in the Qur'an, but Muslim scholars teach that Jews and Christians have corrupted these original revelations.

God
God (Allah) is One. The greatest sin in Islam is *shirk*, or associating anything with God. Many Muslims think that Christians believe in three gods and are therefore guilty of *shirk*. Human attributes such as fatherhood cannot be associated with God.

Jesus
Jesus (*Isa* in Arabic) is one of the most respected of over 124,000 prophets sent by Allah. Jesus was sinless, born of a virgin, and a great miracle worker, but not the Son of God. His virgin birth is like Adam's creation. Jesus is not God, and God is not Jesus. He was not crucified. Jesus, not Muhammad, will return for a special role before the future judgment day, perhaps turning Christians to Islam.

Holy Spirit
Allah has or is a spirit. Muslims reject the biblical concept of the Trinity.

Salvation
Humans are basically good, but fallible and need guidance. The balance between good and bad deeds determines eternal destiny in paradise or hell. Allah's mercy may tip the balances to heaven, as his will is supreme.

Death
Resurrection of bodies. Fear of eternal torment is a prevalent theme of the Qur'an. Paradise includes a garden populated with *houris*, maidens designed by Allah to provide sexual pleasures to righteous men.

Other Beliefs
Followers are called Muslims. Go to mosque for prayers, sermons, counsel. Holy efforts to spread Islam (*jihad*). Five pillars of Islam: Confess that Allah is the one true God and that Muhammad is his prophet. Pray five times daily facing Mecca. Give alms (money). Fast during the month of Ramadan. Make pilgrimage to Mecca (once in a lifetime).

Nation of Islam

Founder

Founded by Wallace D. Fard (1891–?) in Detroit in 1930, but led by Elijah Muhammad (1897–1975) since 1934. Current head is Louis Farrakhan (born 1933). Headquarters in Chicago, Illinois.

Writings

Publicly, the Holy Qur'an is authoritative and the Bible is quoted often, but *Message to the Blackman in America, Our Saviour Has Arrived,* and other books by Elijah Muhammad supply its distinctive views. Current teachings are in *The Final Cal* newspaper and speeches of Minister Farrakhan.

God

Officially, there is one God, Allah, as described in the Qur'an. But Elijah Muhammad's teachings are also true: God is a black man, millions of Allahs have lived and died since creation, collectively the black race is God, and Master Fard is the Supreme Allah and Saviour.

Jesus

Officially, Jesus is a sinless prophet of Allah. Privately, Jesus was born from adultery between Mary and Joseph, who was already married to another woman. Jesus was not crucified, but stabbed in the heart by a police officer. He is still buried in Jerusalem. Prophecies of Jesus' return refer to Master Fard, Elijah Muhammad, or to Louis Farrakhan.

Holy Spirit

The Holy Spirit is not significant to their belief, but is generally regarded as the power of God or as the angel Gabriel who spoke to the prophet Muhammad.

Salvation

People sin, but are not born sinful; salvation is through submission to Allah and good works. Older beliefs still held: Fard is the saviour, salvation comes from knowledge of self and realizing that the white race are devils who displaced the black race.

Death

There is no consciousness or any spiritual existence after death. Heaven and Hell are symbols. Statements about the resurrection refer to awakening "mentally dead" people by bringing them true teachings.

Other Beliefs

Farrakhan's public messages coexist with earlier, esoteric doctrines. Elijah Muhammad's older views (such as polytheism, God as the black race, Master Fard as Allah incarnate, whites as devils bred to cause harm) are still distributed, but public preaching now focuses on Islamic themes (one eternal God, non-racial emphasis) with frequent use of the Bible.

Bahá'í World Faith

Founder

Siyyid 'Alí-Muhammad, "the Báb" (1819–1850) and Mírzá Husayn-'Alí, "Bahá'u'lláh" (1817– 1892). Founded 1844 in Iran. Headquarters in Haifa, Israel.

Writings

Writings of Bahá'u'lláh and 'Abdu'l-Bahá, including *Kitáb-i-Aqdas* ("Most Holy Book") and *Kitáb-i-Íqán* ("Book of Certitude"). The Bible, interpreted spiritually to conform to Bahá'í theology.

God

God is an unknowable divine being who has revealed himself through nine "manifestations" (religious leaders), including Adam, Moses, Krishna, Buddha, Jesus, Muhammad, and Bahá'u'lláh. No Trinity.

Jesus

Jesus is one of many manifestations of God. Each manifestation supersedes the previous, giving new teachings about God. Jesus, who superseded Moses, was superseded by Muhammad, and most recently by the greatest, Bahá'u'lláh ("Glory of Allah"). Jesus is not God and did not rise from the dead. He is not the only way to God. Jesus has returned to earth in the form of Bahá'u'lláh.

Holy Spirit

Holy Spirit is divine energy from God that empowers every manifestation. "Spirit of Truth" refers to Bahá'u'lláh.

Salvation

Faith in the manifestation of God (Bahá'u'lláh). Knowing and living by Bahá'u'lláh's principles and teachings.

Death

Personal immortality based on good works, with rewards for the faithful. Heaven and hell are conditions, not places.

Other Beliefs

Bahá'í originated as an Islamic sect and is severely persecuted in Iran. Bahá'í teaches that all religions have the same source, principles, and aims. Stress on oneness and world unity. Regular local gatherings called "feasts," administrative meetings called "spiritual assemblies." "Universal House of Justice" in Haifa, Israel, is the ultimate governing body.

Judaism

Founder

Abraham of the Bible, about 2000 BC, and Moses in the Middle East. There are three main branches of Judaism—Orthodox, Conservative, and Reform—each with its own beliefs.

Writings

The Tanakh (Old Testament), and especially the Torah (first five books of the Bible). The Talmud (explanation of the Tanakh). Teachings of each branch. Writings of sages, such as Maimonides.

God

God is spirit. To Orthodox Jews, God is personal, all-powerful, eternal, and compassionate. To other Jews, God is impersonal, unknowable, and defined in a number of ways. No Trinity.

Jesus

Jesus is seen either as an extremist false messiah or a good but martyred Jewish rabbi (teacher). Many Jews do not consider Jesus at all. Jews (except Messianic Jews and Hebrew Christians) do not believe he was the Messiah, Son of God, or that he rose from the dead. Orthodox Jews believe the Messiah will restore the Jewish kingdom and eventually rule the earth.

Holy Spirit

Some believe the Holy Spirit is another name for God's activity on earth. Others say it is God's love or power.

Salvation

Some Jews believe that prayer, repentance, and obeying the Law are necessary for salvation. Others believe that salvation is the improvement of society.

Death

There will be a physical resurrection. The obedient will live forever with God, and the unrighteous will suffer. Some Jews do not believe in a conscious life after death.

Other Beliefs

Meeting in synagogues on the Sabbath (Sabbath is Friday evening to Saturday evening). Circumcision of males. Many holy days and festivals, including Passover, Sukkoth, Hanukkah, Rosh Hashanah, Yom Kippur, Purim. Jerusalem is considered the holy city.

Hinduism

Founder	No one founder. Many sects. Began 1800–1000 BC in India.
Writings	Many writings, including the Vedas (oldest, about 1000 BC), the Upanishads, and the *Bhagavad-Gita*.
God	God is "The Absolute," a universal spirit. Everyone is part of God (Brahman) like drops in the sea, but most people are not aware of it. People worship manifestations of Brahman (gods and goddesses).
Jesus	Jesus Christ is a teacher, a guru, or an avatar (an incarnation of Vishnu). He is a son of God as are others. His death does not atone for sins and he did not rise from the dead.
Holy Spirit	The Holy Spirit is not part of this belief.
Salvation	Release from the cycles of reincarnation. Achieved through yoga and meditation. Can take many lifetimes. Final salvation is absorption or union with Brahman.
Death	Reincarnation into a better status (good karma) if person has behaved well. If one has been bad, he can be reborn and pay for past sins (bad karma) by suffering.
Other Beliefs	Some disciples wear orange robes, and have shaved heads. Many Hindus worship stone and wooden idols in temples. Some gurus demand complete obedience. Disciples meditate on a word, phrase, or picture. Yoga involves meditation, chanting, postures, breathing exercises. Foundation of New Age and Transcendental Meditation.

Hare Krishna
(ISKON)

Founder	The International Society for Krishna Consciousness, founded by A.C. Bhaktivedanta Swami Prabhupada (1896–1977) in 1965 in New York, is based on Hindu teachings from 16th century AD.
Writings	*Back to Godhead* magazine. Prabhupada's translations of and commentaries on Hindu scriptures, especially *Bhagavad-Gita, As It Is*.
God	God is Lord Krishna. Krishna is a personal creator; the souls of all living things are part of him. ISKCON teaches that what Krishna does freely for his own pleasure (intoxication, sex outside of marriage) is prohibited to his devotees.
Jesus	Jesus is not important to this group. He is usually thought of as an enlightened vegetarian teacher who taught meditation. He is not an incarnation of God. Some Krishna devotees consider Jesus to be Krishna. Others say he is a great avatar (teacher).
Holy Spirit	The Holy Spirit is not part of this belief.
Salvation	Chanting Krishna's name constantly, total devotion to Krishna, worshipping images, and obeying the rules of ISKCON throughout many reincarnated lives, releases a follower from bad karma.
Death	Those who are unenlightened continue in endless reincarnation (rebirth on earth) based on the sinful acts of a person's previous life.
Other Beliefs	Public chanting of Hare Krishna mantra, yoga, food offerings, soliciting donations. Vegetarian diet. No intoxicants, no gambling. Sex for procreation only. ISKCON (International Society for Krishna Consciousness) attracts new members through feasts and Indian cultural programs. Followers are given new names, and often cut family ties.

Transcendental Meditation (TM)

Founder	Maharishi Mahesh Yogi (1917–2008). Founded 1955–1958 in India, based on Hinduism and karma yoga. Headquarters in the Netherlands. Also called World Plan Executive Council.
Writings	Hindu scriptures, including the *Bhagavad-Gita*. *Meditations of Maharishi Mahesh Yogi, Science of Being and the Art of Living*, other writings by the founder.
God	Each part of creation makes up "God" (Brahman). Supreme Being is not personal. All creation is divine; "all is one."
Jesus	Jesus is not uniquely God. Like all persons, Jesus had a divine essence. Unlike most, he discovered it. Christ didn't suffer and couldn't suffer for people's sins.
Holy Spirit	The Holy Spirit is not part of this belief.
Salvation	Humans have forgotten their inner divinity. Salvation consists of doing good in excess of evil in order to evolve to the highest state (final union of the self with Brahman) through reincarnation.
Death	Reincarnation based on karma (reaping the consequences of one's actions) until loss of self into union with Brahman. No heaven or hell.
Other Beliefs	Mentally recite a mantra (word associated with a Hindu god). Meditate twice a day to relax and achieve union with Brahman. Maharishi University in Iowa offers advanced T.M. programs in "levitation" and "invisibility." Practices include yoga, Hindu astrology, use of crystals, and idol worship (offerings of flowers, fruit, and cloth for Maharishi's dead teacher, Guru Dev).

Buddhism

Founder

Gautama Siddhartha, (563–483 BC), also known as the Buddha ("Enlightened One"). Founded in modern-day Nepal and India as a reformation of Hinduism.

Writings

The *Mahavastu* ("Great Story," a chaotic collection covering the Buddha's life story), the *Jataka Tales* (550 stories of the former lives of the Buddha), the *Tripitaka* ("Three Baskets"), and the *Tantras* (as recorded in Tibetan Buddhism).

God

The Buddha himself did not believe in the existence of God. Others speak of the Buddha as a universal enlightened consciousness or as a god.

Jesus

Jesus Christ is not part of the historic Buddhist worldview. Buddhists in the West today generally view Jesus as an enlightened teacher, while Buddhists in Asia believe Jesus is an *avatar* or a *Bodhisattva* (but not God).

Holy Spirit

The Holy Spirit is not part of this belief. Buddhists do believe in spirits, and some practice deity yoga and invite spirit possession.

Salvation

Goal of life is *nirvana*, to eliminate all desires or cravings, and in this way escape suffering. The Eightfold Path is a system to free Buddhists from desiring anything.

Death

Reincarnation. People do not have their own individual souls or spirits, but one's desires and feelings may be reincarnated into another person.

Other Beliefs

Eightfold path recommends right knowledge, intentions, speech, conduct, livelihood, right effort, mindfulness, and meditation. Some Buddhist groups talk about an "eternal Buddha" (life-force). Through the "Doctrine of Assimilation" the belief systems of other religions are blended into their form of Buddhism.

Nichiren Shoshu Buddhism

Founder

Nichiren Daishonin (1222–1282). Nichiren Shoshu sect founded in Japan in 1253. Soka Gakkai founded in 1930 by Tsunesaburo Makiguchi (1871–1944).

Writings

The *Lotus Sutra* (a sutra is a discourse of the Buddha as recorded by his disciples). *The Major Writings of Nichiren Daishonin*, plus writings of Daisaku Ikeda.

God

There is no god in Nichiren Shoshu. Followers hold to a monistic worldview, believing that there is no separation between Creator and creature and that they are protected by Buddhist, Hindu, and Shinto gods that they regard as spiritual forces.

Jesus

Jesus Christ is not part of this belief.

Holy Spirit

The Holy Spirit is not part of this belief.

Salvation

Enlightenment, prosperity, and healing come from chanting *nam-myoho-renge-kyo, a mantra* (phrase) expressing devotion to the law of karma. Fulfilling worldly desires brings enlightenment, which can be achieved in one lifetime.

Death

Repeated reincarnation until one awakens to one's Buddha nature, then enters nirvana (escaping the cycle of rebirth). Heaven and hell are two of ten states of existence. After death, one enters a suspended state called *Ku.*

Other Beliefs

Worship of a scroll called the *Gohonzon* by chanting *nam-myoho-renge-kyo* (roughly translated, "hail to the mystic law of cause and effect"). *Shakubuku* (literally, "the tearing and crushing of other faiths") is their form of proselytizing, which they believe helps them change their karma. Soka University is their main educational institution in the United States.

Spiritualism/Spiritism

Founder

Ancient belief popularized by sisters Kate and Margaret Fox, 1848, Hydesville, New York. Many small groups, no official headquarters.

Writings

Spiritualist Manual, Aquarian Gospel of Jesus the Christ, Oahspe, the Bible (selected portions), and others.

God

God is infinite intelligence. Impersonal power controlling the universe.

Jesus

Jesus was a man, not God. While on earth, he was a prophet or an advanced medium (one believed to communicate with the spirit world). Jesus is now a spirit that one can communicate with in the spirit world.

Holy Spirit

The Holy Spirit is not part of this belief. However, some use the term to refer to the spirit of a holy person who once lived.

Salvation

Knowledge and good works enhance one's status in the afterlife.

Death

After life on this earthly plane, life continues in the spirit world, where one's spirit may progress from one level to another. Heaven and hell are states of mind. Some believe in reincarnation.

Other Beliefs

Séances to contact the dead. Psychic demonstrations. Church services with singing, music, sermon, spirit messages from the dead, and prophecies. May use Ouija™ boards. Often attracts grieving people who hope for contact with a deceased loved one.

Liturgical Churches
In order by date

	Catholic Church	Orthodox Churches	Lutheran Churches
Founder and Date	Catholics consider Jesus' disciple Peter (died ca. AD 66) the first pope; Gregory the Great (pope, AD 540-604) was a key figure in the pope's office. At that time, the pope came to be viewed as ruling over the whole church.	330: Emperor Constantine renamed the city of Byzantium "Constantinople," which became the city of the leading patriarch in the "Great Schism" of 1054.	1517: Martin Luther's "95 Theses" (challenges to Catholic teaching) usually mark the beginning of the Protestant Reformation. 1530: The Augsburg Confession is the first formal Lutheran statement of faith.
Adherents in 2000	About 1 billion worldwide; 62 million, USA	About 225 million worldwide; 3-5 million, USA	About 60 million worldwide (all branches; see below); over 8 million, USA
Scripture	The Scriptures teach without error the truth needed for our salvation. Scripture must be interpreted within the Tradition of the Church. The canon includes 46 books for the Old Testament including deuterocanonical books (the Apocrypha) and 27 books for the New Testament.	The Scriptures are without error in matters of faith only. Scripture is to be interpreted by Sacred Tradition, especially the seven Ecumenical Councils which met from AD 325-787. The canon includes 49 Old Testament books (the Catholic Bible plus three more) and the 27 New Testament books.	Scripture alone is the authoritative witness to the gospel (some parts more directly or fully than others). Conservatives view Scripture as inerrant. The standard Protestant canon of 39 Old Testament books and 27 New Testament books is accepted.
God	The one Creator and Lord of all, existing eternally as the Trinity (Father, Son, and Holy Spirit).	The one Creator and Lord of all, existing eternally as the Trinity (Father, Son, and Holy Spirit).	The one Creator and Lord of all, existing eternally as the Trinity (Father, Son, and Holy Spirit).
Jesus	The eternal Son incarnate, fully God and fully man, conceived and born of the virgin Mary, died on the Cross for our sins, rose bodily from the grave, ascended into heaven, and will come again in glory to judge us all.	The eternal Son incarnate, fully God and fully man, conceived and born of the virgin Mary, died on the Cross for our sins, rose bodily from the grave, ascended into heaven, and will come again in glory to judge us all.	The eternal Son incarnate, fully God and fully man, conceived and born of the virgin Mary, died on the Cross for our sins, rose bodily from the grave, ascended into heaven, and will come again in glory to judge us all.
Salvation	Christ died as a substitutionary sacrifice for our sins; God by his grace infuses a supernatural gift of faith in Christ in those who are baptized, which is maintained by doing works of love and receiving Penance and the Eucharist.	In Christ, God became human so that human beings might be deified (theosis), that is, have the energy of God's life in them. Through baptism and participation in the church, God's people receive the benefits of Christ's redeeming work as they persevere.	We are saved by grace alone when God imputes to us his gift of righteousness through faith alone (sola fide) in Christ, who died for our sins. Good works are the inevitable result of true faith, but in no way the basis of our right standing before God.
Afterlife	The souls of the faithful go to heaven either immediately or, if imperfectly purified in this life, after purgatory. The souls of the wicked at death are immediately consigned to eternal punishment in hell.	At death, the souls of the faithful are purified as needed (a process of growth, not punishment), then get a foretaste of eternal blessing in heaven. The souls of the wicked get a foretaste of eternal torment in hell.	The souls of believers upon dying go immediately to be with Christ, and at Christ's return, their bodies are raised to immortal, eternal life. The souls of the wicked begin suffering immediately in hell.
The Church	The church is the Mystical Body of Christ, established by Christ with the bishop of Rome (the pope), who may at times pronounce dogma (doctrine required of all members) infallibly, as its earthly head. It is united (*one*) in a sacred (*holy*) worldwide (*catholic*) community through the succession of bishops whose ordination goes back to the apostles (*apostolic*); Christians not in communion with the Catholic Church are called "separated brethren."	The church is the Body of Christ in unbroken historical connection to the apostles, changelessly maintaining the faith of the undivided church as expressed in the creeds. It is one, holy, catholic, and apostolic, with churches organized nationally (Armenian, Greek, Russian, and so forth) with its bishops under the leadership of patriarchs (the pope being recognized as one of several), of which that of Constantinople has primacy of honor.	The church is the congregation of believers (though mixed with the lost) in which the gospel is taught and the sacraments rightly administered. All believers are "priests" in that they have direct access to God. All ministers are pastors; some serve as bishops. Historically, apostolic succession has been rejected.
Sacraments	Baptism removes original sin (usually in infants). In the Eucharist, the substances (but not the properties) of bread and wine are changed into Jesus' body and blood (transubstantiation).	Baptism initiates God's life in the one baptized (usually infants). In the Eucharist, bread and wine are changed into Jesus' body and blood (a Mystery to be left unexplained).	Baptism is necessary for salvation; in it both adults and infants are given God's grace. The Lord's Supper remains truly bread and wine but also becomes truly Jesus' body and blood (consubstantiation).
Other Beliefs and Practices	Mary was conceived by her mother immaculately (free of original sin), remained a virgin perpetually, and was assumed bodily into heaven. She is the Mother of the Church and is considered an object of devotion and veneration (a show of honor that stops short of worship).	Mary conceived Jesus virginally. She remained a virgin perpetually, and (in tradition, not dogma) was assumed bodily into heaven. Icons (images of Christ, Mary, or the saints) are objects of veneration through which God is to be worshiped.	The church's liturgy is similar to the Episcopal. Conservative Lutherans generally affirm that God chooses who will be saved before they believe. In 2009 the ELCA opened the ministry to gay and lesbian pastors in committed relationships.
Divisions and Trends	About one-fourth of Catholics are doctrinally conservative. Many priests and members tend to accept liberal, pluralist beliefs contrary to church teaching.	A significant proportion are doctrinally conservative. Most Orthodox bodies are members of the World Council of Churches, whose liberal leanings have long caused concern.	The Evangelical Lutheran Church in America (ELCA) is the mainline church. The Lutheran Church—Missouri Synod is doctrinally conservative.

www.rose-publishing.com

Liturgical Churches
In order by date

	Anglican Churches		Presbyterian Churches		Methodist Churches
Founder and Date	1534: King Henry VIII was declared head of the Church of England. 1549: Thomas Cranmer produced the first Book of Common Prayer.	Date	1536: John Calvin writes Institutes of the Christian Religion. 1643-49: Westminster Standards define Presbyterian doctrine. 1789: Presbyterian Church (USA) first organized (see below).	Date	1738: Conversion of John and Charles Wesley, already devout Anglican ministers, sparks Great Awakening. 1784: USA Methodists form separate church body.
Adherents in 2000	Some 45-75 million worldwide; 2.3 million, USA	No.	Some 40-48 million worldwide; 3-4 million, USA	No.	Some 20-40 million worldwide; 12 million or more, USA
Scripture	Scripture contains the truth that is necessary for salvation and is the primary norm for faith, but must be interpreted in light of tradition and reason. The canon includes 39 Old Testament books and 27 New Testament books (the Apocrypha is respected but not viewed as Scripture).	Scripture	Historic view: Scripture is inspired and infallible, the sole, final rule of faith. PCUSA: Scripture is "the witness without parallel" to Christ, but in merely human words reflecting beliefs of the time. The standard Protestant canon is accepted.	Scripture	Historic view: Scripture is inspired and infallible, the sole, final rule of faith. United Methodist Church: Scripture is "the primary source and criterion for Christian doctrine," but (for most) not infallible. The standard Protestant canon is accepted.
God	The one Creator and Lord of all, existing eternally as the Trinity (Father, Son, and Holy Spirit).	God	The one Creator and Lord of all, existing eternally as the Trinity (Father, Son, and Holy Spirit).	God	The one Creator and Lord of all, existing eternally as the Trinity (Father, Son, and Holy Spirit).
Jesus	The eternal Son incarnate, fully God and fully man, conceived and born of the virgin Mary, died on the Cross for our sins, rose bodily from the grave, ascended into heaven, and will come again in glory to judge us all.	Jesus	The eternal Son incarnate, fully God and fully man, conceived and born of the virgin Mary, died on the Cross for our sins, rose bodily from the grave, ascended into heaven, and will come again in glory to judge us all.	Jesus	The eternal Son incarnate, fully God and fully man, conceived and born of the virgin Mary, died on the Cross for our sins, rose bodily from the grave, ascended into heaven, and will come again in glory to judge us all.
Salvation	Christ suffered and died as an offering for sin, freeing us from sin and reconciling us to God; we share in Christ's victory when in baptism we become living members of the church, believing in him and keeping his commandments.	Salvation	We are saved by grace alone when God imputes to us his gift of righteousness through faith alone (sola fide) in Christ, who died for our sins. Good works are the inevitable result of true faith, but in no way the basis of our right standing before God.	Salvation	We are saved by grace alone when God regenerates and forgives us through faith in Christ, who died for our sins. Good works are the necessary result of true faith, but do not obtain forgiveness or salvation.
Afterlife	The souls of the faithful are purified as needed to enjoy full communion with God, and at Christ's return they are raised to the fullness of eternal life in heaven. Those who reject God face eternal death.	Death	The souls of believers upon dying go immediately to be with Christ. At Christ's return, their bodies are raised to immortal, eternal life. The souls of the wicked begin suffering immediately in hell.	Death	The souls of believers upon dying go immediately to be with Christ; and, at Christ's return, their bodies are raised to immortal, eternal life. The wicked will suffer eternal punishment in hell.
The Church	The church is the Body of Christ, whose unity is based on the "apostolic succession" of bishops going back to the apostles, of whom the bishop of Rome is one of many. It is one, holy, catholic, and apostolic. The Anglican communion is a part of the church, whose unity worldwide is represented by the archbishop of Canterbury. The church in the USA is known as the Episcopal Church.	The Church	The church is the body of Christ, including all whom God has chosen as his people, represented by the visible church, composed of churches that vary in purity and corruption. Christ alone is the head of the church. Congregations choose elders to govern them. Regional groups of elders (presbyteries) meet in denomination-wide General Assemblies.	The Church	The church is the body of Christ, represented by visible church institutions. Bishops oversee regions and appoint pastors. In the United Methodist Church, clergy and laity meet together in a national "General Conference" every four years. All pastors are itinerant, meaning they move from one church to the next as directed by the bishop (on average once every four years).
Sacraments	The sacraments are "outward and visible signs of an inward and spiritual grace." Infants and converts are made part of the church in baptism. Christ's body and blood are really present in Communion.	Sacraments	Baptism is not necessary for salvation but is a sign of the new covenant of grace, for adults and infants. Jesus' body and blood are spiritually present to believers in the Lord's Supper.	Sacraments	Baptism is a sign of regeneration and of the new covenant and is for adults and children. Jesus is really present, and his body and blood are spiritually present, to believers in the Lord's Supper.
Other Beliefs and Practices	Members are free to accept or reject the Catholic doctrines of Mary. The Book of Common Prayer is the norm for liturgy. Priests may marry. In 1976 the Episcopal Church approved the ordination of women. In 2009 the Episcopal Church approved the ordination of gay bishops and allowed bishops to bless same-sex unions.	Beliefs	Conservatives affirm the "five points of Calvinism": humans are so sinful that they cannot initiate return to God; God chooses who will be saved; Christ died specifically to save those whom God chose; God infallibly draws to Christ those whom he chooses; they will never fall away.	Beliefs	"Entire sanctification" is a work of the Spirit subsequent to regeneration by which fully consecrated believers are purified of all sin and fit for service—a state maintained by faith and obedience. Methodists are Arminian, i.e., they disagree with all five points of Calvinism.
Divisions and Trends	In the USA, most belong to the Episcopal Church. The 39 Articles (1571) are the doctrinal basis for conservative splinter groups, such as the Reformed Episcopal Church and the Anglican Church in North America.	Trend	The Presbyterian Church (USA), or PCUSA, is the mainline church. The Presbyterian Church in America (PCA) is the largest doctrinally conservative church body.	Trend	United Methodist Church (8.5 million) and the African Methodist Episcopal church bodies (about 4 million) are mainline churches. The Free Methodists are a small conservative body.

Non-Liturgical Churches

	Anabaptist Churches	Congregational Churches	Baptist Churches
Founder and Date	1525: Protestants in Zurich begin believer's baptism. 1537: Menno Simons begins leading Mennonite movement. 1682: A Quaker, William Penn, founds Pennsylvania.	1607: Members of a house church in England, illegal at that time, who were forced into exile. 1620: Congregationalists called Pilgrims sail on Mayflower to Plymouth (now in Massachusetts).	1612: John Smythe and other English Puritans form the first Baptist church. 1639: The first Baptist church in America established in Providence, Rhode Island.
Adherents in 2000	Perhaps 2 million worldwide; Roughly 600,000, USA.	Over 2 million worldwide; About 2 million, USA.	100 million worldwide (including families); 25-30 million, USA.
Scripture	Most view Scripture as the inspired means for knowing and following Jesus, but not as infallible. Jesus is the living Word. Scripture is the written Word that points to him. The standard Protestant canon is accepted. How believers live is emphasized over having correct doctrine.	Most view Scripture as "the authoritative witness to the Word of God" that was living in Jesus, rather than viewing Scripture as the unerring Word of God. (UCC, see below.) The Bible and creeds are seen as "testimonies of faith, not tests of faith." The standard Protestant canon is accepted.	Scripture is inspired and without error, the sole, final, totally trustworthy rule of faith. The standard Protestant canon is accepted. (Mainline churches vary in the extent to which they continue to view Scripture as without error.)
God	The one Creator and Lord of all, revealed in Jesus through the Holy Spirit. Most affirm the Trinity in some way.	The Eternal Spirit who calls the worlds into being and is made known in the man Jesus.	The one Creator and Lord of all, existing eternally as the Trinity (Father, Son, and Holy Spirit).
Jesus	The Savior of the world, a man in whom God's love and will be revealed by his life of service and his suffering and death. His deity, virgin birth, and resurrection are traditionally affirmed.	The crucified and risen Savior and Lord, in whom we are reconciled to God. (His deity and virgin birth are widely ignored or rejected except in the conservative church bodies.)	The eternal Son incarnate, fully God and fully human, conceived and born of the virgin Mary, died on the Cross for our sins, rose bodily from the grave, ascended into heaven, and will come again in glory to judge us all.
Salvation	Salvation is a personal experience in which, through faith in Jesus, we become at peace with God, moving us to follow Jesus' example as his disciples by living as peacemakers in the world.	God promises forgiveness and grace to save "from sin and aimlessness" all who trust him, who accept his call to serve the whole human family.	We are saved by grace alone when God imputes to us his gift of righteousness through faith alone (sola fide) in Christ, who died for our sins. Good works are the inevitable result of true faith, but in no way the basis of our right standing before God.
Afterlife	No official view of what happens immediately after death. At Christ's return God's people will be raised to eternal life and the unrepentant will be forever separated from God (the traditional view).	Those who trust in God and live as Jesus' disciples are promised eternal life in God's kingdom. No position is taken on the future of the wicked (most reject the idea of eternal punishment).	The souls of believers upon dying go immediately to be with Christ; and, at Christ's return, their bodies are raised to immortal, eternal life. The wicked will suffer eternal punishment in hell.
The Church	The church is the body of Christ, the assembly and society of Christ's disciples who follow him in the power of the Spirit. It is to be marked by holiness, love, service, a simple lifestyle, and peacemaking. No one system of church government is recognized; leadership is to be characterized by humble service and is primarily but not exclusively local.	The church is the people of God living as Jesus' disciples by serving humanity as agents of God's reconciling love. Each local church is self-governing and chooses its own ministers. The United Church of Christ is not part of the "Churches of Christ" but was formed in 1957 as the union of the Congregational Christian Churches and the Evangelical and Reformed Church, a liberal Protestant body.	The church (universal) is the body of Christ, which consists of the redeemed throughout history. The term "church" usually refers to local congregations, each of which is autonomous, whose members are to be baptized believers and whose officers are pastors and deacons. Churches may form associations or conventions for cooperative purposes, especially missions and education.
Sacraments	Baptism is for believers only, a sign of commitment to follow Jesus. The Lord's Supper is a memorial of his death. Most Quakers view sacraments as spiritual only, not external rites.	Congregations may practice infant baptism or believer's baptism or both. Sacraments are symbols of spiritual realities.	Baptism is immersion of believers only as a symbol of their faith in Christ. The Lord's Supper is a symbolic memorial of Christ's death and anticipation of his return.
Other Beliefs and Practices	Anabaptists and similar bodies are "peace churches," teaching nonresistance and pacifism (the view that all participation in war is wrong). Doctrine is deemphasized, and liberal views with social emphasis prevail in some church bodies, including most Quaker churches.	The United Church of Christ (UCC) is one of the most theologically liberal denominations in the USA. Individual ministers and churches vary widely in belief. The United Church of Christ ordains openly homosexual men and women to ministry.	Most Baptist bodies emphasize evangelism and missions. Church and state are to be separate. Baptists include both Calvinists (dominant in the Southern Baptist Convention) and Arminians (dominant in mainline bodies and the Free-Will Baptist bodies).
Divisions and Trends	The Mennonite Church and Church of the Brethren are the largest bodies; the Amish (1693) are a variety of Mennonites. Quakers (Friends) originated separately but share much in common with Anabaptists.	United Church of Christ (1.5 million) is staunchly liberal. The National Assn. of Cong. Christian Churches (110,000) is a mainline body. The Conservative Congregational Christian Conference (38,000) is evangelical.	Southern Baptist (15 million), a conservative body, are the largest Protestant denomination in the USA. American Baptists (1.5 million) and the National Baptists (5-8 million) are mainline churches.

N o n - L i t u r g i c a l   C h u r c h e s In order by date

	Churches of Christ	Adventist Churches	Pentecostal Churches
Founder and Date	1801: Barton Stone holds his Cane Ridge Revival in Kentucky. 1832: Stone's Christians unite with Thomas and Alexander Campbell's Disciples of Christ. They have different beliefs in some areas.	1844: William Miller's prediction that Christ's "advent" (return) would occur in 1844 failed. It was later interpreted as a heavenly event, not as an actual return. 1863: Seventh-day Adventist Church is organized.	1901: Charles Fox Parham's Kansas Bethel Bible College students speak in tongues. 1906: The Azusa Street revival (led by William J. Seymor in Los Angeles) launches Pentecostal movement. 1914: Assemblies of God organize.
Adherents in 2000	Perhaps 5-6 million worldwide; 3-4 million, USA.	Over 18 million worldwide (plus members of much smaller bodies); over 1 million USA.	500 million worldwide (estimates vary); roughly 10 million, USA.
Scripture	"Where the Scriptures speak, we speak; where the Scriptures are silent, we are silent." Churches of Christ view Scripture as the inerrant word of God; Disciples of Christ generally view Scripture as witness to Christ but fallible. The standard Protestant canon is accepted.	Scripture is inspired and without error, the final, totally trustworthy rule of faith. The standard Protestant canon is accepted; *The Clear Word* paraphrase is favored. Ellen G. White, an early Seventh-day Adventist leader, was a prophet; her writings are a "continuing and authoritative source of truth."	Scripture is inspired and without error, the final, totally trustworthy rule of faith. The standard Protestant canon is accepted. Some church bodies view certain leaders as prophets with authoritative messages that are to be confirmed from Scripture.
God	The one Creator and Lord of all. The creeds are rejected, but most conservatives accept the idea of the Trinity.	The one Creator and Lord of all, "a unity of three co-eternal Persons" (Father, Son, and Holy Spirit).	The one Creator and Lord of all, existing eternally as the Trinity (Father, Son, and Holy Spirit).
Jesus	The Son of God, fully God and fully human, conceived and born of the virgin Mary, died on the Cross for our sins, rose bodily from the grave, ascended into heaven, and will come again in glory to judge us all.	The eternal Son incarnate, fully God and fully human, conceived and born of the virgin Mary, died on the Cross for our sins, rose bodily from the grave, ascended into heaven, and will come again in glory to judge us all.	The eternal Son incarnate, fully God and fully human, conceived and born of the virgin Mary, died on the Cross for our sins, rose bodily from the grave, ascended into heaven, and will come again in glory to judge us all.
Salvation	Churches of Christ: A person must hear the gospel, believe in Christ, repent, confess Christ, be baptized, and persevere in holiness to be saved. Disciples of Christ: God saves human beings (possibly all) by his grace, to which we respond in faith.	To be saved, we repent, believe in Christ as Example (in his life) and Substitute (by his death), and so by grace are made right with God and sanctified and empowered by the Spirit to live in obedience to God's commandments. Those found obedient at the end will be saved.	We are saved by God's grace, by Christ's death for our sins, through repentance and faith in Christ alone, resulting in our being born again to new life in the Spirit, as evidenced by a life of holiness.
Afterlife	Churches of Christ: Believers immediately go to be with Christ and at his return are raised to immortality; the wicked will suffer eternally in hell. Disciples: Most believe in personal immortality but not hell.	Death for all people is an unconscious state. At Christ's return the righteous will be raised for life in heaven. After a Millennium, the wicked will be raised only to be annihilated; the righteous will live forever on a new earth.	The souls of believers upon dying go immediately to be with Christ, and at Christ's return their bodies are raised to immortal, eternal life. The wicked will suffer eternal punishment in hell.
The Church	Churches of Christ: The church is the assembly of those who have responded rightly to the gospel; it must be called only by the name of Christ. Only such churches are part of the restoration of true Christianity. Each local church is autonomous and calls its own pastors. Disciples of Christ have a similar form of church government but are ecumenical, and thus do not claim to be the sole restoration of true Christianity.	The universal church includes all who believe in Christ. The last days are a time of apostasy during which a remnant (the Seventh-day Adventist Church) keeps God's commandments faithfully. The General Conference, composed of delegates from regional "union missions," governs the whole church.	The church is the body of Christ, in which the Holy Spirit dwells, which meets to worship God, and which is the agency for bringing the gospel of salvation to the whole world. Most church bodies practice a form of church government similar to Baptists.
Sacraments	Baptism is immersion of believers only, as the initial act of obedience to the gospel. Many Churches of Christ recognize baptism in their own churches only as valid. The Lord's Supper is a symbolic memorial.	Baptism is by immersion, contingent upon affirmation of faith in Jesus and Adventist doctrines, and is into the Seventh-day Adventist Church. The Lord's Supper is a symbolic memorial of Christ's death, practiced quarterly, follows foot-washing.	Baptism is immersion of believers only, as a symbol of their faith in Christ. The Lord's Supper is a symbolic memorial of Christ's death and anticipation of his return.
Other Beliefs and Practices	Many but not all Churches of Christ forbid the use of instrumental music in worship. International Churches of Christ teaches that its members alone are saved and is widely reported to strongly influence its members.	In 1844 Christ began the Investigative Judgment, a work in heaven of determining who among the dead and living are true, loyal believers obeying God's law. Rest and worship on Saturday is an essential element of that obedience. When the Judgment work is done, Christ will return.	Pentecostals in the strict sense view speaking in tongues as the initial evidence of baptism in the Holy Spirit (a second work of grace akin to entire sanctification in Methodism). Charismatics accept tongues but don't view it as the only initial evidence of baptism in the Holy Spirit.
Divisions and Trends	Churches of Christ (about 2 million) are conservative, some militantly and others not. Christian Church (Disciples of Christ) (about 1 million) is the mainline church body.	The Seventh-day Adventist Church by far the largest body, followed by SDA Reform Movement. Most of the smaller offshoots reject the Trinity and other historic Christian doctrines.	Assemblies of God (2.5 million USA, historically white) and Church of God in Christ (3 million USA, historically black) are the largest church bodies. "Oneness" churches reject the Trinity.

Family Tree of Denominations

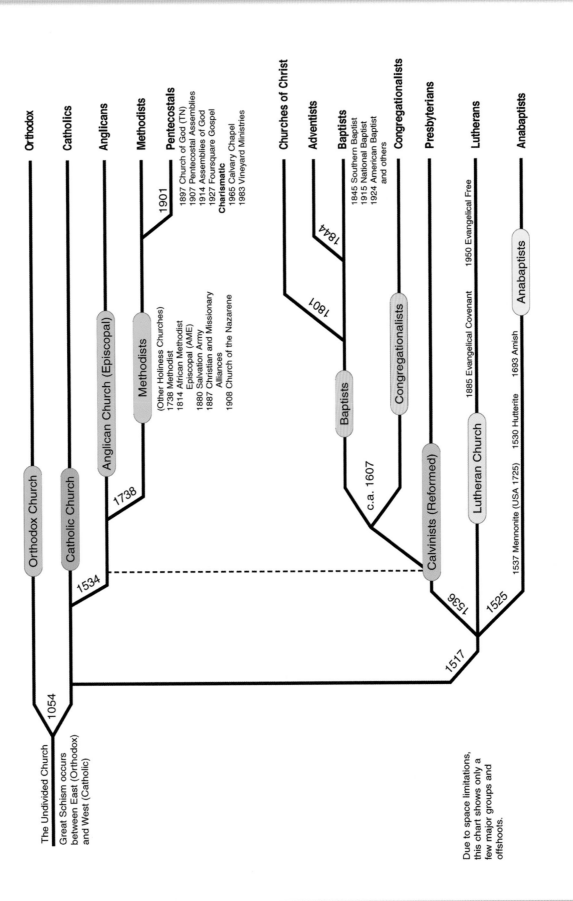

The Undivided Church

1054

Great Schism occurs between East (Orthodox) and West (Catholic)

Due to space limitations, this chart shows only a few major groups and offshoots.

Orthodox Church

Catholic Church

1534

Anglican Church (Episcopal)

1738

Methodists

(Other Holiness Churches)
1738 Methodist
1814 African Methodist Episcopal (AME)
1880 Salvation Army
1887 Christian and Missionary Alliances
1908 Church of the Nazarene

1901

Orthodox

Catholics

Anglicans

Methodists

Pentecostals

1897 Church of God (TN)
1907 Pentecostal Assemblies
1914 Assemblies of God
1927 Foursquare Gospel
Charismatic
1965 Calvary Chapel
1983 Vineyard Ministries

Churches of Christ

1801

Adventists

1844

Baptists

1845 Southern Baptist
1915 National Baptist
1924 American Baptist
and others

Baptists

c.a. 1607

Congregationalists

Congregationalists

Presbyterians

Calvinists (Reformed)

1536

1950 Evangelical Free

1885 Evangelical Covenant

Lutherans

Lutheran Church

1525

1537 Mennonite (USA 1725)

1530 Hutterite

1693 Amish

Anabaptists

Anabaptists

1517

What Christians Believe About the Trinity

In the simplest of terms, Christians believe:

There is only one God, and this one God exists as one essence in three Persons.

The three Persons are:
- God the Father
- God the Son (Jesus Christ)
- God the Holy Spirit (also called the Holy Ghost)

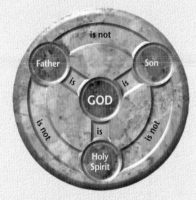

Early Christians used this diagram to explain the Trinity. The Father, Son, and Holy Spirit are all God, but they are not three names for the same Person.

The Persons are distinct:
- The Father is not the Son.
- The Son is not the Holy Spirit.
- The Holy Spirit is not the Father.

God is one absolutely perfect divine Being in three Persons. His *being* is what God is, in relation to the universe he created. The three are called Persons because they relate to one another in personal ways.

When Christians talk about believing in one God in three Persons (the Trinity), they do NOT mean:

1 God in 3 Gods, or
3 Persons in 1 Person, or
3 Persons in 3 Gods, or
1 Person in 3 Gods

Rather, they mean:

1 God in 3 Persons

Therefore,
- The Father is God—the first Person of the Trinity.
- The Son is God—the second Person of the Trinity.
- The Holy Spirit is God—the third Person of the Trinity. (The title "Holy Ghost" is an older English expression for "Holy Spirit." Each is an acceptable translation of the phrase in the Bible.)

Why do Christians Believe in the Trinity?

The Bible clearly teaches that there is only one God, yet the Bible calls all three Persons "God."

There is only one God:
- *Hear, O Israel: The LORD our God is one LORD. (Deuteronomy 6:4)*
- *Before me there was no God formed, neither shall there be after me. (Isaiah 43:10)*

The Father is God:
- *Grace unto you, and peace, from God our Father and from the Lord Jesus Christ. (1 Corinthians 1:3; 8:6; Ephesians 4:4-6)*

The Son is God:
- *The Word was God. (John 1:1-5, 14)* Jesus is identified as "the Word."
- *I and the Father are one. (John 10:30-33)*
- Jesus' disciple Thomas addressed Jesus as *"My Lord and my God." (John 20:28)*

Jesus did not tell Thomas he was mistaken; instead Jesus accepted these titles. Other people in Scripture, notably Paul and Barnabas (Acts 14), refused to accept worship as gods.

- *But unto the Son he saith, Thy throne, O God, is for ever and ever: a sceptre of righteousness is the sceptre of thy kingdom. (Hebrews 1:6-8)*

- *Wherefore God also hath highly exalted him, and given him a name which is above every name: That at the name of Jesus every knee should bow, of things in heaven, and things in earth, and things under the earth; and that every tongue should confess that Jesus Christ is Lord, to the glory of God the Father. (Philippians 2:9-11)*

Paul, the writer of Philippians, is saying about Jesus what Isaiah 45:23 says about the LORD, and then Paul concludes that Jesus is LORD, that is, the same LORD God of the Old Testament.

See these passages about Jesus' deity: Isa. 7:14; Isa. 9:6; John 1:1; John 1:18; John 8:58, 59; John 10:30; Acts 20:28; Rom. 9:5 & 10:9-13; Col. 1:15, 16; Col. 2:9; Titus 2:13; Heb. 1:3, 8; 2 Pet. 1:1; 1 John 5:20.

The Holy Spirit is God:
- *But Peter said, Ananias, why hath Satan filled thine heart to lie to the Holy Ghost? ...Thou hast not lied unto men, but unto God. (Acts 5:3-4)* This verse equates the Holy Spirit (Holy Ghost) with God.

- *Now the Lord is that Spirit. (2 Corinthians 3:17)*

"The Lord" here refers to "the LORD" in the Old Testament verse (Exodus 34:34) Paul had just quoted in the previous verse (2 Corinthians 3:16).

More than 60 Bible Passages mention the three Persons together

- Matthew 3:16, 17 "And Jesus, when he was baptized, went up straightway out of the water: and, lo, the heavens were opened unto him, and he saw the Spirit of God descending like a dove, and lighting upon him: And lo a voice from heaven, saying, This is my beloved Son, in whom I am well pleased."

- Matthew 28:19 "Go ye therefore, and teach all nations, baptizing them in the name of the Father, and of the Son, and of the Holy Ghost."

- 2 Corinthians 13:14 "The grace of the Lord Jesus Christ, and the love of God, and the communion of the Holy Ghost, be with you all."

- Ephesians 4:4-6 "There is one body, and one Spirit, even as ye are called in one hope of your calling; one Lord, one faith, one baptism, one God and Father of all, who is above all, and through all, and in you all."

See also John 3:34, 35; John 14:26; John 15:26; John 16:13-15; Rom. 14:17, 18; Rom. 15:13-17; Rom. 15:30; 1 Cor. 6:11, 17-19; 1 Cor. 12:4-6; 2 Cor. 1:21, 22; 2 Cor. 3:4-6; Gal. 2:21-3:2; Gal. 4:6; Eph. 2:18; Eph. 3:11-17; Eph. 5:18-20; Col. 1:6-8; 1 Thes. 1:1-5; 1 Thes. 4:2, 8; 1 Thes. 5:18,19; 2 Thes. 3:5; Heb. 9:14; 1 Pet. 1:2; 1 John 3:23, 24; Titus 3: 4-6; 1 John 4:13, 14; and Jude 20, 21.

Misunderstandings About the Trinity

Misunderstandings About the Trinity

Misunderstanding #1: "The word 'Trinity' does not appear in the Bible; it is a belief made up by Christians in the 4th century."

Truth: It is true that the word "Trinity" does not appear in the Bible, but the Trinity is nevertheless a Bible-based belief. The word "incarnation" does not appear in the Bible either, but we use it as a one-word summary of our belief that Jesus was God in the flesh.

The word "Trinity" was used to explain the eternal relationship between the Father, the Son, and the Holy Spirit. Many Bible passages express the Trinity.
False beliefs flourished during the early days of Christianity, and still do. Early Christians constantly defended their beliefs. The following early church leaders and/or writings all defended the doctrine of the Trinity long before AD 300:

Approximate Dates:

AD 96	**Clement**, the third bishop of Rome
AD 90-100	**The Teachings of the Twelve Apostles,** the "Didache"
AD 90?	**Ignatius,** bishop of Antioch
AD 155	**Justin Martyr,** great Christian writer
AD 168	**Theophilus,** the sixth bishop of Antioch
AD 177	**Athenagoras,** theologian
AD 180	**Irenaeus,** bishop of Lyons
AD 197	**Tertullian,** early church leader
AD 264	**Gregory Thaumaturgus,** early church leader

Misunderstanding #2: "Christians believe there are three Gods."

Truth: Christians believe in only one God.

Some people might believe that Christians are polytheists (people who believe in many gods) because Christians refer to the Father as God, the Son as God, and the Holy Spirit as God. But Christians believe in only one God. The Bible says there is only one God. But it also calls three distinct Persons "God." Over the centuries people have tried to come up with simple explanations for the Trinity. There are limits to every illustration, but some are helpful. For example, it has been said that

God is not	1 + 1 + 1 = 3
God is	1 x 1 x 1 = 1

The Trinity is a profound doctrine that must be accepted by faith. Accepting a doctrine by faith does not exclude reason, but it also means that we cannot always apply the same logic that we use in mathematics. Without the Trinity, the Christian doctrine of salvation cannot stand. Some religious groups that claim to believe in the God of the Bible, but reject the Trinity, have an understanding of salvation that is based on good works.

St. Patrick is believed to have used the shamrock as a way of illustrating the Trinity. He asked, "Is this one leaf or three? If one leaf, why are there three lobes of equal size? If three leaves, why is there just one stem? If you cannot explain so simple a mystery as the shamrock, how can you hope to understand one so profound as the Holy Trinity?" Even though this is an overly simple way to explain the Trinity, some teachers find it helpful.

Misunderstanding #3: "Jesus is not God."

Truth: Jesus is God, the Second Person of the Trinity.

1. Jesus' own claims
• **He forgave sin.** We may forgive sins committed against us, but we cannot forgive sins committed against others. Jesus has the authority to forgive any sin. (Mark 2:5-12; Luke 5:21)

• **He accepted worship as God and claimed to deserve the same honor as the Father.** (Matthew 14:33; 28:17, 18; John 5:22, 23; 9:38; 17:5)

• **He claimed to be the divine Son of God,** a title the Jews rightly understood to be a claim to equality with God. (John 5:17, 18; John 10:30-33; John 19:7)

2. Jesus and God share traits (see chart).

Traits Unique to God	Traits of Jesus
Creation is "the work of his hands"—alone (Genesis 1:1; Psalm 102:25; Isaiah 44:24)	Creation is "the work of his hands"—all things created in and through him (John 1:3; Colossians 1:16; Hebrews 1:2, 10)
"The first and the last" (Isaiah 44:6)	"The first and the last" (Revelation 1:17; 22:13)
"Lord of lords" (Deuteronomy 10:17; Psalm 136:3)	"Lord of lords" (1 Timothy 6:15; Revelation 17:14; 19:16)
Unchanging and eternal (Psalms 90:2; 102:26, 27; Malachi 3:6)	Unchanging and eternal (John 8:58; Col. 1:17; Heb. 1:11, 12; 13:8)
Judge of all people (Genesis 18:25; Psalms 94:2; 96:13; 98:9)	Judge of all people (John 5:22; Acts 17:31; 2 Cor. 5:10; 2 Tim. 4:1)
Only Savior; no other God can save (Isaiah 43:11; 45:21, 22; Hosea 13:4)	Savior of the world; no salvation apart from him (John 4:42; Acts 4:12; Titus 2:13; 1 John 4:14)
Redeems from their sins a people for his own possession (Exodus 19:5; Psalm 130:7, 8; Ezekiel 37:23)	Redeems from their sins a people for his own possession (Titus 2:14)
Hears and answers prayers of those who call on him (Psalm 86:5-8; Isaiah 55:6, 7; Jeremiah 33:3; Joel 2:32)	Hears and answers prayers of those who call on him (John 14:14; Rom. 10:12, 13; 1 Cor. 1:2; 2 Cor. 12:8, 9)
Only God has divine glory (Isaiah 42:8, 48:11)	Jesus has divine glory (John 17:5)
Worshipped by angels (Psalm 97:7)	Worshipped by angels (Heb. 1:6)

Misunderstandings About the Trinity

Misunderstanding #4: "Jesus is a lesser God than the Father."

Truth: Jesus is co-equal with God the Father. People who deny this truth may use the following arguments and verses. (These heresies date back to Arius, AD 319.)

Verses wrongly used to teach that Christ was created:

1. Colossians 1:15: If Christ is "the first born of all creation," was he created?

   Answer: "Firstborn" cannot mean that Christ was created, because Paul says that all of creation was made in and for Christ, and that he exists before all creation and holds it together (Col. 1:16, 17). The "firstborn" traditionally was the main heir. In context Paul is saying that Christ, as God's Son, is the main heir of all creation (verses 12-14).

2. John 3:16: Does "only begotten Son" mean Jesus had a beginning?

   Answer: "Only-begotten" does not mean that Jesus had a beginning; it means that Jesus is God's "unique" Son. In Hebrews 11:17, Isaac is called Abraham's "unique" son, even though Abraham had other children (Gen. 22:2; 25:1-6). Jesus is God's unique Son because only Jesus is fully God and eternally the Father's Son (John 1:1-3, 14-18).

3. Proverbs 8:22: Does this mean that Christ ("Wisdom") was "created"?

   Answer: This is not a literal description of Christ; it is a personification of wisdom. For example, Christ did not dwell in heaven with someone named Prudence (verse 12); he did not build a house with seven pillars (9:1). This verse says in a poetic way that God used wisdom in creating the world (see Prov. 3:19, 20).

Verses wrongly used to teach that Jesus is inferior to the Father:

1. John 14:28: If "the Father is greater than" Jesus, how can Jesus be God?

   Answer: In his human life on earth Jesus voluntarily shared our natural limitations in order to save us. After he rose from the dead, Jesus returned to the glory he had with the Father (John 17:5; Philippians 2:9-11).

In that restored glory, Jesus was able to send the Holy Spirit and empower his disciples to do even greater works than Jesus did while he was here in the flesh (John 14:12, 26-28).

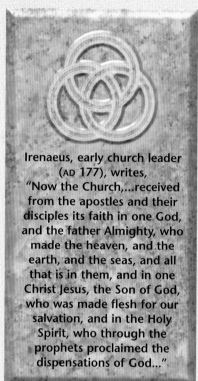

Irenaeus, early church leader (AD 177), writes, "Now the Church,...received from the apostles and their disciples its faith in one God, and the father Almighty, who made the heaven, and the earth, and the seas, and all that is in them, and in one Christ Jesus, the Son of God, who was made flesh for our salvation, and in the Holy Spirit, who through the prophets proclaimed the dispensations of God..."

2. 1 Corinthians 15:28: If Jesus is God, why will he be subject to the Father?

   Answer: Jesus humbly and voluntarily submits himself to the Father's will for a time (Philippians 2:5-11). But, as the pre-existent and eternal Son, he is co-equal with God the Father.

3. Mark 13:32: If Jesus is God, how could he not know when he would return?

   Answer: Jesus voluntarily lowered himself to experience the limitations of human life. Paradoxically, while Jesus continued to be God, he chose to limit his access to knowledge (John 16:30). Paradoxes like this (not contradictions) are exactly what we would expect if, as the Bible says, God chose to live as a real human being (John 1:1, 14).

Misunderstanding #5: "The Father, the Son, and the Spirit are just different titles for Jesus, or three different ways that God has revealed himself."

Truth: The Bible clearly shows that the Father, Son, and Holy Spirit are distinct persons.

Some people think that the doctrine of the Trinity contradicts the truth that there is only one God. They argue that Jesus alone is the one true God, and therefore that Jesus is "the name of the Father and the Son and the Holy Spirit" (Matt. 28:19), and not just the name of the Son. While it is certainly true that there is only one God, we must allow the Bible to define what this means. And the Bible makes it quite clear that the Father, Son, and Holy Spirit are distinct persons:

- The Father sends the Son (Gal. 4:4; 1 John 4:14)
- The Father sends the Spirit (John 14:26; Gal. 4:6)
- The Son speaks, not on his own, but on behalf of the Father (John 8:28; 12:49)
- The Spirit speaks, not on his own, but on behalf of Jesus (John 16:13-15)
- The Father loves the Son, and the Son loves the Father (John 3:35; 5:20; 14:31)
- The Father and the Son count as two witnesses (John 5:31-37; 8:16-18)
- The Father and the Son glorify one another (John 17:1,4, 5), and the Spirit glorifies Jesus the Son (John 16:14)
- The Son is an Advocate for us with the Father (1 John 2:1; Greek, *parakletos*); Jesus the Son sent the Holy Spirit, who is another Advocate (John 14:16, 26)
- Jesus Christ is not the Father, but the Son of the Father (2 John 3)

In Matthew 28:19, Jesus is not identifying himself as the Father, Son, and Holy Spirit. He is saying that Christian baptism identifies a person as one who believes in the Father, in the Son whom the Father sent to die for our sins, and in the Holy Spirit whom the Father and the Son sent to dwell in our hearts.

Misunderstanding #6: "Jesus wasn't really fully God and fully man."

Throughout history many people have balked at the idea that Jesus is both fully God and fully man. They have tried to resolve this paradox by saying that Jesus was a mere man through whom God spoke, or that he was God and merely appeared to be human, or some other "simpler" belief. Admittedly the idea that in Jesus, God became a man, is difficult for us to comprehend. But the Incarnation—the truth that God became flesh—is the ultimate proof that nothing is too hard for God (Genesis 18:14; Luke 1:37). And this truth is clearly taught in the Bible.

How Early Christians Dealt with These Misunderstandings

The Bible clearly shows that Jesus was fully human:

As a child, he grew physically, intellectually, socially, and spiritually (Luke 2:40, 52).

He grew tired; he slept; he sweat; he was hungry and thirsty; he bled and died; his body was buried (Matthew 4:2; 8:24; Luke 22:44; John 4:6, 7; 19:28-42).

After he rose from the dead, he ate and drank with people and let them see his scars and touch his body (Luke 24:39-43; John 20:27-29; Acts 10:41).

The Bible also clearly shows that Jesus was fully God:

Jesus did on earth what only God can do: he commanded the forces of nature (Matthew 8:23-27; 14:22, 33), forgave sins (Mark 2:1-12); claimed to be superior to the Sabbath law (John 5:17, 18); and gave life to whomever he pleased (John 5:19-23).

Paul said that God purchased the church with his own blood (Acts 20:28).

Paul also said that the rulers of this world unwittingly crucified the Lord of glory (1 Corinthians 2:8).

All the fullness of God's nature and being resides in Jesus' risen body (Colossians 2:9).

Early Christian theologians of the first two centuries wrote many works defending Christianity from several threats:

- Persecution from the Roman Empire. Until the early A.D. 300s, Christianity was illegal and often Christians were viciously persecuted.
- Heresies attacking basic Christian beliefs, especially the deity of Jesus Christ and the nature of God.

The Apostles' Creed was one of the earliest statements of faith Christian leaders crafted to clarify basic Christian beliefs. It emphasizes the true humanity—including the physical body—of Jesus, which was the belief the heretics of the time denied.

I believe in God, the Father almighty, creator of heaven and earth.

I believe in Jesus Christ, his only Son, our Lord. He was conceived by the power of the Holy Spirit and born of the Virgin Mary. He suffered under Pontius Pilate, was crucified, died, and was buried. He descended to the dead. On the third day he rose again. He ascended into heaven, and is seated at the right hand of the Father. He will come again to judge the living and the dead.

I believe in the Holy Spirit, the holy catholic Church, the communion of saints, the forgiveness of sins, the resurrection of the body, and the life everlasting. Amen.

The Nicene Creed was written by church leaders in AD 325, and was later expanded somewhat. It was written to defend the church's belief in Christ's full deity and to reject formally the teachings of Arius, a man who claimed that Jesus was a created, inferior deity.

We believe in one God, the Father, the Almighty, maker of heaven and earth, of all that is, seen and unseen.

We believe in one Lord, Jesus Christ, the only Son of God, eternally begotten of the Father, Light from Light, true God from true God, begotten, not made, of one Being with the Father; through him all things were made. For us and for our salvation he came down from heaven; by the power of the Holy Spirit he became incarnate from the virgin Mary and was made man. For our sake he was crucified under Pontius Pilate; he suffered death and was buried; on the third day he rose again in accordance with the Scriptures; he ascended into heaven. He is seated at the right hand of the Father, he will come again in glory to judge the living and the dead, and his kingdom will have no end.

We believe in the Holy Spirit, the Lord, the giver of life, who proceeds from the Father and the Son; with the Father and the Son he is worshiped and glorified; he has spoken through the prophets. We believe in one holy catholic and apostolic Church. We acknowledge one baptism for the forgiveness of sins. We look for the resurrection of the dead, and the life of the world to come.

Note: The Greek word from which the word *catholic* is derived means "universal." The "catholic Church" means the ancient church that agreed with the whole of the apostles' teaching, as opposed to false teachers that followed a "secret revelation" or emphasized only one part of the first century apostles' teachings.

Divine Attributes	Father	Son	Holy Spirit
Eternal	X Romans 16:26, 27	X Revelation 1:17	X Hebrews 9:14
Creator of all things	X Psalm 100:3	X Colossians 1:16	X Psalm 104:30
Omnipresent (capable of being all places at once)	X Jeremiah 23:24	X Ephesians 1:23	X Psalm 139:7
Omniscient (knows all things)	X 1 John 3:20	X John 21:17	X 1 Cor. 2:10
Wills and acts supernaturally	X Ephesians 1:5	X Matthew 8:3	X 1 Cor. 12:11
Gives life	X Genesis 1:11-31 see also John 5:21	X John 1:4 see also John 5:21	X Romans 8:10, 11 see also John 3:8
Strengthens believers	X Psalm 138:3	X Philippians 4:13	X Ephesians 3:16

The Church and the Creeds

The **Athanasian Creed**, written about AD 400 and named after Athanasius, a great defender of the Trinity, says the three Persons are not three Gods, but only one.

This is what the catholic faith teaches: we worship one God in the Trinity and the Trinity in unity.

We distinguish among the persons, but we do not divide the substance.

A simple illustration:
Ice, Water, Steam
All have the same nature, water.
(But of course, the Father, Son, and Holy Spirit are God at the *same* time.)

For the Father is a distinct person; the Son is a distinct person; and the Holy Spirit is a distinct person. Still the Father and the Son and the Holy Spirit have one divinity, equal glory, and coeternal majesty. What the Father is, the Son is, and the Holy Spirit is.

The Father is uncreated, the Son is uncreated, and the Holy Spirit is uncreated. The Father is boundless, the Son is boundless, and the Holy Spirit is boundless. The Father is eternal, the Son is eternal, and the Holy Spirit is eternal.

Nevertheless, there are not three eternal beings, but one eternal being. Thus there are not three uncreated beings, nor three boundless beings, but one uncreated being and one boundless being.Likewise, the Father is omnipotent, the Son is omnipotent, and the Holy Spirit is omnipotent. Yet there are not three omnipotent beings, but one omnipotent being.

Thus the Father is God, the Son is God, and the Holy Spirit is God. But there are not three gods, but one God. The Father is Lord, the Son is Lord, and the Holy Spirit is Lord. There as not three lords, but one Lord.

For according to Christian truth, we must profess that each of the persons individually is God; and according to Christian religion we are forbidden to say there are three Gods or three Lords.

The Father is made of none, neither created nor begotten. The Son is of the Father alone; not made nor created, but begotten. The Holy Spirit is of the Father and of the Son; neither made, nor created, nor begotten, but proceeding.

So there is one Father, not three Fathers; one Son, not three Sons; one Holy Spirit, not three Holy Spirits. And in this Trinity none is afore, nor after another; none is greater, or less than another.

But the whole three persons are co-eternal, and co-equal. So that in all things, as aforesaid, the Unity in Trinity and the Trinity in Unity is to be worshipped.

The **Chalcedonian Creed**, written in AD 451 by church leaders to defend the faith against false teachings, says that Jesus is fully God and fully man.

Therefore, following the holy fathers, we all with one accord teach men to acknowledge one and the same Son, our Lord Jesus Christ, at once complete in Godhead and complete in manhood, truly God and truly man, consisting also of a reasonable soul and body; of one substance (homoousios) with the Father as regards his Godhead, and at the same time of one substance with us as regards his manhood; like us in all respects, apart from sin; as regards his Godhead, begotten of the Father before the ages, but yet as regards his manhood begotten, for us men and for our salvation, of Mary the Virgin, the God-bearer (theotokos); one and the same Christ, Son, Lord, Only-begotten, recognized in two natures, without

confusion, without change, without division, without separation; the distinction of natures being in no way annulled by the union, but rather the characteristics of each nature being preserved and coming together to form one person and subsistence, not as parted or separated into two persons, but one and the same Son and Only-begotten God the Word, Lord Jesus Christ; even as the prophets from earliest times spoke of him, and our Lord Jesus Christ himself taught us, and the creed of the Fathers has handed down to us.

For Further Reading

Beisner, E. Calvin. *God in Three Persons*. Wheaton: Tyndale House, 1984. Popular overview of the historical development of the doctrine.
Bickersteth, Edward H. *The Trinity*. Grand Rapids: Kregel, 1957. Classic exposition of the doctrine from a multitude of biblical texts.
Bowman, Robert M., Jr. *Why You Should Believe in the Trinity*. Grand Rapids: Baker, 1989. Answers to various criticisms of the doctrine.
Boyd, Gregory A. *Oneness Pentecostals and the Trinity*. Grand Rapids: Baker, 1992. Biblical critique of the belief held by Oneness Pentecostals that Jesus is the Father, Son, and Holy Spirit.
Bray, Gerald. *Creeds, Councils and Christ*. Downers Grove, IL: InterVarsity Press, 1984. More advanced analysis of the origins and biblical basis of the creeds.
Christianity, Cults & Religions. Torrance, CA: Rose Publishing, 1994. 19" by 26" wall chart comparing the beliefs of 18 religions and cults. Topics include: God, Jesus, the Holy Spirit, salvation, what happens after death, and more.
Reymond, Robert L. *Jesus, Divine Messiah: The New Testament Witness*. Phillipsburg, NJ: Presbyterian & Reformed, 1990. Advanced biblical study, defending Christ's deity primarily against modern critical theories.
Rhodes, Ron. *Christ Before the Manger*. Grand Rapids: Baker, 1992. What the Bible says about Jesus before he became a man. Also see Rhodes's book *The Complete Book of Bible Answers*.

Helpful Websites

http://www.watchman.org/subindex.htm
Watchman Fellowship, P.O. Box 13340, Arlington, TX 76094, Ph. (800) 769-2824 Specializes in teaching biblical interpretation and in tracking numerous religious groups that deny the Trinity and other essential Christian doctrines (Scroll down to *Trinity* in this alphabetical list of topics.)
http://home.earthlink.net/~ronrhodes/
Reasoning from the Scriptures Ministries (contact: Ron Rhodes), P.O. Box 2526, Frisco, TX 75034 Ph. (214) 618-0912 Specializes in giving basic answers to commonly asked questions (See "Answers to Common Questions.")
http://www.apologeticsindex.org/t10.html
Apologetics Index (contact: Anton Hein) Online literature explaining a variety of Christian doctrines.
http://www.irr.org/mit/trinity1.html
Institute for Religious Research (contact: Luke P. Wilson), 1340 Monroe Ave. NW, Grand Rapids, MI 49505 Ph. (616) 451-4562

Religious History

Who is God?

What Muslims Believe

Islam, the Original Religion
Muslims believe that Islam (meaning submission to Allah) is the original religion since the creation of Adam, the first prophet. Since the beginning of time, all people who submit to Allah are called Muslims. Over the centuries, Allah appointed thousands of prophets to warn and guide mankind. Prominent among them were *Ebrahim* (Abraham), *Musa* (Moses), *Dawud* (David), and *Isa Al Masih* (Jesus the Messiah).

Muhammad, the Final Prophet
Mankind habitually strayed from the way of Allah revealed through the prophets. About AD 610 in Arabia, Allah sent the last prophet, Muhammad, who united the tribes of Arabs and turned them from idolatry to Islam.

The Spread of Islam
After the death of Muhammad in AD 632, Sunni Islam rapidly spread from Arabia under the leadership of the first four "rightly guided" rulers (*caliphs*) who were close companions of Muhammad. Shia Islam began to rapidly spread through the teachings of "infallible" Imans from the bloodline of Muhammad. To Muslims, the military and economic expansion of Islam liberated people suffering under the corrupt Byzantine and Persian Empires.

What Muslims Believe

Allah is One
The absolute Oneness of Allah is primary to Muslims. The greatest sin is to associate any partner with Him. This sin is called *shirk*. Muhammad's message advocating one God was courageous because idolatry was the established religion of Arabia. Muhammad challenged this system and finally prevailed with the message of monotheism. Islam is rooted in this commitment to the belief in one God.

Allah Cannot be Compared
Allah is transcendent and cannot be compared to humans or any other created thing. Allah's character and attributes are revealed through His 99 Arabic names, the two most common being "The Merciful" and "The Compassionate." Allah is never described in Islam by using human family terms such as "father " or "son." In the Quran he reveals his will for mankind to obey, not his person for mankind to relate with and know.

Allah's Ultimate Attribute: His Will
Allah creates and sustains all life, spiritual and material. His will is absolute and cannot be questioned by his creation. He is our final judge without a mediator. The best chance on Judgment Day is for those who live lives of righteousness and submission to Allah's will—*Insha Allah* (God willing).

What Christians Believe

Adam and Jesus
Christians also trace their religious history back to Adam, who brought the curse of sin upon all mankind. (Gen. 1-3) In the Bible, Jesus is known as the second Adam, who came to remove this curse of sin. (Rom. 5)

Abraham and Jesus
God's plan unfolded carefully over history. Abraham (*Ebrahim* in Arabic) was promised the blessing to carry out God's eternal purposes. He was blessed so he could be a blessing to all the families of the earth. (Genesis 12:1-3; Galatians 3) Jesus is the promised seed of Eve who would crush the head of Satan (*Shaytan* in Arabic - Genesis 3:15) and bring the blessing of the "Good News" (*Injil* in Arabic).

The Victory of Jesus
A great war has been raging throughout the Creation, a struggle in which Satan has twisted all good things—even religion—into weapons to discredit God. The decisive battle of this war was won on the cross when Jesus destroyed Satan's power and overcame the curse of sin. By rising from the dead, Jesus conquered death, a consequence of the curse, and thereby offers the blessing of eternal life to mankind.

What Christians Believe

God: A Unity, not a Unit
The Bible teaches that God is One, but He is a complex unity, not just a simple unit. He is completely unique, a personal God who existed in relationship from eternity.

God the Father, God the Son, God the Holy Spirit
Scriptures reveal God as the ultimate Father, in name, character, and person, but always as the Creator, never with sexual references. God also reveals Himself as the Eternal Word, who became flesh when the Holy Spirit overshadowed the Virgin Mary and conceived Jesus, the Messiah, who is also called the Son of God in the Bible. In His teaching, Jesus further reveals God the Holy Spirit, who was sent by the Father and Himself.
The Bible presents a mystery of three persons revealed as one God. Although the word "Trinity" is not in the Bible, the term captures Bible truths about God. The Father, the Son, and the Holy Spirit are God, not just three parts of God or three names for the same person. God reveals Himself as a Tri-Unity.

God's Ultimate Attribute: His Love
The Bible says, "God is Love." This love existed from eternity as the Father loved the Son even before the foundation of the world. God's love is expressed through creation. God does not simply choose to love; His Love chooses to act. "God so loved the world that He gave His Son..." (John 3:16)

How to Correct Misunderstandings

The Misunderstandings
Religious history between Christians and Muslims is covered with blood and war, much like all of human history. God's name has been used by both sides to justify murder and mayhem. Several key events in history continue to affect the perceptions of Christians and Muslims. These events include the Islamic expansion (AD 600 to 800's), the Crusades (AD 1000 to 1200's), the establishment of the state of Israel in 1948, the attack on the World Trade Center, the Gulf Wars of 1991 and 2003, and many other events.

Correcting the Misunderstandings
Historians have pointed out that these "holy wars" of history were more about economics than faith. Yet economic struggle cannot explain the intense hatred, cruelty and malicious evil of a Crusader, Nazi, or suicide bomber. Behind these horrors is a deeper spiritual war and a vindictive enemy, namely Satan. Christian and Muslims should not lose sight of Satan, the "enemy of souls." By recognizing the common enemy, Christians and Muslims can create a context in which they can build relationships.

How to Correct Misunderstandings

The Misunderstandings
Most Muslims consider Christians to be polytheists (people who believe in many gods) because of the Trinity. A popular misunderstanding of the Trinity is that Christians believe that a Father God had sex with a Mother God (Mary) to produce their "Son of God." No Christian believes this. Educated Muslims understand this false Trinity is not what Christians believe, but they still do not understand how the math can show God's unity. To them it is simple: $1+1+1=3$; Father + Son + Holy Spirit = Three Gods. This is not what Christians believe.

Correcting the Misunderstandings
Rather than an analogy of adding units ($1+1+1=3$), the Trinity has been explained as multiplied wholeness ($1 \times 1 \times 1=1$). Concerning the divinity of Jesus (*Isa al Masih* in Arabic), the Quran (Islam's holiest book) highly exalts Him and confirms His miracles, even raising the dead. The Quran also affirms His virgin birth.

The Bible says Jesus forgave sin (Luke 5:21) and accepted worship. (John 5:22, 23) Jesus is unique, fully divine, fully human.

Holy Scriptures

Prophets

What Muslims Believe

The Only Trustworthy Scripture
According to Muslims, there is only one trustworthy Holy Scripture, the Quran. Many prophets before Muhammad were also given Allah's Word, among them: *Musa* (Moses) given the *Taurat* (Torah), *Dawud* (David) given the *Zabur* (Psalms), and *Isa* (Jesus) given the *Injil* (Gospel). However, Muslims are taught that all these writings were corrupted, so Allah appointed Muhammad to receive the Quran in order to correct this corruption.

How Muslims Got the Quran
In AD 610, Allah sent the angel Gabriel to Muhammad in Mecca, Saudi Arabia. Over the next 22 years Gabriel revealed *suras* (chapters) to Muhammad with the command to recite it to others. Shortly after Muhammad's death in AD 632 his followers gathered the suras into the Quran. The third caliph, Uthman, had scholars compile an official Quran, in written form, and had all other variant texts burned.

The Quran Today
The Quran is considered divine in its original Arabic form, and Muslims memorize and recite it only in this pure language.

What Muslims Believe

Muhammad, The Seal of the Prophets
To Muslims, the Prophet Muhammad, called the "seal of the prophets," is the last of over 124,000 prophets going back to Adam. His name means "praised one," and he is commended by Allah in the Quran.

Muhammad, The Reformer
Mecca was a center of idol worship in AD 610 when Muhammad first challenged the people to forsake idolatry and embrace Islam. Most Meccans rejected his message and many began to persecute the early Muslims, causing them to flee to Medina in AD 622. (This flight is known as the *hijara* and marked the first year on the Islamic calendar.) Medina was more receptive to Muhammad and from this city, through battles and diplomacy, Islam was spread to the entire Arabian Peninsula before Muhammad died in AD 632.

Muhammad, the Perfect Example to Follow
Muslims try to follow Muhammad's example known as his *sunna*, or his way, in every detail possible. Everything is prescribed, from ritual washings before prayer to hygienic practices in the bathroom. Such detailed behavior is known through large collections of *hadith*, accounts of Muhammad's life, words, and behavior passed on by his early followers.

What Christians Believe

How Christians Got the Bible
Followers of Jesus believe the Bible is the authoritative, inspired word of God, composed of 66 different books, transmitted through at least 40 prophets, apostles, and holy men. The first 39 books, written before the coming of Christ, are called the Old Testament. The Old Testament was written over many centuries by various authors in diverse cultures using the Hebrew and Aramaic languages. The remaining 27 books after Christ are called the New Testament. They were written in Greek, the dominant language of the first century. The New Testament contains collections of eye-witness reports of the life and teachings of Jesus followed by a history of His disciples over the next 50 years, including letters from His apostles, and a vision of the end times called the "Revelation."

Inspiration
The Christian view of inspiration is that God "breathed" His Word through many people. Therefore the Bible reflects cultures as diverse as Abraham's nomadic lifestyle to the royal court of King David. The result is the Book of beautiful human diversity interwoven with divine unity.

What Christians Believe

Old Testament Prophecy
New Testament writers proclaimed Jesus as the fulfillment of the Law of Moses (Taurat) and the predictions of Old Testament prophets. These prophets are quoted in the New Testament. For instance, Matthew quotes various prophets concerning Jesus' birth in Bethlehem (Micah 5:2), his mother being a virgin (Isaiah 7:14), and even the killing of baby boys by King Herod. (Jeremiah 31:15) The prophets also detail the suffering, death, and resurrection of Jesus. (Isaiah 53; Psalm 16:8-11) The Bible points out that God carefully planned and carried out the details of the coming of Jesus in history. (Luke 24:27; Acts 3:18)

Christ's Warning About False Teachers
The Bible contains numerous warnings about false teachers and prophets. Jesus predicts the end times will be full of these. (Matthew 24:11) Therefore, every teaching must be judged against the truth already revealed in the Bible. Jesus also promised that the Holy Spirit ("The Spirit of Truth") would guide truth seekers into all truth. (John 14–16)

How to Correct Misunderstandings

The Misunderstandings
Muslims feel sorry that Christians follow a corrupted book and most Muslims avoid the Bible. Even among Western-educated Muslims, the great diversity of Bible versions and translations adds to their belief that the Bible is corrupted.

Correcting the Misunderstandings
Muhammad did not question the accuracy of the Bible. The accusation that the Bible had been corrupted came centuries after Muhammad, at a time when Muslim scholars realized there were contradictions between the Quran and the Bible. Yet the Quran points to the Bible as truth over 120 times. The text of the Bible is better preserved than the writings of Plato and Aristotle. Furthermore, the discovery of the Dead Sea Scrolls confirmed the reliability of the Bible.

To think it is possible for any man to corrupt the actual Word of God is to diminish God. By His reputation God is committed to protect His Word. (Psalm 138:2) The best defense of the Bible's integrity is the nature, power, and reputation of God.

How to Correct Misunderstandings

The Misunderstandings
In conversation with Muslims, do not attack Muhammad. Since so much is determined by imitating their prophet, to insult Muhammad is to attack their entire life and culture.

Correcting the Misunderstandings
It is wise to find common ground and agree that Muhammad has much in common with Old Testament prophets. Like David and Solomon, he was a political and military leader with multiple wives. Like Moses and Joshua, he united tribes and led them in battle. Like Elijah and many other prophets, he destroyed idols and confronted the corrupt political and economic powers of his day.

Just as Old Testament prophets looked forward to the coming Messiah, Muhammad looked back with respect and admiration to Jesus as the Messiah. The Quran calls *Isa Al Masih* (Jesus) "God's word" and a "Spirit from Him." (Surah 4:171) It affirms His virgin birth and special role in the end times.

Followers of Jesus do not have to deny or embrace Muhammad in order to exalt the Messiah. It is important to lift up Jesus, not tear down Muhammad.

Practices & Rituals

Salvation & Paradise

What Muslims Believe

The Five Pillars
The ritual practices of Islam are the pillars of their religious system. Although beliefs are important, the substance of their religion is the accomplishment of these five pillars (see details on back of chart).

- Confessing the Faith (*Shahada*)
- Prayer (*Salat*)
- Fasting (*Sawm*)
- Giving of Alms (*Zakat*)
- Pilgrimage to Mecca (*Hajj*)

The Muslim's objective is to follow Muhammad's pattern (his exact words, motions, and timing) found in the sunna as they accomplish the pillars.

Jihad
Some Muslims would include a sixth pillar, Holy Struggle (*Jihad*). This struggle could be internal (a struggle in the soul to do the right thing) or external (an effort against the enemies of Islam). The interpretation of jihad can determine the difference between moderate and radical Muslims.

Judgment Day
Their belief in the nature of the final Judgment Day motivates Muslims to faithfully accomplish these pillars. In the Quran, these practices are of great importance.

What Christians Believe

The Gift of Salvation
The Bible teaches that salvation is a gift from God through faith in Jesus Christ (Isa Al Masih) and there are no rituals or practices that anyone can do in order to get right with God. (Ephesians 2: 8, 9)

Jesus' Seven Commands
Even though no one can be saved by good works, followers of Jesus serve him, imitate him, and do what he commanded because they are filled with the Holy Spirit. Jesus said, "If you love me you will keep my commands, and my commands are not burdensome." He gave seven specific commands:

- Repent and Believe (a turn of heart)
- Pray (as a lifestyle, from the heart)
- Be Baptized (with water)
- Make Disciples (among all peoples)
- Love God and Others (greatest command)
- Celebrate the Lord's Supper (remember Jesus)
- Give (with a joyful heart)

Making disciples involves worship, fellowship, fasting, studying Scripture, and sharing the good news. Jesus said that his disciples would be recognized by their love for one another. (John 13:35)

How to Correct Misunderstandings

The Misunderstandings
A Muslim can be confused by Christian symbols and rituals, such as the cross (considered a military symbol to Muslims) and the Lord's Supper when using wine (alcohol is prohibited in Islam). Christians are confused by some of the Muslim rituals as well.

Correcting the Misunderstandings
If Christians and Muslims can communicate and completely understand the meaning behind these symbols and rituals, meaningful relationships can be built and truth-sharing can take place.

Following the "Sermon on the Mount" (Matthew 5–7) is perhaps the best way for Christians to imitate Jesus and share with Muslims. The "Sermon on the Mount" challenges all followers of Jesus to live a righteous lifestyle of humility and love. Unfortunately, today in Western culture, Christian practices such as prayer, fasting, and giving are not emphasized. Muslims need grace-motivated Christian friends who follow the disciplines of Jesus. Jesus calls his followers to pray as a lifestyle, frequently and effectively. By confronting evil and bringing healing, believers can introduce Christ to their Muslim friends.

What Muslims Believe

Reward and Penalty
The Quran says, "For those who reject Allah, there is a terrible penalty: but for those who believe and work righteous deeds, there is forgiveness and a magnificent reward" (Surah 35:7). This great reward is *janna*, a garden paradise, an eternal place of sensual and spiritual pleasures.

No Savior, but Mercy Is Possible
In Islam, there is no savior. That is not to say salvation is impossible, for Allah is merciful and compassionate. He can always forgive—for Allah's will is supreme—but He is primarily the judge. There are many descriptive warnings about hellfire and punishment in the Quran.

Judgment Day: A Motivation to Righteous Deeds
All men should fear Judgment Day, in which each person's deeds will be weighed on a scale. "Recording angels" keep a list of every deed, both good and bad. Islamic teachers assign credits to deeds related to the pillars of Islam. It is unthinkable for many Muslims to abandon their accumulation of credits and trust a Savior.

Guarantee of Paradise?
Muslim terrorists manipulate the Quran to suggest that paradise is guaranteed for jihad martyrs. Most Muslim scholars and leaders reject the terrorists' definitions of jihad and martyrdom.

What Christians Believe

Judgment Day
Christians believe that after death, all people await the final Judgment when both believers and unbelievers will be resurrected. All will be judged according to the deeds they have done, but believers will be saved because God removed the record that contained the charges against them. He destroyed it by nailing it to the cross of Jesus. (Colossians 2: 14) This would remove the list of bad deeds kept by any Muslim's "recording angel."

The Gift of Salvation
Even if one's list of good deeds outweighed their list of bad deeds, it would not make them acceptable to God. The Bible says this would only cause boasting and pride, as though someone could impress God by their good deeds. (Ephesians 2: 8-10) Instead God has credited us with the righteousness of Christ, so salvation is a gift, not earned by anyone, not even martyrs, but bought with a great price (Jesus' blood).

A Renewed Relationship With God
In addition to this great gift, God the Father adopts those He saves into His family so they may live with Jesus in Heaven. To be saved involves being "born again" into a new relationship with God. (John 3:5)

How to Correct Misunderstandings

The Misunderstandings
Thinking about Allah as Abba-Father is difficult for some Muslims. Any negative view of the earthly father role will twist one's view of God. In Western cultures, parenting trends err toward permissiveness (more love than discipline). In the East, fathers tend to be negligent or authoritarian (more discipline than love). God is a Father, who shows both love and discipline. He wants loving followers, not just slaves or spoiled children.

Correcting the Misunderstandings
This view of fatherhood makes it easier to relate to God as Abba and to come to Him as a humble child, ready to be loved and disciplined. Jesus said one must enter God's kingdom as a little child.

The final book of the Bible describes the future scene of a huge family gathering with many from every tribe, tongue, people, and ethnic group gathered around the throne of God. (Revelation 5) Boasting of good deeds would be unthinkable, because Jesus, the Lamb of God, sits upon the throne. Everyone in this great crowd honors Jesus as their substitute sacrifice, just as God pictured beforehand when He provided a ram to die in place of Abraham's son. (Genesis 22)

Role of Women

Religion & Culture

What Muslims Believe

The Perspective of Muslim Women
Muslim women generally consider themselves protected and satisfied within their culture. Their fulfilling social life is usually gender-separated and happens primarily within extended families and some close neighbors.

The Protection of Muslim Women
Women are valued in Islam. In fact, Muhammad brought an end to the practice of female infanticide, widely practiced before his time. The honor of women is a major concern in Muslim societies. The reputation of the family is linked with the women. Islam helps maintain roles and expectations that predate Muhammad. The modest dress code is to protect women. If seen without loose clothing or a veil, men might judge a woman based on her appearance or may try to abuse her. Muslim women do not need to wear a veil or loose clothes at home or when only women are present.

Polygamy
Since marriage and child bearing are highly valued in the Middle East, polygamy is allowed and yet controlled. Islam limits a man to four wives and requires equal treatment for each.

What Muslims Believe

The Muslim Holistic Worldview
Muslims understand religion as a whole and integrated way of life. Secular, Christian-influenced cultures can confuse and even anger Muslims who see things through their holistic worldview. They often view "Hollywood sexuality" as "Christian," or a military action as a "Crusade." To them, the cross is a military symbol.

The Islamic Community
In Islam, brotherhood and consensus is emphasized, and individualism is avoided. The "community of the faithful" is responsible to enforce the moral code. This can explain how a lone Muslim, outside a community support structure, does not feel as guilty when breaking the code. However, bringing shame on his family or community would be a great sin.

Avoiding shame and protecting honor are primary motivations of most Muslims. Shame and honor are community-related, as contrasted to an individual sense of guilt.

Radical Muslims, known as Islamists or Jihadists, use this sense of community honor and shame to recruit and motivate their followers.

What Christians Believe

The Perspective of Christian Women
Christians believe that the Bible teaches that both man and woman were created in God's image, had a direct relationship with God, and shared jointly the responsibilities of bringing up children and ruling over the created order. (Gen. 1:26-28) Christian husbands and wives are to mutually submit to one another. Women are to respect their husbands; husbands are to sacrificially and selflessly love their wives, just as Jesus Christ loves His church. (Ephesians 5:21-25)

The Protection of Christian Women
Christian women are to dress modestly (1 Timothy 2:9), and all followers of Jesus are to flee from sexual immorality. (1 Corinthians 6:18)

Not Conforming to the World
Followers of Jesus believe that they must be transformed by renewing their minds and avoid conforming to the patterns of the secular world. (Romans 12:2) Problems arise when Christians adapt to the Western secular culture more than to the Bible. When this happens there is a decline in morality which leads to an increase in sexual immorality, drunkenness, deceit, selfishness, rage, and other sins.

What Christians Believe

The Western Worldview
Followers of Jesus believe that they are to impact culture for Christ by going into all parts of the world to bring the message of Jesus to the people that live there. (Matthew 28:19, 20) In the West, a division exists between culture and religion. Religion is separated from government, and some people object to any influence of religion on state institutions and symbols.

Community in the West
Followers of Jesus do influence Western culture and institutions, but they seem to be a shrinking influence. Western culture affirms individualism and some people avoid community responsibility. Tolerance of sin and unbiblical practices continue to dilute the true Christian message; evolutionism and atheism also continue to influence the increasingly secular West. Only a minority of those in the West consider themselves followers of Jesus Christ. Most simply consider themselves Christian by name only, and do not follow the teaching of the Bible, of which they are largely ignorant. Generally, Western culture does not have a sense of the "community of the faithful."

How to Correct Misunderstandings

The Misunderstandings
Western values conflict with Muslims regarding women perhaps more than any other category. There are several problems in Muslim societies in regard to women. However, secularism and women's liberation have brought the "Christian" West several problems as well.

Correcting the Misunderstandings
Christians, often focused on the plight of Muslim women, fail to see that many Western "solutions" are more to be feared than the problems they address. Many Muslim women prefer their lifestyle to lonely singleness, sexual exploitation, and the desire for money that makes home and family unimportant.

Societies long dominated by Islam have problems which need to be addressed, but before Christians can address these issues they must deal with their own cultural problems. As Jesus said, "You hypocrite, first take the plank out of your own eye, and then you will see clearly to remove the speck from your brother's eye." (Matthew 7: 5)

How to Correct Misunderstandings

The Misunderstandings
Recently, Time magazine ran a cover article asking the question: "Should Christians Convert Muslims?" The artwork featured a militant-looking clenched fist holding a metal cross reminiscent of a Crusader's sword. This imagery correctly symbolizes some typical Muslim misunderstandings, especially when viewed with the cigarette advertisement on the back cover. The advertisement features a sensual goddess-like model with men fawning at her feet. These pictures display some fears of Muslims: to be dominated militarily and corrupted morally by "Christianity."

Correcting the Misunderstandings
The challenge is to present a correct view of the cross. Mel Gibson's movie, "The Passion of the Christ," has been seen by Muslims all over the world. They have seen the cross as a symbol of suffering, not as a military or political icon. Followers of Jesus, through their words and actions, are called to show Muslims that God loves all people so much that Jesus died on the cross. He also defeated Satan and death by rising from the grave. Jesus made it possible for all of God's children to live with Him forever. This "good news" should be attractive to Muslims.

Map Index

Subject Index

*T= fold out Bible Time Line (front cover)